New Perspectives on Association Football in Irish History

This book assesses association football's history and development in Ireland from the late 1870s until the early twenty-first century. It focuses on four key themes—soccer's early development before and after partition, the post-Emergency years, coaching and developing the game, and supporters and governance. In particular, it examines key topics such as the Troubles, Anglo-Irish football relations, the failure of a professional structure in the Republic and Northern Ireland, national and regional identity, relationships with other sports, class, economics and gender. It features contributions from some of today's leading academic writers on the history of Irish soccer while the views of a number of pre-eminent sociologists and economists specialising in the game's development are also offered. It identifies some of the difficulties faced by soccer's players and administrators in Ireland and challenges the notion that it was a 'garrison game' spread mainly by the military and generally only played by those who were not fully committed to the nationalist cause. This is the first edited collection to focus solely on the progress of soccer in Ireland since its introduction and adds to the growing academic historiography of Irish sport and its relationship with politics, culture and society.

The chapters in this book were originally published as a special issue in *Soccer & Society*.

Conor Curran is Irish Research Council Postdoctoral Research Fellow at Trinity College Dublin, Ireland, and has taught sports history at De Montfort University, Leicester, UK. He has published two books, *The Development of Sport in Donegal, 1880–1935* (2015) and *Irish Soccer Migrants: A Social and Cultural History* (2017).

David Toms is an independent scholar based in Norway. Previously, he taught sports history at University College Cork, Ireland, and his monograph, *Soccer in Munster: A Social History, 1877–1937*, was published in 2015.

Sport in the Global Society: Contemporary Perspectives

Edited by
Boria Majumdar, *University of Central Lancashire, UK*

The social, cultural (including media) and political study of sport is an expanding area of scholarship and related research. While this area has been well served by the *Sport in the Global Society* series, the surge in quality scholarship over the last few years has necessitated the creation of *Sport in the Global Society: Contemporary Perspectives*. The series will publish the work of leading scholars in fields as diverse as sociology, cultural studies, media studies, gender studies, cultural geography and history, political science and political economy. If the social and cultural study of sport is to receive the scholarly attention and readership it warrants, a cross-disciplinary series dedicated to taking sport beyond the narrow confines of physical education and sport science academic domains is necessary. *Sport in the Global Society: Contemporary Perspectives* will answer this need.

Recent titles in the series include:

A Social and Political History of Everton and Liverpool Football Clubs
The Split, 1878–1914
David Kennedy

Football Fandom in Italy and Beyond
Community through Media and Performance
Matthew Guschwan

Numbers and Narratives
Sport, History and Economics
Wray Vamplew

Healthy Stadia
An Insight from Policy to Practice
Daniel Parnell, Kathryn Curran and Matthew Philpott

Young People and Sport
From Participation to the Olympics
Edited by Berit Skirstad, Milena M. Parent and Barrie Houlihan

Reviewing the AFL's Vilification Laws
Rule 35, Reconciliation and Racial Harmony in Australian Football
Sean Gorman, Dean Lusher and Keir Reeves

The State of the Field
Ideologies, Identities and Initiatives
Edited by David Kilpatrick

Global and Transnational Sport
Ambiguous Borders, Connected Domains
Edited by Souvik Naha

New Perspectives on Association Football in Irish History
Going beyond the 'Garrison Game'
Edited by Conor Curran and David Toms

Major Sporting Events
Beyond the Big Two
Edited by John Harris, Fiona Skillen and Matthew McDowell

For more information about this series, please visit: www.routledge.com/series/SGSC

New Perspectives on Association Football in Irish History
Going beyond the 'Garrison Game'

Edited by
Conor Curran and David Toms

LONDON AND NEW YORK

First published 2018
by Routledge
2 Park Square, Milton Park, Abingdon, Oxon, OX14 4RN, UK

and by Routledge
711 Third Avenue, New York, NY 10017, USA

Routledge is an imprint of the Taylor & Francis Group, an informa business

© 2018 Taylor & Francis

All rights reserved. No part of this book may be reprinted or reproduced or utilised in any form or by any electronic, mechanical, or other means, now known or hereafter invented, including photocopying and recording, or in any information storage or retrieval system, without permission in writing from the publishers.

Trademark notice: Product or corporate names may be trademarks or registered trademarks, and are used only for identification and explanation without intent to infringe.

British Library Cataloguing in Publication Data
A catalogue record for this book is available from the British Library

ISBN13: 978-0-8153-9927-8

Typeset in TimesNewRomanPSMT
by diacriTech, Chennai

Publisher's Note
The publisher accepts responsibility for any inconsistencies that may have arisen during the conversion of this book from journal articles to book chapters, namely the possible inclusion of journal terminology.

Disclaimer
Every effort has been made to contact copyright holders for their permission to reprint material in this book. The publishers would be grateful to hear from any copyright holder who is not here acknowledged and will undertake to rectify any errors or omissions in future editions of this book.

Contents

Citation Information vii
Notes on Contributor ix

1 Introduction to 'going beyond the 'garrison game':
  new perspectives on association football in Irish history' 1
  Conor Curran and David Toms

2 Association Football in the Shamrock Shire's *Hy Brasil*:
  The 'Socker' Code in Connacht, 1879–1906 10
  Paul I. Gunning

3 'Who were the Shoneens?': Irish militant nationalists and
  association football, 1913–1923 33
  Aaron Ó Maonaigh

4 'Inciting the roughs of the crowd': soccer hooliganism in
  the south of Ireland during the inter-war period, 1919–1939 50
  Mark Tynan

5 Football unity during the Northern Ireland Troubles? 65
  Cormac Moore

6 Linfield's 'Hawk of Peace': pre-Ceasefires reconciliation
  in Irish League football 81
  Daniel Brown

7 Harry Cannon: a unique Irish sportsman and administrator 95
  Tom Hunt

8 How it all began: the story of women's soccer in sixties Drogheda 110
  Helena Byrne

CONTENTS

9 The development of schoolboy coaching structures for association football in Ireland, 1945–1995 132
   Conor Curran

10 Pedagogy, game intelligence & critical thinking: the future of Irish soccer? 148
   Seamus Kelly

11 Supporter ownership as a method of football governance: the concept of a Supporters' Trust and its operation within England and the Republic of Ireland 170
   Shane Tobin

12 Rule changes and incentives in the League of Ireland from 1970 to 2014 187
   David Butler and Robbie Butler

Index 203

Citation Information

The chapters in this book were originally published in *Soccer & Society*, volume 18, issues 5–6 (2017). When citing this material, please use the original page numbering for each article, as follows:

Chapter 1
Introduction to 'going beyond the 'garrison game': new perspectives on association football in Irish history'
Conor Curran and David Toms
Soccer & Society, volume 18, issues 5–6 (2017) pp. 599–607

Chapter 2
Association Football in the Shamrock Shire's Hy Brasil: *The 'Socker' Code in Connacht, 1879–1906*
Paul I. Gunning
Soccer & Society, volume 18, issues 5–6 (2017) pp. 608–630

Chapter 3
'Who were the Shoneens?': Irish militant nationalists and association football, 1913–1923
Aaron Ó Maonaigh
Soccer & Society, volume 18, issues 5–6 (2017) pp. 631–647

Chapter 4
'Inciting the roughs of the crowd': soccer hooliganism in the south of Ireland during the inter-war period, 1919–1939
Mark Tynan
Soccer & Society, volume 18, issues 5–6 (2017) pp. 648–662

Chapter 5
Football unity during the Northern Ireland Troubles?
Cormac Moore
Soccer & Society, volume 18, issues 5–6 (2017) pp. 663–678

CITATION INFORMATION

Chapter 6
Linfield's 'Hawk of Peace': pre-Ceasefires reconciliation in Irish League football
Daniel Brown
Soccer & Society, volume 18, issues 5–6 (2017) pp. 679–692

Chapter 7
Harry Cannon: a unique Irish sportsman and administrator
Tom Hunt
Soccer & Society, volume 18, issues 5–6 (2017) pp. 693–707

Chapter 8
How it all began: the story of women's soccer in sixties Drogheda
Helena Byrne
Soccer & Society, volume 18, issues 5–6 (2017) pp. 708–729

Chapter 9
The development of schoolboy coaching structures for association football in Ireland, 1945–1995
Conor Curran
Soccer & Society, volume 18, issues 5–6 (2017) pp. 730–745

Chapter 10
Pedagogy, game intelligence & critical thinking: the future of Irish soccer?
Seamus Kelly
Soccer & Society, volume 18, issues 5–6 (2017) pp. 746–767

Chapter 11
Supporter ownership as a method of football governance: the concept of a Supporters' Trust and its operation within England and the Republic of Ireland
Shane Tobin
Soccer & Society, volume 18, issues 5–6 (2017) pp. 768–784

Chapter 12
Rule changes and incentives in the League of Ireland from 1970 to 2014
David Butler and Robbie Butler
Soccer & Society, volume 18, issues 5–6 (2017) pp. 785–799

For any permission-related enquiries please visit:
http://www.tandfonline.com/page/help/permissions

Notes on Contributors

Daniel Brown is based at the Department of History, Queen's University Belfast, UK.

David Butler is based at the School of Economics, National University of Ireland – University College Cork, Ireland.

Robbie Butler is a Lecturer at the School of Economics, National University of Ireland – University College Cork, Ireland.

Helena Byrne is a Project Member at Drogheda Local Voices, Drogheda Museum Millmount, Ireland.

Conor Curran is Irish Research Council Postdoctoral Research Fellow at Trinity College Dublin, Ireland, and has taught sports history at De Montfort University, Leicester, UK. He has published two books, *The Development of Sport in Donegal, 1880–1935* (2015) and *Irish Soccer Migrants: A Social and Cultural History* (2017).

Paul I. Gunning is an independent scholar.

Tom Hunt is an independent social and sports historian based in Waterford, Ireland.

Seamus Kelly is Director of the UCD Centre for Sports Studies, Dublin, Ireland.

Aaron Ó Maonaigh is post-primary teacher at the Department of Education and Skills, Dublin City University, Ireland.

Cormac Moore is a graduate student at the Department of History, De Montfort University, Leicester, UK.

Shane Tobin is an independent scholar.

David Toms is an independent scholar based in Norway. Previously, he taught sports history at University College Cork, Ireland, and his monograph, *Soccer in Munster: A Social History, 1877–1937*, was published in 2015.

Mark Tynan is an independent scholar based at Portlaoise, Ireland.

Introduction to 'going beyond the 'garrison game': new perspectives on association football in Irish history'§

Conor Curran and David Toms

This special issue began to take shape more than 18 months ago over the course of a telephone conversation between both editors. This took place, appropriately, at half-time during a UEFA Europa League game. During our conversation, we decided that there needed to be an outlet for much of the new emerging research on football coming out of Ireland. For a decade and more now, the growth of academic and non-academic publications relating to the history of sport, and football in particular, in the Irish context has been extraordinary. When both of us began our Ph.D. research a number of years ago, there was a paucity of available works to consult when it came to Irish soccer historiography. 1999 saw the publication of Mike Cronin's *Sport and Nationalism in Ireland: Gaelic games, Soccer and Irish Identity since 1884*, while five years later, Neal Garnham completed the first in-depth examination of the early development of soccer in Ireland.[1] Although focusing largely on events in East Ulster and in Dublin, Garnham's *Association Football and Society in pre-partition Ireland* can be compared to Tony Mason's seminal work on English football, *Association Football and English Society, 1863–1915* in its contribution to the historiography of Irish soccer.[2]

However, the volume of work published on soccer in Ireland has changed considerably since the opening years of the twenty-first century. In 2015 alone, there were some five books published on various aspects of Irish sport history, a high-water mark for monographs in the field, with soccer featuring heavily in four of these.[3] This extraordinary flowering of research has been driven by the wider development of sport history in Ireland, a sub-discipline whose growth has been greatly aided by the establishment in 2005 of the Sport History Ireland annual conference and the growing number of research and doctoral studies on various aspects of Irish sport history being conducted in both Ireland and the United Kingdom. This is not the first special issue to appear in a journal that takes Irish sport as its organizing theme.[4] What makes this issue unique is that it is the first to focus solely on the game of association football. Perhaps as recently as five years ago, such a special issue as we are presenting here would have been scarcely imaginable. Yet, here we are.

---

§For an assessment of the meaning of the term 'garrison game' and the endurance of the common view that soccer and the British military had a strong linkage in Ireland, see Garnham, *Association Football and Society*, 18 and 205–6.

NEW PERSPECTIVES ON ASSOCIATION FOOTBALL IN IRISH HISTORY

That this special issue exists at all is doubly to be celebrated since the circumstances in which many of the scholars who answered our call for research papers, and then undertook that research and the writing up of their work, were less than propitious, given the current academic climate. In Ireland, and in the United Kingdom, continued recession and public service cuts to higher education coupled with growing numbers of postgraduate and doctoral graduates entering a shrinking jobs market has meant that many of those who work as scholars in the field especially of sport history or sport studies do so not as professional academics, but as adjuncts, part-timers and in their spare time away from their main source of income. For this reason, the high quality of the scholarship and the articles here presented ought to be highlighted. Limited access to resources and scarcity of time to devote to such research has been overcome by many of the contributors to provide us editors, and you readers, with fresh perspectives on the history and development of association football in Ireland. The establishment of a research centre in Ireland for the study of sports history and culture would help further strengthen the development of this growing aspect of history, although given the lack of interest expressed by most history departments within Ireland's universities in taking on courses dealing with the subject and its relationship with society, this still seems a long way off.

This special issue however extends beyond the reach of the historical, while retaining the history of the game at its core. While there has been a great and significant flourishing of sport history, sport in general has also received wider academic attention in Ireland in recent times. This is why we chose not to limit the scope of this special issue to just historical articles on football. We have also included new research on Irish football from the fields of sociology, social studies, economics and coaching and pedagogy. In doing so, we hope that as well as going beyond the garrison game, we open up a broader conversation about the role football plays in Irish life that sees it not merely as a sport but as a shaper of historical and contemporary social and civic identity, and as a force to be reckoned with in Irish life; one that touches many aspects of people's lived experiences past, present and future.

We want this special issue to show what can be achieved by scholars producing work when examining a topic that might otherwise be dismissed as trivial. We hope this special issue will generate debate about Irish soccer domestically and internationally, historically and contemporarily. Most of all, we hope that this special issue will both inform and inspire, as well as move forward, these debates. What should be clear from the wide-ranging focus of each of these articles is that far from being a story well told and well trodden, the story of association football on the island of Ireland is one whose surface has barely been scratched. Helena Byrne's article on women's indoor soccer in the 1960s raises questions about the gender imbalance in our understanding of not just football's history in Ireland and not only sport's history in Ireland, but the history of women in Ireland full-stop. The economic work of David and Robert Butler gives us further pause for thought about why it is that Ireland's domestic league, despite its competitiveness, still lags so far behind in terms of attendance despite many attempts to improve people's engagement with the domestic game. Shane Tobin's case study looking at Cork City FC's Supporters' Trust and their role in reviving that club in the past ten years offers us potential new ways for people to re-engage with their domestic league that are concerned less about the on-field action and more about people's sense that their club is a part of their community.

Important questions about the potential for both of Ireland's footballing bodies to unify are posed by the work of Cormac Moore and Daniel Brown. Whether or not such unification ever was or is feasible, to say nothing of desirable, remains a fraught subject. Both Moore and Brown's articles offer no easy solutions, but both offer the potential to better understand firstly, where such efforts erred in the past, and second, what, if any difference, is perceived by those who might have to play in such a unified team.

The north-south divide in Irish soccer, unique in Irish sporting administration, ought not to detract however from the fact that the development of soccer on the island was not a simple transference from north to south. Rather, as Paul Gunning's article illustrates, by looking westward, we may need to re-evaluate our understanding of how football culture has developed on the island of Ireland. Likewise, Mark Tynan's article on hooliganism in the interwar period provides us with a unique new perspective on how football saw itself and how it was seen in Ireland at a crucial phase in its development following the establishment of the Irish Free State. The career of one of the early stars of the Free State soccer team and Bohemians FC, Harry Cannon, is examined in detail by Tom Hunt within the context of the game in Ireland and the army in the opening decades of the fledgling State. That soccer was the garrison game is a notion put under further pressure thanks to the work of Aaron Ó Maonaigh, who shows in his case study of some IRA members fighting during the War of Independence, there was to them nothing particularly national or unnational in their choice of sport.

Likewise, the development of the game at grassroots level was not a straightforward process, as the contributions from Curran and Kelly show. Curran's work focuses our minds on the historical development of the discipline of coaching in Ireland, north and south of the border, showing both the lack of development in schools and the disparate attempts to develop a coherent coaching strategy with the only very recent emergence of what might be termed a proper coaching programme for all regions. Kelly's work, which notes the same strategies currently coming under revision, posits many interesting questions for those involved in coaching as a form of teaching and learning and pushes the debate about the role of coaching in the development of the game domestically forward in a constructive, player-centric way.

An Agenda for Future Research

And yet, there is much still to be uncovered about the development of soccer and other codes and what they can tell us about life in Ireland and associational culture. In particular, while it has been well established that association football was first played in Ireland in the late 1870s, what came in the years directly before it is not so clearly established. A few historians have asserted that folk-football in Ireland was largely in decline by the opening decades of the 1800s.[5] But there were some exceptions. There is strong evidence, for example, that in Donegal, matches 'under the association rules' in the 1880s contained elements of folk-football or pre-codified forms of the game.[6] Therefore, if folk-football was in decline before the Great Famine of 1845–52, then why was it still present in the minds of those attempting to play the new game in the late nineteenth century, and exactly how much folk-football was being played in other counties in the period from the 1830s until the late 1870s? A trawl through provincial newspapers for that period might clarify matters further, if only to confirm its absence. The historiography of soccer in Ireland lacks the type of debate currently ongoing within academic circles in Britain, particularly in regard to the notion that the game originated with the public schools and universities, a theory which has been challenged by those who take the approach that the working-classes had a strong role to play in the game's development, and that there was more continuity between traditional and modern forms of soccer than has been acknowledged.[7]

Additionally, little has been written about the role of the game in educational institutes in Ireland in the late nineteenth and early twentieth century. We have, for example, an excellent study of the role of Gaelic games within Irish colleges.[8] But what of the Collingwood Cup, the traditional competition played annually by Irish college selections, said to have its origins in the 1913–14 season?[9] Similarly, initial attempts to develop the game in primary and secondary schools have not yet received the attention they deserve. In addition, a complete history of professional football in Ireland remains to be written, and the game's development at grassroots level is still the subject of ongoing research. There is also a surprising lack of academic assessment of the history of the game in Derry city, despite the prominence of soccer there since the late 1880s.

This overall neglect of the history of Irish soccer is perhaps reflective of the general lack of engagement with Anglo–Irish football relations within academia. Much has been written about the role of the GAA within the Irish diaspora but there has been less emphasis on soccer players who emigrated and found solace in playing the game and participating in its related social activities.[10] Men such as Niall Staunton of Clondalkin, who managed a Boston-based soccer club made up of Irish and British players which greeted a Shamrock Rovers selection on their arrival to participate in the United Soccer Association league in 1967, have not yet received the acknowledgement which their efforts have merited.[11] In the last few years, both editors have attempted to redress this imbalance by assessing the role of Irish football migrants within English league football and the challenges they have faced. We know that Cardiff City's 1927 FA Cup winning goalkeeper was an Irishman with republican sympathies, while post-war Irish football migrants have also been the subject of a number of recently published articles and a new book reflecting on their experiences will soon be available.[12] As well as opening up questions about the relationship between Britain and Ireland where soccer is concerned, this work helps us to reframe a huge portion of the history of Irish soccer into wider narratives about migration and labour. Few forms of migratory labour can be said to be so sought after, so desirable, because the potential rewards are so high. Yet, the consequences of such a form of migration can nonetheless be deeply negative for those who try to 'make it' in football across the water.

In 2010, one alcohol company's usage of television advertising and billboards throughout Dublin to proclaim that 'This is Rugby Country' was probably somewhat baffling to anyone with even a basic understanding of Irish sport.[13] Association football's promoters and advertisers have not yet publicly dared to make such bold statements, despite the interest the game enjoys throughout much of Ireland. While the GAA's contribution to Irish society has been well documented, particularly in the early twenty-first century, much remains to be written about Ireland's early soccer pioneers and stars, but also its less prominent players and its largely unrecognized organizers. Like those involved in the GAA, many of these people participated on a voluntary basis within their local communities. At times, their victories were celebrated with marching bands, escorts and dances until the early hours; the GAA did not enjoy a monopoly on this type of local celebration and engagement with the local community, contrary to popular belief.[14] Yet even historical television documentaries on Irish sport have been dominated by those concerned with commemorating the GAA. In the spring of 2016, the GAA announced its plans to tie in its Gaelic football National League finals with *Laochra* (Heroes), a celebration of the centenary of the 1916 Rising, to be held on 24 April 2016. It was stated in a television advertisement that the GAA was inviting 82,000 men, women and children to Croke Park to 'commemorate 1916 and celebrate our national identity' by participating in this event.[15] Such blatant linkage with Ireland's nationalist history is nothing new to the GAA, but it is worth noting that the 1966 FAI Cup Final had in attendance 'some 200 survivors who fought in Dublin' in the Rising having accepted invitations from the FAI to attend the Shamrock Rovers and Limerick decider at Dalymount Park.[16] Despite a commemorative ceremony taking place before kick-off, the Republic of Ireland's soccer organizers have generally showed restraint in linking the game to the struggle for Irish independence. They did, however, more discreetly, highlight the contribution of Oscar Traynor to the game with a feature and a front page photograph on the match programme for the March 2016 home match against Switzerland.[17]

In addition, the GAA can boast of a television series commemorating it's *Laochra Gael* (Gaelic heroes), featuring mainly the stars of yesteryear from Gaelic football and hurling. Shown repeatedly on the Irish language channel TG4, although ironically often using analysts contributing through the medium of English, it is another media celebration of these national and local giants of Gaelic games. Boxing's Dan Donnelly has also received some attention, but George Best remains the most documented professional footballer from Northern Ireland or the Republic, with the death in 2005 of the former European Footballer of Year being acknowledged through an unofficial state funeral in Belfast.[18] But where are the other *Laochra Sacair*? There was, for example, no television documentary to chronicle the life of Davy Walsh, a member of the Ireland team which beat England at Goodison Park in 1949, after his death in March 2016.[19] And yet, the GAA great Paidí Ó Sé had, prior to his death in 2012, already been subject to a television documentary, while another celebrating his achievements soon followed.[20] To date, there has been one documentary produced on Patrick O'Connell, the former Manchester United and Ireland player generally credited with having saved CF Barcelona during the Spanish Civil War. O'Connell's background was acknowledged by the erection of a plaque by Dublin City Council in his native Drumcondra last year.[21] An RTÉ television documentary, which focused on the history of the island of Ireland's two national teams, was broadcast in 2012 but gave little indication of how the game spread in the Irish countryside, with the role of the military in the game's development reiterated by one leading Irish historian.[22] A few other programmes have focused on aspects of Irish football and English clubs such as *The Rod Squad* and *Premier Ambitions*.[23] At the time of writing, in the months preceding the 2016 European Championship finals in France, it would be very surprising if the Republic and Northern Ireland soccer teams did not become the subject of another more comprehensive historical television programme.

More analysis also needs to be undertaken on how the so-called 'foreign game' was encouraged through the media in Ireland. By the late 1960s, domestic soccer in Ireland was still struggling to attract radio attention at times, with FAI President and then Minister for Health, Donogh O'Malley, critical of Raidio Éireann's decision not to broadcast the aforementioned cup final in 1966.[24] Was the televising of the 1966 World Cup really the major turning point in raising interest in soccer in regional Ireland?[25] Newspaper evidence suggests that it was already there in many areas, but the game did not get the State support necessary to develop fully. What of areas such as Clones, said to be 'the home of soccer' in County Monaghan by 1935, where localized leagues and cups were in place at various stages in the twentieth century?[26] A league for minors was established in Mullingar, County Westmeath, by 1946; in Carrickmacross, County Monaghan, an under-fourteen street league was operational in 1959, while a league for juveniles was in place in Clones in 1963.[27] A league for juveniles had also been established in Longford town by the summer of 1948, again highlighting the interest in soccer in regional parts of the country.[28] Admittedly, attempts at establishing competitions do not appear to have spread throughout these counties until much later. In Cavan town, a local selection entered the FAI's Youth Cup for the first time in 1965, which would again suggest more interest in the countryside than has been acknowledged.[29]

Clearly, the GAA's dominance of sport in Ireland was not as cut and dried as some commentators would have us believe, and there is strong evidence that Gaelic football experienced a decline in that decade, and not just because of an upsurge in interest in soccer with the televising of English football. While acknowledging the advent of televised soccer matches, one provincial GAA writer felt in 1967 that there was not enough 'skilled, open, attacking football' being displayed, and that cynical tactics were also creeping in at minor and colleges' level. This was reflected in Gaelic football's lowest crowd since the war at an All-Ireland semi-final that year, with just 28, 370 present at the Cork versus Cavan match.[30] Yet, domestic soccer failed to capitalize on this decline or challenge the GAA's strong parish and county identity at that time, and still struggles to do so.

The 1970s did see the permanent establishment of association football leagues in counties such as Donegal, Kerry and Roscommon.[31] However, interest in domestic professional football in the Republic of Ireland was hindered by the coverage of English soccer on television, particularly when matches were staged on Sunday afternoons, with a decline of 60% in League of Ireland attendances over four years noted in a Football Commission report published on 10 May 1973.[32] Soccer organizers in the Free State, and later Republic of Ireland, faced not only having to deal with the GAA's Ban on its members taking part in 'foreign games' until the early part of that decade when it was finally removed in 1971; the GAA was also the sporting organization which enjoyed the most governmental and church support throughout the twentieth century. As David Goldblatt has stated, 'there was no official enthusiasm and less money available to the game in de Valera's Irish Free State' after Fianna Fáil formed its first government in 1932.[33]

Soccer organizers also faced subtler social pressure in their attempts to further the so-called 'garrison game.' In 1929, the pavilion at the Sligo Agricultural Society's Show Grounds was said to have been deliberately damaged with some indication given in the press that this was done as a result of soccer being played there.[34] In turn, some junior soccer clubs, such as the West Donegal Gweedore Celtic club in 1976 and 1977, have had their property vandalized, such was the opposition to the playing of soccer from some sections of society.[35] Social pressure was also exerted to prevent the development of soccer grounds, with the award of £150 to Mayo club Westport FC by the local Urban District Council for work to be undertaken on a playing field they were developing bringing protest from the local GAA club in the winter of 1948.[36] The grant was later overruled by the Department of Local Government, who ruled that 'the park was not dedicated to the public and the site did not belong to the Council.'[37]

The question therefore remains, how long will it be until the level of State and social discrimination against the playing of the sport of soccer and its advocates (the aforementioned Davy Walsh, suspended by the GAA as a schoolboy for playing soccer, amongst them) in twentieth century Ireland becomes more publicly acknowledged? Will players such as Jim Harte, exposed in the local press by one GAA writer as a dual player in 1929 for Raphoe's Gaelic football club and Lifford United, ever receive a (post-humous) apology for this type of public humiliation?[38] The argument will be made that nobody forced these footballers to play, but given the lack of alternative sporting and social activities available in most parts of rural Ireland and the small populations in many villages, engagement with local GAA and soccer clubs and teams was likely to have been seen as a highly enjoyable experience and a fundamental way of keeping healthy, mentally and physically. These developments are some of the key themes within the historiography of Irish sport which have yet to be fully examined, and perhaps one day, a book examining the experiences of 'banned' players themselves and the infamous Rule 27 will be published in full.

We hope this publication will encourage others to engage with these questions, along with others presented in this journal, in the future. In all then, we believe that this compilation of articles will enhance our understanding of the game in Ireland: its history, economic, social and sporting value. As editors, we will measure this present collection a success if it generates debates, responses and new research. Though modest, those are our hopes and aims in presenting this special issue.

Disclosure statement

No potential conflict of interest was reported by the authors.

Notes

1. Cronin, *Sport and Nationalism*; and Garnham, *Association Football*.
2. Mason, *Association Football and English Society*.
3. Toms, *Soccer in Munster*; Moore, *The Soccer Split*; Curran, *The Development of Sport in Donegal*; Rouse, *Sport & Ireland*; and Ó Tuathaigh ed., *The GAA & Revolution*.
4. Cronin and Ó Conchubhair, eds., 2013. *Éire-Ireland*, 48 (1 & 2), Spring/Summer; and Hassan and McElligott, eds., 2016. *Sport in Society: Cultures, Commerce, Media, Politics,* 19 (1).
5. Garnham, Association Football, 3–4; and Kelly, *Sport in Ireland*, 282.
6. Curran, *The Development of Sport*, 164.
7. Taylor, *Association Football*, 20–31.
8. McAnallen, *The Cups that Cheered*.
9. *Sunday Independent*, December 9, 1956.
10. Darby and Hassan, *Emigrant Players*; Darby, *Gaelic games*; and Redmond, *The Irish*.
11. *Irish Press*, May 12, 1967.
12. Toms, 'Notwithstanding the discomfort involved,' 516; Curran, 'The Migration;' 'Post-playing careers' (2015); and 'The Geography of Irish-born.'
13. See 'Guinness This is Rugby Country Advertisement.' Available at https://www.youtube.com/watch?v=ElMEi_TlPmM.

14. Toms, 'Notwithstanding the discomfort involved,' 510; and Curran, *The Development of Sport*, 183.
15. 'Laochra-the GAA celebrates 1916.' Available at https://www.youtube.com/watch?v=IiKToDEu-Kw.
16. *Irish Independent*, April 22, 1966.
17. 'The FAI pays great tribute to soccer playing hero of 1916 in Switzerland programme.' Available at http://www.balls.ie/football/the-fai-pays-great-tribute-to-soccer-playing-hero-of-1916-in-switzerland-programme/328473.
18. 'Hail and Farewell: the people of Belfast salute a fallen hero.' Available at http://www.theguardian.com/uk/2005/dec/05/football.northernireland.
19. 'Michael Walker: Final Whistle sounds for the redoubtable Davy Walsh.' Available at http://www.irishtimes.com/sport/soccer/michael-walker-final-whistle-sounds-for-the-redoubtable-davy-walsh-1.2587376.
20. See for example, 'Marooned.' Available at https://www.youtube.com/watch?v=Tv2EbjhAf-I.
21. 'Dublin City Council Honours Patrick O'Connell, Legendary Footballer and Manager.' Available at http://www.dublincity.ie/dublin-city-council-honours-patrick-o%E2%80%99connell-legendary-footballer-and-manager.
22. 'Green is the Colour-Irish Television Documentary.' Available at https://www.youtube.com/watch?v=EUvdg7FoQLA.
23. 'The Rod squad.' Available at https://www.youtube.com/watch?v=zbGQwcGhVxE and 'Premier Ambitions.' https://www.youtube.com/watch?v=_EcmP1uHEIk (accessed April 19, 2016) This might be contrasted with depictions from an earlier age of League of Ireland soccer in the RTÉ documentary 'In My Book You Should Be Ahead' first aired in 1975. Available at https://www.youtube.com/watch?v=VHY76Me6PuA.
24. *Irish Independent*, April 25, 1966.
25. *Irish Independent*, January 25, 1972.
26. *Anglo-Celt*, May 18, 1935 and May 24, 1958.
27. *Westmeath Examiner*, May 4, 1946; *Anglo-Celt*, July 4, 1959 and August 10, 1963.
28. *Longford Leader*, June 19, 1948.
29. *Anglo-Celt*, December 11, 1965.
30. *Sunday Independent,* August 13, 1967.
31. Curran, 'The Geography of Irish born', 87–88.
32. *Irish Examiner*, December 29, 1973.
33. Goldblatt, *The Ball is Round*, 105.
34. *Connacht Sentinel*, April 29, 1929.
35. *Derry People and Donegal News*, August 28, 1976 and May 7, 1977.
36. *Connaught Telegraph*, November 6, 1948 and *Western People*, November 13, 1948.
37. *Connaught Telegraph*, December 11, 1948.
38. Curran, *The Development of Sport*, 218.

References

Cronin, M. *Sport and Nationalism in Ireland: Gaelic Games, Soccer and Irish Identity since 1884*. Dublin: Four Courts Press, 1999.

Cronin, M., and B. Ó Conchubhair, eds. *Éire-Ireland*. Vol. 48, no. 1–2, Spring/Summer. New Jersey: The Irish-American Cultural Institute, 2013.

Curran, C. *The Development of Sport in Donegal 1880–1935*. Cork: Cork University Press, 2015.

Curran, C. 'The Migration of Irish-born Footballers to England, 1945–2010'. *Soccer & Society* 16, no. 2–3 (2015): 360–76.

Curran, C. 'Post-playing Careers of Irish-born Footballers in England, 1945–2010'. *Sport in Society* 18, no. 10 (2015): 1273–86.

Curran, C. 'Irish-born Players in England's Football Leagues, 1945–2010: An Historical and Geographical Assessment'. *Sport in Society* 19, no. 1 (2016): 74–94.

Darby, P. *Gaelic Games, Nationalism and the Irish Diaspora in the United States*. Dublin: UCD Press, 2009.

Darby, P., and D. Hassan, eds. *Emigrant Players: Sport and the Irish Diaspora*. Oxon: Routledge, 2008.

'Dublin City Council Honours Patrick O'Connell, Legendary Footballer and Manager'. Available online at http://www.dublincity.ie/dublin-city-council-honours-patrick-o%E2%80%99connell-legendary-footballer-and-manager.

Garnham, N. *Association Football and Society in Pre-Partition Ireland*. Belfast: Ulster Historical Foundation, 2014.

Goldblatt, D. *The Ball is round: A Global History of Football* [Paperback edition]. London: Penguin, 2007.

'Green is the Colour-Irish Television Documentary'. Available online at https://www.youtube.com/watch?v=EUvdg7FoQLA.

'Guinness This is Rugby Country Advertisement'. Available online at https://www.youtube.com/watch?v=ElMEi_TlPmM.

'Hail and Farewell: the people of Belfast salute a fallen hero'. Available online at http://www.theguardian.com/uk/2005/dec/05/football.northernireland.

Hassan, D., and R. McElligott, eds. *Sport in Society: Cultures, Commerce, Media, Politics*, 19, no. 1. Abingdon: Taylor and Francis, 2016.

'In My Book You Should Be Ahead'. Available online at https://www.youtube.com/watch?v=VHY76Me6PuA.

Kelly, J. *Sport in Ireland 1600–1840*. Dublin: Four Courts Press, 2014.

'Laochra-the GAA celebrates 1916'. Available online at https://www.youtube.com/watch?v=liKToDEu-Kw.

'Marooned'. Available online at https://www.youtube.com/watch?v=Tv2EbjhAf-I.

Mason, T. *Association Football and English Society, 1863–1915*. Brighton: Harvester Press, 1980.

McAnallen, D. *The Cups That Cheered: A History of the Sigerson, Fitzgibbon and Higher Education Gaelic Games*, Cork: Collins Press, 2012.

Moore, C. *The Irish Soccer Split*. Cork: Cork University Press, 2015.

Ó Tuathaigh, G. ed. *The GAA & Revolution in Ireland, 1913–1923*. Cork: The Collins Press, 2015.

'Premier Ambitions'. Available online at https://www.youtube.com/watch?v=_EcmP1uHEIk.

Redmond, P. *The Irish and the Making of American Sport, 1880–1935*. Jefferson: McFarland & Company, 2014.

Rouse, P. *Sport & Ireland: A History*. Oxford: Oxford University Press, 2015.

Taylor, M. *The Association Game: A History of British Football*. Harlow: Pearson Education Limited, 2008.

'The FAI pays great tribute to soccer playing hero of 1916 in Switzerland programme'. Available online at http://www.balls.ie/football/the-fai-pays-great-tribute-to-soccer-playing-hero-of-1916-in-switzerland-programme/328473.

'The Rod Squad'. Available online at https://www.youtube.com/watch?v=zbGQwcGhVxE.

Toms, D. 'Notwithstanding the Discomfort Involved': Fordson's Cup Win in 1926 and How 'the Old Contemptible' Were Represented in Ireland's Public Sphere during the 1920s'. *Sport in History* 32, no. 4 (2012): 504–25.

Toms, D. *Soccer in Munster: A Social History 1877–1937*. Cork: Cork University Press, 2015.

Walker, Michael. 'Final Whistle Sounds for the Redoubtable Davy Walsh'. Available online at http://www.irishtimes.com/sport/soccer/michael-walker-final-whistle-sounds-for-the-redoubtable-davy-walsh-1.2587376.

Association Football in the Shamrock Shire's *Hy Brasil*: The 'Socker' Code in Connacht, 1879–1906

Paul I. Gunning

> Connacht was the only Irish province outside the penumbral aura of a Victorian-era Irish Football Association (IFA) division. Throughout the Gaelic Renaissance, this western province quintessentially represented the primitivistic and joyful aesthetic trope of *Hy Brasil*. It informed the transmundane thinking of those Celtophiles who classified soccer as a 'garrison game'. Though the historiography of soccer in this isolated outpost is an impoverished habitus, within key urban sportive oubliettes resided sequestered soccer pioneers. This paper considers themes to include the introduction, agency, lucid diffusion and participation of the 'socker code' in Connacht. Its inherently bottom-up organization, responses to top-down oppositional nativist fusillades, local mythos (often amid complex class and regional sporting allegiances) are expressed through multivocal identities and ethno-religious *mentalities*. The belated *fin-de-siècle* fizzle of rural soccer and veracity of perpetuated contentions regarding the British military's key role as soccer's sole provincial emissary are also appraised.

Introduction

Stoddart's assertion that Irish soccer's position apropos themes of Ireland's nationhood, patriotism and identity generates 'complex and bitter contest'[1] also pertains to Connacht's emergent late Victorian soccer arena. Marginal locations within the 'last asylum of Celtism'[2] were articulated through essentialist concepts of emancipatory Gaelic nativism versus pervasive British imperialism, however the Manichaean duality representing Ireland through the binate of 'commercial east' and 'subsistence west' is not always tenable.[3] Ethnic considerations were infused into Irish soccer which was considered 'suitable to none but Scotchmen' and 'too calculating and canny for the impulsive Irish temperament'.[4] Soccer was manifest in Connacht by 1879 (four years before it was demonstrated at the Hospital for Incurables, Dublin) when exhibited by Sligo's naturalized Scoto-Irish merchant community. By 1901, soccer was arguably the national game within a majority of larger towns throughout counties Sligo, Roscommon, Mayo and Leitrim – assisted by the Gaelic Athletic Association's (GAA) provincial collapse – while county Galway now experienced a more capricious journey. Taylor's panegyric assessment of Garnham's 'particularly nuanced account' of Irish identity in 'all its complexity related to soccer'[5] is diminished somewhat considering the latter named authoritative author largely forsook Connacht's inaugural soccer decades. Provincial urban Ireland's sportive identity was not hermetically sealed and therefore Taylor's[6] reliance on Cronin's uncalibrated assertion soccer was invariably 'identifiable with a specific sector of Irish society,'[7]

Figure 1. 'Remarkable "Feat" on the Football Field'.
Source: *Roscommon Herald*, 5 May 1900, 1.

namely Unionists, though sustainable in key specific instances, often requires the reification of *post hoc* fallacies to be sustained nationally and ignores the discrete margins of sportive contact demonstrable in Connacht between its Nationalist and Unionist proto-soccer communities.

Initial efforts that 'Raised football in Connaught out of the mud, aye!'
Though Connacht, like much of provincial Ireland,[8] was often bereft of the conducive circumstances required to embrace soccer[9], nevertheless, certain western towns were not insensate to soccer's advance. Bairner's assertion soccer had spread 'from Ulster…to other parts of Ireland'[10] fails to appreciate interest and involvement in certain provincial nodes pre-dating the IFA's 1880 formation in Belfast – with the latter body termed 'the Ulster Association.'[11] In 1877, arising from Edinburgh Hibernian FC's[12] success, *Town Gossip* implored the Catholic Reading Room Committee in Tuam, county Galway to establish a football club and ensure the code was 'Association by all means.' Having procured a 'patron and promoter … players and playing pitch' the projected cost to establish a club was 'one pound sterling.'[13]

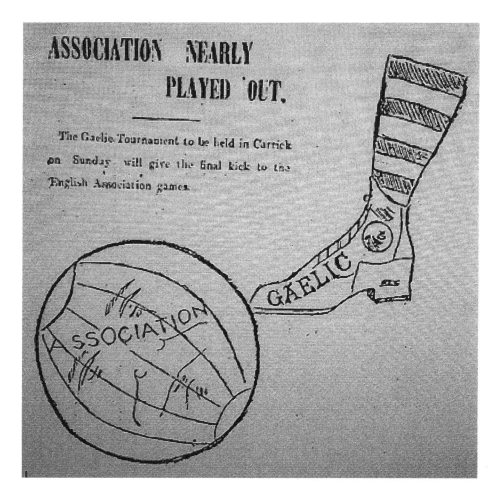

Figure 2. 'Association Nearly Played Out'.
Source: *Roscommon Herald*, 21 May 1904, 1.

By way of cultural reversal, Sligo Borough's leading pan-Protestant sportive community (spearheaded by its close-knit Scoto-Irish cohort) on St Patrick's Day 1879 organized a match between 'The Commercials of Sligo Foot Ball Club' and 'Eleven of The Rest.'[14] This group contained merchants (who traded heavily from Sligo's Butter Market to Glasgow) central to the Sligo United YMCA's executive committee and local Presbyterian congregational conversazione.[15] By 1880, soccer in Sligo was sustained by Mr Eade's *Diocesan School FC*, the Roman Catholic *Marist Brothers FC* and *Sligo FBC*[16] allied with the recently arrived 105th *Madras Light Infantry*. By January 1885, county Roscommon's Castlerea FC, founded by the irrepressible Orlando R. Coote,[17] contained a membership of professionals involved in law, banking and medicine but more predominately land agency. Resident at Arm Lodge, Castlerea,[18] Coote's coaching may have incorporated tactics demonstrated in elite English educational bastions and the club enlivened Castlerea (population 1,229)[19], described as 'the dullest…of its size in Ireland' with young men compelled to parade 'the long, straggling, dreary street' or frequent 'the public-house.'[20]

Figure 3. 'Giant and Dwarf'.
Source: *Roscommon Herald*, 29 November 1902, 1. 'Gaelic football which is only about 12 months revived has almost wiped Association'.

Early competition included Michael Cunningham's Boyle FC who in turn played the exclusively Protestant Boyle Academicals.[21] Railway trips were required to play at Athlone's Ranelagh School Grounds against county Offaly's Banagher FC, Tullamore FC, Dublin Association FC and Athlone FC from 1886 to 1888.

Candidates who potentially initiated soccer in county Mayo by 1886 include Ballinrobe FC, Castlebar FC, Ballyhaunis FC[22] and possibly a Border Regiment team.[23] Acceptance that Castlebar FC, a rugby club, when established by Dr Willie D'Exeter Jordan in December 1885, was a Gaelic football team appears misplaced while an overlap with 'Castlebar Association FC'[24] indicates either less affluent members played soccer or these clubs operated in parallel. Amongst county Mayo's pioneers of Gaelic football, Towerhill FC established in January 1885, by Lieut. Valentine J Blake of the 6th Batt. Connaught Rangers (the latter regiment's colours being red with a green facing), provides further uncertainty regarding selected football codes. The Blakes were significant landowners and vocal supporters of Roman

Figure 4. 'Go on De Wet'.
Source: *Sligo Star*, 3 January 1901, 5. When Sligo Light Blues' played in Longford on St Stephen's Day 1900, 'intense merriment' was caused by the 'antics of an old countryman, who planted himself in the centre of a lot of soldiers. Every time the ball received a vigorous kick he indulged in a buck-jump and bellowed '*Go on, De Wet*!'

Catholic rights but increasingly ran counter to Nationalist land-based politics.[25] Capt VJ Blake sourced players from 'a confederacy' of surrounding teams[26] that quite conceivably benefitted from its founding fathers' sportive influence in one of England's elite Catholic educational bastions where the *Stonyhurst Rules* reigned.[27]

Diffusion was aided by the 'crack' Welsh Fusiliers, often led by their band and 'historic goat' as mascot,[28] who played Castlebar in July 1888.[29] Soccer 'arrived from London' to Headford, county Galway (population 779[30] with 69 troops) when Walter Allen offered to teach 'town boys' the code.[31] In December 1887, Tuam (township population of 3,567)[32] possessing some of the province's top cricketers was urged to form a football team to compete against 'Galway and other provincial towns' and advised to play 'Rugby or Association, *not* gaelic.' By April 1888, Tuam FC with 110 members was regarded as 'second to none' in Connacht with rivals including Castlerea FC, Ballinrobe and Dunmore Robert Emmets, while *Fiat Justitia Ruat Caelem* vowed this club's patriotic ardour was 'purer and more honest' than Dunmore GAA's whose 'professed patriotism' was 'a cloak for selfish purposes.'[33] In December 1889, the Welsh Fusiliers' band's team, based in Galway town, travelled to play Tuam FC while the province's football *la tier monde* apparently was facilitated by Athenry (Dr Croke) FC.[34] Falteringly, soccer emerged in county Leitrim when Mohill Cricket and FC were established not 'in opposition' to the local Faugh-a-Ballagh GAA but 'inaugurated at the same time, if not sooner.'[35]

Rebooting From *Year Zero*, 1879

Unlike Ireland's *Linenopolis,* namely: the soccer hotbed of Belfast, Connacht possessed low urbanization and little manufacturing base. By 1881, 8% of Connacht's population lived in towns exceeding 2,000 inhabitants[36], being reliant upon agriculture and or its consumer-oriented economy.[37] An appraisal of Connacht's 'principal port towns' Galway, Sligo and Westport decried their lack of 'well-directed energy and legitimate enterprise.'[38] Scant sportive facilities were available, soccer promoters rarely emerged and melancholic sheets of rain often kept 'indoor toilers' interested in the winter game 'caged up.'[39] More fundamentally, with Home Rule agitation and crypto-revolutionary agrarian demands bestirred, a threatened distress of similar intensity to the 'Famine slaughter' experienced during *Black 1847*[40] now engulfed provincial urban Connacht. Yet, its pillarized sportive condition was evident when its soccer pioneers, by chasing the bounding ball, coterminously demonstrated the ethos of Muscular Christianity and a cultural connection with the British Empire's sportive landscape. Soccer's early advance in Connacht was fitful and disjointed, beset with logistical difficulties and without a centralized regional or even local administration, but not utterly without emergent promoters possessive of a 'drive for success.'[41]

The *'Garrison Game'* Game

Though soccer in Connacht emanated through a multi-causal agency and experienced varying gradations of diffusion, the impeachment of Irish soccer as 'traditionally known as the *garrison game*' due to its 'popularity within British garrison towns'[42] is buttressed by Holmes' observation that 'pockets of enthusiasm' outside of Ireland's major urban areas seemed 'to coincide' with the presence of army barracks.[43] Such assertions epitomize generalized contentions – often without adequate empirical evidence – generally resolve to demonstrate soccer in Ireland was borne from an uncompromising cultural sportive binate. Featherstone claims soccer though less modulated by 'the class interests of imperial administration' was 'originally imported by British soldiers at the expense of *indigenous* Gaelic sports.'[44] Cronin, when asserting soccer was synonymous with 'the forces of unionism' and connoted with 'West Britonism' reiterated a barb that the IFA was 'a symbol of British imperialism,' further perpetuates a simplistically interpretation that 'the soccer authorities in southern Ireland had a problem' in promoting 'a banned game in the minds of GAA followers and many other political and cultural nationalists.' This reframed narrative appears to be predicated upon the existence of a putative existential crisis amongst Irish soccer advocates concerning national identity and sportive participation as Cronin's conjectures (albeit it avowedly pursuing soccer's imprint upon nationalist Ireland) provide an almost Kaffaseque transference when imprecisely opining soccer had to 'justify'[45] itself to anointed sportive opponents, despite the latter being arguably inherently 'Anglophobic and anti-colonial.'[46] The context and alimentation for the former's astigmatic analysis are further crystallized by way of parsing Sugden and Bairner's mutable argument, concerning soccer's role in Irish society as a foreign sport, which locates soccer as a vaguely qualified ethno-sectarian conductive when maintaining most of 'the indigenous community' viewed soccer as 'an anathema.'[47] Pre-existing argumentation which attenuates such contentions includes a declaration 'socie football was in Sligo before Gaelic [football] was thought of'[48] demonstrates Victorian-era soccer's capacity for voluntary participation ran contrary to the decried mantra regarding the 'tyranny of imported and enforced' sportive mores. By the Edwardian-era, imperious and sardonic denunciations of soccer had escalated, with soccer condemned as a 'sham conflict' promoted by the British army's 'recruiting sergeant' to bait the nets of 'red man-stealers' for 'valiant defenders of the Empire.'[49] But such condemnatory critiques were not readily apparent in late Victorian Connacht and must be considered alongside countervailing considerations to include the GAA's slide into provincial abyss, the vibrancy of 1890s' Dublin's soccer culture amongst its elite Roman Catholics and/or particularist provincial urban sporting mores. When stung into responding to unrestrained charges regarding soccer's unpatriotic character, a provincial aficionado pilloried the GAA as 'a sink of absurdity, a nest of hypocrisy and an arsenal of humbug.'[50]

Despite wide-ranging mooted assumptions concerning Irish repellence towards the British Army, Irish soldiers in 1870 represented 27.9% of its recruits and 13.2% by 1898.[51] While football was considered the army's 'only outdoor amusement' where 'the officers and nonce rank... mix promiscuously'[52], the military were rarely associated with attempts to promote or advocate football amongst civilians in provincial urban Ireland.[53] Divergent extrapolations concerning the engagement of Connacht's respective militias with soccer are evinced. In Galway, Castlebar and Boyle, militia training was considered 'inconvenient' with young men 'greatly required' for 'harvest operations'[54], while the 'scarcity of men' at Sligo Harbour was due to the latter's assembly[55], with the latter regiment being the only such military unit in Connacht to play soccer when challenging the 2nd Bttn North Lancashire in February 1893.

An analysis of the military's comparative numerical strength[56] to local civilian populations when assessing the garrison's respective roles in soccer's adhesion in Connacht's two largest towns, Galway[57] and Sligo (populations, respectively, in 1891, 13,800 and 10,274), demonstrates arrant bifurcation. Outside of Dublin's metropolitan area, Galway's township in 1881 was Ireland's 7th most populated area, while Sligo's municipal borough was correspondingly the 12th largest.[58] The former town's soldiers were quartered at the Connaught Rangers' depot at Renmore, the Upper Citadel Barracks near Eyre Square and the Shambles Barracks at West

Bridge with Sligo containing the Forthill Barracks.[59] Castlebar, county Mayo with 3,855[60] inhabitants and a garrison of 354 soldiers, represented that county's highest military to overall population figure at 9.18%, with Ballinrobe (population 2,286[61] and military 177, 7.74%), Ballaghaderreen (1,496[62] and 60, 4.01%) and Westport, (4,469[63] and 68, 1.52%) demonstrating a relatively vibrant (if late arriving) soccer arena. Ballina, the county's most populous town (5,760[64] and 67, 1.16%), did not experience a Victorian-era working-class soccer habitus. The highest military-to-overall-population percentage in Connacht was observable in Oughterard, county Galway (834[65] and 100, 11.99%). By the mid-1890s, Oughterard Celtic FC was amongst the province's elite having defeated various military teams based in Galway town. Headford, with a military presence of 8.86%, enjoyed an evanescent soccer role. County Galway's second largest town, Tuam (3,567[66] and 66, 1.85%), developed a more vibrant Nationalist soccer scene but with no discernible military connection regarding the club's formation. Connacht now increasingly embroiled within the Land War witnessed barracks being temporarily reopened. Athenry (population 1,030)[67] by December 1882 with 2 officers and 50 non-commissioned soldiers was typical of the province's small town military presence. By 1891, Galway (13,800[68] and 477, 3.46%), though hosting Connacht's single largest garrison, experienced an enervated soccer network, while north Connacht's largest town, Sligo (10,274[69] and 93, 0.91%), saw the game thrive.

Keystone Local Mythos Disassembled

The mythos regarding Sligo's foundational soccer match provides a rare provincial example where the '*garrison game* played by the soldiers of a British colonial regime'[70] narrative was readily incorporated into its localized folklore. Holmes' averment 'the first football match played in Sligo featured soldiers from the Lancashire Regiment billeted in the town'[71] mirrors Reid's assertion: the 'British army regiments' introduced soccer and locals 'quickly took to the game.'[72] Nevertheless, such assessments fall considerably short of accurately delineating soccer's introduction or contextualizing its phased gestation. When commenting upon the 'apathy and indifference of a sizeable section' of Sligo town's population towards Gaelic games and corresponding preference for soccer, McTernan's observation, that the reasons for same are 'not altogether clear'[73], resounds more consistently with the contradictions which pervade Sligo's often anamorphic 'soccer-garrison' narrative.

The central local legend is principally fabricated upon a strident, though anachronistic, assertion that Sligo's first game of soccer occurred in 1883 when the 'Lancashire Regiment' played the Hare and Hounds FC. This bedevilling exemplum has long rapt historians and journalists[74] who have relied upon a generally faithful article detailing Sligo's soccer pioneers.[75] Problematically, by early 1883, the Forthill barracks (but for the possible presence of local militia permanent staff) were temporarily abandoned and not reoccupied until January 1886.[76] Further, the Hare and Hounds FC had reverted to rugby, while the East Lancashire regiment, upon their arrival to Sligo in January 1886, predominately played rugby and formed the Sligo Lilywhites RFC[77] – supplemented by affluent resident Protestants. After the GAA's hiatus into Sligo's burgeoning soccer scene by 1890–1891, the East Lancashires re-emerged playing GT Pollexfen's, Sligo 'Black and Blues' Gaels FC and the Volunteers – the first and latter teams containing influential local conservative Unionist sportsmen.

An extrication from key, though deceptively subtle, scribal errors contained within an obsequies appreciation of John Lambert[78] – formerly a foreman linotype-setter with the *Sligo Champion* – is key to unravelling the circumstances, surrounding the conflation of dates and matches, contained within the 1883 conundrum. Lambert, having figured with Sligo Commercials GAA, more importantly, most likely organized the Sligo Amateurs FC match against the East Lancashires in 1891.[79] Tellingly, the 1939 article failed to specify Sligo's putative foundational game's date but if, as later contested, it occurred in 1883, Lambert was then a callow 10-year-old lad. The 1939 article's contention football was previously a 'mixture of many codes' and it was only when games with British regiments took place that 'soccer came to Sligo' is more indicative of provincial urban Nationalists' interaction with British army elite teams (though also implicitly drawing attention to the newly agreed international codified soccer rules). Sligo's pillarized localized soccer landscape was evident as local labour more readily found enthusiastic competition amongst British military soccer teams (comprised of working-class men some with identifiably Irish surnames) than local elite conservative Unionist or pan-Protestant educational or business establishments. Competition against rural Gaelic football enthusiasts, based on recent experience, was a preposterous proposition.

Soccer's ready embrace of dissimulated origins – when compounded with ardent oppositional top-down criticisms of soccer as 'almost entirely' played 'by the Garrison' who were 'more English than the English' and representing a status as military recruiter[80] – more often generated an internalized mutated identity loop that reinforced *post hoc* and spurious identifiers. Contrariwise, generalized argumentation *ex silentio* conflating a supposed desire by soccer enthusiasts for approval or justification from within the penumbral prohibitions of oppositional cultural sportive authorities, culminating in a wish to establish putatively desired 'nationalist credentials' and thereby not be viewed as 'traitors,'[81] concerning key sub-groups is a deductive fallacy concerning sportive identifications. In short, western urban provincial soccer's often deeply insular folkloric tradition ensured simplistic and or commingled contentions, crystallized around vernacular approved myths, were accepted. Its actual adherents more repeatedly demonstrated an often fatalistic disinclination, though not inability, to rekindle old ideological arguments. Resultantly opaque and misdiagnosed assertions in Connacht bestowing certain agents putative pioneering roles, be they civilian or military, could be sustained and evade scrutiny, particularly following pan-Protestant elites' subsequent disengagement from soccer.

Little Belfast, Sligo v *Old Spanish Colony*, Galway

When further assessing the specificity of urban Connacht's multi-causal soccer agency, the province's two largest towns demonstrate significantly divergent engagements amongst both its working classes and elite commercial milieu. Despite a trifling late Victorian garrison presence and with no touring regiments during the Edwardian era, Sligo was nominated *post factum* as amongst those towns whose garrison status was central to soccer's emergence.[82] Due to the often sectarian demeanour of Sligo's urban character, it was ominously dubbed 'Little Belfast'[83], with the town's predominant commercial character largely informed by its port. In 1791, a French consul had noted upon the comparatively distinct 'world of Presbyterian merchants' in urban Sligo[84] and by 1879, this community's willingness to embrace soccer was arguably yet another component of their wider Scotticized identification. Sligo municipal borough's population of 10,670 in 1871 included 8,220 Roman Catholics, 1,712 Episcopalian Protestants and 304 Presbyterians. *Nichevo* remarked its 'substantial Scottish colony' imbued Sligo with a 'character and culture... unique among provincial towns'[85] and on 24 March 1881, the *Freeman's Journal* noted Sligo's inhabitants were predominately 'true Conacians and thoroughbred Irishmen in blood and sympathy' while the town partook the 'look and manner of an Ulster town, being on the borderland.' Sligo's 'shipping trade' and customs returns were 'sufficient to establish its superiority over Galway' and status as Connacht's 'commercial capital.'[86] In 1875, a visiting Wesleyan Preaching Missionary thrilled at Sligo's 'surrounding scenery,' 'commercial stir' and above all its 'Protestant influence' which contrasted 'very favourably with the Roman Catholic town of Galway.'[87]

Sligo's Caledonian sportive acculturation accelerated the often pillarized state of soccer as determined by the past and present students of Mr Eades' Diocesan School, Primrose Grange FC and the Sligo FBC who damned Home Rule as 'that dreadful apparition'[88], though club member RB M'Neilly opined the 'difference of opinion amongst certain farmers and landlords' made 'no difference on the question of Unionism.'[89]

Galway established by Englishmen was now Ireland's 'most essentially Irish town.' The 'vulgar tongue' of Connacht, namely Irish, was 'almost exclusively' employed by its tradesmen, leading shops and the gentry both colloquially and of 'necessity.'[90] Galway's streetscape, more appropriate to the Bay of Biscay, was elegiacally termed an 'old Spanish colony'[91] and a chimera of former trading glories with continental Europe. In 1871, Galway township's population of 15,597[92] included 14,424 Roman Catholics; Episcopalian Protestants, 846; and 171 Presbyterians.[93] Occasionally, sportive regiments in Galway played soccer but found little ready competition within the *Citie of the Tribes* as typified when the Welsh Fusilier's band's team, based at the Renmore Barracks, travelled to play Tuam in December 1889 and the East Kent's travelled to play Oughterard FC.[94] The county town's general disinclination to play soccer also applied to its celebrated garrison when the Connaught Rangers' 1st Batt. established a rifle and cricket club in 1892[95] and a nine-hole golf course in 1895.[96] Hurling[97] was the most popular codified game locally, with Gaelic football fleetingly demonstrated when the Galway Commercials GAA played Athenry GAA on George Cottingham's field at Prospect Hill.[98] Galway possessed Connacht's only university, though a speculative classification of an 1865 football game as 'resembling...soccer'[99] was more likely a 20-aside 'Varsity-styled rugby match involving Queens College and the Corrib rowing club.[100] Garnham notes soccer 'largely failed to take root' in Ireland's provincial public schools and colleges citing Galway Queens College FC folded due to the lack of available games and a 'general lack of enthusiasm' amongst students.[101] Dr Richard Biggs, headmaster of the Erasmus Smith school and president of the Connaught Rugby Union, was representative of local sportive elites' control of the province's rugby, cricket and hockey organizations. In contrast, Sligo's intermediate schools, namely Mr Eades' Diocesan School, (formerly an Erasmus Smith school) and the Primrose Grange (run by the Incorporated Society for the Promotion of Protestant Education), were critical to promoting competing the credos of *mens sano* and 'the animal-man'[102] through soccer.

By 1879 soccer in Sligo emerged but by 1882, its first phase had ceased, when after 15 years in existence, the Sligo FBC had split (when Sligo Wanderers formed). *Sport* on 21 October 1882, warned neither club was 'strong enough to stand alone,' and considered it strange in a 'small place as Sligo' that its banking and commercial factions were 'antagonistic.' When the Sligo FBC, captained by James Sinclair (of a Scoto-Irish family that owned Sligo's largest grocery warehouse), in February 1882, played Lissadell, this was most likely the last notable game of Sligo soccer's inaugural phase. Lord Kilmarnock (selected for Scotland against England in 1872) had lined out alongside his cousin Sir Henry Gore-Booth, a regarded Artic expeditioner and game shot, of Lissadell House.

In 1887, a remarkable series of 12-aside games varyingly reported as conducted under 'constitution' or 'association' rules saw soccer re-emerge when the Hare and Hounds, though 'out of practice at the Association game,' played Jack Shiels'[103] Black and Blues – a newly formed Gaelic football team. Mr Shekleton's Primrose Grange and Mr Eade's Diocesan School[104] in March 1887 demonstrated their central importance to sustaining soccer locally with competition sourced from within Sligo's pan-Protestant community, particularly its leading shipping agents and mill owners as in late 1889. G.T. Pollexfens' best men as 'followers of the pen' were considered scarcely 'nimble enough,' for Mr Shekleton charges whose muscles were well-developed when scaling Knocknarea's prominent hills.[105] Crucially, the fatality of James Acheson, when playing rugby for Primrose Grange FC in January 1890, most likely convinced Shekleton (secretary of Sligo's *Light of West* Freemason Lodge and a leading Unionist)[106] his students should exclusively play soccer. The local arena was further invigorated by Alex Munro's XI (a Sligo student of Trinity College, Dublin who figures in James Joyce's *Ulysses*)[107], who played Primrose Grange FC in December 1899 along with various matches involving Willie Campbell BL, a goalkeeper for Cambridge University and Corinthians FC. Campbell subsequently played for Dublin's Bohemians FC and a Leinster provincial selection[108] and was listed as an out-field player for Sligo Light Blues against Richmond Rovers, Dublin. Intriguingly, it appears Campbell kept goals for Dublin city's Freebooters FC, an elite Dublin club for Roman Catholics.[109] His controversial non-selection for Ireland drew forth the customary accusation this privilege was largely 'confined to Belfast men.'[110]

Subsequent to the GAA's effective 1886–1890 rise and demise in Sligo, soccer though embraced by aspirant nationalists enjoyed a largely apolitical disposition[111] but displayed a pillarized character. Its pan-Protestant sportive commercial class were less likely to engage overtly nationalist teams that included Sligo Celtic FC while societal distinctions would arguably debar the Grassyhill Pirates and the Barroe Emmets.[112] The former teams, drawn from the subterranean habitués of Sligo's dock and labouring community, were interspersed with charismatic artisans of yeoman stock from nearby Holborn Hill and Barrack Street – the latter arguably being most demonstrative of a Protestant working-class habitus in Connacht.[113] Meanwhile, in the predominately Nationalist east ward, the Sligo Amateurs FC, as the town's premier combination, were fixed to play Primrose Grange and Mr William Campbell's XI.

Sham Patriotism – a Helter-Skelter-Kick-or-Miss Business

The hypothesis that 'soccer had to work twice as hard as the GAA to prove its nationalist credentials'[114] arguably resounds of paradigmic blindness when eschewing calibrated assessments that soccer was not invariably considered unpatriotic. Crucially such assessments fail to gradate wider perspectives of patriotism amongst Nationalists who perceived and engaged in soccer as legitimate sportive entertainment. The Edwardian era ushered in a reassertion of the GAA's erstwhile *lex talionis,* with authoritarian and hegemonic nationalist sportive neo-elite hard-line positions reasserted[115] and renewed exclusionary membership laws enforced if found playing or encouraging 'imported games.' Nevertheless, a stubborn soccer subculture objected to the 'curtailment of individual freedom' with the GAA characterized as 'a kind of intermediate grub between sycophant and oppressor' whose magisterium was rebuffed with the *ad hominem* insult they 'never possessed brains enough to master the intricacies of…an intensely scientific game as Association football.'[116] Advanced Irish nationalist sentiment didn't universally consider soccer a negative branding upon Irish patriotic identity. In 1882, Hibernians FC (whom the IFA's JM M'Alery congratulated as 'Irishmen' who competed with 'the best players in Scotland and England')[117] were feted by the Ladies Land League in Blackburn, England.[118] A discourse by Hassan, McCullough and Moreland that soccer when 'established in Belfast rather than Dublin' from 'its inception…sat apart from other sports in Ireland'[119] fails to acknowledge M'Alery's goodwill, encouragement and hope to see 'a few good clubs in the metropolis' and/or sportive identity's participatory fluidity as when Michael Cusack assembled Dublin's *Gitanos* to play county Roscommon's Strokestown and District FC in rugby.[120]

Arguably, it was subsequent to the GAA's engagement with football that soccer experienced the chilling effect of class (as much as nationalistic) animosity as exhibited by *One of the Snubbed Football Kickers* who denounced Castlerea FC as a 'snobocracy' that refused to socialize with its 'rag tag and bob tail' membership or dine with the 'vulgar lot' – presumably meaning the team's less affluent members and/or their Boyle FC opponents. This 'exclusive club' due to a lack of numbers was 'horrors of horrors' forced to admit 'shopkeepers and constabulary.'[121] On 4 February 1888, the *Tuam Herald* reported the baptism of Tuam FC at Parkmore before several thousand spectators by the long-standing Ballyhaunis FC. This resulted in 'phenomenal' interest with the former club's committee 'positively embarrassed' when trying to select '12 of the best men.' A return match upon a pitch resembling a 'battlefield' with several 'ugly pits' up to four feet deep[122] was a mere bagatelle compared to heated committee skirmishes regarding the patriotic sportive allegiances of 'true' Irishmen. However, by April 1888, its secretary (now also a GAA member) had sought to resign and its chairman also felt, Tuam FC should exclusively play Gaelic football.[123] Yet, despite unspecified rough opposition and prejudices, the club enjoyed steady progress with support from a Glasgow-born journalist.[124] Less ideological justifications to play soccer were espoused by *Irish Sportsman* who labelled Gaelic football a 'helter-skelter-kick-or-miss business.'[125] The GAA was advised to 'frame new laws' more cognizant of player safety or permit conversions to soccer amongst 'patriotic men.'[126] Violence in Gaelic football was a regular feature. The Castlebar Mitchells – drawn finalists in Connacht's inaugural 1888 GAA final against Shiel's Black and Blues – though familiar with both soccer and rugby, had never experienced such brutal treatment during a tempestuous encounter against local rivals, Balla GAA describing the latter as 'savages.'[127]

Sligo's soccer acculturation unarguably was facilitated via its busy dock with regular shipping to Glasgow and Liverpool. When Morrison's 18-aside Sligo Wanderers played 'The Emmet Gaelic Athlone Club' in January 1886, it was representative of an unpublicized sportive *oubliette* inhabited by dock stevedores and trades unionists.[128] It also entreats an intriguing enquiry as to whether the shibbolethic one-parish-one-club rule was demonstrated in Sligo, as in Boyle, county Roscommon[129] and county Leitrim[130] or contrariwise whether urban Sligo demonstrated an early disavowal of Gaelic football. Increasingly, internal Nationalist class bifurcation was evident. During a dock strike, the founding father of Sligo borough's GAA, Michael Milmoe TC, condemned farmers' 'dastardly conduct' in taking union men's jobs,[131] and though townsmen previously were 'willing to fight for their brothers in the country,' they now 'expected' a quid pro quo[132] entreating *Quay Porter* to rhetorically enquire 'what has the UIL done for home industries [and] … the labourer of the towns…?'[133]

Return migration was another incipient factor that promoted soccer. Migratory contact through Westport, Ballina and Sligo to and from Glasgow and Greenock in pursuit of wages in Caledonia's manufacturing cities or harvesting fields was commonplace. Sligo-born Charlie Gorevan of The Celtic FC quite likely previously played for Whitefield FC against Scotland's elite Queen's Park at Hampden Park.[134] Though Celtic FC's founder was a native of Ballymote, county Sligo – unlike as demonstrated in Athlone, a garrison town which integrated a faulty Marist Brother legend into its soccer heritage[135] – (despite possessing a Marist Brother's soccer team in 1880) no contemporaneous association between Gorevan and/or Brother Walfrid regarding the source of soccer's origins in Sligo are detectable. A rare example of a work-based Nationalist soccer team was Alderman Edward Foley's Brewery FC in 1899, though more typical were work combinations sourced from Sligo's generally more affluent Protestant-owned commercial community, particularly the Scoto-Irish Pettigrew firm.

In November 1888, Ballina's nationalists of consequence formed a lawn tennis and football club at Francis Street which comprised many legal and banking professionals with notables including Simon H Scroope – captain of Dublin's Freebooters FC (formed amongst elite Irish Roman Catholics, educated in England). The Scroope family's involvement embodied Connacht's cultural sportive nexus between O.R. Coote's legacy and the *Stonyhurst Rules*.[136] Henry Scroope, a bank manager who formerly figured with Castlerea FC, quite likely was responsible for organizing a game of 'English football' in April 1888 between Ballina and Castlerea in which Scottish international, Walter Arnott of Queens FC – and subsequently of Linfield FC, Belfast – lined out for Ballina FC. Similar to Tuam's 1880s' sportive setting, Ballina's bustling Roman Catholic professional base when concurrently holding key executive positions in local Gaelic League, cricket and tennis clubs[137] promoted soccer in the Moy-side town which was further invigorated by enthusiastic educationalists such as W.R. Hatte of Ballina Intermediate FC.

A proposed Connacht Union

With the growth and spread of Irish soccer both 'chronologically and geographically' uneven[138], by 1895, after another 'serio-comic' international defeat, it was pessimistically opined 'soccer would never catch on in Ireland.'[139] Consistent with such saturnine assessments, football in Connacht was alternately conducted on an *ad hoc*, local and sub-regional basis. Castlebar FC proposed the establishment of a Connacht Union and provincial championship 'under Association rules' with Sligo's Light Blues FC, in welcoming this scheme, also hopeful of establishing a county championship in October 1896. Though a self-constituted regional Connacht AFU failed to materialize, in the IFA's absence, teams associated with the Army Football Association (AFA) now disported upon Connacht's soccer fields.

The presence in 1892–1893 of 'The Buffs,' 2nd Batt East Kent, with 150 soldiers in Castlebar and 80 in Galway[140] certainly facilitated interest in soccer. Leading regimental soccer teams in Connacht included the 1st Batt South Lancashire and 1st Batt Kings Own Yorkshire Light Infantry. The North Lancashires in February 1894 'out-witted' the Sligo Amateurs FC on 'all points' and exposed them as being 'woefully deficient in the arts of dribbling and passing' and responsible for shot-taking of 'the wildest order.'[141] In one week, the Yorkshires played Sligo Celtic Rangers FC and Sligo Wanderers FC and sought a replay against the Light Blues FC (having in January 1896 lost to this crack team and where good feeling was demonstrated). Ougtherard in county Galway experienced stronger soccer fellowship with regiments garrisoned in the *Citie of the Tribes* than the latter's inhabitants when in February 1893, Oughterard Celtic FC played The Buffs at Renmore, Galway, with a return match fixed for the popular fishing and tourist base. In 1881, this session town and police headquarters contained 834 residents[142] with 100 soldiers accommodated in Ougtherard Fort. The town's soccer team was sourced from local artisan, hospitality and fishing communities with a marginal cross-over membership with the local cricket team. The club's secretary, John Ferris, most probably a Church of Ireland Protestant[143], was reported as a Fishery Inspector.[144]

The arrival of a new detachment of *The Buffs* in Castlebar by September 1894 coincided with Westport FC's formation. Westport, set amid sentinel mountains and likened to 'a little Alpine town'[145], was county Mayo's second most populous town with 4,469[146] residents and garrison of 68 soldiers.[147] Their inaugural match was a win over *The Buffs* which elicited 'hurras of enthusiasm ... unbounded' from the enormous attendance.[148] Ougtherard Celtic FC's 'very successful career' included 'one-sided' victories against the South Lancashire's 'crack team' in November 1893 and the East Yorkshires in January 1895. Relations with the military were cordial and typified when entertainments with the South Lancashires concluded with a rendition of 'Auld Lang Syne.'[149] But in October 1894, with the club's prospects considered 'rosey,' the evacuation of *The Buffs* arguably curtailed Oughterard's blossoming soccer scene and conversely greatly strengthened the Dublin association. Meanwhile, in 1898, key personnel representing Derry-based North West FA were amenable to joining the Leinster FA and AFA to 'prevent a half-a-dozen teams in Belfast practically ruling the game in Ireland.'[150] Connacht, typically, continued its soccer sojourn in provincial isolation.

Rural *Coloeur Locale*

If the GAA's collapse assisted provincial Irish soccer, more particularly, it awakened football interest in deepest rural Connacht. The sportive theatricality of cultural nationalism now percolated soccer's *coloeur locale*. In south Leitrim, never was 'so great an interest aroused in football' when Mohill's Faugh-a-Ballagh played Carrick Emmets, in a 'friendly game of the *national pastime*' that ushered in a commemorative year to honour the 'glorious' 1798 Rising.[151] The interiorization and folklorization of soccerized former Gaelic teams continued apace. In September 1900, Ballinrobe FC was renamed 'Major McBride AFC' as 'a token of admiration of that gallant' Irishman's role against the British during the Boer War.[152] Appropriated

Gaelic football customs were integrated into rustic soccer including off-field pomp, on-pitch pageantry and vituperate newspaper battles concerning parish broils. Large contingents from Ballinamore, Dromod, Bornacoola and Cloone, in county Leitrim and county Cavan, where soccer was previously 'unheard of,' took the train to see Mohill play Longford.[153] Small, now more market-orientated, towns, including Mohill (population of 1,117 and 52 military, 4.66%) and Carrick-on-Shannon, headquarters of Leitrim Rifles militia, population 1,284[154] with a touring military presence of 52 representing 3.89%, were bolstered with competition from towns such Longford and Boyle (population of 2,994 and 69 military[155] 2.31%) engaged in association football. Soccer was now the most popular codified sport throughout much of urban north Connacht.

Clubs assisted in key fundraisers as when Ballaghaderreen's Faugh-a-Ballaghs donated proceeds to repair the Roman Catholic Diocese of Achonry's cathedral. Sligo's Light Blues 'the well-known exponents of the socker code in the west'[156] along with Castlerea, Tobbercurry, Boyle and Ballymote were invited to this tournament where levity was provided when a 'hairy legged ... holy terror' in a 'fit of athletic enthusiasm' dispensed of his boots and sprinted after the leather with his *'Remarkable Feat'* illustrated. Various Roman Catholic schools now encouraged soccer as when the Presentation Brothers of Boyle and Carrick-on-Shannon organized matches.[157] *Bon homie* was regularly demonstrated as Ballinrobe FC, though comprehensively defeated 6–0 by their 'old rivals' Castlebar FC enjoyed post-match hospitalities at the Christian Brothers' school.[158] Meanwhile, pillarization was apparent, with the astringent whiff of loyalist exclusivity perceptible, when the Excelsior FC (a club patronized by the YMCA, Church of Ireland clergy, military men and notables to include Bill Campbell BL) voted to consider changing its name to Victoria FC,[159] while in rural county Sligo, Ballymote Rovers (comprising wholly of young Protestant men) played The Wanderers in 1900.[160]

'The Lemonaders' and social respectability

Soccer in Nationalist Connacht now ventured into the quest for personal salvation in the struggle against the powerful foe 'King Alcohol.'[161] In September 1900, erstwhile members of the United Irish League (UIL), the defunct Light Blues FC (borne out of Shiels' Black and Blues FC), a vigorous independent Parnellite rump (including the influential ME Gilgan), and Summerhill's College FC converged to create Temperance FC. Facetiously termed 'The Lemonaders,' this club represented an important constituent of the local Gaelic League. Religious aspirations were sartorially demonstrated with the 'sacred heart' affixed to their blue jersey and red sash. With 100 public houses in Sligo, the Roman Catholic Bishop of Elphin proclaimed Irishmen when abstaining from alcohol were 'more than a match for Saxon or Tueton' however, Nationalist internecine squabbles, based on divergent societal *mentalities* and personality clashes, exhumed class stratifications. In March 1902, Temperance FC lost 6–4 to Sligo United FC before 4–5000 spectators in a match billed to decide the town's premiership, when the latter's star performer Andy Kilfeather[162] (secretary of Sligo Borough's UIL branch and a Sligo County Council clerk) was repeatedly targeted and then 'heaved' by 'Easkey Brennan' (formerly a bodyguard for CS Parnell in Sligo) hostilities ensued. Though held within an 'enclosed' ground and admission set at a meagre three pence, the prevalent phenomena of wall-climbing resulted in a poor financial return for this record local attendance.

A Sojourn in blessed isolation: Connacht in the IFA

Without a governing provincial body, when a 'grand football tournament' for the 'Championship of Connacht' was advertised in February 1902, Ballinrobe, Boyle Freebooters, Ballyhaunis and Castlerea were reported as Connacht's elite teams with Galway's Queens College and Carrick-on-Shannon also scheduled to participate. A disgruntled and uninvited Sligo United FC – having 'raised football' in the province 'out of the mud, aye!'[163] – refused to recognize the victors as Connacht's premier team. In 1898, the Sligo Light Blues FC after matches against Boyle, Castlerea, Longford and Athlone drew with Dublin's elite junior team Richmond Rovers (Leinster's Junior cup holders) when welcomed to Dublin as the 'Connacht cup-holders.' Their relative success signalled soccer's arrival in Connacht and participation could be encouraged if competition against 'good teams' from Belfast and Dublin was secured.[164] With the Munster FA's formation announced, western soccer towns were urged by *Sport*[165] to 'come into line' as only a 'few good heads' were needed to form a Connacht body.

In September 1901, Sligo AFC was formed with a specific intention, namely: individual honour in pursuit of the IFA Junior Cup (IJC). Though defeated during successive seasons in the IJC semi-final and the Irish Intermediate cup final, when presented with the Chichester Plate, an IFA junior secretary declared Ireland had no 'pluckier' junior team[166] while rivals acrimoniously styled this side 'The Boastful Sligo United FC.'[167] When Sligo St Marys in March 1906 lost in the IJC after a replayed final against Linfield Pirates FC, advancements included the establishment of the Sir Josslyn Gore-Booth league cup, managed by its self-constituted North Sligo Football Association (NSFA). Sir Josslyn, whose liberal-Unionist politics were fused with socialist tendencies, *noblesse oblige* and philantrophic patriotism, was also a coach and player with Lissadell AFC and president of Sligo Athletic AFC. In September 1906, Sligo no longer sojourned in 'blessed isolation' when J.P.Gillin, Fermanagh FA's secretary[168], confirmed the newly assigned Fermanagh and Western FA would include Sligo, Manorhamilton, Ballyshannon, Donegal, Bundoran and Kiltycloghert. This represented the IFA's first significant intervention to promote soccer in Connacht. A £50 grant to defray the league's costs resulted in GAA opponents 'trying to appear vexed over the matter,' being castigated as 'weak kneed pessimists.'[169] The 'True Blues' of Sligo United YMCA FC (sourced from its 100 strong fraternal membership was inaugurated at Protestant Hall) and Sligo Athletic FC were affiliated to this Fermanagh-controlled joint provincial league. In October 1906, Westport Hearts FC (affiliated with the North West FA) were defeated by Sligo AFC in Connacht's first inter-county IJC fixture. These teams were amongst a select provincial few, possessive of the desire to secure sportive arête and regional silverware while sustaining the significant logistical burdens of elite junior football. Sligo's various IFA cup campaigns occasionally generated accusations of on-field bias against the Conacians (and, admittedly rarer, incidents of off-field sectarianism) when 'trying to wrench' the IJC 'from the bullies of the North.'[170] More pointed was the prang of western mores and Ulster rectitude referable to Sabbatarianism with the IFA's junior division informed strict enforcement would result in Sligo's secession.

But by now, soccer's provincial landmass was receding. The GAA was facilitated by the Gaelic League throughout north Connacht[171] with Dr Douglas Hyde declaring rugby, soccer and hockey had succeeded the games of 'Fionn and his warriors,' but these 'alien games' would be banished.[172] In 1902, the battleground of sportive allegiance was vividly interpreted in a cartoon, entitled '*Giant and Dwarf*' depicting a herculean Gaelic footballer insouciantly threatening a miniature socerite. After 12 months' revival, Gaelic football had almost wiped out the dribbling code. Soccer's position vis-à-vis Irish nationalist identity was increasingly marginalized. Nevertheless, a rational aesthete – representative of those long practised in negotiating the ethno-religious and cultural intolerances demonstrable in sportive Ireland – admitted 'socie' football hadn't arrived in Ireland emblazoned with shamrocks or under 'false colours' which couldn't be said for the 'fine old English game known hereabouts as *Gaelic [football]*'.[173]

Conclusion

Connacht experienced a multi-causal agency with important participants including Sligo's Scoto-Irish immigrant community, the landocracy of county Roscommon, intermediate schools (both Protestant and Roman Catholic), clerical classes and the military. Incipient factors include the potential of reverse Nationalist migration from Scotland, along with increased literacy, provincial *ennui* and a quest for modernity. Soccer was more popular in urban Connacht than its rural outlines. The focus of oppositional *ressentiment* amongst Muscular Celticists concerning soccer's association with the military was often culturally *post scriptum* and hyperbolic. Participation in soccer – though largely apolitical – exhibited a pillarized condition when backed by Protestant civic leadership or urban Nationalists. Rural Nationalists exhibited asymmetrical cultural sportive political obliquities to include a strident naming policy. Provincial participation was characterized by localized self-organized bottom-up approach. The standard of play was further hampered by logistical difficulties and distance from Ireland's principal soccer centres. Though often lacking official emblems of civic identity, soccer was an important component of Ireland's persona and a symbol of respective urbanized communities' multi-vocal sportive ambitions and identity of place. Away from parish sportive squabbles, soccer provided spectators with entertainment and players with rivalry that encouraged them to demonstrate 'more science and give up ungentlemanly play.'[174]

Disclosure statement

No potential conflict of interest was reported by the author.

Notes

1. Featherstone, *Postcolonial Cultures*, 88.
2. Rasche, '… A Strangle Spectacle …: , 99.
3. Proudfoot, "Ireland: Markets and Fairs, c 1600–1853'…, 93.
4. *Sport,* April 22, 1881.
5. Taylor, *The Association Game: A History of British Football.* 105.
6. Ibid.
7. Cronin, *Sport and Nationalism in Ireland: Gaelic Games, Soccer and Irish Identity since 1884,* 121.
8. The Highlands of Connacht were regarded as the 'most neglected region in the most neglected country in Europe.' See Rasche, '… A Strangle Spectacle …: , 90–94. For the general economic condition of Connacht post the 1840s and legislative responses, see Lane, 'The Impact of the Encumbered Estates Act,' 45.

9. Curran, *Sport in Donegal, A History*, 22.
10. Regarding the contrasting socio-economic conditions and origins of soccer in Britain and Ireland, see. Bairner, 1996, 57–76.
11. *Sligo Champion,* March 29, 1902.
12. Hibernian FC consisted 'entirely of Irishmen,' Nation, March 18, 1882. Regarding 'pillarisation,' see. Morton, *Ourselves and Others: Scotland 1832–1914*, 240–241. Regarding 1890s' working-class Irish and Scottish ethnic 'machismo' and sportive tensions, highlighted by Neil Tranter, see Callum, *Sport in Europe: Politics, Class Gender*, 171–73. It was argued Irishmen in Edinburgh and Dundee were indifferent regarding Irish politics and 'think more of the game of football than of trying to increase the happiness of the land that gave them birth' (Nation, December 4, 1880), though 'kick the Papishes, every one' sectarian tensions were apparent in the Scottish FA (Nation, September 27, 1884).
13. *Tuam Herald,* February 12, 1877.
14. *Sligo Independent,* March 29, 1879.
15. *Sligo Chronicle,* January 25, 1879.
16. The 'Eleven of the Rest,' formed from Sligo FBC, included two Roman Catholics, the Kilgallen brothers.
17. *Roscommon Messenger,* January 25, 1885.
18. Interview with Anthony Touhy, Main Street, Castlerea, December 2, 2011.
19. Census of Ireland... 1881, 457.
20. *Roscommon Messenger*, October 10, 1883.
21. *Roscommon Herald*, February 25, 1885.
22. *Mayo Examiner,* December 4, 1886.
23. Ibid, January 7, 1887.
24. Ibid.
25. The Blakes were leading members of County Mayo's Landlords and Incumbrances Association branch and the South Mayo Hunt along with the beleaguered Captain Boycott.
26. *Ballinrobe Chronicle*, April 17, 1886.
27. *The Stonyhurst Magazine, Vol XIII, 1457.* Gruggen and Keating 1901, 156. Cullen, 2014 , 25; Football at Clongowes College, near Dublin, 'owed its origins to...the distinctive Stonyhurst Rules' played at the Jesuit College in Lancashire 'resembling soccer.' See Peter [ed. Garnham], 1999, 3–4.
28. *Mayo Examiner,* August 27, 1887.
29. Ibid, July 7, 1888.
30. Census of Ireland... 1881, 38.
31. *Tuam Herald,* September 11, 1886. The short-lived club ended by October 1886.
32. Census of Ireland...Galway...Table XXXI ... 1881, 180.
33. *Roscommon Herald,* June 8, 1888.
34. *Tuam Herald,* June 15, 1889. Athenry, whose barracks formerly were local cloisters, contained a 'cluster of hovels...on a bleak hill rising out of the bog.' See Rasche A Strangle Spectacle ...: , 92.
35. *Leitrim Advertiser,* February 12, 1889.
36. Clark, *Social Origins of the Irish Land War,* 136.
37. Proudfoot, Ireland: Markets and Fairs, c 1600–1853,' 93.
38. *Freeman's Journal*, September 14, 1871.
39. *Roscommon Messenger,* February 3, 1900.
40. *Freeman's Journal,* December 8, 1879.
41. Garnham, *Association Football and Society in Pre-partition Ireland.* 199.
42. Bradley, 'British and Irish Sport: the Garrison Game and the GAA in Scotland,' 81.
43. Holmes, 'Symbols of National Identity and Sport: The Case of the Irish football team,' 88.
44. Featherstone, *Postcolonial Cultures*, 76.
45. Cronin, *Sport and Nationalism in Ireland: Gaelic Games, Soccer and Irish Identity since 1884*, 120–23.
46. Garnham, 'Professionals and Professionalism in Pre-Great War Irish Soccer,' 77.

47. Hassan, McCullough and Moreland, 'North or South? Darron Gibson and the issue of player eligibility within Irish soccer'..., 46.
48. *Sligo Independent,* 4 August 1906.
49. *Sligo Champion,* April 15 1906.
50. *Sligo Independent,* August 18, 1906.
51. Spiers, *The Late Victorian Army, 1868–1902,* 131. By 1891, Connacht contained 13 military barracks with 2072 troops, though 1032 were based in Athlone.
52. *Freeman's Journal,* November 22, 1879.
53. Garnham, *Association Football and Society in Pre-partition Ireland,* 19. The 15th Battalion's *Beverley Rovers* efforts and invitation to teach Mullingar's inhabitants to soccer had little avail. For military involvement in promoting soccer, see Curran, Sport in Donegal, 65 and 74.
54. *Galway Observer,* March 5, 1898.
55. *Sligo Independent,* June 9, 1877.
56. The British Army strength throughout Ireland contained: Dublin, 14,700; Cork, 13,300; and Belfast 3,000. *Dublin Daily Express,* February 16, 1882.
57. Census of Ireland 1891 ... Table V, 10.
58. Census of Ireland 1911... Galway, Table XXV (Part II), 57: ....Sligo, Table V, 2.
59. Census of Ireland 1891 ... Galway ... Table IX, 17 ... Sligo Table IX, 567.
60. Census of Ireland 1881 ... Mayo ... Table V, 280.
61. Ibid., Table VII, 330.
62. Ibid., 316.
63. Ibid., Table V, 280.
64. Ibid.
65. Ibid.... Galway ... 97.
66. Ibid. Table V, 10.
67. Ibid. Table VII, 18.
68. Census of Ireland 1891 ...Table V, 10.
69. Ibid ... Sligo .. Table V, 534.
70. Holmes and Storey, 'Who Are The Boys In Green? Irish Identity and Soccer in the Republic of Ireland'..., 88.
71. Holmes, 'Symbols of National Identity and Sport: The Case of the Irish football team,' 88.
72. Reid, *History of Sligo Rovers,* 1–4.
73. McTernan, *Sligo GAA: A centenary history 1884–1984,* Foreword.
74. See Deignan, *The Protestant Community in Sligo,* 1914–49, 339; Gallagher, *The Streets of Sligo,* 195; Gunning and Feehily, *Down Gallows Hill....,* 195; Holmes, Symbols of National Identity and Sport: The Case of the Irish football team'..., 88; Gray, *The Game's Never Over,* Foreword; Reid, *History of Sligo Rovers,* 1–4.
75. *Sligo Champion Centenary Supplement,* 'Pioneers of Sligo Soccer,' 43.
76. *Sligo Independent,* February 20, 1886.
77. *Sligo Independent,* March 6, 1886; *Sport,* March 27, 1886.
78. *Sligo Champion,* October 21, 1939.
79. *Sligo Champion,* November 28, 1891.
80. *The Leader...,Vol 8. 1904, 26.#.*
81. Cronin, Sport and Nationalism, 123–124.
82. Deignan, *The Protestant Community in Sligo,* 1914–49, 339; Holmes, 'Symbols of National Identity and Sport: The Case of the Irish football team,' 88.
83. Jordan, *WB Yeats: Vain, glorious, lout; a maker of modern Ireland,* 80.
84. Chinneide, 'A Frenchman's Tour of Connacht in 1791'..., 30–43.
85. *Sligo Independent,* February 1, 1936.
86. *Sligo Chronicle,* October 18, 1851; *Sligo Independent,* September 6, 1862.
87. *Sligo Independent,* April 24, 1875.
88. *Sligo Independent,* April 10, 1886.
89. *Sligo Independent,* March 30, 1895.
90. The Christian Examiner, 'The Utility of the Irish Language,' 295.
91. Grousset, *Ireland's Disease: Notes and Impressions,* 234.
92. Census of Ireland 1871...Table V. 614 ... Table XXXI, 679.

93. Census of Ireland 1871…Table XXXII, 169: Table V, 614.
94. *Galway Express,* February 11, 1893.
95. *Weekly Freeman's Journal,* May 28, 1892.
96. http://www.galwaygolf.com/uploadedfiles/Chapter-1.pdf (accessed December 1, 2015).
97. Hurling, 'Belhare,' only existed in Munster and Connaught. Football was played in Leinster. Ulster's Presbyterians were 'scandalized' by Sunday games. See Chinneide, 'Conquebert' s Impression of Galway City and County…1791,' 11.
98. *Galway Express,* February 17, 1894.
99. Cunningham, *'A Town Tormented by the Sea': Galway, 1790–1914,* 307.
100. *Galway Express* December 9, 1865.
101. Garnham, *Association Football and Society in Pre-partition Ireland,* 24.
102. See Mangan and Walvin, *Manliness and Morality: Middleclass Masculinity In Britain and America, 1800–1940,* 142.
103. John Shiels was Sligo's largest wholesale butter exporter when agent for Shiels and McTigue at Hope Street, Glasgow and later Sligo Borough Town Clerk.
104. Primrose Grange School in 1889 had 30 pupils. In 1879 Mr Eade's Diocesan School had 30 pupils.
105. *Sligo Independent,* November 30, 1889.
106. WA Shekelton was a member of Sligo's Irish Loyal and Patriot Union branch.
107. http://www.jjon.org/jioyce-s-people/wheelmen (accessed December 2, 2015).
108. *Belfast Newsletter,* May 11, 1895; and *Dublin Daily National,* January 14, 1899.
109. Regarding Irish-born students at Stonyhurst and Freebooters FC, see. O'Neill, *Catholics of Consequence…,* 103.
110. *Sligo Independent,* 12 August 1905.
111. Farry, *The Aftermath of Revolution, Sligo 1921–23,* 141).
112. *Sligo Champion,* February 8, 1896.
113. (http://www.census.nationalarchives.ie/pages/1901/Sligo/Sligo_Town_in_19_files/Barrack_Street/.
114. Cronin, *Sport and Nationalism in Ireland: Gaelic Games, Soccer and Irish Identity since 1884,* 124.
115. Regarding the 'anglophobic' nature of the GAA and exclusionary membership rules, see. Garnham, 'Professionals and Professionalism in Pre-Great War Irish Soccer,' 77–93.
116. *Sligo Independent,* August 18, 1905.
117. *Freeman's Journal,* September 22, 1880.
118. *Blackburn Standard,* April 8, 1882.
119. Hassan, McCullough and Moreland, 'North or South? Darron Gibson and the issue of player eligibility within Irish soccer'…, 46.
120. *Dublin Daily Express,* December 21, 1880.
121. *Roscommon Messenger,* March 14, 1885.
122. *Tuam Herald,* March 3, 1888.
123. Ibid., April 21, 1888.
124. Regarding John McAdam, a leading National League committee member, nationalist newspapers, Presbyterianism and the military in South Donegal, see Curran, *Sport in Donegal, A History,* 65–70.
125. *Tuam Herald,* March 3, 1888.
126. Ibid.
127. *Connaught Telegraph,* May 11, 1889.
128. *Sligo Champion,* January 30, 1886.
129. *Roscommon Herald,* October 26, 1889.
130. *Leitrim Advertiser,* June 27, 1889.
131. *Sligo Independent,* December 26, 1891.
132. *Sligo Star,* February 28, 1901.
133. *Sligo Champion,* October 22, 1898.
134. *Glasgow Herald,* 4 October 1886.
135. Lynch, *The History of Athlone Town first 101 years,* 8.
136. *Western People,* August 11, 1894.
137. *Tuam Herald,* February 23, 1889; *Tuam Herald,* August 25, 1889.

138. Garnham, *The Origins and Development of Football in Ireland*, 8. For further analysis regarding the military's role in promoting soccer in 'rural areas,' see the latter, pp 30.
139. *Morning Post,* March 11, 1895.
140. *Galway Express*, September 2, 1893.
141. *Sligo Independent,* February 10, 1894.
142. Census of Ireland 1881 ... Table IX, 114.
143. http://www.census.nationalarchives.ie/pages/1901/Galway/Oughterard/Faugh_East/1394867/ (accessed April 8, 206).
144. *Galway Express,* November 30, 1895.
145. *Connaught Telegraph,* 6 September 1879.
146. Census of Ireland 1871 ... Table XXXII, 679.
147. Census of Ireland 1881 ... Table IX, 355.
148. *Mayo News*, October 13, 1894.
149. *Galway Express,* November 18, 1893.
150. *Derry Journal,* November 11, 1898.
151. *Roscommon Herald,* January 8, 1898.
152. *Connaught Telegraph*, September 29, 1900.
153. *Roscommon Herald,* January 14, 1899.
154. Census of Ireland 1881 ... Leitrim, 233 [Mohill]; Ibid. , ... 226; [Carrick-on-Shannon, part of].
155. Census of Ireland 1881 ... Table V, 426, [Boyle].
156. *Roscommon Herald,* December 9, 1900.
157. *Roscommon Herald,* December 29, 1900.
158. *Ballinrobe Chronicle,* December 21, 1895.
159. *Sligo Independent,* April 27, 1901.
160. *Roscommon Herald,* December 29, 1900.
161. *Sligo Independent,* December 24, 1902.
162. During the mid-1930s, Andrew Kilfeather was credited with overseeing Sligo Rovers FC entry into Ireland's professional ranks – the first such club in Connacht. Allegedly, he was responsible for illicitly hoisting in 1898 the Irish flag over Sligo Courthouse – the first such occurrence.
163. *Sligo Champion,* March 29, 1902.
164. Ibid., April 23, 1898.
165. *Sport,* December 7, 1901.
166. *Sligo Champion,* January 31, 1902.
167. *Roscommon Herald,* March 1, 1906.
168. *Sligo Champion,* September 22, 1906. The Fermanagh FA was formed in 1904 and by 1907 Sligo AFC supported Enniskillen's efforts to stave off Derry NFA's efforts to control all matters in the North West of Ireland.
169. *Sligo Independent,* 15 September 1906. Regarding respective positions vis-à-vis soccer and Gaelic, see Garnham, *The Origins and Development of Football in Ireland*, 30.
170. *Roscommon Herald,* February 22, 1902.
171. Egan, *Castlebar Mitchels, 1885–1895*, 44.
172. *Mayo News,* February 16, 1901.
173. *Sligo Independent,* September 15, 1906. Football was 'not an indigenous game, but a lowly-valued cultural offshoot of the English presence in the kingdom.' See Kelly, *Sport in Ireland – 1600–1840*, 273.
174. *Sligo Champion,* March 22, 1902.

References

Bairner, Alan. 'Ireland, sport and empire', An Irish Empire? In *Aspects of Ireland and the British Empire*. ed. Keith Jeffrey, 57–76. Manchester: Manchester University Press. 1996.

Bradley, Joseph 'British and Irish Sport: The Garrison Game and the G.A.A. in Scotland'. *The Sports Historian* 19, no. 1 (1999): 81–96.

Brown, Callum G. 'Sport and the Scottish Office in the Twentieth Century: The Control of a Social Problem'. In *Sport in Europe: Politics, Class, Gender*, ed. JA Mangan. London: Frank Cass. 1999.

Census of Ireland. 1871. Her Majesty's Stationary Office: A Thom. Dublin. 1877.
Census of Ireland. 1881. *Province of Connaught,* Vol IV. Her Majesty's Stationary Office, A. Thom. Dublin. 1882.
Census of Ireland. 1891. *Province of Connaught*, Vol IV. Her Majesty's Stationary Office, A Thom. Dublin, 1892.
Census of Ireland. 1901. Her Majesty's Stationary Office, A Thom, Dublin. 1902.
Clark, Samuel. *Social Origins of the Irish Land War.* Princeton, NJ: Princeton University Press, 1979.
Coogan, Tim Pat. *Michael Collins: The Man Who Made Ireland.* New York: Palgrave, 2002.
Cronin, Mike. *Sport and Nationalism in Ireland: Gaelic Games, Soccer and Irish Identity since 1884.* Dublin: Four Courts Press, 1999.
Cullen, Brendan. 'The History of Gravel Football', Coiseanna'. *The Journal of Clane Local History Group.* Kildare: Clane Local History Group, 2014.
Cunningham, John. *'A Town Tormented by the Sea': Galway, 1790–1914.* Dublin: Geography Publications, 2004.
Curran, Conor. *Sport in Donegal, A History.* Dublin: History Press, 2010.
DeBurca, Marcus. *The GAA. A History of the Gaelic Athletic Association.* Dublin: Gill and Macmillian, 2000.
Deignan, Padraig. *The Protestant Community in Sligo, 1914–49.* Dublin: Original Writing, 2010.
Egan, Liam. *Castlebar Mitchels, 1885–1895.* Castlebar. 1985.
Farry, Michael. *The Aftermath of Revolution, Sligo 1921–23.* Dublin: UCD Press, 2000.
Featherstone, Simon. *Postcolonial Cultures.* Edinburgh: Edinburgh University Press, 2005.
Gallagher, Fiona. *The Streets of Sligo.* Sligo: Fiona Gallagher, 2008.
Garnham, Neal. *The Origins and Development of Football in Ireland.* [Reprint]. Belfast: Ulster Historical Foundation, 1999.
Garnham, Neal. 'Professionals and Professionalism in Pre-Great War Irish Soccer'. *Journal of Sport History* 29, no. 1 (2002): 77–93. University of Illinois Press.
Garnham, Neal. *Association Football and Society in Pre-partition Ireland* Belfast: Ulster Historical Foundation, 2004.
Gray, Jim. *The Game's Never Over.* Sligo: Jim Gray, 1990.
Grousset, Paschal. *Ireland's Disease: Notes and Impressions.* London: Glasgow, 1888.
Gruggen, George, and Joseph Keating. *Stonyhurst: Its Past History and Life in the Stonyhurst.* London: Trubner, 1901.
Hassan, David, S McCullough, and E Moreland. 'North or South? Darron Gibson and the issue of player eligibility within Irish soccer'. In *Why Minorities Play or Don't Play Soccer: A Global Exploration, North or South?* ed. Kausik Bandypadhyay, 44–57. Oxon: Routledge. 2010.
Holmes, Michael. 'Symbols of National Identity and Sport: The Case of the Irish Football Team'. *Irish Political Studies* 9 (1994): 81–98.
Holmes, Michael, and David Storey. 'Who Are The Boys In Green? Irish Identity and Soccer in the Republic of Ireland'. In *Sport and National Identity In the Post-War World,* ed. Dilwyn Porter and Adrian Smith, 88–104. London: Routledge. 2004.
Hunt, Tom. *Sport and Society in Victorian Ireland: The Case of Westmeath.* Cork: Cork University Press, 2007.
Jordan, Athony. *WB Yeats: Vain, glorious, lout; a maker of modern Ireland.* Westport: Westport Books, 2003.
Kelly, James. *Sport in Ireland – 1600–1840.* Dublin: Four Courts Press, 2014.
Lane, Padraig G. 'The Impact of the Encumbered Estates Act of 1849 on Counties Galway and Mayo'. *Journal of Galway Archaeological and Historical Society (1981–1982),* ed. Martin Coen, 45–58, 1972.
Leach, Cristín. (Private correspondence with author, 2016).
Lynch, Frank. *The History of Athlone Town first 101 years.* Athlone: Frank Lynch, 1991.
Mangan, J.A., and James Walvin. *Manliness and Morality: Middleclass Masculinity In Britain and America, 1800–1940.* New York: St Martin's Press, 1987.
McTernan, J. *Sligo GAA: A centenary history 1884–1984.* Sligo: John McTernan, 1984.
Morton, Graeme. *Ourselves and Others: Scotland 1832–1914.* Edinburgh: Edinburgh University Press, 2012.

Ni Chinneide, Sile. 'Conquebert' s Impression of Galway City and County…1791'. *Journal of the Galway Archaeological and Historical Society* XXV, no. 1–2 (1952), 1–15.

Ni Chinneide, Sile. 'A Frenchman's Tour of Connacht in 1791'. *Journal of the Galway Archaeological and Historical Society* ed. Martin Coen. (1977): 30–43.

O'Neill, Ciaran. *Catholics of Consequence*. Oxford: Oxford University Press, 2014.

Paul, Gunning, and Paraic Feehily. *Down Gallows Hill*. Sligo: Sligo Heritage Group, 1995.

Proudfoot, Lindsay. 'Ireland: Markets and Fairs, c 1600–1853'. In *Provincial Towns in Early Modern England and Ireland: Change, Convergence and Divergence* ed. Peter Borsay and Linsay Proudfoot, Oxford: Oxford University Press. 2002.

Rasche, Hermann. 'A Strangle Spectacle …: German Travellers in The West 1828–1858'. *Galway Archaeological and Historical Society Journal* ed. Joe O'Halloran. 47 (1995): 87–107.

Reid, T. *History of Sligo Rovers*. Dublin: T. Reid, 1981.

Sligo Champion. *Centenary Supplement, 1836–1936*. Sligo: Sligo Champion, 1936.

Spiers, Edward M. *The Late Victorian Army, 1868–1902*. Manchester, NH: Manchester University Press, 1992.

Sugden and Bairner. *Sport, Sectarianism and Society*. Leicester: Leicester University Press, 1993.

Taylor, M. *The Association Game: A History of British Football*. Harlow: Pearson Longman, 2008.

The Stonyhurst Magazine. February 1916. Vol. XIII (Part 2) No. 204. Stoneyhurst College, Clitheroe.

'The Utility of the Irish Language', *The Christian Examiner and Church of Ireland magazine*. Vol II. Dublin: Curry. 1826.

'Who were the Shoneens?': Irish militant nationalists and association football, 1913–1923

Aaron Ó Maonaigh

No other sporting organization on the island of Ireland has received the historical attention which the Gaelic Athletic Association (GAA) continues to enjoy. The disproportionate amount of historical writing on the GAA has sidelined accounts of other sports on the island such as association football, rugby and cricket; although recent publications have made some headway in the reversal of this trend (For instance, see: Hunt, *Sport and Society in Victorian Ireland: the Case of Westmeath*; Garnham, *Association Football and Society in pre-partition Ireland*; and Curran, *The Development of Sport in Donegal.*). A knock-on effect of the aforementioned historical trend is the suppression of the involvement of Ireland's revolutionary 'soccerites' in the early twentieth century. This article attempts to fill the gap in historical writing regarding these individuals, and the difficulties and opposition faced by those who chose to play non-Gaelic games during the Irish Revolution 1913–1923.

Introduction

The conflation of one's choice of sporting activities with one's political sympathies was something which was, in many instances, vehemently stressed by many influential figures throughout the Gaelic Revival period (late nineteenth to early twentieth century), an era which saw a revitalization of Irish sports, literature and language through the establishment of several organizations dedicated to rejuvenating the prominence of said cultural forms. As such it was a frequent topic of discussion in many periodicals throughout the early twentieth century in Ireland.[1] However, as association football was perceived as British in origin, the assignation of political values to one's sporting choice presented a difficult conundrum for the scores of Irish nationalist revolutionaries who chose the sport as their main athletic activity. Refuting the validity of the conflation of politics and sports, the ex-Irish Republican Army Commandant and ardent soccer enthusiast Oscar Traynor commented in 1928 that 'the game a man played did not influence his convictions one iota.'[2] Traynor's robust retort was written as a response to those who questioned the patriotism of Ireland's association football players. As a former association football player and commandant of the IRA's Dublin Brigade, such criticism had a personal resonance for Traynor.

Association football found itself in a precarious situation during the early years of the nascent Irish Free State (1922–1937). Frequently, along with rugby and cricket, the game was seen as a foreign interloper upon the soil of the newly formed state; which consequently had a knock-on effect upon the perception of enthusiasts of these games. As one historian remarked, 'these games had no part to play in the concept of Irish identity as promulgated by the Irish Free State government, the Gaelic revivalists and the Gaelic Athletic Association.'[3] At times, the criticism of Ireland's soccer enthusiasts drew vitriolic remarks from cultural nationalists who questioned and derided their sporting choice. Speaking of the Dublin soccer cohorts, founder of the GAA, Michael Cusack derisively referred to them as 'the foreign faction, the Orange Catholics [and] the West Britons' who played association football in Dublin's Phoenix Park.[4] An equal opportunities critic, Cusack once referred to the Irish Amateur Athletics Association during one particular spat as a 'ranting, impotent, West British abortion.'[5] The establishment of the GAA on 1 November 1884 provided the various other sporting bodies on the island with their most potent opponent. Recent research on County Westmeath has found that the wave of cultural nationalism which occurred in the late nineteenth and early twentieth century virtually obliterated the once popular sport of cricket in the region. As Tom Hunt has remarked '... the GAA removed the men from the turf-boats, replaced their cricket bats with hurleys and provided the hurling pitch as the stage for some of the young men of rural Westmeath to express their athletic talent.'[6] Thus, throughout the late 1800s and into the early 1900s sport in Ireland became increasingly embroiled in the prevailing politics of that era.[7] Throughout this period a considerable effort was afoot to promote and disseminate traditional Irish or Gaelic games, often at the expense of what were termed 'foreign games', such as association football, cricket and rugby; games which were frequently associated with British culture and politics, the antithesis of the emergent Irish nationalist culture of the Gaelic Revival. As Brian Hanley has perceptively noted, many of the GAA's members

> regard themselves as Irish nationalists and see their support for Gaelic games as an integral part of [their sense of national and cultural identity] ... however even at the highpoint of the independence struggle from 1919 to 1921 there were Republicans who either had little interest in the GAA or who followed what it considered 'foreign games.'[8]

A garrison game?

The view that association football, or soccer, was an inherently British game and therefore 'un-Irish' was prevalent throughout the Irish Revolutionary period; most notably in Irish nationalist circles. The origin of this viewpoint appears to have stemmed from the earlier years of association football's development in Ireland, whereby the military was an important tool in the dissemination of the game, and in setting the standards of play. Although vehemently opposed to the game by principle, nationalist organizations such as the GAA were not alone in characterizing military participation in sports as 'a thorough nuisance', as Neal Garnham has observed 'local civilians ... resented the success of military teams, and the growing alienation of the military from civil society may ultimately have been reflected in some areas of rejection of both the army and their pastimes'.[9] Thus military association football teams faced a dual pronged opposition from civilians who envied their physical advantage and various Irish nationalist groupings who disagreed with their participation on political and cultural grounds. Reflecting upon the nationalistic character of his native Derry City during the War of Independence (1919–1921), IRA Volunteer

Neil Gillespie regarded an association football game which occurred between a local team and another comprised of members of the British Army's Dorsetshire regiment as a sign of the city's national weakness.[10] In 1897 the GAA council introduced a motion, Rule 21[11] which explicitly banned members of the Royal Irish Constabulary, British armed forces or police from becoming members of the organization, and thus further exacerbating the relationship between the Gaels and the garrison. Although former Royal Irish Constabulary constable and later IRA member, Tom Carney recalled one incident of cordial relations between the local GAA and the police force. Speaking to Ernie O'Malley in 1950, Carney recounted,

> When I was [stationed] in Dovea (Co. Tipperary) the local hurlers kept their hurleys in the barracks and they played in a field in front of us and they also played football. If I were the barracks orderly I would be out to play hurley with the lads while a sedate countryman would be left in the barracks to look after the rifles for me.[12]

The British military's participation in Irish Association football reached its zenith in the 1890s, after which its participation waned considerably in the intervening years and their eventual withdrawal from the Irish Free State in 1922. Despite this however, the moniker of 'garrison game' continued to see usage long after the departure of the force; particularly as a derisive sneer applied to Irish adherents of the game.[13]

As Neal Garnham has noted, 'by the summer of 1914, association football was in a remarkably buoyant position in Ireland'.[14] However the halcyon days of association football in Ireland came to an end in the wake of the First World War and the subsequent revolutionary violence witnessed in Ireland in the ensuing years. During this period the GAA grew to eclipse, notwithstanding some local exceptions, all other sports on the island. Despite the perceived 'Britishness' of association football several members of Dublin City association football clubs joined the ranks of the Irish Volunteers, Irish Citizen Army, and later the IRA. Throughout the various conflicts these men remained several steadfast abstentions from the allure of the GAA, who despite the pressure of conformity, chose to play non-Gaelic games. The following section will look at the opposition faced by Irish revolutionaries who played association football from various advanced nationalists groups who sought to thwart the spread of what they perceived as 'foreign games' and pastimes.

Who are the Shoneens?

The variety of sportsmen who took part in the 1916 Easter Rising[15] is apparent from the recollection of Dublin Volunteer Robert Holland, who remarked that interned alongside the various Gaelic Athletes in Knutsford prison, England 'was a good sprinkling of [men from] "Strandville," "Distillery" and "St. James' Gate" Association Football Teams'.[16] Oscar Traynor too recalled his amazement at '… the number of old soccer colleagues who were daily appearing [at Frongoch internment camp, Wales]'.[17] John Shouldice, inter-county GAA player and member of the 1st Battalion, Dublin Brigade, IRA remarked that '[the GAA] had been a great recruiting ground for … the Volunteers and IRA' although he was also keen to stress that 'other sporting and non-sporting bodies, or members of them, contributed their quota to the Volunteers and I.R.A. soccer, rugby, Gaelic League, National University, literary and press organisations were represented, especially in Dublin where these bodies were strong'.[18] It is not surprising that the IRA's Dublin Brigade contained a considerable number of association football players due to the sport's popularity in the capital city, although Gerald Boland's assertion that 'more than half of the Dublin Brigade 1918–1921 were soccer men', must be taken with a pinch of salt.[19]

However, despite the plethora of varying sportsmen interned in Frongoch internment camp only Gaelic games were permitted to be played, a decision which was arrived at by the Irish Volunteers' appointed camp commandants.[20] Internment camps such as Frongoch in Wales were utilized by their republican internees as a space in which a separatist national identity could be fomented, inculcated and shaped through various means, thus the decision to play Gaelic games exclusively during their internment was a considered one, rather than one based upon the personal preferences of the internees. The decision was the manifestation of national sentiment and an outward expression of the internees' 'separateness', or as one historian has commented 'the concentration on Gaelic games was intended as a symbolic statement of the prisoners' commitment to Irish nationalism and a rejection of Britain.'[21] It was not until the Irish Civil War of 1922–1923 that a relaxation in camp rules regarding the codes of sport which were permitted came to pass. Todd Andrews believed this change came about as a the result of a higher proportion of Dubliners among the internees, although it is more likely that as their jailers were Irish Free State forces rather than British ones there was less impetus for internees to project a sense of Gaelic nationalism.[22]

Despite having taken part in the 1916 Easter Rising and subsequent Irish War of Independence, Ireland's revolutionary soccer players were not immune from criticism or chastising from their comrades, on account of their sporting preference. Irish revolutionaries who chose to play 'foreign games' faced expulsion in some cases from nationalist organizations as a result of their dalliances with the former. Newry Volunteer Patrick McCann recalled in his Bureau of Military History statement that an Irish cultural society was established in the town in early 1905 or late 1904 which 'made war on all manifestations of 'seoininism[23] and West Britainism' and attendance at a foreign dance or a soccer football match would have entailed expulsion.'[24] McCann explained that 'most of the [society's] members thought it a violation of principle to attend any form of entertainment that did not conform to the Irish Ireland ideal' and as such any manifestation of pro-British sentiment whether cultural or political was aggressively opposed by the County Down society.[25] When McCann's fellow county-man and Irish Volunteers member Patrick Rankin returned to Ireland after a brief sojourn to Canada in 1915, he established no fewer than six GAA teams in the area.[26]

Opposition to non-Gaelic games was given an extra impetus by the strength and growth of soccer in the Ulster region in comparison to the GAA which struggled to make ground in some Ulster counties at the turn of the twentieth century; a fact which Irish cultural nationalists were all too keenly aware of.[27] Despite its gains across the island, the province of Ulster remained somewhat of stumbling block for the GAA in its early years due to the split demographic between nationalists and unionists, religious opposition to games on the Sabbath, and the early successes of the association football movement in the region. Historian Conor Curran's work has highlighted the strength of soccer in Donegal during the period currently under discussion, commenting that 'while at least fourteen Donegal GAA clubs fielded Gaelic football teams from 1905 to 1907 these were not of a sufficient number to mount any serious challenge to association football.'[28] The strength and popularity of soccer in the region is echoed by the recollection of Donegal Volunteer Joseph Murray, who recalled of his time spent as a school teacher during this period in Bundoran,

Co. Donegal 'I commenced to organize the G.A.A. and Gaelic League where, up to this, it had not previously existed. At this period, County Donegal had got away from Gaelic games, football, hurling etc., and soccer was the popular game.'[29] In its 6 October 1917 issue, the nationalist publication *The Leader* reported with optimism the advancements made by visiting committees of the GAA to several colleges and schools in County Dublin. The purpose of said visits was part of a concerted effort to encourage the schools to take up the playing of Gaelic games in their institutions. The GAA were clearly aware of the opportunity that schools could provide in spreading the national games and inculcating a sense of Irish nationalist identity. Interestingly two of the delegates send forth by the GAA were Irish Volunteers and 1916 veterans, John Shouldice and Harry Boland.[30] The choice of Shouldice and Boland as mascots for the GAA played upon the rising tide of Irish nationalism and the reputation of the men as men who 'were out during Easter week.'[31]

Depending on the prevailing fortunes of association football and Gaelic football, players in the Ulster region often switched between both codes. When the IRA's Glasslough Company, Co. Monaghan established a Gaelic football club in 1918, Officer Commanding J. H. McKenna noted that many of their recruits had previously played soccer; similar crossovers between GAA and association football teams occurred in the neighbouring County Cavan in the early twentieth century.[32] Despite the overlap in players across both codes, advanced nationalists in Ulster took a rather jaundiced view of the situation.

Frequently, newspaper editorials throughout the first two decades of the twentieth century carried a myriad of attacks from advanced nationalists upon association football. Insults directed towards soccer teams and their players such as 'shoneen, empty-headed dandies, and nincompoops' litter the letters pages of the County Cavan based *Anglo-Celt*.[33] Lamenting the dismal showing by the Fermanagh inter-county GAA team against Ulster rivals County Down in 1916 the *Anglo-Celt's* 'Sports and Athletics' columnist blamed the 'strong West-British element' in the county and declared it a soccer stronghold.[34]

As a soccer player I had a poor opinion of Gaelic football

The various memoirs, witness statements and personal correspondence of Ireland's revolutionary soccer players provide valuable insight into life during the tumultuous years of 1913–1923. Whilst often focused almost exclusively upon their military and nationalist activities, glimpses of their lives outside these realms frequently pervade the texts. These fleeting glimpses shed a light on what it meant to be an Irish revolutionary and simultaneously, a soccer player. In the first of his wonderfully perceptive and oft cited two-part autobiography, *Dublin Made Me*, Dublin Brigade IRA Volunteer (1917–1923) Christopher Stephen 'Todd' Andrews provides a valuable insight into the life of a Republican whose sporting preference was that of the 'foreign' persuasion. Andrews' sporting choice was an apolitical one, owing more to the socio-economic factors of his upbringing and his sense of belonging to the lower middle-class of Dublin's north inner city, rather than any considered political statement or nationalist allegiance. For Todd Andrews, reflecting back upon his upbringing, the distinction between the individual social classes of the Dublin of his youth was demarcated by, among many things, their chosen sporting preference. At the 'top of the Catholic heap' as Andrews put it, were the 'Castle Catholics' or Catholic upper middle-class, disparagingly referred to as such for their social aspirations and their perceived mimicry of the Protestant upper-class.[35] To Andrews these 'Castle Catholics' were denoted by their preference for foreign games such as golf, rugby, cricket, tennis, hockey and croquet, sports which required financial means and social connections that for the most part excluded the classes which occupied the lower rungs of the proverbial social ladder.[36]

The diary of Alfred Fannin, a Methodist and managing director of a medical and surgical supplies business situated on Dublin's Grafton Street, provides an illuminating portrait of the disparate attitudes and indeed lifestyles of the prevalent social classes of early twentieth century Ireland. On Easter Tuesday 1916, Fannin and his family decamped to Greystones, Co. Wicklow for several rounds of golf. Upon trying to place a phone call to the city-centre during lunch, Fannin was informed that the lines had been cut by 'Sinn Féiners' and that rebellion had broken out in the city; interestingly, the reaction of the Fannin family was to continue playing golf, finishing off nine rounds before making their way back into the city![37] Nestled on the rung below the so-called Castle Catholics were the 'middle class' who engaged in the playing of rugby, cricket, and tennis but did not however indulge in the fineries of golf and croquet. Lower down the social scale were the shop assistants, clerks and publicans of the lower middle-class, the socio-economic grouping of which Andrews was a self-declared member. The children of the lower middle classes played association football and cricket, as they dismissed golf and croquet as 'effeminate games,' and rugby as the preserve of the Protestants and the Castle Catholics. Most interestingly for a grouping which supplied many a willing IRA volunteer, Andrews perceived Gaelic games such as hurling and Gaelic football as follies solely fit for the 'country goms!'[38]

Andrews' lowly opinion of Gaelic games stemmed from what he perceived as the game's inherent lack of skill and its brutish nature, an issue upon which Andrews was not shy to express his views, declaring that 'Gaelic football is technically a bad game; to me it is a spectator sport to be avoided.'[39] Interestingly both Andrews and fellow Dubliner Frank Henderson, claimed that such a view was common among the 'Jackeens' of early twentieth century Dublin. In his memoir Henderson recalled that there was some consensus among Dubliners at the turn of the nineteenth century, that Gaelic games were rough and dangerous, resulting in them being held in scorn and contempt by his fellow city folk.[40] The argument of which of the two codes was the more skilful or spectator friendly was not confined to Ireland's capital city, as debates in the local Donegal press concerning the Evans Cup testify, quite a considerable amount of commentary was abound concerning the 1906 association football tournament, particularly within the nationalist newspapers and from advanced nationalists who used the medium of the press to chastise the county's association football teams.[41]

According to Andrews, the lower middle-class denizens of Dublin City spent what minimal recreational time they had following the city's principal association football teams such as Bohemians and Shelbourne, Andrews himself was a lifelong supporter of the former; Henderson too, attested to the popularity of soccer and rugby among the boys and men of Dublin City.[42] Indeed Andrews had a somewhat vested interest in his preference for the Phibsboro-based Bohemians, as his younger brother Paddy was a player with the club. Paddy, who Andrews described as 'a natural athlete ... equally successful hurler, Gaelic footballer, and when he grew up, a soccer player', became captain of the Bohemians team and gained one full International cap for Ireland over the course of his footballing career.[43]

Andrews was not alone in categorizing association football as game of the lower classes. The County Tyrone nationalist and Sinn Féin judge Kevin O'Shiel remarked in his memoirs that 'the game that was played by and appealed to the proletariat – Protestant and Catholic – was Association Football'.[44] Andrews left Dalymount Park and soccer behind, albeit only briefly in early 1918, and joined his local GAA club, Terenure Sarsfields, as he put it, 'in pursuit of principle'.[45] Andrews' brief flirtation with the GAA, outside internment camps, amounted to little more than a handful of junior football matches, a mid-match bust up and a subsequent missed appointment with the disciplinary board. When called upon to explain himself to the local GAA council Andrews, having neither the inclination nor the time, declined to offer up an appearance in his defence which ultimately brought his short GAA career to a close.[46] Henderson, however, became a zealous GAA convert within a few short years. The once proud soccer and rugby player cited the influence of the avowedly nationalist periodicals, *The United Irishmen*, *The Leader*, and *An Claidheamh Soluis* as the motivating factor for his transformation from 'Gall' to 'Gael'.[47] Urged on by the propaganda of the aforementioned papers and the GAA's ban on so-called 'foreign games', Henderson turned his back on rugby and soccer and took up hurling with the Ard Craobh club before joining St. Laurence O'Tooles Gaelic football club, of which many of his friends were member.[48] Brian Ó hUiginn, who made several unsuccessful attempts to entice a young Henderson to join the IRB throughout the revolutionary period, would later go on to establish the staunchly republican journal, *The Wolfe Tone Annual*. In the same fashion as Sceilig's (J.J. O'Kelly) *Catholic Bulletin*,[49] albeit in more pronounced and often vitriolic form, Ó hUiginn's *Wolfe Tone Annual* espoused the virtues of a sanctimonious conception of Irishness, pure, rounded, and free from Anglo influence.[50]

Other Volunteers were less susceptible to nationalistic propaganda, such as Thomas Pugh of the Dublin Brigade IRA's B Company Second Battalion. Recalling the wave of national spirit in the pre-1916 period Pugh stated 'we used to get all the National papers, "United Irishmen" and others … but I was more interested in the soccer crowd, I was secretary of a football team'.[51] Pugh's statement is an interesting one as it reveals an attitude not unlike his contemporary Oscar Traynor, who refused to acknowledge the supposed incompatibility of his Irish republicanism with his preference for soccer. Proving that politics were not always synonymous with sporting preferences inner-city Dublin born ICA man, Frank Robbins recalled that

> I was very often on the receiving end of smart remarks and made to feel I was being just about tolerated as far as national politics were concerned. My continual advocacy of the rights of the working class gained me amongst my football colleagues the nickname of 'Liberty.'[52]

Despite the disapproval of his political endeavours by many of his fellow St. Vincent's AFC clubmen, Robbins could at least draw solace from one of his teammates, Michael 'Tiger' Smith.[53] Smith shared many of Robbins' political sentiments and was an active member of the Irish Volunteers. Frank Robbins was not the only revolutionary whose politics were a source of comedic relief for their sporting teammates, as Dubliner Thomas Pugh of B Company, Second Battalion recalled of one particular drilling session

> The worst assignment I had was one day I was doing recruits drill and my football team was playing in the next field. At half-time all the boys congregated on the ditch between the two fields and made a laugh of me.[54]

Andrews' musings on his own influences and opinions on the debate between association and Gaelic football highlight the popularity of the former among the working-class of Dublin, in terms of sociological composition, the revolutionaries listed herein match the profile of Irish Volunteers and IRA members established by JoostAugusteijn in his 1996 study *From Public Defiance to Guerrilla Warfare: The Experience of Ordinary Volunteers in the Irish War of Independence 1916–1921*. Almost all of the revolutionary soccer players were young males (20–29 years old), educated by the Christian Brothers, and came predominantly from the working and lower middle classes (See Appendix 1 table). What differentiated them from their revolutionary brethren was a simple love of the 'Garrison Game'.

The game a man played did not influence his convictions one iota

Oscar Traynor, a man of impeccable Republican credentials who saw action throughout the 1916 Easter Rising, Irish War of Independence and subsequent Civil War began his successful football career at Dublin's Frankfort before transferring to Strandville, North Strand and eventually completing a move to the County Antrim side, Belfast Celtic.[55] From 1948 until his death in 1963 he was president of the Football Association of Ireland.[56] As mentioned in his Bureau of Military History statement, Traynor's short but relatively successful footballing career was interrupted by the formation of the Irish Volunteers which occurred towards the end of the 1912–1913 Irish football season; it was shortly after the Howth Gun-running in 1914 that Traynor gave up football completely to focus on his volunteer activities.[57] In the late 1920s, Oscar Traynor utilized the publication *Football Sports Weekly*, the de facto organ of the Football Association of the Irish Free State, as a means of rebutting the claims of those who sought to question the nationalist credentials of the game's adherents. In one 1927 article entitled *Who are the Shoneens?*, Traynor began by stating that 'soccer players, officials, and fans played a very important part in the fight for freedom, 1916–1921', before going on to list several Dublin-based clubs whose members contributed their services throughout the revolutionary period.[58]

Although Traynor referred to the men solely by their ranks and club affiliations, it can be ascertained that among the men to whom he was referring were Emmet Dalton, Michael Chadwick, Jim Slattery, and himself.[59] Emmet Dalton is the man referred to as 'a prominent member of Bohemians FC'. Emmet and his brother Charles both played for Bohemians, with the former serving as club president in 1926. Michael Chadwick is the man referred to as Vice-OC of the South Dublin 6th Battalion IRA.[60] Clareman and member of Michael Collins' Squad, Jim Slattery is the man referred to as having lost the use of his arm. Slattery lost a hand during the IRA's destruction of the Custom House.[61] Sam Robinson was another member of the 'Squad' who had a distinguished soccer career. Robinson played with both Bohemians and Drumcondra football clubs.[62] Such was his ire, Traynor signed off the article by stating that it would require a publication several times the size of *FootballSports Weekly* in order for him to detail the large contribution to the independence movement by 'Éire's soccerites'.

Traynor followed up 'Who are the Shoneens?' on 11 February 1928 with a lengthier piece for *Football Sports Weekly* entitled 'The Crime of Playing Soccer'. In this piece Traynor addressed, head on, the supposed incompatibility of his Irish republicanism with his preference for soccer. Traynor argued that soccer was 'a

Gaelic game, pure and simple, having its origins in the highlands of Scotland'. Traynor went on to assert that a preference for sports, even foreign ones, was no motivating factor when the call of national duty rang out. Using Cathal Brugha and Kevin Barry as examples of republican patriots who indulged in foreign games, Traynor asked if soccer's critics dared question the integrity of those particular men. Traynor was not the sole pro-soccer revolutionary who took issue with the repeated criticisms of Ireland's soccer enthusiasts. Henry McGowan of Ballybofey, County Donegal issued a letter to the editor of the Derry Journal on 5 October 1928, in which he accused members of the Donegal GAA's county board of conducting a concerted and protracted campaign of abuse against those who were interested in association football in the county; a proverbial war of words which was played out throughout the regional newspapers.[63]

Popular myth holds that the Alton United side that won the 1923 Irish Free State Cup was largely comprised of IRA personnel, drawing their membership and support from the largely nationalist Falls Road area of West Belfast. In his *Football Sports Weekly* column on 11 February 1928 Oscar Traynor quotes an article by contributor 'Mount Divis' in the same issue of *FSW* which referred to the Belfast side as 'The Gunmen', going on to state that such a moniker was a honour for a side whose players earned it for their part in defending the nationalist population of Belfast during the 'Belfast Pogroms', during which, a spate of sectarian killings took place in the city.[64] Whilst Traynor's inferences imply that Alton's 1923 IFS Cup side was composed of IRA Volunteers from Belfast's City battalion, records of the battalion's membership prove otherwise. In a display more resplendent of a GAA fixture than a soccer one, the dramatic arrival of Alton United's team in Dublin for the 1922–1923 Irish Free State Cup final replay underlined the precarious conditions of a sport operating amidst the outward trappings of war. The Belfast side were escorted upon arrival at Amien's Street station to Dalymount by an armed guard provided by the IRA; an event which mirrored earlier displays by the Irish Volunteers at GAA fixtures, such as that which occurred on 5 July 1914 when Austin Stack marched 700 members of the Tralee branch of the County Kerry Irish Volunteers to the town's railway station to welcome the visiting Wexford GAA team.[65]

Despite the military grandeur of Alton's arrival, on 19 March the *Freeman's Journal* happily reported that 'despite rumours and alarms, everything passed off peacefully and enjoyably'. Facing the heavily favoured Dublin side Shelbourne, Alton surprised all and sundry by finishing the game one-nil winners. Although the Alton players received their winners' medals, the tumultuous state of affairs in the newly established Six County statelet prevented the cup travelling north. However, of the side that faced Shelbourne in the 1923 IFS Cup, only two Alton players were active members of the Belfast IRA. These men were Vice O/C Michael Brennan, of Belfast's First Battalion Staff and C Company Volunteer James Maginnis.[66] Alton's dramatic arrival was not the first time that the IRA and the FAIFS crossed paths. The previous year's (1921–1922) IFS cup final saw a post-match dispute settled by an IRA member brandishing a gun. A mass brawl broke out between the players and supporters of the opposing sides which culminated in the invasion of the St. James' Gate dressing room by incensed Shamrock Rovers fans and players. During the ensuing mayhem the brother of one of the St. James Gate players took a gun from his belt and fired into the roof, dispersing the Rovers players.[67]

The events of the 1922 and 1923 IFS Cups cannot be seen in isolation, such events were resplendent of the prevailing internecine conflict, the Irish Civil War.

Such events demonstrated that the violence of the era crossed all boundaries of public life and was not restricted exclusively to Gaelic orientated endeavours.[68] Oscar Traynor's and Henry McGowan's responses highlight the vilification of Ireland's soccerites during the early years of the nascent Irish Free State, offering an interesting counterbalance to the view that the GAA alone, was at the fore of the Irish Revolution.

Conclusion

Quarter-master general of 'F' Company, Fourth Battalion Dublin Brigade, Peadar S. Doyle astutely recalled how the men who comprised the volunteers that turned out for the Easter Rising of 1916 were drawn from a whole host of occupations, sporting organizations and interests including 'Soccer and foot-ball [sic] and Rugby men … staff of the Abbey Theatre, as well as from the ranks of the Trades Union'.[69] Historian Peter Hart would later arrive at the same conclusion in his article on the social structures of the IRA during the period 1916–1923. Hart deduced that 'the IRA drew members from every walk of life and from every sector of the Irish economy. The appeal of militant republicanism crossed all occupational boundaries'.[70] Despite this however, militant Irish nationalists who played non-Gaelic games have tended to dwell upon the fringes of the historiography of the period until quite recently. Sport provided Irish militant nationalists with a difficult conundrum to negotiate, frequently torn between an allegiance to the nationalist ethos of their peers in the form of the GAA, or the derisively termed 'garrison game'. It is clear from their reminiscences that several Irish Republicans who played association football felt an undue pressure to conform to a myopic definition of Gaelic or Irish nationalism which forbade the playing of such games; this view was espoused both by their peers and also by the nationalist press.[71] Irish soccer organizers and players had to work 'twice as hard' as their peers in the GAA to prove their nationalist credentials.[72]

The legacy of the GAA's ban on non-Gaelic sports and the attitudes of advanced Irish nationalists towards the adherents of said sports is a most striking feature of this period of Irish history. Evidently, despite their commitment to the cause of Irish political independence, Irish revolutionary soccer players experienced sustained criticism from their advanced cultural nationalist peers who deemed their sporting choice as irreconcilable with their political values. Although the traditional narrative of the Irish Revolution promulgated a script which was predominantly Gaelic in almost every aspect, the truth is that there were several active individuals who transcended such a myopic definition.[73] As Oscar Traynor stated, 'Faithful to Éire, we have answered her call, Soccer men, Gaelic men, Rugger, and Hurley men, true-hearted sporting men, Irishmen all'.[74]

Disclosure statement

No potential conflict of interest was reported by the author.

Notes

1. Curran, 'Sport and Cultural Nationalism: The conflict between Association and Gaelic football in Donegal, 1905–1934', 81; and McElligott, *Forging a Kingdom: The GAA in Kerry 1884–1934.*

2. *Football Sports Weekly,* February 11, 1928.
3. McCabe, 'Football Sports Weekly and Irish Soccer: 1925–1928', 148.
4. [Dublin] *Evening Telegraph*, March 21, 1896.
5. *Freeman's Journal*, June 5, 1885.
6. Hunt, 'Classless Cricket? Westmeath 1880–1905', 26.
7. For a case study of the relationship between the GAA and politics during the revolutionary period, see: Hassan and McGuire, 'The GAA and Revolutionary Irish Politics in late Nineteenth- and Early Twentieth-Century Ireland'.
8. Hanley, 'Irish Republican attitudes to sport since 1921', 175.
9. Garnham, *Association Football*, 21; and University College Dublin Archives Department, Fallon papers, [Hereafter UCDAD].
10. MacEoin, *Survivors*, 162.
11. Rule 21 which explicitly banned members of the Royal Irish Constabulary, British armed forces or police from becoming members of the GAA remained in force from 1897 to 2001. The GAA introduced another motion officially known as Rule 27, euphemistically titled 'The Ban' this rule banned all GAA members from taking part in non-Gaelic games. In addition, it also banned them from watching non-Gaelic sports, taking part in social events organized by such games, or furthering their cause. This rule remained in place from 1902 to 1971.
12. UCDAD, O'Malley notebooks, (UCDAD, P17b/109/29L&29R).
13. Garnham, *Association Football*, 18–9.
14. Ibid., 161.
15. The Easter Rising was an armed insurrection which took place in Ireland during Easter Week April 1916. The Rising was launched by several advanced Irish nationalist and socialist groups in an attempt to end British rule in Ireland and establish an independent Irish Republic. In its aftermath up to 3400 civilians and rebels were arrested, and ca. 1800 were interned in various prisons in Britain; it is this experience which Holland, Traynor and Shouldice are recounting.
16. National Archives of Ireland, Bureau of Military History, Robert Holland witness statement 371 [Hereafter NAI, BMH WS].
17. *Football Sports Weekly*, February 11, 1928.
18. John Shouldice, witness statement (NAI, BMH WS 679).
19. *Irish Times*, October 19, 1968.
20. For a contemporary account of the post-1916 Rising internments, and a detailed description of the day-to-day running of the camps, see: Brennan-Whitmore, *With the Irish in Frongoch*.
21. Murphy, 'The GAA during the Irish Revolution, 1913–1923', 71.
22. Andrews, *Dublin Made Me*, 317.
23. A 'seoinín', anglicized as 'shoneen', is a derogatory term for an Irish person who is perceived as being overly anglophilic in matters of culture or politics. The term West Brit carries the same connotations.
24. Not to be confused with the GAA's ban, it is expulsion from the Newry Gaelic cultural society rather than the GAA which McCann is seemingly implying in this instance.
25. Patrick McCann, witness statement (NAI, BMH WS 171).
26. Murray, 'A Rebel Returned: The Story of Patrick Rankin, who Took Part in the Rising', 32.
27. Curran, 'Networking Structures and Competitive Association Football in Ulster, 1880–1914', 75.
28. Curran, 'Sport and Cultural Nationalism: The conflict between Association and Gaelic football in Donegal, 1905–1934', 81.
29. Joseph Murray, witness statement (NAI, BMH WS 1566).
30. *The Leader*, October 6, 1917.
31. Boland and Shouldice were two of the 302 Dublin GAA members who took part in the Easter Rising 1916. Dublin GAA members comprised ca. 20% of the estimated 1500 rebels who took part in the rising in Dublin; see: Nolan, *The Gaelic Athletic Association in Dublin 1884–2000*.
32. J.H. McKenna, witness statement (NAI, BMH WS 575); and *Anglo-Celt*, October 18, November 9 and December 21, 1901.

33. The debate carried on for over two months, see: *Anglo-Celt,* December 26, 1908, January 2, 23, 1909.
34. *Anglo-Celt*, August 6, 1916.
35. Andrews, *Dublin Made Me*, 5.
36. Ibid., 5.
37. Warwick-Haller, *Letters from Dublin 1916: Alfred Fannin's Diary of the Rising*, 13–4.
38. Andrews, *Dublin Made Me,* 113.
39. Ibid., 113.
40. Henderson, *Frank Henderson's Easter Rising: Recollections of a Dublin Volunteer*, 21.
41. Curran, 'Networking Structures and Competitive Association Football in Ulster, 1880–1914', 4.
42. Andrews, *Dublin Made Me*, 5–6; and Henderson, *Frank Henderson's Easter Rising,* 21.
43. Ireland's International Players.
44. Kevin O'Shiel, witness statement (NAI, BMH WS 1770).
45. Andrews, *Dublin Made Me*, 117.
46. Ibid., 117.
47. Gall' is the Gaeilge term for a foreigner.
48. Henderson, *Frank Henderson's Easter Rising*, 21.
49. Murphy, 'Telling the Story of 1916: *The Catholic Bulletin* and *Studies*', 51.
50. O'Neill, 'National Consciousness', 14.
51. Thomas Pugh, witness statement (NAI, BMH WS 397).
52. Robbins, *Under the Starry Plough:Recollections of the Irish Citizen Army*, 35.
53. O'Farrell, *Who's Who in the Irish War of Independence and Civil War: 1916–1923*, 145.
54. Thomas Pugh, witness statement (NAI, BMH WS 397).
55. Skinner, *Politicians by Accident*, 231; Flynn, 'First Hoops for Belfast Celtic's Minister of Defence', 6–7.
56. Coleman, 'Oscar Traynor'.
57. Oscar Traynor, witness statement (NAI, BMH WS 340).
58. Early histories of the GAA were keen to stress the connections between the organization and various Irish revolutionary endeavours. In his article Traynor makes a direct assault on the GAA's monopolizing of the popular history of sport and the Irish Revolution and the organization's inflated ego regarding the matter. For instance, see: O'Toole, *The Glory and the Anguish*, de Búrca, *The GAA: A History*. However, recent contributions to the historiography of the GAA have produced more nuanced portraits of the organization. See, Ó Tuathaigh, ed., *The GAA & Revolution in Ireland 1913–1923*.
59. *Football Sports Weekly*, April 9, 1927.
60. Irish Military Archives, 6th Battalion, Dublin I Brigade nominal rolls (MA IE, MSPC/RO/07), [Hereafter MA IE].
61. O'Mahony, *The Burning of the Custom House in Dublin 1921*, 18.
62. Bohemian Graves at Glasnevin Cemetery.
63. Curran, 'Sport and Cultural Nationalism', 85.
64. McKenna, *Facts and Figures of the Belfast Pogroms, 1920–1922*.
65. Ryan and O'Rourke, *Gillette Book of the FAI Cup*, 13–14; and Gaughan, *Austin Stack: Portrait of a Separatist*, 30–31.
66. IMA, 3rd Northern Division, 1st Brigade (Belfast), 1st Battalion nominal rolls (MA IE, MSPC/RO/403).
67. Rice, *We Are Rovers*, 35.
68. Kissane, *The Politics of the Irish Civil War*, 69.
69. Peadar S. Doyle, witness Statement (NAI, BMH WS 155).
70. Hart, 'The Social Structure of the Irish Republican Army, 1916–1923', 207.
71. Henderson, *Frank Henderson's Easter Rising*, 21.
72. Cronin, *Sport and Nationalism in Ireland: Gaelic games, soccer and Irish identity since 1884*, 124.
73. Hanley, 'Oscar Traynor and "The Crime of Playing Soccer"', 48–49.
74. *Football Sports Weekly*, April 9, 1927.
75. Andrews, *Dublin Made Me*; id., *Man of No Property*; C.S. Andrews, Military Service Pensions files(MA IE, MSP/34/REF57554 and 34D/1920); Tom Garvin, Andrews, Christopher Stephen ('Todd').

76. Census of Ireland 1901; John Fagan, Military Service Pensions files (MA IE, MSP/34/REF20598 and W34/E5021);Thomas Smart (NAI, BMH WS 255); and Information from Thomas Tormey.
77. Frank Henderson, witness statement (NAI, BMH WS 249 & 821); Ruaidhri Henderson, witness statement (NAI, BMH WS 1686); Dempsey and Boylan, 'Henderson, Frank'; and Henderson, *Frank Henderson's Easter rising*.
78. Census of Ireland 1911; Michael Smyth, Military Service Pensions files (MA IE, MSP/34/REF1264 and W34/D1619); Robbins, *Under the Starry Plough;* O'Farrell,*Who's Who in the Irish War of Independence and Civil War: 1916-1923*; and Fox, *The History of the Irish Citizen Army*.
79. A Gaelscoil is an Irish language medium school.
80. Coleman, 'Traynor, Oscar'; Oscar Traynor, witness statement (NAI, BMH WS 340); Oscar Traynor voice recording, circa 1950/51 (NAI, BMH VR/03); Oscar Traynor interview, Ernie O'Malley notebooks (UCDAD, P17b 96, 98, 101); Skinner, *Politicians By Accident*; and Flynn, 'First Hoops for Belfast Celtic's Minister of Defence', 6–7.
81. Census of Ireland, 1901; Baptism Records of St. Mary's Pro Cathedral, Dublin; Thomas Pugh, witness statement (NAI, BMH WS 397); Matthews, *The Irish Citizen Army*; and Fox, *The History of the Irish Citizen Army*.
82. Census of Ireland 1901; Frank Robbins, witness statement (NAI, BMH WS 585); Robbins, *Under the Starry Plough*; Matthews, *The Irish Citizen Army*; Angela Murphy, 'Robbins, Francis ("Frank")'; and Fox, *The History of the Irish Citizen Army*.
83. White, 'Boland, Gerald'; Boland and McInerney, 'Gerald Boland's Story: Contemporaries and New Men'; and Maher, *Harry Boland: A Biography*.

References

Andrews, Christopher Stephen. *Dublin Made Me*. Dublin: Lilliput Press, 2001.
Andrews, Christopher Stephen. *Man of No Property*. Dublin: Lilliput Press, 2001.
Augusteijn, Joost. *From Public Defiance to Guerrilla Warfare: The Experience of Ordinary Volunteers in the Irish War of Independence 1916–1921*. Dublin: Irish Academic Press, 1996.
Bohemian Graves at Glasnevin Cemetery.
Boland, Gerald, and McInerney, Michael. 'Gerald Boland's Story: Contemporaries and New Men'. *Irish Times*, October 19, 1968.
Bureau of Military History. Doyle, P.S. Witness Statement (National Archives of Ireland [hereafter NAI], BMH/WS/155).
Bureau of Military History. Henderson, F. Witness statement (NAI, BMH WS 249 & 821).
Bureau of Military History. Henderson, R. Witness statement (NAI, BMH WS 1686).
Bureau of Military History. Holland, R. Witness statement (NAI, BMH/WS/371).
Bureau of Military History. McCann, P. Witness statement (NAI, BMH/WS/171).
Bureau of Military History. McKenna, J.H. Witness statement (NAI, BMH/WS/575).
Bureau of Military History. Murray, J. Witness statement (NAI, BMH/WS/1566).
Bureau of Military History. O'Shiel, K. Witness statement (NAI, BMH WS 1770).
Bureau of Military History. Pugh, T. Witness statement (NAI, BMH WS 397).
Bureau of Military History. Robbins, F. Witness statement (NAI, BMH WS 585).
Bureau of Military History. Shouldice, J. Witness statement (NAI, BMH/WS/679).
Bureau of Military History. Smart, T. Witness statement (NAI, BMH WS 255).
Bureau of Military History. Traynor, Oscar. Witness statement (NAI, BMH/WS 340).
Census of Ireland returns 1901 & 1911. National Archives of Ireland.
Coleman, Marie. 'Oscar Traynor'. In *Dictionary of Irish Biography*, ed. J. McGuire and Quinn J., Cambridge: Cambridge University Press, 2009. http://dib.cambridge.org.dcu.idm.oclc.org/viewReadPage.do?articleId=a8626&searchClicked=clicked&quickadvsearch=yes
Cronin, Mike. *Sport and Nationalism in Ireland: Gaelic games, soccer and Irish identity since 1884*. Dublin: Gill & Macmillan, 1999.
Curran, Conor. 'Sport and Cultural Nationalism: The conflict between Association and Gaelic football in Donegal, 1905–1934'. *Éire-Ireland* 48, no. 1 (2013): 79–94.

Curran, Conor. 'Networking Structures and Competitive Association Football in Ulster, 1880–1914'. *Irish Economic and Social History* 41 (2014): 74–92.

Curran, Conor. *The Development of Sport in Donegal 1880–1935*. Cork: Cork University Press, 2015.

de Búrca, Marcus. *The GAA: A History*. Dublin: Gill & Macmillan, 2000.

Dempsey, Pauric J., and Shaun Boylan. 'Frank Henderson'. In *Dictionary of Irish Biography*, ed. James McGuire and James Quinn, Cambridge: Cambridge University Press, 2009. http://dib.cambridge.org.dcu.idm.oclc.org/viewReadPage.do?articleId=a3921&searchClicked=clicked&quickadvsearch=yes

Derry Journal on 5 October 1928.

[Dublin] *Evening Telegraph*, March 21, 1896.

Flynn, Martin. 'First Hoops for Belfast Celtic's Minister for Defence'. *History Ireland* 18, no. 2 (March–April 2010): 6–7.

Fox, Richard Michael. *The History of the Irish Citizen Army*. Dublin: J. Duffy & Co., limited, 1944.

Freeman's Journal, June 5, 1885.

Freeman's Journal, March 19, 1923.

Garnham, Neal. *Association Football and Society in pre-partition Ireland*. Belfast: Ulster Historical Foundation, 2004.

Garvin, Tom. 'Christopher Stephen ("Todd") Andrews'. In *Dictionary of Irish Biography*, ed. James McGuire and James Quinn, Cambridge: Cambridge University Press, 2009. http://dib.cambridge.org.dcu.idm.oclc.org/viewReadPage.do?articleId=a0155&searchClicked=clicked&quickadvsearch=yes#

Gaughan, John Anthony. *Austin Stack: Portrait of a Separatist*. Dublin: Kingdom, 1977.

Hanley, Brian. 'Oscar Traynor and "The Crime of Playing Soccer"'. *History Ireland* 24, no. 1 (January–February 2016): 48–9.

Hanley, Brian. 'Irish Republican attitudes to sport since 1921'. In *The Evolution of the GAA: Ulaidh, Éire agusEile*, ed. Donal McAnallan, David Hassan, and Roddy Hegarty, 175–84. Belfast: Stair Ulaidh, 2009.

Hart, Peter. 'The Social Structure of the Irish Republican Army, 1916–1923'. *Historical Journal (Cambridge)* 42, no. 1 (1999): 207–31.

Hassan, David, and Andrew McGuire. 'The GAA and Revolutionary Irish Politics in late Nineteenth- and Early Twentieth-Century Ireland'. *Sport in Society: Cultures, Commerce, Media, and Politics* 19, no. 1 (2015): 1–11.

Henderson, Frank. 'Recollections of Frank Henderson (1)'. In *Frank Henderson's Easter Rising: Recollections of a Dublin Volunteer*, ed. Michael Hopkinson, 13–27. Cork: Cork University Press, 1998.

Hunt, Tom. '"Classless Cricket?" Westmeath 1880–1905'. *History Ireland* 12, no. 2 (2004): 26–30.

Hunt, Tom. *Sport and Society in Victorian Ireland: the Case of Westmeath*. Cork: Cork University Press, 2007.

'Ireland's international players'. A list of players who represented the Republic of Ireland in official international matches.

Irish Military Archives. 3rd Northern Division, 1st Brigade (Belfast), 1st Battalion Nominal Rolls (MA IE, MSPC/RO/403).

Irish Military Archives. 6th Battalion, Dublin I Brigade nominal rolls (MA IE, MSPC/RO/07).

Irish Military Archives. Christopher Stephen Andrews, Military Service Pensions files (MA IE, MSP/34/REF57554 and 34D/1920).

Irish Military Archives. John Fagan, Military Service Pensions files (MA IE, MSP/34/REF20598 and W34/E5021).

Irish Military Archives. Michael Smyth, Military Service Pensions files (MA IE, MSP/34/REF1264 and W34/D1619).

Irish Military Archives. Oscar Traynor voice recording, circa 1950/51 (MA IE, BMH VR/03).

Kissane, Bill. *The Politics of the Irish Civil War*. Oxford: Oxford University Press, 2005.

Kitching, G. 'The Origins of Football: History, Ideology and the Making of "the People's Game"'. *History Workshop Journal* 79, no. 1 (Spring 2015): 127–53.

MacEoin, Uinseann, ed. *Survivors*. Dublin: Argenta, 1980.
McCabe, Conor. 'Football Sports Weekly and Irish Soccer: 1925–1928'. *Media History* 17, no. 2 (2011): 147–58.
McElligott, Richard. *Forging a Kingdom: The GAA in Kerry 1884–1934*. Cork: Collins Press, 2013.
Maher, Jim. *Harry Boland: A Biography*. Cork: Mercier, 1998.
Mandle, William Frederick. *The Gaelic Athletic Association and Irish National Politics 1884–1924*. Dublin: Gill and Macmillan, 1987.
Matthews, Anne. *The Irish Citizen Army*. Cork: Mercier, 2014.
McKenna, G.B. (Father John Hassan). *Facts and Figures of the Belfast Pogroms, 1920–1922*. Dublin: O'Connell Publishing Company, 1922.
Murphy, Brian. 'Telling the Story of 1916: The "Catholic Bulletin" and "Studies"'. *Irish Quarterly Review* 101, no. 401 (2012): 47–56. Irish Studies.
Murphy, William. 'The GAA during the Irish Revolution, 1913–1923'. In *The Gaelic Athletic Association 1884–2009*, ed. Mike Cronin, William Murphy, and Paul Rouse, 61–76. Dublin: Irish Academic Press, 2009.
Murray, Joe. 'A Rebel Returned: The Story of Patrick Rankin, who Took Part in the Rising'. In *The Rising Centenary: Louth 1916/2016*, 32–6, ed. Anne Campbell. Drogheda: Drogheda Independent and The Argus, 2009.
National Library of Ireland. 'Michael Cusack, Maurice Davin and the Gaelic Athletic Association'. In *The 1916 Rising, Personalities and Perspectives: An Online Exhibition*. National Library of Ireland, 1916. http://www.nli.ie/1916/exhibition/en/content/stagesetters/culture/cusack-davin/
National Library of Ireland. James L. O'Donovan to Daniel O'Donovan, 16 February 1923. (NLI, James L. O'Donovan papers, MS 22, 306).
National Library of Ireland. W.G. Fallon to F.B. Dineen, Chairman GAA Athletics Council, 26 April 1907, Draft letter (Fallon papers, NLI, MS 22,577).
Nolan, William, ed. *The Gaelic Athletic Association in Dublin 1884–2000*. Dublin: Geography Press, 2000.
O'Farrell, Padraic. *Who's Who in the Irish War of Independence and Civil War: 1916–1923*. Cork: Mercier Press, 1980.
O'Mahony, Seán. *The Burning of the Custom House in Dublin 1921*. Dublin: 1916–1921 Club in association with Elo Publications, 2000.
O'Neill, C. 'National Consciousness'. In *The Wolfe Tone Annual*, ed. Brian Ó hUiginn, Dublin, 13–5, 1933.
O'Toole, Pádraig. *The Glory and the Anguish*. Galway: Loughrea, 1984.
Ó Tuathaigh, Gearóid, ed. *The GAA & Revolution in Ireland 1913–1923*. Cork: Collins Press, 2015.
Rice, Eoghan. *We Are Rovers*. Dublin: Nonsuch, 2005.
Robbins, Frank. *Under the Starry Plough: Recollections of the Irish Citizen Army*. Dublin: Academy Press, 1977.
Ryan, Seán, and O'Rourke, Terry. *Gillette book of the FAI Cup*. Dublin: Irish Soccer Co-op, 1985.
Skinner, Liam. *Politicians by Accident*. Dublin: Metropolitan Publishing, 1946.
The Leader XXXV, no. 9 October 6, 1917.
Traynor, Oscar. 'Who were the Shoneens?' *Football Sports Weekly*, April 9, 1927.
Traynor, Oscar. 'The Crime of Playing Soccer'. *Football Sports Weekly*, February 11, 1928.
University College Dublin Archives Department. Tom Carney (Former RIC, 3rd Battalion East Mayo Brigade IRA), interview, (UCDAD, Ernie O'Malley notebooks, P17b/109/29L&29R).
University College Dublin Archives Department. Oscar Traynor (Officer Commanding Dublin Brigade I IRA), interview, (UCDAD, Ernie O'Malley notebooks, P17b 96, 98, 101).
Warwick-Haller, Adrian, and Warwick-Haller, Sally, eds. *Letters from Dublin 1916: Alfred Fannin's Diary of the Rising*. Dublin: Irish Academic Press, 1995.
White, Lawrence William. 'Gerald Boland'. In *Dictionary of Irish Biography*, ed. James McGuire and James Quinn, Cambridge: Cambridge University Press, 2009. http://dib.cambridge.org.dcu.idm.oclc.org/quicksearch.do;jsessionid=F07D30662B211EABFC0D9B62AD93FB79

Appendix 1. Sociological composition of Dublin's 'Irish revolutionary soccerites'

Names	Christopher 'Todd' Andrews[75]	John 'Kruger' Fagan[76]	Frank Henderson[77]	Michael Smyth[78]
Rank in the IRA/ICA	Lieutenant 'E' Company 4th Bn., Dublin I (1921)	Volunteer, 'F' Company 1st Bn., Dublin I	Commandant of 2nd Dublin Bn., (1917)	Section Commander 'E' Company 2nd Bn., Dublin I (1921)
Age/D.O.B	6 October 1901	1900	16 April 1886	29 January 1892
Gender	Male	Male	Male	Male
County	Dublin	Dublin	Dublin	Dublin
Occupation	Student	Employee, Lafayette photographers	Clerk	Hotel Servant
Religion	Roman Catholic	Roman Catholic	Roman Catholic	Roman Catholic
Marital status (1913–1923)	Single	Single	Married (1918)	Married (1916)
Rural or urban background	Urban	Urban	Urban	Urban
Education	Christian Brothers School, Gaelscoil,[79] University College Dublin	CBS	CBS	Unknown; Could read and write in English
Influence from Gaelic culture	Attended Pádraig Pearse's Scoil Éanna	None stated	Gaelic League and GAA member	Father and brother both spoke Gaeilge
Played GAA sports/club affiliation	Whilst interned, briefly with Terenure Sarsfields GFC	No	ArdCraobh Hurling Club, St. Laurence O'Tooles GFC	Not stated
Association football affiliation	UCD FC	Shamrock Rovers FC, Football League of the Irish Free State XI	CBS Fairview FC	St. Vincent's FC
Names	Oscar Traynor[80]	Thomas Pugh[81]	Frank Robbins[82]	Gerald Boland[83]
Rank in the IRA/ICA	Officer Commanding Dublin Brigade I IRA (1920)	Volunteer, 'B' Company, 2nd Bn., Dublin I.	Sergeant ICA (1916)	First lieutenant of 'B' Company, 2nd Bn., Dublin I. Commandant 7th Bn., Dublin II (1921)

Age/D.O.B	21 March 1886	9 August 1883	5 July 1895	25 May 1885
Gender	Male	Male	Male	Male
County	Dublin	Dublin	Dublin	Dublin
Occupation	Compositor	Clerk	General labourer	Apprentice fitter
Religion	Roman Catholic	Roman Catholic	Roman Catholic	Roman Catholic
Marital status (1913–1923)	Married (1918)	Single	Single	Married (1915)
Rural or urban background	Urban	Urban	Urban	Urban
Education	CBS	Not stated	CBS	NS
Influence from Gaelic culture	None	Supported various Irish-Ireland causes	None	Gaelic league and GAA member, Celtic Literary Society
Played GAA sports/club affiliation	No	No	No	O'Donovan Rossas GFC, Rathmines Hurling Club
Association football affiliation	Frankfort, Strandville, Belfast Celtic	Not stated	St. Vincent's FC	Not stated

'Inciting the roughs of the crowd': soccer hooliganism in the south of Ireland during the inter-war period, 1919–1939

Mark Tynan

> Hooliganism is not a term readily associated with soccer during the early twentieth century, nor is it a term commonly associated with the sport in Ireland. As such it may come as a surprise to note that the term was in circulation in Ireland during the inter-war period. This article begins by challenging the perception that the soccer-related violence that occurred in Ireland against the backdrop of the Anglo-Irish War (1919–1921) was solely a by-product of sectarian division in the north of the country. During this period violence around soccer was arguably just as prevalent, if less serious, in the south of Ireland, and the article describes how this violence persisted in the south into the 1920s and the 1930s. Finally, the article attempts to identify the root causes of soccer hooliganism in inter-war Ireland by analysing the violence in the context of the wider socio-economic environment.

Introduction

On 27 October 1919, reporting on a violent incident that had just taken place at a soccer match in Dublin, the *Irish Independent* used the term 'hooliganism' to describe the behaviour of those responsible. Today, this term is most associated with the violence perpetrated by English supporters who rampaged their way across Europe during the 1980s in particular, but soccer hooliganism is by no means a new or modern concept. It has in fact existed in some form or another for as long as the game has been played. Soccer hooliganism really came to the fore in Europe during the inter-war period. David Goldblatt cites tension rooted in local and national patriotism, the influence of alcohol and the changing demographic of soccer crowds as contributing factors to a continent-wide upsurge of soccer-related violence during the 1920s and 1930s.[1] Likewise, Eric Dunning and his colleagues at the University of Leicester have tended to focus on the social demographic of soccer crowds in their interpretation of the causes of soccer hooliganism. Drawing from Norbert Elias' theory of the civilization process,[2] Dunning has contended that the historic proliferation of civilized behaviour has yet to fully reach the lower working-classes, the section of society most associated with soccer and soccer hooliganism. In this regard the primeval, male-dominated environs surrounding English soccer in the 1970s and 1980s were social spaces where a lower working-class subculture permeated and thrived. This subculture fostered distinct ideas about masculinity, local identity, aggression and the acceptability of violence that often diverged from mainstream social conventions.[3] The theories of Dunning and the Leicester School of sociology can certainly be applied to soccer hooliganism in Europe during the inter-war period.

In his study of twentieth-century European society, Richard Bessel explains how the geography of leisure was transformed during the inter-war period.[4] Across the continent Europeans engaged with the concept of leisure and recreation like never before; whether it was a night at the theatre, a trip to the cinema or a day out at a sporting event. From the early 1920s, 'a profound need and desire for hedonism and escape, for pleasure and play' took hold among Europeans from all social backgrounds,[5] and for a vast number of people this escape was found in the camaraderie and exhilaration provided by soccer. In the years after the First World War (1914–1918), Europe's working classes made the game of soccer their own. Mirroring what had occurred in Britain during the late nineteenth century, the sport was engendered with an increasingly proletariat character on the continent as greater freedom from the workplace, improving infrastructure and transformation networks, and heightened media coverage contributed to a growing soccer culture among the European masses. Soccer became increasingly popularized in almost all European countries in the years following the First World War. For example, soccer crowds in Austria more than quadrupled in size between 1914 and 1924,[6] and similar trends are visible elsewhere, not least in Ireland. Figures provided by Neal Garnham for the finals of national cup competitions in the north and south of the country give an indication of the growing popularity of the sport in Ireland during the inter-war period.[7] These figures show that just over 5000 people watched the 1923 Irish Cup final in Belfast. By 1930, this figure had risen to over 26,000.[8] In Dublin, the crowd that watched the annual Free State Cup final increased from 14,000 in 1923 to almost 31,000 in 1936.[9] In the south of Ireland, soccer had always been most popular in Dublin. Nevertheless, a strong soccer tradition existed in various parts of the country by the outbreak of the First World War,[10] and this was further built upon during the inter-war period. During the 1920s, soccer was disseminated throughout Southern Ireland, and within 10 years of the formation of the FAI in 1921 it was played in practically all parts of the country.[11]

Soccer's growing popularity with Europe's working-classes occurred against the backdrop of socio-economic struggle. The First World War and the Russian Revolution of 1917 made Europe 'a much poorer place'.[12] During the period, unemployment rates were high throughout Europe, and poverty was an ever-present companion of the demoralized, frustrated and angry working-classes whose sacrifices during the Great War had been quickly forgotten. Harold James has argued that the inter-war depression was 'the most traumatic economic event' of the twentieth century,[13] and it was within this context that fascist politics, and totalitarian regimes, came to the fore in a number of European states. There is no doubt that the soccer hooliganism that took place in inter-war Europe was at least in part a consequence of the continent's wider socio-economic environment. Soccer grounds were chaotic, testosterone-fuelled environments where anti-social behaviour was, if not encouraged, at least accepted. They provided the cover of anonymity for would-be troublemakers, and in many cases people attended soccer matches to vent and to dissent. Moreover, individuals attended soccer matches to feel a sense of belonging. In this regard, soccer served an important social function in inter-war society, one that will be explored in greater detail in the context of Southern Ireland later in this article.

In the Irish context the inter-war period was a particularly violent time. The period began with an armed nationalist insurrection against British rule. During this Anglo-Irish War, a conflict which was fought between January 1919 and July 1921, hooliganism became increasingly common around Irish soccer. Sports historians focusing on the Irish case have traditionally approached the violence witnessed at soccer grounds during this period from the standpoint of the sectarian divisions that shaped society in the north of the country.[14] The early twentieth century was marked by some intense fighting at soccer matches between members of Belfast's Catholic and Protestant communities, and the sheer ferocity involved in these episodes somewhat overshadowed the violence that took place elsewhere. This article challenges the view that Irish soccer hooliganism during the early twentieth century was primarily a northern phenomenon by shedding fresh light on a number of disturbances that took place in Dublin at the time of the Anglo-Irish War. The hooliganism that occurred in both Belfast and Dublin during this period formed a certain impression of soccer supporters in the public consciousness. Soccer supporters were often portrayed as unruly, unpredictable and aggressive, and further bouts of violence that were reported during the 1920s and 1930s did little to alter this perception. This article analyses this violence in the context of the wider socio-economic environment of inter-war Ireland.

Soccer violence during the Anglo-Irish War: A northern phenomenon?

During the latter stages of the First World War, Ireland's political landscape was completely transformed by the rise of an increasingly militant brand of republicanism on the home front. When the Sinn Féin party, the political manifestation of this republican movement, won a landslide victory in the general election of December 1918, the country edged ever closer towards open rebellion, and within a month the first shots were fired in the Anglo-Irish War. Over the course of the next two and a half years, fighting between the forces of the Irish Republican Army (IRA) and the forces of the British crown brought violence to the doorsteps of the Irish people. This was not a war fought on some distant battlefield. This was a war being fought in the countryside, in towns and cities, in the very midst of the civilian population. The IRA's targeting of the security forces, coupled with the British Government's 'heavy-handed' response, often dragged ordinary civilians into the violence.[15] For example, Cork city centre was set on fire by crown forces in December 1920 in retaliation for earlier IRA aggression, and throughout the conflict villages were routinely raided and sacked amid what Roy Foster describes as 'draconian powers of search and arrest'.[16] Diarmaid Ferriter argues that the scale of the violence that civilians were exposed to during the Anglo-Irish War in turn lowered their own collective 'threshold of violence'.[17] Civilians were increasingly likely to themselves behave violently, and on a number of occasions this growing inclination towards violence was witnessed at Irish soccer grounds.

When the First World War ended in late 1918, the cities of Belfast and Dublin were the two main centres of soccer activity in Ireland. After floundering due to the impact of army recruitment during the initial phase of the war, Belfast soccer had recovered somewhat by 1916. The large-scale manufacture of wartime necessities gave the city's economy a much needed boost, and there was enough disposable income in circulation for its soccer followers to once again frequent soccer matches in their droves.[18] The latter stages of the First World War are considered a boom period for Belfast soccer, but in Dublin the game was in a far more precarious position. Between 1915 and 1918, Dublin soccer was decimated by the combined effects of army recruitment, growing nationalist fervour and dwindling interest. During this period, the Dublin game was effectively cut off from the sustenance that Belfast's leading clubs provided. In July 1915, amid much jingoistic fanfare, the Irish League, which was the country's major senior league competition with membership from both Belfast and Dublin, was suspended for the duration of the war. It was not restarted until September 1919, and when it did restart reports of violence at league matches immediately began to surface.

In 1919, the widely held belief among Dublin's soccer fraternity was that soccer hooliganism was a northern phenomenon that followed clubs from Belfast. This belief stemmed largely from an incident that had occurred in Belfast in 1912 when sectarian tension spilled over into violent clashes between the Catholic and Protestant supporters of the Belfast Celtic and Linfield clubs respectively. The clashes led to the hospitalization of 60 people,[19] and the ferocity involved; one person was admitted with injuries caused by a gunshot; left an indelible impression that lingered long in the collective memory. Soccer-related violence was not unknown to Dublin; a serious disturbance borne of a bitter industrial dispute in the city had taken place as recently as 1913[20]; but, nevertheless, it came as quite a surprise when the first serious case of post-war hooliganism occurred at Dalymount Park in Dublin. On 6 September 1919, with 13 minutes left to play in a match between the local Bohemians club and Belfast Celtic, a controversial refereeing decision sparked a pitch invasion that culminated with the assault of the referee, Mr P. Coleton. The morning after the match the *Sunday Independent* was quick to condemn those involved. It commented that 'scenes such as these are, fortunately rare on Dublin pitches. They call for the severest condemnation, and such attacks are cowardly and devoid of the least sporting instinct'. Match reports fail to specify exactly how many intruders made their way onto the pitch, but certainly enough people partook for the *Irish Independent,* on 9 September, to label the incident a 'riot', a word more commonly associated with Belfast soccer.

As it transpired the Dalymount Park 'riot' was not an isolated incident. The following month, at the same venue, a second disturbance took place at an inter-provincial match between teams representing the Dublin-based LFA and the Co. Antrim Football Association, whose headquarters were located in Belfast. With the visitors leading by five goals to nil, a number of spectators once again rushed the pitch to interrupt the match. This time one of the Co. Antrim players was the victim of an assault which appears to have been borne of frustration with the scoreline. While the overriding feeling in Dublin was one of shock after the first incident, this second disturbance caused nothing short of outrage. Again a *Sunday Independent* article, published on 26 October 1919, led the charge by calling for 'the culprit, or culprits, if apprehended, [to be] made an example of'. This was a sentiment echoed a day later in the *Irish Independent*, which noted that 'the blackguards who were the cause of the first scenes escaped, and if an example had been made of them it might have prevented the recurrence of hooliganism which will soon turn respectable supporters away from the game'. This was a fair point. Had the perpetrators of the earlier violence been held accountable it would have gone a long way to discouraging others from following their lead. As it was, spectators intent on trouble were all too aware that they were unlikely to face any consequences or punishments.

In the wake of this latest incident, Dublin newspapers began to acknowledge what appeared to be a growing culture of violence within the local game. It could no longer be reasonably argued that soccer hooliganism was solely a northern concern, a reality which was portrayed by the *Freeman's Journal* on 18 December 1919 in an article that warned its readers against 'the dangers of inciting the roughs of the crowd, who nowadays need very little excuse for mobbing'. Although violence was clearly on the rise at soccer in Dublin, events in Belfast continued to cast the longest shadow. The most serious case of soccer hooliganism to occur anywhere in Ireland during the inter-war period took place in Belfast in 1920. While combat during the Anglo-Irish War was largely confined to exchanges between the IRA and crown forces in the rest of the country, in Belfast the fighting spread to civilian communities. This civilian violence was sectarian in nature, and although it did not begin in earnest until July 1920 an extremely tense atmosphere prevailed in the city when Belfast Celtic met Glentoran, another club boasting a large Protestant following[21] in an Irish Cup semi-final at the Oval ground on 13 March. During the match, sectarian chanting and flag-waving stung sections of the crowd 'to fraternal fury',[22] and around the pitch and in the stands fighting broke out between opposing sets of supporters. For the second time in less than a decade the sound of gunfire reverberated at a Belfast soccer match. Miraculously, there were no fatalities after six shots were unloaded into the crowd at point blank range.

The behaviour of supporters during this incident, which was later dubbed 'the Battle of Belfast', was clearly more sinister and far more disturbing than anything that was witnessed in Dublin the previous year. Not to be outdone, however, a disturbance at a soccer match at Shelbourne Park just two weeks later focused the spotlight firmly back on the capital. On 27 March 1920, at an unofficial Irish Cup final between Shelbourne and Glentoran,[23] the referee, Mr W. Moore, sustained a wound above his eye when he was struck by a stone thrown from the crowd. Two days later the *Irish Independent* described how the play was subsequently stopped, and how spectators rushed the pitch forcing the Glentoran players to take refuge inside the pavilion. There they hid for a further two hours while a bloodthirsty mob waited outside. Eventually, the players made a hasty escape to their bus through a hail of stones. This latest episode led some commentators, including 'Northerner' in the *Irish Independent*, to imply that violence was now just as likely to occur in Dublin as it was in Belfast. There were others that strongly refuted this assertion however. Some soccer commentators in Dublin appear to have been unwilling to consider the growing trend of hooliganism objectively. One particular account of the incident actually had the temerity to suggest that the crowd's behaviour was justified by the spoiling tactics utilized by the Glentoran team, while another contributor to the *Irish Independent* on 30 March 1920, identified only as 'Eyewitness', dismissed the criticism of the Dublin game by raising the age-old adage that 'rioting at football matches was instituted in Belfast some years ago as a popular pastime'. In truth this was an argument that no longer carried much weight.

Though the Dublin hooliganism appeared to be indiscriminate in terms of sectarian motivation, with the Belfast Celtic and Glentoran clubs representing opposite sides of Belfast's religious divide, there was at least an anti-northern dynamic to the violence. In this regard, Anglo-Irish War politics were clearly at play. Anti-northernism was rife in the south of the country during the Anglo-Irish War. The north was associated with unionism and Protestantism, and an underlying resentment towards all things northern only intensified with reports of the harassment and displacement of Belfast Catholics during the early 1920s.[24] Fearing further outbreaks of violence, the management of the Belfast Celtic club decided to completely withdraw from soccer during the summer of 1920. Shelbourne and Bohemians soon followed suit, as, apparently, it was 'not judicious [for Belfast teams] to come to Dublin under present circumstances'.[25] On 29 August 1920, the *Sunday Independent* mournfully lamented that 'prejudice has invaded the realm of sport, hitherto considered sacred to such baneful influence', but there is no doubt that the decision to stop Belfast teams from coming to the capital was the correct one. In 5 May 1920, the *Freeman's Journal* had reported on the murder of a referee who had been set upon by a horde of spectators at a match in Italy, and all things considered it was quite conceivable that a similar incident could occur in Dublin. Within the space of a year, the atmosphere surrounding Dublin soccer had been completely altered. The excitement that had existed as preparations were being made for the return of the Irish League in the summer of 1919 had long been replaced by an air of fear and foreboding. Hooliganism had unceremoniously reared its head amid the politics of the Anglo-Irish War, and the days when Dublin soccer enthusiasts cast judgmental glances towards Belfast, and its culture of soccer violence, had long since passed.

The 'terrorism' of soccer supporters in the south of Ireland, 1921–1939

By the time that a truce brought the fighting in the Anglo-Irish War to an end in July 1921, Irish soccer had been partitioned between north and south.[26] The acrimony and bitterness involved in the split between the IFA and the FAI meant that no official matches were played between teams from Belfast and Dublin until late 1923.[27] In Belfast, hooliganism did persist at soccer grounds during the early 1920s against the backdrop of political and social unrest.[28] For example, during late 1922 disturbances at soccer matches in Belfast were being reported on an almost weekly basis, with the authorities threatening individual clubs with ground closures if they could not gain control of the situation.[29] In the south of the country, instability rooted in the wider political and social environment also made an impression on Dublin soccer pitches. In April 1922, at the end of the replayed final of the inaugural FAI Cup competition, supporters of the Shamrock Rovers club entered the pitch to attack the victorious St James's Gate players as they celebrated. When a number of the St James's Gate players were subsequently pursued to their dressing room, a revolver was brandished in a threatening manner to stave off the attack. The revolver allegedly belonged to Jack Dowdall, the brother of a St James's Gate player, and a man who had been involved in the IRA campaign during the Anglo-Irish War.[30] That people went about their daily routines in the possession of firearms was, if nothing else, a sign of the times, but the irony in this instance was that the appearance of the revolver probably prevented more serious violence from occurring.

Though the worst of the hooliganism witnessed at soccer matches during the inter-war period took place at the time of the Anglo-Irish War, the sport continued to be associated with violent behaviour throughout the 1920s and 1930s. Often players were just as culpable as spectators when it came to bouts of violence. They were, after all, young men pumping with adrenaline in the heat of battle, and it is hardly surprising that tempers sometimes boiled over into confrontations on the field of play. The minute books of the FAI's disciplinary committees reveal that rough play and general bad behaviour was endemic within the sport during the period. For transgressions committed on the pitch, players were usually punished with a suspension or a small fine, but in some cases the penalties could be much more severe. After a 21-year-old player was fatally injured during a match in Dublin's Phoenix Park in December 1924, three men appeared at court accused of his murder. The deceased player, Samuel O'Brien, had himself been sent off for an incident that occurred during the match. Upon leaving the pitch he began fighting with an opposing player, and was subsequently rounded upon and kicked on the ground. He later succumbed to his injuries at a local hospital.[31]

The responsibility for controlling the behaviour of players during matches fell on the shoulders of the referee, but in many ways this was a thankless task. As a general rule referees commanded very little respect, either from the players they officiated over or from administrative bodies such as the LFA or the FAIFS; the FAI having changed its title in 1923 to that of the Football Association of the Irish Free State in an effort to enhance its claim for international recognition from FIFA.[32] Certainly referees were not respected by supporters. This article has already described a number of incidents in which referees were specifically targeted by spectators, but despite this, there was very little empathy with referees. The press was often guilty of dehumanizing referees, portraying them as a sort of pantomime villain to be scorned and ridiculed. Satire parodying referees regularly appeared in newspaper columns. One joke, published in the *Irish Independent* on 21 November 1926, went as follows: 'The present football season has, we are told been unusually free from foul play. In fact we understand that so far most of the referees attending hospitals are merely outpatients'. Another from the same publication on 17 April 1927 light-heartedly suggested that referees required 'a suit of armour' to protect themselves against violence. This kind of coverage was obviously amusing to readers, but for referees the peril they encountered was no laughing matter. Certainly there was nothing humorous about an incident that occurred in 1930 in Bray in County Wicklow in which a referee was chased to a local Garda station by up to two hundred irate soccer supporters.[33]

On 14 December 1925, the *Irish Independent* spoke of the 'terrorism' perpetrated by the supporters of soccer clubs in the Irish Free State. On this occasion the newspaper was referring to a common, and most irritating, tendency of spectators who would purposely cause the abandonment of matches with the intention of preventing their team from losing. During the inter-war period, the supporters of certain clubs gained particular notoriety for their predilection for violence. During the early 1920s, the supporters of clubs such as Shamrock Rovers and Bray Unknowns were maligned for their menacing behaviour. By the late 1920s, the supporters of the Dundalk GNR club had become the most infamous in the Irish Free State. This reputation was borne of two incidents in particular, incidents which perhaps stand as the most serious cases of soccer hooliganism to occur in the south of the country since the Anglo-Irish War. Both incidents took place in Dundalk. The first, reported in the *Anglo-Celt* on 8 October 1927, saw the match referee and linesman kicked and punched by supporters who had entered the field of play. This disturbance prompted a bullish FAIFS to issue a caution to the Dundalk club. Its management committee was ordered to erect notices around its ground warning spectators against any further violence,[34] a warning which was not heeded. Six months later, on 31 March 1928, the *Irish Independent* reported that a referee was again assaulted at a match in Dundalk. The referee was apparently struck twice, and then kicked on the ground, after as many as one hundred supporters invaded the pitch. This time the FAIFS came down hard on the Dundalk club. The association held the club's management committee accountable for failing to protect the referee, and imposed on it a huge fine of £100.[35] If a severe punishment such as this did not act as a deterrent against future violence, it was reasoned, nothing else would. Dundalk supporters were certainly not alone in causing trouble at soccer matches. In fact, the violence witnessed in Dundalk in March 1928 was the culmination of a sequence of minor disturbances that occurred at soccer grounds around the country earlier in the year. In the context of Southern Ireland, it appeared as though a concerted wave of soccer hooliganism was for the first time on the rise outside of Dublin. In this regard, the negative perception of soccer supporters that had been formed in the public consciousness by events during the Anglo-Irish War was further broadened and solidified.

A number of incidents that were reported in national and regional newspapers during the 1930s did little to dispel this perception. In Waterford in September 1930, a bad-tempered match between Waterford and Shelbourne descended into chaos when spectators rushed the field to become involved in fighting that had broken out between both sets of players. The referee was allegedly assaulted in the ensuing melee, before a large Garda force intervened to disperse the crowd. Reporting on this incident on 15 September 1930, the *Irish Independent* noted that scenes like this had become increasingly common at soccer matches over the last number of years. The newspaper attributed the violence to 'partisanship', and even suggested that some Shelbourne supporters, riled by what had taken place in Waterford, had gone in search of further trouble on their return to Dublin later that evening. The next meeting of the clubs in the capital just three months later was marked by more 'ugly' scenes.[36] On this occasion, the Waterford players had to be escorted from the pitch by the Civic Guards when Shelbourne supporters, intent on revenge, invaded the pitch.

In January 1931, the FAIFS encouraged individual clubs to tackle the general 'unpleasantness' that increasingly seemed to surround soccer matches.[37] This unpleasantness was by no means confined to large urban centres such as Dublin and Waterford. On 5 December 1931, the *Leitrim Observer* reported on the abandonment of a match because of crowd trouble in the town of Ardee in County Louth. After the match spectators reportedly took to the streets armed with weapons that included hurling sticks and fire-irons. A fight ensued, and interestingly this exchange involved not only young men, the demographic most associated with hooliganism, but also members of 'the fairer sex' who had been in attendance at the match. During the mid-1930s, a flurry of disturbances was reported from across the Irish Free State. These disturbances usually involved the customary stone-throwing and pitch invasions, while at one match played in Cork in 1935 sods of turf were thrown at a referee.[38] On 17 January 1936, the *Irish Press* reported that Bob Jack, the manager of the Plymouth Football Club, while on a scouting mission at a match in Dublin had been shocked by the behaviour of spectators who had stormed the pitch. Certainly this type of violence was more prevalent within Irish soccer than in England during the inter-war period. Although some English clubs were punished for the behaviour of their followers with grounds closures violence was actually quite rare within the English game. This was largely due to the fact that English soccer supporters tended not to travel to their club's away matches in large numbers.[39] This was not the case in Scotland, where, like Northern Ireland, festering sectarianism led to regular clashes between rival soccer supporters.[40] In the north of Ireland, soccer violence once again came to prominence during the 1930s, and again the scale of this violence somewhat overshadowed what was taking place south of the border. The worst of the violence witnessed at Belfast soccer grounds coincided with the Outdoor Relief Riots of 1932,[41] and sectarian rioting in the city during 1935.[42] Again, this strongly suggests an intrinsic link between soccer hooliganism and civil unrest borne of the wider political and social environment.

By the late 1930s, the followers of the Waterford club had assumed the mantle as the most notorious soccer supporters in Southern Ireland. Throughout the decade, crowd trouble was reported with alarming regularity at matches in Waterford. Some incidents were more serious than others; on 20 February 1937, the *Irish Independent* reported that the club's chairman, Gerard Whelan, had been knocked unconscious by rampaging supporters, while an article from the same publication on 11 May 1937 described spectators with 'blood-streamed faces' fighting each other with glass bottles in scenes that were more reminiscent of a battlefield than a soccer match. The FAIFS had a zero tolerance approach to violence at soccer matches, but no punishment that its disciplinary committees could muster proved to be an effective deterrent. Clubs were often threatened, fined or in some cases completely banned from competitions, but the reality was that they were in the unenviable position of being powerless to stop spectator violence. Again, Irish soccer clubs simply did not have the resources to deploy enough stewards to deal with an outbreak of violence among spectators should it occur, while the fees demanded by the Gardaí to preside at soccer matches, which could be as high as £2 per match,[43] discouraged clubs from acquiring their services.

Deconstructing the growing trend of violence at soccer in the south of Ireland

Each case of hooliganism described above was unique in itself, and this makes it rather difficult to identify any clear and definitive trends that would tend to explain, in its entirety, the upsurge of spectator violence witnessed at Irish soccer grounds during the inter-war period. Certainly there were a number of intertwining and overlapping factors at play. Generally speaking, soccer hooliganism occurred in Ireland for much the same reasons as it did elsewhere in Europe. Dunning contends that soccer hooliganism is resultant of, among other variables, 'the major fault-lines' that define the political, social and economic landscape of particular countries.[44] For example, reported violence in Spain in 1924, between followers of the Barcelona and Espanyol clubs, was rooted in regional politics surrounding Catalonian identity, while the violent scenes that were witnessed at soccer matches in Vienna during the early 1920s were linked to the 'influx of the proletariat' to the sport. Other cases of crowd violence in Europe were caused by differing factors. In Sweden excessive alcohol consumption around soccer was forwarded as the cause of a rising number of pitch invasions during the inter-war period, while an incident in Italy that saw gun shots fired between soccer supporters from Genoa and Bologna in 1925 was caused by partisanship boiling over.[45]

A number of the newspaper reports depicting hooliganism in the south of Ireland also cite partisanship as the primary cause of disturbances. Over the course of the last decade or so a great deal of outstanding academic research has been conducted around the community function that the GAA provides in Ireland.[46] This work has shown how in rural Ireland, the association's one club per parish policy had the effect of turning local GAA clubs into the sporting embodiment of their communities by creating a nucleus around which the community gathered, socialized and played. In larger urban centres, such as Dublin, Cork, Limerick and Waterford, soccer clubs could also provide this function. For those that supported them soccer clubs undoubtedly represented the local, and were a visible embodiment of regional identities. Though the players that played for a club were not necessarily from the local community the clubs themselves certainly were, and people connected with them for this reason. The strengthening of regional identities naturally spawns regional rivalries however, and there is no doubt that some of the hooliganism described in this article can be attributed to this.

The references to partisanship in the newspaper reports in question hint at what appears to have been a growing fanaticism for the game among soccer supporters during the inter-war period. As previously noted, the sport exploded in popularity in the south of Ireland from the early 1920s. Analysis of various newspaper reports show that during the early 1920s, the matches played by Dublin's more popular clubs, namely Bohemians, Shelbourne, Shamrock Rovers and St. James Gate, were watched by somewhere between four and 6000 spectators. By 1926, the average attendances at important matches in the Free State League, Southern Ireland's premier soccer league, reached somewhere in the region of 12,000. For highly important league fixtures this could rise to upwards of 16,000. Crowds increased further as the period progressed. At the beginning of the 1930s there are reports of up to 30,000 people attending matches in Dublin, while in 1932 it was estimated that around 60,000 people were attending soccer matches in the capital on a weekly basis. Large crowds also watched matches in provincial centres such as Cork, Dundalk, Waterford and Sligo as regional clubs joined the Free State League during the 1920s and 1930s. For example, crowds of up to 9000 regularly attended the matches of the Fordson club of Cork when it joined the league in 1924, while in Waterford somewhere in the region of 5000 spectators regularly watched the local senior team during the 1930s.

Inter-war soccer supporters were fanatics in the truest sense of the word. They were passionate and demanding in equal measure. Supporters proudly adorned their club colours on hats, scarves and coat lapels when they went to matches,[47] and played their part in community singing on the terraces and embankments.[48] As transportation networks improved, Irish soccer supporters began to travel over larger distances in support of their team, and for those that undertook these journeys the weekend excursion to a soccer match was a highly anticipated social event. When the journey was not undertaken supporters were known to huddle outside the offices of local newspaper companies to hear the latest results from far off fields.[49] Inter-war soccer supporters were extremely vocal. They cheered their team on loudly when it was winning, and by the same token could be the harshest of critics when things were going badly on the pitch. Tellingly, some of the most serious cases of hooliganism seen during the period involved the supporters of teams that were losing heavily on the day. A 1999 Council of Europe Parliamentary Assembly report on the causes of modern hooliganism in Britain suggests that the actual match results are unimportant to hooligans who are intent on trouble whether their team wins or loses.[50] This was not the case in Ireland during the inter-war period. Much of the violence witnessed at soccer grounds in the south of Ireland was reactionary. It was rarely planned or premeditated. It happened organically, in the heat of the moment, which in turn made it even more difficult to prevent.

Goldblatt's assessment of the root causes of inter-war soccer hooliganism also refers to the changing demographic of the people that were watching the sport.

Though soccer in the south of Ireland retained a measure of its middle-class persona, most notably in the staunch amateur ethos of the Bohemians club and in the inter-varsity Collingwood Cup, it was, by the inter-war period, largely associated with urban working class culture. Soccer was certainly the sport of choice for industrial workforces in the Irish Free State.[51] It was played, illegally, in the limited space afforded by city thoroughfares and cramped back alleys. It was played on the cobbled streets of towns across the state, and in urban parklands. As was the case on the continent, inter-war soccer hooliganism took place in Ireland against the backdrop of socio-economic tumult. During the 1920s, economic growth occurred at a slower rate in the Irish Free State than in any of the new nation states that emerged in Europe in the aftermath of the First World War. In 1923, 14% of the Free State's industrial workforce was unemployed, and it is estimated that fewer than 5000 new jobs were created by the beginning of the 1930s. According to Ferriter, working-class communities were 'forgotten and marginalized' by a government that was more concerned with issues of rurality than with driving industrial growth in urban areas.[52] Throughout the history of the game, violence has peaked at soccer grounds at times of economic downturn and high unemployment and in this regard inter-war Ireland was no different. Historically, young, unemployed males in group settings have been potentially volatile entities. Their difficult circumstances render them socially alienated and disaffected, and this in turn leads to disgruntlement and the possibility of violent outbursts. David Toms, in his work on the history of soccer in the Munster province, has demonstrated how a culture of violence can prevail within organized unemployment groups that are dissenting against their position in society,[53] and in times of economic hardship bands of soccer followers can also be considered in this context.

In many ways, soccer gave a voice to people that found themselves forgotten and marginalized by mainstream society. It allowed them to be heard. Soccer supporters were part of distinct imagined communities based on shared interests and ideals.[54] Galeano theorizes that individuals that find themselves rejected by society can gain a sense of identity and belonging within the group construct of soccer communities.[55] This in turn leads them to strong feelings of loyalty and solidarity towards the group, and on occasions when violence breaks out individuals are more than willing to participate to defend the very thing that provides them with their identity. There is no doubt that some supporters were drawn into the violence in a quest for approval from their peers. Misplaced bravado was undoubtedly a factor, as was excessive alcohol consumption. Alcohol was prominent within working-class culture in inter-war Ireland. Social events of any kind rarely took place without alcohol, and soccer matches were no different. Although alcohol was generally not sold at soccer matches in the south of Ireland there was certainly a strong drinking culture around the game, a culture which was of particular concern to temperance movements who became concerned by reports of youngsters breaking their Confirmation pledges.[56] Sunday drinking hours, whereby the public houses were closed between the hours of three and five o'clock, perfectly coincided with the scheduling of soccer matches in the south of Ireland.[57] Soccer supporters indulged in drinking before and after matches, and there is no doubt that many of those who made their way to soccer grounds were under the influence of alcohol. Naturally, this made them more likely to behave anti-socially.

The incidents described in this section of the article formed a negative impression of soccer supporters in the public psyche, but it is perhaps worth noting at this juncture that the vast majority of soccer matches played in the south of Ireland passed off without any hint of trouble whatsoever. In this regard, the reputation for anti-social behaviour that soccer supporters acquired as a group can be considered to be quite harsh. It was suggested from some quarters that some of the hooliganism depicted in the media during the inter-war period was exaggerated. Did sections of the media have an agenda against soccer? This is a question that cannot be answered fully within the confines of this article. Certainly violence occurred at other sports during the inter-war period. Newspaper reports from around the country suggest that disturbances were quite common at GAA matches, while fighting was also reported at international rugby matches during the 1920s. On closer inspection it appears as though there may have been some class bias at play in terms of the public perception of soccer, but, again, this is a question for a wider research project. While outlandish accusations that individuals associated with the GAA, individuals who had an agenda against soccer, were attending matches with the sole intention of inciting violence can be discounted as folly,[58] it is clear that ordinary, well-behaved soccer supporters were being cast in a villainous light by the actions of a small section of their peers. For all the reports of violence at soccer grounds there were many others that depicted a jovial and welcoming atmosphere around matches. It is an unfortunate reality, however, that negative incidents live longest in the collective memory, and it is even more unfortunate that the actions of a small number of people impacted so heavily on the representation of the vast majority that had no inclination whatsoever towards violence.

Conclusion

The soccer hooliganism that became embedded in the culture of the sport in inter-war Ireland was in many ways a reflection of wider society. The violence that occurred at Irish soccer grounds amid the chaos and instability of the Anglo-Irish War was clearly a by-product of the political tensions that prevailed in the country. While this violence was at its most severe when soccer supporters from Catholic and Protestant backgrounds clashed in Belfast, there is no doubt that a hooligan problem also existed in the capital during this bloody period in Irish history. The hooliganism witnessed in Dublin during 1919 and 1920, which was primarily borne of the strong anti-northern outlook that prevailed in the city, was considered far less serious than that which occurred in Belfast. Nonetheless, it was on a scale that had previously not been seen in Dublin, and by the summer of 1920 the sport's administration was forced to concede that the threat of violence made the city altogether too unsafe to host northern soccer teams. Though the partition of Irish soccer in 1921 eliminated the threat of anti-northern violence at soccer matches hooliganism was not eradicated from the sport in the south of the country. Comparatively, it was small-scale and infrequent after partition, but it did occur with enough regularity during the 1920s and 1930s to tarnish the image of soccer, and the people that supported it. Again, this hooliganism must be considered in the context of the forces that were shaping Irish society. As was the case elsewhere in Europe during the inter-war period, soccer hooliganism in the south of Ireland can be attributed to growing partisanship around the sport, as well as issues concerning class, community and local identity. It was also reflective of a wide range of socio-economic issues such as unemployment, poverty, social disaffection and alcohol consumption. There is no definitive, all-encompassing rationalization that would explain the hooliganism witnessed at soccer in the south of Ireland during the inter-war period in its entirety. Ultimately, each individual case was a unique event. That said, these cases had the combined effect of forming a negative perception of soccer supporters in popular culture, a perception that was unfair on the majority of supporters who peacefully attended matches purely for entertainment and for love of the game.

Disclosure statement

No potential conflict of interest was reported by the author.

Notes

1. Goldblatt, *The Ball is Round*, 220.
2. Norbert Elias (1897–1990) was a German sociologist. From the 1960s, his most famous work, *The Civilizing Process* (1939), became the basis for theories of figurational sociology such as those forwarded by Eric Denning and the Leicester School in its interpretation of soccer hooliganism.
3. Dunning, 'Violence and Sport', 916; Spaaij, 'Football Hooliganism as a Transnational Phenomenon', 416–7.
4. Bessel, 'European Society in the Twentieth Century', 248.
5. Goldblatt, *The Ball is Round*, 177.
6. Ibid., 193.
7. The split between the Irish Football Association (IFA), Irish soccer's national governing body since 1880 and the Leinster Football Association (LFA) in 1921 partitioned Irish soccer between north and south. This split coincided with the political boundary that was established firstly by the Government of Ireland Act (1920), and ultimately by the failure of the Boundary Commission in 1925. After the 1921 split, two separate national soccer associations existed in Ireland; the Belfast-based IFA governed over soccer in Northern Ireland, while the newly formed Football Association of Ireland (FAI) governed the game in the territory that would become the Irish Free State in December 1922. As such two separate national cup finals were played in Ireland from 1922. For a fuller discussion of the split between the IFA and the LFA see Garnham, *Association Football in Pre-Partition Ireland*. See also Moore, *The Irish Soccer Split*.
8. Garnham, 'Ein Spiel in zweiNationen?', 73.
9. Ibid., 81.
10. Before the Great War, soccer was more popular in some part of Ireland than in others for various reasons. For example, a lengthy tradition of seasonal migration existed between West Donegal, Sligo, Mayo and Scotland, and this is often forwarded as an explanation for the popularity of soccer in these areas. Likewise, soccer was extremely popular in large provincial towns in Leinster, such Athlone, Mullingar, Tipperary, Dundalk and Drogheda, and indeed many other towns and villages. In some cases, this was due to the presence of a large British military presence in these areas during the late nineteenth century. Conversely, soccer was not as strong in Munster where the sports promoted by the Gaelic Athletic Association (GAA) held reverence.
11. Tynan, 'Association Football and Irish Society during the Inter-War Period'.
12. Bessel, 'European Society in the Twentieth Century', 236.
13. James, 'Fall & Rise of the European Economy', 191.
14. For a discussion on the impact of sectarian and religious division on sport in Northern violence see Cronin, *Sport and nationalism in Ireland*. See also Sugden and Bairner, *Sport, Sectarianism and Society in a Divided Ireland*. For a particular discussion of sectarian violence at soccer in Belfast during the early twentieth century see Moore, *The Irish Soccer Split*.
15. Foster, *Modern Ireland*, 496.
16. Ibid., 499.
17. Ferriter, *The Transformation of Ireland*, 233.
18. Garnham, *Origins and Development of Football in Ireland*, 24.

19. Moore, *The Irish Soccer Split*, 56.
20. 'Baton Charges – Wild Scenes Last Night'. *Irish Independent*, September 29, 1913.
21. Moore, *The Irish Soccer Split*, 56.
22. 'Football Riot'. *Freeman's Journal*, March 18, 1920.
23. The Shelbourne club had previously been awarded the trophy without playing a final match because both the Belfast Celtic and Glentoran clubs were disqualified from the Irish Cup as punishment for issues arising from the aforementioned 'Battle of Belfast' match.
24. Ferriter, *The Transformation of Ireland*, 275; Foster, *Modern Ireland*, 526–7; Farrell, *Northern Ireland: The Orange State*.
25. 'Belfast Clubs and 'Feeling' in Dublin'. *Irish Independent*, August 21, 1920.
26. See note 7.
27. When relations between the IFA and the FAI thawed slightly after discussions between the two associations took place in Liverpool in 1923, clubs from north and south of the border were once again permitted to organize exhibition matches against each other. These matches were sometimes referred to as 'olive-branch' matches as they were considered to be building relationships between soccer enthusiasts in the IFA and FAIFS jurisdictions.
28. Ferriter, *The Transformation of Ireland*, 278; Foster, *Modern Ireland*, 529.
29. 'Belfast Football Scene'. *Irish Independent*, November 9, 1922.
30. Keogh, *Twentieth Century Ireland*, 36.
31. 'Footballer's Death'. *Irish Independent*, December 9, 1924.
32. By adopting this title, the FAIFS was attempting to distinguish itself from the IFA as FIFA refused to recognize two national soccer associations from the same country.
33. 'Waterford Wins at Bray'. *Munster Express*, November 14, 1930.
34. 'Association'. *Irish Independent*, November 8, 1927.
35. 'Dundalk F.C. Fined £100'. *Irish Independent*, May 11, 1928.
36. 'Hectic Game Between Waterford and Shelbourne'. *Munster Express*, December 12, 1930.
37. 'Cup-Tie Forecasts – Appeal to Clubs and Followers'. *Irish Independent*, January 10, 1931.
38. 'Sods for Referee'. *Southern Star*, March 2, 1935.
39. Goldblatt, *The Ball is Round*, 187–8; and Taylor, *The Association Game*, 145–53.
40. Goldblatt, *The Ball is Round*, 187–8.
41. The Outdoor Relief Riots of 1932 were a cross-community protest in Belfast against harsh government policy surrounding unemployment benefits. This policy involved the public shaming of recipients of relief, and the dispersion of credit notes in lieu of money. This meant that unemployment relief could not be used to pay rent. In 1932, 47% of Belfast's workforce was unemployed.
42. Gray, *Ireland This Century*, 128–9.
43. 'An Garda Síochána: claim against Cork Bohemian FC'.
44. Dunning, 'Towards a Sociological Understanding of Football Hooliganism', 141–62.
45. Goldblatt, *The Ball is Round*, 195–220.
46. The GAA's Oral History Project, a Boston College-Ireland-based project commissioned by the GAA in 2009 to mark the association's 125th anniversary, has produced a number of fascinating publications that look at the various functions that the GAA occupied in Irish society. Among these functions is the GAA's role within the local community, which is examined in Cronin, Duncan and Rouse, *The GAA: A People's History*.
47. 'Bohemians Complete 'Double'. *Sunday Independent*, March 18, 1928; 'The Magic of the Cup Ties'. *Irish Independent*, February 2, 1938.
48. 'Fitting Draw in F.S. Cup Final'. *Irish Independent*, March 18, 1927.
49. 'Free State League'. *Sunday Independent*, October 3, 1926.
50. Committee of Culture and Education, 1999.
51. Soccer was played widely in industrial settings in the south of Ireland during the interwar period. In fact, three of the Irish Free State's largest industrial employers, the world-renowned Guinness brewery and the Jacobs biscuit factory in Dublin, and the Ford motor factory in Cork, were represented by affiliated soccer teams in the Free State League during the 1920s and 1930s.
52. Ferriter, *The Transformation of Ireland*, 311–4.

53. Toms, *Soccer in Munster*, 177.
54. The concept of an imagined community as is applied in this article derives from Benedict Anderson's 1983 publication, *Imagined Communities: Reflections on the Origin and Spread of Nationalism*.
55. McGinniss, *The Miracle of Castel di Sangro*, 239.
56. 'Future of Temperance Cause'. *Irish Independent*, June 26, 1926.
57. 'Position of Clubs – Hours and Regulations'. *Irish Independent*, February 12, 1927.
58. Garnham, *Association Football and Society in Pre-partition Ireland*, 195.

References

'An Garda Síochána: Claim Against Cork Bohemian Football Club in Respect of Services'. National Archives of Ireland, 90/5/43, 1934–1935.

Bessel, Richard. 'European Society in the Twentieth Century'. In *The Oxford History of Modern Europe*, ed. T. C. W. Blanning, 234–59. Oxford: Oxford University Press, 2000.

Council of Europe Parliamentary Assembly. 'Report of Committee of Culture and Education: Football Hooliganism', 30 September 1999, http://www.assembly.coe.int/nw/xml/XRef/X2H-Xref-ViewHTML.asp?FileID=8749&lang=en (accessed December 25, 2015).

Cronin, Mike. *Sport and Nationalism in Ireland*, Dublin: Four Courts Press, 1999.

Cronin, Mike, Mark Duncan, and Paul Rouse. *The GAA: A People's History*. Dublin: Collins Press, 2009.

Dunning, Eric. 'Towards a Sociological Understanding of Football Hooliganism as a World Phenomenon'. *European Journal on Criminal Policy and Research* 8 (2000): 141–62.

Dunning, Eric. 'Violence and Sport'. In *International Handbook of Violence Research*, eds. Wilhelm Heitmeyer and John Hagan, 903–20. London: Springer, 2003.

Farrell, Michael. *Northern Ireland: The Orange State*. New York: Urizen, 1976.

Ferriter, Diarmaid. *The Transformation of Ireland 1900–2000*. London: The Overlook Press, 2005.

Foster, R. F. *Modern Ireland: 1600–1972*. London: Penguin, 1989.

Garnham, Neal. *The Origins and Development of Football in Ireland: Being a Reprint of R. M. Peter's Irish Football Annual 1880*. Belfast: Ulster Historical Foundation, 1999.

Garnham, Neal. *Association Football and Society in Pre-partition Ireland*. Belfast: Ulster Historical Foundation, 2004.

Garnham, Neal. 'Ein Spiel in zweiNationen?Fußball in Irland, 1918–1939'. In *Fußballzwischen den Kriegen: Europa 1918–1939* [Football Between the Wars: Europe 1918–1939], eds. Christian Koller and Fabian Brändle, 65–85. Munster: Lit-Verl (Verlag), 2010.

Goldblatt, David. *The Ball is Round: A Global History of Football*. London: Penguin, 2006.

Gray, Tony. *Ireland This Century*. London: Little, Brown, 1994.

James, Harold. 'The Fall & Rise of the European Economy in the Twentieth Century'. In *The Oxford History of Modern Europe*, ed. T. C. W. Blanning, 186–213. Oxford: Oxford University Press, 2010.

Keogh, Dermot. *Twentieth Century Ireland*. Dublin: Palgrave McMillan, 2005.

McGinniss, Joe. *The Miracle of Castel di Sangro: A Tale of Passion and Folly in the Heart of Italy*. New York: Broadway Books, 2000.

Minute Book of the Protest and Appeals and Emergency Committees of the Football Association of Ireland. University College Dublin, P137/14, 1921–1932.

Moore, Cormac. *The Irish Soccer Split*. Cork: Atrium, 2015.

Spaaij, Ramón. 'Football Hooliganism as a Transnational Phenomenon: Past and Present Analysis: A Critique – More Specifically and Less Generally'. *The International Journal of the History of Sport* 24, no. 4 (April 2007): 411–31, doi:10.1080/09523360601157156.

Sugden, John, and Alan Bairner. *Sport, Sectarianism and Society in a Divided Ireland*. London: T & T Clarke, 1993.

Taylor, Matthew. *The Association Game: A History of British Football*. London: Routledge, 2007.

Toms, David. *Soccer in Munster: A Social History, 1877–1937*. Cork: Cork University Press, 2015.

Tynan, Mark. 'Association Football and Irish Society during the Inter-war Period, 1918–1939.' PhD diss., Maynooth University, 2013.

Football unity during the Northern Ireland Troubles?

Cormac Moore

> This article looks at the attempts during the 1970s and early 1980s between the Irish Football Association and the Football Association of Ireland to heal the split that had been in place in Irish soccer since 1921. These attempts were made against the backdrop of the Northern Ireland Troubles of 1968–1998. This paper explores the reasons why the talks took place at this juncture. It examines the main issues discussed at the conferences that took place from 1973 to 1980 between these national governing bodies for football and assesses the main factors leading to their ultimate failure.

Introduction

The study of soccer history in Ireland has been a topic much ignored by academics until recent years. There has been a dramatic explosion of interest and works from scholars over the last few years, though, clearly manifested in three publications focusing on soccer published by Cork University Press in 2015.[1] The relationship between football and the Northern Ireland Troubles has been the subject of many works with particular focuses on Derry City's secession from the Irish Football League in 1972 and sectarianism within football.[2] The relationship between the Irish Football Association (IFA) and the Football Association of Ireland (FAI) and the efforts between both associations to bring about one international team for Ireland was the subject of a chapter in *The Irish Soccer Split*.[3] This article is an expansion of that chapter.

The IFA was formed in 1880 to govern soccer for the whole island of Ireland. It was founded and headquartered in Belfast. An uneasy alliance existed between the governing body in Belfast and the different regional divisions for over 40 years, particularly the regional division encompassing Dublin, the Leinster Football Association. Some regional divisions were established long after the IFA was, for example, Munster in 1902. This tawdry union was ended in 1921 when the Leinster Football Association seceded from the IFA and subsequently formed the FAI. The FAI changed its name to the Football Association of the Irish Free State (FAIFS) in 1923, reverting to its original name in 1936. A number of attempts were made throughout the 1920s and early 1930s to heal the division and bring about one governing body for soccer on the island of Ireland again. These attempts were made against the changed political backdrop in Ireland. Ireland had subsequently been partitioned by the Government of Ireland Act of 1920, divided through six counties making up Northern Ireland and the other twenty-six making up the Irish Free State. It has been ascertained that the primary reason for the split and the failure to re-unify in Irish soccer was the prevailing political climate at the time.[4] Politics certainly played a major part. Many senior IFA figures were prominent unionists including the IFA chairman James Wilton and *Belfast Telegraph* editor Thomas Moles. The political climate in Ireland in the early 1920s had seen the withdrawal of the Dublin teams from the Irish Football League. Incidents of violence at matches, manifested most notoriously at an Irish Cup tie between Glentoran and Belfast Celtic in 1920 where a mass brawl ensued and revolvers were used, demonstrated the link between football and the bitterness between nationalist and unionist communities in Belfast.[5] Soccer was the only major sport in Ireland governed from Belfast. This posed problems for many. Due to pogroms in Belfast from 1920 to 1922 that led to the deaths and removal from homes and jobs of Catholics on a wide scale, Sinn Fein organized a boycott on goods and companies from Belfast.[6] Under such circumstances, it became increasingly unfeasible for Leinster football to be governed from Belfast. Although politics contributed to division, the main factor leading to and maintaining the split was power and a struggle to govern soccer for all of Ireland. The conferences of the 1920s and 1930s demonstrated this.[7] The IFA, the fourth oldest football association in the world, looked to maintain its status, to concede as little as it could. The FAI ultimately would not agree on a settlement unless it was granted on total equality.

After the last conference in 1932, no serious attempt was made for decades to solve the differences between both Irish associations and bring about union.[8] The relationship between the IFA and FAI was coloured by rancour and distrust. The IFA, seeing itself as the governing body for soccer for the whole island of Ireland, played under the name 'Ireland' and selected players born in the Irish Free State for international fixtures right up until 1950.[9] The situation was clarified by the Fédération Internationale de Football Association (FIFA) in 1953, ruling that for football purposes the 26 counties would be known as the Republic of Ireland and the six counties known as Northern Ireland.[10] Both bodies had minimal interaction with each other for years, such was the level of misgivings between the Irish associations. Interestingly, it was soon after the Troubles of Northern Ireland commenced in the late 1960s that real efforts were attempted to bring about union. This paper will explore the reasons why these talks took place at this juncture, when Northern Ireland became engulfed in a bitter conflict that lasted for 30 years. It will examine the main issues discussed at the conferences that took place from 1973 to 1980 between the IFA and FAI and assess the main factors leading to the ultimate failure of the conferences.

Towards an all-Ireland side?

By the late 1960s, the animosity that had coloured the relationship between the IFA and FAI for decades had been replaced by a more conciliatory one. IFA representatives were in attendance at an international match between the Republic of Ireland and Poland in 1964. It was agreed in 1965 to inaugurate an annual fixture between youth teams from the North and the South[11] and in 1967 'the Blaxnit All-Ireland' cup competition was launched with four teams representing the FAI and four teams the IFA, participating.[12] Despite these advances and the calls from illustrious players such as George Best enthusiastically supporting an all-Ireland international team, it was still believed unification was far off due to the 'internal politics of Irish soccer'.[13] A motion was defeated at a council meeting of the FAI in 1969 to approach the IFA with a view to the establishment of an all-Ireland soccer team.[14]

The escalating violence in the North of Ireland from the late 1960s appeared to scupper any chances of healing the split in Irish soccer with the Blaxnit Cup considered to be in jeopardy as a viable entity in early 1970 due to The Troubles.[15] It was reported, though, that the FIFA president, Stanley Rous, 'would welcome any move to fuse the Football Association of Ireland and the Irish Football Association' and the IFA secretary, William Drennan 'agreed that both Irish bodies should be working towards an all-Ireland side'.[16] In 1970, George Best reiterated his call for an all-Ireland international team claiming he had 'talked to several players from the South and they all want to see a full Irish team. I know the Northern Ireland players think the same way'.[17] Best was a Protestant from Belfast who had joined the Orange Order as a boy but in adulthood steered clear of politics. Perhaps playing for Manchester United, the perceived Irish Catholic club of Manchester, also afforded him an open-minded view on connections with the Republic of Ireland.[18] Another prominent Northern Ireland footballer who actively campaigned for an all-Ireland team was Derek Dougan.[19] Dougan claimed there was a need, for competitive reasons, for an all-Ireland team, and in comparing most other sports to football, stated 'it makes so much sense to combine in Rugby, Boxing, Hockey, Cricket, and Swimming while remaining polarised in the game of soccer'.[20] Footballers in the Republic of Ireland such as John Giles and Liam Brady would have relished an all-Ireland team too. Brady in his 1980 autobiography *So Far So Good: A Decade in Football* claimed that every footballer, north and south, 'wants the same thing – a united Ireland team'.[21] The book devoted a full chapter to the woes of having two teams on the island, imagining what the team could achieve 'if united with the players from the other side of some wooden pole or sentry box – usually imaginary'.[22] With administrators from both associations and international footballers more open to reconciliation, the fans and the new political realities of Northern Ireland would intervene to maintain the chasm. At the Blaxnit Cup Final of 1971 between Linfield and Cork Hibernians, held in Dalymount Park, crowd trouble coloured the match. The Linfield supporters waved Union Jacks whilst shouting 'Up the UVF' leading to both sections of supporters throwing bottles and stones at each other. The rioting continued after the match.[23]

The nationalist leaning club Derry City was dealt a significant blow when its ground, the Brandywell, close to the Bogside in Derry, scene of many riots, was considered too dangerous to host games and the club was forced to play its 'home' games in Coleraine, 40 miles from the city in late 1971.[24] Derry City, in refusing to play Linfield in its home ground, Windsor Park in November 1970 was fined £300 with the match awarded to Linfield. No action was taken against Protestant leaning clubs for cancelling fixtures for similar reasons.[25] Derry City was required to go to Windsor Park when it reached the Irish Cup final in 1971. In what has been described as 'The Silent Final', just 6000 spectators turned up, a mere 180 Derry City fans travelled by train to Belfast. Unsurprisingly, the club was beaten 3–0 in the final by Distillery.[26] The club decided to withdraw from Irish league football in 1972, following in the footsteps of its predecessor, Belfast Celtic.[27] One of the primary reasons cited by the club for withdrawing was the belief that it was increasingly rejected by the rest of the clubs in the Irish Football League and by the IFA itself who appeared to be unsympathetic to Derry City's plight.[28] Even though the security authorities had described the Brandywell as safe as any other Northern

Ireland ground in 1972, the Irish Football League refused to allow fixtures to be played there.[29]

The FAI commissioned a report on association football which was published in May 1973 on the ills that beset the game in the country. It was chaired by Fianna Fáil TD, David Andrews. On the prospect of reunification, the report stated 'that in the long term a country wide league competition, including teams from Northern Ireland, be considered'. It also recommended 'that the possibility of fielding an All-Ireland team be examined ... The Football Association of Ireland should set up machinery with the Irish Football Association with a view to the establishment of a country-wide association'. It concluded by stating 'problems involved in fielding an All-Ireland team can be overcome ... the Football Association of Ireland should look ahead and attempt to create an atmosphere of conciliation'.[30]

One event that happened just months later offered encouragement to those who dreamed of an all-Ireland team. Such a team comprising of players from Northern Ireland and the Republic of Ireland did play together in July 1973 as a 'Shamrock Rovers All-Ireland XI' against Brazil, a team considered the greatest of all time, having won its third World Cup three years previously.[31] It was organized by Louie Kilcoyne for charity, who with the support of his brother-in-law, John Giles and Derek Dougan assembled a team together. Although not receiving the support of the IFA, Dougan had no difficulty in convincing Northern Ireland internationals, Pat Jennings, David Craig, Alan Hunter, Martin O'Neill, Liam O'Kane and Brian Hamilton who all 'grabbed the chance' to play against the World Champions.[32] Dougan claimed that Harry Cavan, IFA president, actively canvassed FIFA to cancel the match and was responsible for the team being called a 'Shamrock Rovers Select Eleven' and not an 'All-Ireland Eleven'.[33] He also believed his international career was ended with Northern Ireland, 'being made a citizen of the coldlands of isolation and exclusion', due to his participation in the fixture against Brazil.[34] The game that ended four-three to the Brazilians was enthusiastically supported by 34,000 attendees at Lansdowne Road who heard a rendition of 'A Nation Once Again' by the St. Patrick's Brass and Reed band beforehand.[35] Many observers believed the event would lead to 'an all-Ireland team in action in world competition' in the not too distant future.[36]

Talks begin

The FAI subsequently sent the IFA a letter requesting a meeting 'to discuss matters of mutual interest', a meeting the IFA unanimously agreed to attend.[37] At that conference, held in Belfast on 2 October, 'a very lengthy and amicable discussion' was held, in stark contrast to many of the failed attempts between both associations in years past.[38] Two of the main topics discussed were the possibility of all-Ireland competitions with European ramifications and the possibility of an all-Ireland International team either under the jurisdiction of a joint Committee or under the jurisdiction of one.[39] At the conclusion of the meeting, it was agreed that 'further joint meetings of office bearers be arranged'.[40] The next meeting between both associations took place in Dublin in January 1974. On the issue of an all-Ireland league competition, it was felt this venture would not be possible without 'very substantial sponsorship'.[41] On the primary issue of the possibility of an all-Ireland team, Harry Cavan 'pointed out that both Associations at present have the right of entry to the World Cup Competition and the European Football Championship. If there was an

All Ireland team, there could only be one entry to both these Competitions'.[42] The FAI suggested

> The possibility of the Irish FA calling on Southern born players for the British International Championship and the FA of Ireland calling on Northern Ireland born players for friendly matches arranged by the FA of Ireland. After further consideration it was agreed that the Irish FA would ascertain the views of the other British Associations ... and Mr. Cavan would also enquire from FIFA about their reaction to such an arrangement.[43]

Although no agreement was reached, talks were still in progress some months later. In deploring the failure of the Scottish Football Association to send its international team to Belfast, the Northern Ireland Minister for Community Relations, Ivan Cooper commented in March 1974 that discussions were ongoing between the FAI and IFA 'with a view to the possible creation of an all-Ireland soccer team'.[44] By 1974, no international team had played in Northern Ireland due to The Troubles for three years, the last team to visit was the Soviet Union in 1971.[45] The Northern Irish soccer team ultimately played 10 'home' game in mainland Britain from 1972 to 1978 due to civil unrest.[46] The talks of 1973–1974 ultimately failed on the IFA looking for the FAI to amalgamate back into the IFA, something the southern body was unwilling to do.[47] It is important to note that the IFA–FAI talks were taking place the same time as the Sunningdale Agreement was reached, an attempt in late 1973 to introduce power-sharing between unionists and nationalists in the governing of Northern Ireland, an attempt that also failed, collapsing in May 1974 due to widespread unionist opposition.[48]

In 1976, the Irish Universities Football Union comprising of 12 universities and colleges from Northern Ireland and the Republic of Ireland, including five from the North, sought grant aid from the IFA and FAI to allow the body to fulfil its remaining fixture against Wales that year.[49] Both associations contributed £100 towards the travelling expenses of the team. The Irish Universities international team was the only all-Ireland soccer team in existence and this was the first occasion it was funded by both associations, another indication the possibility of reunion was a distinct possibility.[50]

Two teams in a small country like this was nonsensical

The IFA agreed to meet after another request was made by the FAI in 1977 'to discuss the possibility of an All Ireland International team'.[51] Cavan, who was also a vice-president of FIFA, said 'he saw no reason why there should not be further discussions on the matter' even if 'there were "practical difficulties"' involved. He also mentioned that 'there might be some difficulty in convincing FIFA of the feasibility of fielding just one national team, representative of two different associations, for competitive games such as the World Cup and European Championship ties'.[52] Commenting on the renewal of talks, David Andrews who had become the Republic of Ireland's Parliamentary Secretary (Minister of State) to the Minister for Foreign Affairs earlier in the year, believed it was 'one of the most encouraging and significant developments on the Irish soccer front in recent years'. He was in favour of a federation of Irish football where a team chosen from both associations would 'play two international friendly matches every year against the top teams in Europe'.[53]

Coinciding with the renewal of talks was the pairing of Northern Ireland with the Republic of Ireland in Group One of the 1980 European Championship qualifiers in late 1977. England was also drawn in the same group. Considered by the *Irish Times* as 'a nice touch of irony at a time when moves are afoot to explore the possibility of fielding just one international soccer team', it would lead to the first clash between both teams at the senior international level.[54] The first concern that came to most peoples' minds was the security concerns the clashes in Dublin and Belfast would pose due to the ongoing violence that had engulfed Northern Ireland over the previous eight years. One commentator called it 'the worst thing that could possibly happen to soccer football in this country' saying it could 'set the scene for the most serious football riots of all time since a war broke out over the result of a match in South America (the "Football War" of 1969 between Honduras and El Salvador)'.[55]

Liam Brady claims that when both Irelands were drawn against each other, six Irishmen playing at Arsenal (Brady, David O'Leary and Frank Stapleton from the Republic of Ireland and Pat Jennings, Sammy Nelson and Pat Rice from Northern Ireland) 'sat down and faced up to a sickening and depressing reality … there we were, born on the same island yet destined to come face to face in combat and, as it turned out, wreck each other's chances of reaching the Italy-based Finals'.[56]

It was envisaged the talks would be ongoing over months, perhaps years, to reach an agreement satisfactory to both the IFA and FAI. The most likely solution, it was believed, was an 'all-Ireland Control body which, while guaranteeing the sovereignty of the two associations, will enable them to co-operate for the purpose of promoting international football'.[57] The first session of the 'newest, and clearly, the most determined campaign so far, to attain the long cherished goal of an all-Ireland team in international football' took place in Dundalk on 2 February 1978. After the four-hour-long meeting, a joint communique was issued to the Press:

> Several options were considered, including the possibility of an All-Ireland Football Federation which would be responsible for international matches. It was agreed that a joint paper be produced setting out these options and the possible difficulties which might arise. The discussions will be continued during the period of the European championship in which the two associations are drawn against each other. The representatives agreed that the meeting had been extremely positive and worthwhile. A further meeting has been arranged for March 8th in Dublin.[58]

The FAI had succeeded in having the emphasis switched from an outright merger of the two associations to the consideration for an all-Ireland Football Federation, something which would be unprecedented in world football. Cavan gave a qualified endorsement of the outcome of the first day of talks, declaring that 'a lot of points were agreed today but obviously some areas will present problems'.[59] The problems he envisaged that could crop up included economics, with a joint team only playing half of the fixtures both associations played each year resulting in a corresponding drop in income. He also believed it would be hard for the League of Ireland and the Irish League to retain their separate representation in the three European club competitions if only one Irish team was entered in international tournaments. He felt the forthcoming European championship matches between the Republic of Ireland and Northern Ireland could have a profound influence 'for good or bad' on the talks, the attitude of fans would reflect the feelings at the grass root level for a unified team.[60] He concluded on a note of optimism, stating that 'our presence here today is proof that we are convinced there is enough common ground between these two associations to warrant the closest examination of the present situation'.[61] Cavan was also reported as saying he was 'delighted with the way it went and I have high hopes that something good will come out of the talks'.[62]

Frank Davis, the FAI president, was very upbeat after the first session, stating, 'With the goodwill shown around the table today, I believe that, whatever the timing, an all-Ireland team must now come into being ... The fact that we are drawn together in the European championship is another means of bringing us closer and getting to know each other's options'.[63]

Commenting on the unity talks between the two Irish associations, the *Kerryman* newspaper compared the divide in Irish soccer to hockey in Ireland, where a 32 county Irish team was due to compete in the men's World Cup Hockey Finals in Argentina that summer. The soccer World Cup Finals were also due to be played in Argentina in 1978. Neither Irish team qualified for the soccer World Cup. The Hockey Association was involved in a controversial episode with the GAA who banned four of its members from participating in a fundraising function for the Irish hockey team as the latter 'uses "Danny Boy" instead of "Amhrán na bhFiann" as an anthem, and substitutes the flag of the Four Provinces for the Tricolour as a national flag'. The newspaper claimed an all-Ireland soccer team would be good enough to be going to Argentina too and if the price of that unity was 'Danny Boy' and a flag of the Four Provinces, it was a price worth paying.[64]

The second session held a month later in Dublin was also considered a positive meeting with the discussions 'taking place in a friendly, cordial atmosphere and that some progress had been made'.[65] Security arrangements were discussed for the upcoming clashes between both Irish associations with the consensus being that the matches posed 'no insurmountable problems'.[66] The meeting concluded with the arrangement for a third meeting in Belfast a month later.[67] At the IFA AGM of 1979, Harry Cavan, 'the man whom many people in the Republic thought was the principal opponent of the move' for an all-Ireland team, claimed 'that two teams in a small country like this was nonsensical, but he warned that anyone who thought that a united Ireland team would win the World Cup was living in cuckoo land'.[68]

All-Ireland dream killed by naked tribalism

The meetings stuttered along at a torturous pace over the following months. The European championship clashes between both of the Irish teams passed almost without incident. There was a hoax bomb scare close to the border train line as well as some minor skirmishes between rival fans at the Dublin encounter in September 1978.[69] Liam Brady recalled that the game 'was played in a good spirit, leading to a lot of spectators to label the game an anti-climax'.[70] At the Belfast fixture in November 1979, a stone-throwing incident led to the forced substitution of Republic of Ireland player Gerry Daly due to an ugly gash at the back of his head.[71] It was a club match, a European Cup tie between Linfield and Dundalk in 1979 that demonstrated the precarious nature of soccer on the island, and its close links to the political conflict in Northern Ireland, causing one journalist to claim that the 'All-Ireland dream (was) killed by naked tribalism'.[72] The match was preceded days earlier by the killings of Lord Mountbatten and others in his party on a boat off the coast of Mullaghmore in County Sligo as well as the deaths of 18 British soldiers in Warrenpoint, County Down by the Irish Republican Army (IRA), the highest death toll suffered in a single incident by the British Army throughout the Troubles.[73] The match which was held in Oriel Park, Dundalk, had not even started before trouble broke out. Over 3000 Linfield fans converged on Dundalk.[74] Linfield fans destroyed a pub before the match. Their buses were stoned by Dundalk supporters. Throughout the match, Linfield fans continuously threw stones and sought confrontation. Cliftonville fans had travelled from Northern Ireland just to clash with the Linfield supporters. Midway through the second half, Linfield fans attempted to pull down the Tricolour flying over the unreserved stand, prompting the Gardai to baton charge and clear the Linfield contingent from the ground.[75] One Dundalk player, Mick Lawlor described the chaotic scenes that night, when he stated that 'I turned away from a Linfield player with the ball and ran directly into a policeman'.[76] On the way back to their buses, the Linfield fans continued on their rampage, smashing every window within sight. Seventy people were injured from the rioting.[77] UEFA considered the Linfield fans to be the primary culprits with the Northern club forced to play its 'home' leg, the return fixture, in a neutral venue outside of Ireland or Britain. That match took place in Haarlem in the Netherlands.[78] Journalist Peter Byrne referred to the end of the match in Harlem as 'less the closing of a chapter in the ongoing strife of north-south relations as an emphatic thumbs down to the whole concept of all-Ireland club soccer'.[79] The FAI, in referring to the 'recent unfortunate occurrences', claimed the incidents at Oriel Park would not de-rail its unification talks with the IFA.[80]

The sixth meeting (since the talks had resumed in 1978) took place between the IFA and the FAI in Belfast in November 1979 on the eve of the Northern Ireland and Republic of Ireland match held in Windsor Park.[81] The campaign to attain an all-Ireland team was considered 'to be almost as difficult as achieving political unity and, in some respects, even more treacherous'.[82] The main stumbling blocks appeared not to be on the sensitive issues of flag and anthem but on money and the financial dilemma the halving of revenue from international fixtures would cause. It still was agreed to meet again in January 1980, grounds for optimism according to Peadar O'Driscoll, FAI secretary, who claimed, 'the longer the talks progress, the better the chances of a solution'.[83]

The following round of talks held in Dublin in January 1980 would prove to be a turning point, though, bringing the venture that had started in earnest in 1973 'close to total breakdown'.[84] The primary reason for the pessimism was the ongoing conflict in Northern Ireland, manifested during the Linfield Dundalk riot the previous year. Cavan commented on the

> Major problem of community feeling in the North. I went on record a few years ago as saying that something positive in the All Ireland context would be achieved by the IFA's centenary year, which is this year. I didn't realise at the time that the community unrest would still be such a huge problem in 1980.[85]

The problem of reconciling the concept of an all-Ireland team with the rules of FIFA was also mentioned as an obstacle, with FIFA rules prohibiting the formation of one team for competitive purposes where a political border exists between two countries.[86]

Despite attempts by the FAI to renew talks in 1981,[87] the divides were 'still so great, the difficulties so complex and the avenues of finding a solution so long', for any more meaningful attempt to be made at union.[88] Derek Brookes, secretary of Linfield, summed up the main obstacle to unity

> The problem with people who speak glibly of unity in Irish soccer ... is that they tend to ignore the facts of life here in the North of Ireland. The concept of one Ireland

football team may be exciting but, unfortunately, it does not take account of the fact that we are living in troubled times. People must live six days a week in that environment. It is unreasonable to expect that football can be immune on the seventh.[89]

The political factor was eventually acknowledged by the FAI as the primary hindrance to overcome. Its president, John Farrell stated in 1983, 'there will be no settlement of the split in Irish soccer until such time as the political problems which divide the North and the Republic have been solved'.[90]

The 1980s would see fortunes improve for both associations at the international level. The Northern Irish soccer team won the British Home Championship in 1980 and 1984, the last year it was ever held. The 1981 championship was abandoned due to the civil unrest in Northern Ireland surrounding the hunger strikes in the Maze Prison with the English and Welsh teams refusing to travel to Belfast.[91] Under Billy Bingham, the international side also qualified for the World Cups of 1982 and 1986, causing one of the biggest upsets in the 1982 competition by defeating the host nation, Spain.[92] The results Northern Ireland was experiencing led Harry Cavan to comment, 'with results like we have had over the last two years, who needs a United Irish soccer side?'[93] Such comments would suggest Cavan's interest in an all-Ireland team had been lukewarm at best. Qualification for the World Cup in 1986 would mark the end of Northern Ireland's highly successful run. The team did not qualify for an international tournament until 2015, qualifying for its first European Championship finals in France in 2016.

By contrast, just two years after Mexico '86, the Republic of Ireland made its introduction at international tournaments at the European Championship of 1988 in West Germany. In qualifying for the World Cups in 1990 and 1994, the southern body had overtaken its Northern rival on the field. It also would lessen the appetite from the FAI for unity. Louie Kilcoyne, the FAI president, commenting in 1995 on the prospect of re-union stated, 'if it ain't broken, don't fix it'.[94]

Sectarian tensions fuelled by the conflict in Northern Ireland also spilled over to soccer during the 1980s and 1990s. When Northern Ireland reached the World Cup finals in 1982 and 1986, virtually all of Northern Ireland, including most of the Catholic minority, rallied to the team. According to Alexander Wolff, the relationship between the Northern Ireland football team and the Catholic and nationalist community changed dramatically from the late 1980s

> After the signing of the Anglo-Irish Agreement (of 1985) pledging greater cooperation between Great Britain and the Republic, Protestant Ulster felt increasingly isolated and began to cling more desperately to symbols of its separateness from the South. About the same time, an Englishman named Jack Charlton took over the Republic's theretofore mediocre team and made a great success of it, going all the way to the final eight of the Cup in 1990. After years of immersion in Gaelic games – parochial pastimes like hurling and Gaelic football – Irish Catholics could now use soccer as well to proclaim their Irishness to the world. Over this span the number of Catholics on the Northern Ireland team dwindled, and its successes on the field became more modest. And the mood at Windsor Park, where Northern Ireland plays, became increasingly sectarian.[95]

This was echoed by John Sugden and Alan Bairner who claimed in 1991 that, although open to selecting players from both communities, the choice of Windsor Park, 'laden with loyalist imagery', as Northern Ireland's home venue made it increasingly difficult for Catholics to support the team and in many cases they changed their allegiance to the team from the Republic.[96]

At an Irish Cup tie between Linfield and nationalist leaning club, Donegal Celtic, at Windsor Park in 1990, crowd disturbances led to the intervention of the RUC who fired plastic bullets into the crowd. Forty-five RUC officers and fifteen civilians were injured.[97] The match had originally been scheduled to be played in Donegal Celtic's home ground in West Belfast. The RUC had felt it couldn't secure public safety in West Belfast. The IFA decided to reschedule the match to Linfield's home ground, Windsor Park, leading the *Irish News* to condemn the IFA for its 'disgracefully cavalier attitude in riding roughshod over the views of the Donegal Celtic management'.[98] In 1991 Donegal Celtic was drawn at home against Ards, who had a predominantly Protestant following, in the Irish Cup. Again, the RUC ruled it was too unsafe to stage the match in West Belfast and again the IFA agreed. Donegal Celtic was ordered to play the tie at the Ards ground in Newtownards. Refusing to do so, Donegal Celtic decided to withdraw from the competition. The club's application for membership to the FAI, following the footsteps of Derry City who joined the FAI governed League of Ireland in 1985, was rejected due to the danger associated with West Belfast.[99] In 1989, an attempt by Derry City to schedule a benefit match with Linfield was rejected as it was believed both clubs' fans 'would see a Linfield–Derry City friendly as a contradiction in terms'.[100] Buses carrying Derry City fans returning from the FAI Cup Final that year were stoned by Protestant youths carrying Ulster Flags.

A survey conducted in 1990 amongst Northern Ireland soccer supporters demonstrated the huge gulf between Catholic and Protestant supporters at the time. One hundred Catholic and one hundred Protestants from the greater Belfast area were surveyed by University of Ulster student N.P. McGivern, who asked whom they would prefer to see win a British-Irish tournament staged among the two Irish teams, England, Scotland and Wales.[101] Ninety-one per cent of Catholics wanted the Republic of Ireland to come first, with only eight per cent opting for Northern Ireland. Eighty-eight per cent of Protestants wanted Northern Ireland to win the tournament with over sixty per cent desiring for the Republic of Ireland to be placed fourth or last.[102] Eighty-five per cent of Catholics were in favour of an all-Ireland team compared to forty-two per cent of Protestants. Forty-three per cent of Protestants desired an all-UK team.[103] A recent University of Ulster study appears to suggest there is less appetite for an all-Ireland team now, with fifty-four per cent of people in Northern Ireland desiring an all-Ireland team, seventy per cent from the Catholic community and thirty-nine per cent from the Protestant community.[104]

The treatment by fans of Northern Ireland international players who joined Glasgow Celtic, such as Anton Rogan, Allen McKnight (a Protestant) and most notoriously, Neil Lennon helped to solidify the belief that the Northern Ireland team was available for just one community in Northern Ireland.[105] Their treatment was considered mild, though, in comparison to the 24-hour police protection BixenteLizarazu had to receive following death threats he received by Basque separatists for playing for France, Lizarazu being of Basque origin.[106]

A frightening example of the deep hatred many in Northern Ireland held towards the Republic of Ireland was starkly demonstrated at the World Cup qualifier between the two Irish international teams in Windsor Park in November 1993. The match was played in a poisonous atmosphere throughout. The match was preceded by some of the worst atrocities of the Troubles with the IRA bombing of a fish shop on the Shankill Road in Belfast on 23 October, killing eight people, being followed by Ulster loyalists killing seven customers at the Rising Sun bar in Greysteel, County

Derry seven days later. Twenty-six people were fatal victims of the Troubles in the last week of October 1993 alone.[107] A change of venue from Windsor Park to a neutral location was seriously considered at one juncture by FIFA.[108] After interventions from the IFA and the FAI, the game did go ahead in Winsdor Park. To avoid unnecessary provocation, it was decided not to fly the Irish tricolour in the ground nor to play the Irish national anthem, *Amhrán na bhFiann*.[109] A 'terrible tension' engulfed the stadium.[110] Fans with southern accents were advised to keep quiet throughout the match. The *Irish Times* journalist Fintan O'Toole was in the crowd that night:

> To be a Republic supporter in that stand, is to live in a surreal, semi-conscious dream. You have to be somebody else, to divest yourself of your voice and still your reaction. To put your conscious, waking self into a state of suspended animation like a machine with the power on but all the controls turned right down, lest it leap out and betray you. With the Billy Boys left and right, with the screams of 'Fenian scum' and the palpable waves of hatred breaking over your back, you have to act a role. You have to think and feel like them, to be outwardly a Billy Boy yourself.[111]

Republic of Ireland international, Alan McLoughlin who scored the equalizing goal on the night that secured World Cup qualification for the Republic of Ireland for USA 1994, described Windsor Park that evening as 'a very strange place' with 'the safest place' being on the pitch.[112] Although the Northern Ireland manager Billy Bingham came in for strong criticism for his behaviour that night, many of the Northern Ireland players and officials were happy for all of the Republic of Ireland players except one, Roy Keane 'whose verbal abuse of the Northern Ireland players during the game was not appreciated'.[113]

The prospect for union between both associations had never been further from realization. Months later, the draw for the qualifying rounds of the 1996 European championship in England was made with the Republic of Ireland drawn against Northern Ireland yet again. Sean Connolly, FAI secretary remarked, 'This draw doesn't help. We have asked FIFA that in the future the two countries be kept apart'. He was accused by David Bowen, his counterpart in the IFA of 'hysterical scaremongering'.[114]

Tensions have eased in recent years. Republican and loyalist ceasefires, followed by the signing of the Good Friday Agreement in 1998 have seen an end to the wide-scale violence of The Troubles of Northern Ireland. Both Irish teams have seen their fortunes dwindle on the international stage too and have not met in serious competition since the 1990s. In appointing a Community Relations' Officer, the IFA has actively looked to include more people from the nationalist community to its fold[115] and sectarian chants at Northern Ireland matches are now consistently tackled head on through the IFA's 'Football for All – Love Football Hate Bigotry' campaign.[116] There have been disagreements between the IFA and the FAI recently, though, particularly over the eligibility of Northern Ireland born players such as James McClean and Darron Gibson in representing the Republic of Ireland.[117] The eligibility issue has come to the fore after the Good Friday Agreement which has allowed individuals born on the island of Ireland to choose to declare themselves as British or Irish. On selecting players born in Northern Ireland, and with the tacit approval of FIFA, the FAI has risked the ire of the IFA and contributed to a souring of the improved relationship between both bodies.[118] Despite this disagreement, recent years have seen more cordial relations between both associations. The Setanta Cup, the first cross-border competition since the 1980s was inaugurated in 2005 and continues to this day.[119] Both associations have also co-operated on issues such as coaching[120] and schooling in the border regions.[121] There have been, though, no clear overtures from either the FAI or the IFA to reconvene talks on unity in soccer. This may change.

Conclusion

2016 has seen both Irish international teams compete in the finals of a major tournament at the same time for the first time. Despite the many talks that took place between the IFA and the FAI from 1973 to 1980, there still are two teams on the island. There were just too many hurdles of an internal and external nature to overcome. The fact the talks took place at all, considering the violent backdrop in Northern Ireland at the time and the previous history between both Irish associations, is extraordinary. In many ways, it was players such as George Best, Derek Dougan, John Giles and Liam Brady who made the pioneering steps in calling for an all-Ireland team. The administrators, particularly from the FAI, realizing how much the game was suffering in the country, sought to bring a healing, if not an amalgamation, from the split that had dominated the sport in Ireland since 1921. The IFA, in its willingness to fully participate in up to nine conferences with the FAI, demonstrated it too was open and prepared to reach an agreement.

The talks could not escape the political realities of Northern Ireland. The talks began in 1973 as efforts of power-sharing between nationalists and unionists in the governing of Northern Ireland were attempted, albeit unsuccessfully, and ended in 1980, soon after the events at a football match between Linfield and Dundalk showed just how close the linkage between sport and politics were. At junctures where breakthroughs seemed close at hand, sectarian violence within football had a crippling effect. Success also lessened the appetite for union for both Northern Ireland and the Republic of Ireland. The halving of finances and potentially of jobs for the administrators from the IFA and the FAI can also not be discounted as reasons for failure. It was also mooted that FIFA would not allow for one football team for two political entities.

Although the wide-scale violence in Northern Ireland has ended, there still are significant barriers for the community to overcome, not least within football. Many Catholics and nationalists still have more affinity for the Republic of Ireland team than the Northern Ireland team, feeling the latter team still is a Protestant team for a Protestant people. The IFA has made big strides to be more inclusive in welcoming Catholics and nationalists to support its international team, the appointment of Catholic Michael O'Neill as the Northern Ireland manager being a case in point. The relationship between the IFA and FAI has improved considerably since the 1990s with both bodies liaising on many issues regularly now. Despite both teams qualifying for France 2016, the quality of both teams is a pale reflection on the teams both associations had at their disposal in years gone by. Lack of success combined with more cordial relations may see the prospect of an all-Ireland appear on the agenda yet again.

Disclosure statement

No potential conflict of interest was reported by the author.

Notes

1. See Curran, *The Development of Sport in Donegal, 1880–1935*; Moore, *The Irish Soccer Split*; and Toms, *Soccer in Munster: A Social History, 1877–1937*.
2. See Bairner, 'Sports, Politics and Society in Northern Ireland: Changing Times, New Developments'; Cronin, 'Playing Away from Home: Identity in Northern Ireland and the Experience of Derry City Football Club'; Platt, *A History of Derry City Football and Athletic Club, 1929–1972*; Saunders and Sugden, 'Sport and community relations in Northern Ireland'; Hassan, 'A People Apart: Soccer Identity and Irish Nationalists in Northern Ireland'.
3. See Chapter 18 in Moore, *The Irish Soccer Split*.
4. Brodie, *100 Years of Irish Football*, 15.
5. Flynn, *Political Football: The Life and Death of Belfast Celtic*, 80.
6. Lynch, 'The People's Protectors? The Irish Republican Army and the "Belfast Pogrom", 1920–1922', 375.
7. For a detailed study on those conferences see Moore, *The Irish Soccer Split*.
8. The conference in 1932 was the closest football came to union again. However, it collapsed over the potential sharing of the IFA's two seats on the International Football Association Board.
9. Sugden and Bairner, *Sport, Sectarianism and Society in a Divided Ireland*, 74.
10. *Irish Times*, November 28, 1953, 19.
11. *Irish Independent*, October 27, 1965, 14.
12. *Irish Independent*, November 26, 1967, 14.
13. *Irish Times*, November 28, 1967, 3.
14. *Sunday Independent*, November 16, 1969, 15.
15. *Irish Times*, January 3, 1970, 3.
16. *Irish Press*, August 13, 1970, 18.
17. *Irish Press*, August 19, 1970, 18.
18. Bairner, 'Simply the (George) Best: Ulster Protestanism, Conflicted Identity and "The Belfast Boy's"', 35, 37.
19. Dougan, 'The Case for an All-Ireland Team', 19.
20. Dougan, *The Sash He Never Wore ... Twenty Five Years On*, 177.
21. Brady, *So Far So Good: A Decade in Football*, 59.
22. Ibid., 58–64.
23. *Irish Times*, May 22, 1971, 8.
24. Sugden and Bairner, *Sport, Sectarianism and Society in a Divided Ireland*, 85.
25. Duke and Crolley, *Football, Nationality and the State*, 72.
26. Ibid., 72.
27. *Irish Times*, October 14, 1972, 2.
28. Cronin, 'Playing Away from Home: Identity in Northern Ireland and the Experience of Derry City Football Club', 71.
29. Duke and Crolley, *Football, Nationality and the State*, 73.
30. *Irish Times*, May 10, 1973, 3.
31. Tobin, 'All-Ireland Samba: Shamrock Rovers All-Ireland XI 3–4 Brazil Lansdowne Road, Tuesday 3 July 1973', 46.
32. Dougan, *The Sash He Never Wore ... Twenty Five Years On*, 178.
33. Ibid., 176.
34. Ibid., 179.
35. *Irish Times*, July 5, 1973, 3.
36. *Irish Times*, July 4, 1973, 3.
37. IFA Minute Book 1970–1977, D4196/A/11, August 28, 1973.
38. Ibid.
39. Ibid.
40. *Irish Press*, October 3, 1973, 18.
41. IFA Minute Book 1970–1977, D4196/A/11, January 29, 1974.
42. Ibid.
43. Ibid.
44. *Irish Times*, March 8, 1974, 10.
45. *Irish Times*, October 30, 1974, 3.

46. Sugden and Bairner, *Sport, Sectarianism and Society in a Divided Ireland*, 70.
47. *Irish Times*, February 3, 1978, 3.
48. Gillespie, 'Sunningdale and the 1974 Ulster Workers' Council Strike', 47.
49. IFA Minute Book 1970–1977, D4196/A/11, March 30, 1976.
50. *Irish Independent*, March 11, 1976, 11.
51. IFA Minute Book 1970–1977, D4196/A/11, August 30, 1977.
52. *Irish Times*, August 31, 1977, 3.
53. *Irish Times*, October 12, 1977, 3.
54. *Irish Times*, December 1, 1977, 4.
55. *Irish Times*, December 6, 1977, 3.
56. Brady, *So Far So Good: A Decade in Football*, 62.
57. *Irish Times*, February 2, 1978, 3.
58. *Irish Times*, February 3, 1978, 3.
59. *Irish Times*, February 3, 1978, 3.
60. *Irish Times*, February 3, 1978, 3.
61. *Irish Times*, February 3, 1978, 3.
62. *Irish Independent*, February 3, 1978, 13.
63. *Irish Times*, February 3, 1978, 3.
64. *Kerryman*, February 10, 1978, 8.
65. *Irish Times*, March 9, 1978, 3.
66. *Irish Times*, March 9, 1978, 3.
67. *Irish Press*, March 9, 1978, 16.
68. *Donegal News*, July 7, 1979, 5.
69. *Irish News*, September 21, 1978, 1.
70. Brady, *So Far So Good: A Decade in Football*, 62.
71. *Irish News*, November 22, 1979, 1.
72. *Irish Times*, August 30, 1979, 4.
73. *Irish News*, August 28, 1979, 1.
74. Byrne, *My Part of the Day*, 60.
75. *The Argus*, August 31, 1979, 1.
76. Byrne, *My Part of the Day*, 61.
77. *The Argus*, August 31, 1979, 1.
78. *The Argus*, September 7, 1979, 28.
79. Byrne, *My Part of the Day*, 62.
80. *Irish Times*, September 8, 1979, 4.
81. *Irish Press*, November 20, 1979, 7.
82. *Irish Times*, November 23, 1979, 3.
83. *Irish Times*, November 23, 1979, 3.
84. *Irish Times*, January 10, 1980, 3.
85. *Irish Press*, January 10, 1980, 16.
86. *Irish Times*, January 10, 1980, 3.
87. *Irish Times*, June 27, 1981, 22.
88. *Irish Press*, September 10, 1981, 13.
89. *Irish Times*, December 31, 1981, 12.
90. *Irish Times*, May 4, 1983, 1.
91. Samuel, *The British Home Football Championships 1884–1984*, 95, 96, 99.
92. Byrne, *Green is the Colour: The Story of Irish Football*, 229.
93. Agnew, 'Irish Football's Two Contrasting States', 23.
94. *Irish Independent*, March 29, 1995, 13.
95. Wolff, 'Peacefully Done'.
96. Sugden and Bairner, 'The Political Culture of Sport in Northern Ireland', 139.
97. *Irish Times*, February 19, 1990, 11.
98. Sugden and Bairner, *Sport, Sectarianism and Society in a Divided Ireland*, 88.
99. Ibid., 89.
100. McCann, 'Two Tribes on the Terraces?', 25.
101. *Irish Press*, March 29, 1995, 35.
102. Sugden and Bairner, *Sport, Sectarianism and Society in a Divided Ireland*, 79.
103. Ibid., 80.

104. Hargie, Somerville and Mitchell, 'Social Exclusion and Sport in Northern Ireland', 13.
105. Bairner, 'Sport, Politics and Society in Northern Ireland: Changing Times, New Developments', 286.
106. *The Observer*, March 4, 2001.
107. *Irish Times*, November 17, 1993, 5.
108. *Irish Independent*, November 3, 1993, 12.
109. *Irish Press*, November 15, 1993, 21.
110. *Irish Independent*, November 18, 1993, 28.
111. *Irish Times*, November 20, 1920, A1.
112. McLoughlin with Evans, *A Different Shade of Green: The Alan McLoughlin Story*, 18.
113. Ryan, *The Boys in Green: The FAI International Story*, 198.
114. *Irish Voice*, February 1, 1994, 2.
115. Hassan, 'An Opportunity for a New Beginning: Soccer, Irish Nationalists and the Construction of a New Multi-Sports Stadium for Northern Ireland', 345.
116. See the IFA website, http://www.irishfa.com/the-ifa/community-relations/resources/.
117. *Ulster Herald*, November 8, 2007, 12.
118. Hassan, McCullough and Moreland, 'North or South? Darron Gibson and the issue of player eligibility within Irish soccer', 752.
119. *Irish Independent*, January 5, 2005, 1.
120. *Ulster Herald*, December 13, 2007, 76.
121. *Donegal News*, February 20, 2009, 62.

References

Agnew, Paddy. 'Irish Football's Two Contrasting States'. *Fortnight* 200 (1984): 22–3.
Bairner, Alan. 'Sport, Politics and Society in Northern Ireland: Changing Times, New Developments'. *Studies: An Irish Quarterly Review* 90, no. 359 (2001): 283–90.
Bairner, Alan. 'Simply the (George) Best: Ulster Protestanism, Conflicted Identity and "The Belfast Boy(s)"'. *The Canadian Journal of Irish Studies* 32, no. 2 (2006): 34–41.
Brady, Liam. *So Far So Good: A Decade in Football*. London: Stanley Paul, 1980.
Brodie, Malcolm. *100 Years of Irish Football*. Belfast: Blackstaff Press, 1980.
Byrne, Peter. *My Part of the Day*. Dublin: PR Books, 1981.
Byrne, Peter. *Green is the Colour: The Story of Irish Football*. London: Carlton Books Limited, 2012.
Cronin, Mike. 'Playing Away from Home: Identity in Northern Ireland and the Experience of Derry City Football Club'. *National Identities* 2, no. 1 (2000): 65–79.
Curran, Conor. *The Development of Sport in Donegal, 1880–1935*. Cork: Cork University Press, 2015.
Dougan, Derek. 'The Case for an All-Ireland Team'. *Fortnight* 184 (1981): 19.
Dougan, Derek. *The Sash He Never Wore ... Twenty Five Years On*. Antrim: Lagan Books and All Seasons Publishing, 1997.
Duke, Vic, and Liz Crolley. *Football, Nationality and the State*. Essex: Routledge, 1996.
Flynn, Barry. *Political Football: The Life and Death of Belfast Celtic*. Dublin: Nosuch Ireland, 2009.
Gillespie, Gordon. 'Sunningdale and the 1974 Ulster Workers' Council Strike'. *History Ireland* 15, no. 3 (2007): 42–7.
Hargie, Owen, Ian Somerville, and David Mitchell. *Social Exclusion and Sport in Northern Ireland*. Belfast: Ulster University, 2015.
Hassan, David. 'A People Apart: Soccer, Identity and Irish Nationalists in Northern Ireland'. *Soccer & Society* 3, no. 3 (2002): 65–83.
Hassan, David. 'An Opportunity for a New Beginning: Soccer, Irish Nationalists and the Construction of a New Multi-Sports Stadium for Northern Ireland'. *Soccer & Society* 7, no. 2–3 (2006): 339–52.
Hassan, David, Shane McCullough, and Elizabeth Moreland. 'North or South? Darron Gibson and the Issue of Player Eligibility Within Irish Soccer'. *Soccer & Society* 10, no. 6 (2009): 740–53.
Irish Football Association Minute Book 1970–1977, D4196/A/11.

Lynch, Robert. 'The People's Protectors? The Irish Republican Army and the "Belfast Pogrom", 1920–1922'. *The Journal of British Studies* 47, no. 2 (2008): 375–91.

McCann, Eamonn. 'Two Tribes on the Terraces?' *Fortnight* 274 (1989): 25.

McLoughlin, Alan with Bryce Evans. *A Different Shade of Green: The Alan McLoughlin Story*. Wicklow: Ballpoint Press, 2014.

Moore, Cormac. *The Irish Soccer Split*. Cork: Cork University Press, 2015.

Platt, W.H.W. *A History of Derry City Football and Athletic Club, 1929–1972*. Derry: Coleraine Printing Company, 1986.

Ryan, Seam. *The Boys in Green: The FAI International Story*. Edinburgh: Mainstream Publishing Company, 1997.

Samuel, Richard. *The British Home Football Championships 1884–1984*. South Humberside: Soccer Books Limited, 2003.

Saunders, Eric, and John Sugden. 'Sport and community relations in Northern Ireland'. *Managing Leisure* 2, no. 1 (1997): 39–54.

Sugden, John P., and Alan E.S. Bairner. 'The Political Culture of Sport in Northern Ireland'. *Studies: An Irish Quarterly Review*, 80, no. 318 (1991): 133–41.

Sugden, John, and Alan Bairner. *Sport, Sectarianism and Society in a Divided Ireland*. Leicester: Leicester University Press, 1993.

Tobin, Shane. 'All-Ireland Samba: Shamrock Rovers All-Ireland XI 3–4 Brazil Lansdowne Road, Tuesday 3 July 1973'. *History Ireland* 16, no. 4 (2008): 46–7.

Toms, David. *Soccer in Munster: A Social History, 1877–1937*. Cork: Cork University Press, 2015.

Wolff, Alexander. 'Peacefully Done'. *Sports Illustrated* 79, no. 22 (1993): 80.

Linfield's 'Hawk of Peace': pre-Ceasefires reconciliation in Irish League football

Daniel Brown

> In Northern Irish football, Linfield are unrivalled in support and success. Yet historically, the Blues have been dogged by accusations of sectarianism. Controversy at the club in the early 1990s allowed Linfield to improve its unwanted image, and also indicated before the Ceasefires and Agreement, reconciliation was in the air. In late 1991, manager Eric Bowyer stated it was 'almost impossible for us to sign Catholics.' The press, politicians and lobbyists seized upon his words and placed enormous pressure on the club. On the back of the furore, Linfield brought in Catholic player Dessie Gorman – the 'Dundalk Hawk.' His performances helped the Blues to the Irish League title and revolutionized perceptions of the club. The press predicted Linfield fans couldn't stomach supporting a Catholic, yet Gorman was idolized. The political changes, hailed later in the decade, were apparent in the social fibres of local football long before.

From the late-1960s until just before the turn of the Millennium, Northern Ireland was engulfed by a bloody ethno-nationalist conflict, commonly referred to as – 'The Troubles.' All walks of life football included were adversely impacted by this reality. At the heart of 'The Troubles' lay a dispute over the constitutional future of the state. Unionists and loyalists wanted Northern Ireland to remain part of the United Kingdom, whilst Irish nationalists and republicans advocated that the Union with Great Britain should end. The everyday violence of 'The Troubles' was in the main perpetrated by paramilitaries, both republican and loyalist, though state forces were also culpable. During three decades of conflict, this violence led to the loss of more than 3500 lives.[1] Stalemate had characterized the first two decades of 'The Troubles,' but at the beginning of the third, the end of the Cold War dramatically altered the realpolitik at play. According to Thomas Bartlett, the collapse of the Soviet Union as a Superpower 'raised the possibility of the United States becoming more involved … in settling the Irish question.'[2] A new context for those seeking a resolution to 'The Troubles' had thus arisen. This changed dynamic was helpful in bringing about paramilitary ceasefires (on both sides) in 1994, and leading to the 1998 peace settlement – the Belfast Agreement.

It should be noted, that in the years immediately following the end of the Cold War, this changed 'Troubles' context was not always easy to discern. 1992 was particularly turbulent in Northern Ireland. During that year, 91 'Troubles'-related deaths were recorded. An upswing in murders carried out by loyalist paramilitaries (a trend apparent throughout the early 1990s) was a key feature of this statistic, whilst the republican Provisional Irish Republican Army (PIRA) continued its widespread bombing campaign across Northern Ireland and Great Britain. If anything, deadlock seemed to be an overriding feature of 1992. Indeed, the British government's first attempts at roundtable talks (with Provisional Sinn Féin excluded), which aimed at ending 'The Troubles' would conclude in November with very little achieved.[3] If the 1992 prospects for peace looked in many regards bleak, local football appeared to offer a glimpse of optimism for Northern Irish society.

During the 1992/93 season, the *almost impossible* was embraced at the League's most successful and best-supported side. Linfield – a club formed in 1886 by workers at the Ulster Spinning Company Mill – had fielded only one Catholic in over 40 years.[4] This statistic would change in 1992, and one of the players who helped break the mould, Dessie Gorman – the 'Dundalk Hawk' – became idolized on the terraces. Gorman would help inspire Linfield to its first league title in four seasons, and also revolutionized how the club was perceived. Given that Linfield had long been associated with Ulster unionism, loyalism and Protestantism, this was significant. Geoffrey Bell gave an indication of the club's apparent political and religious associations when he stated that the start of 'The Troubles' 'were bad years for the Protestants of Northern Ireland. Their parliament was suspended ... their political leaders compromised, even an occasional Orange March was banned. And, on top of all that, Linfield Football Club managed to win the (Northern) Irish League only once.'[5] Apparent change at Linfield nearly two decades after the period Bell was writing about was thus notable.

Prior to 1992, there were erroneous claims that the club operated a sectarian signing policy. Local entertainer James Young had poked fun at this with his comedy song 'I'm the only Catholic in the Linfield team.' The politics of religion and identity mattered in 'Troubles'-afflicted Northern Ireland. Therefore, the introduction of Catholic players at the club, and the embrace they received, indicated that well before the marked societal changes later in the decade, there were signs of a willingness to move past 'The Troubles' deadlock. The case of Linfield and Gorman is one that the wider historiography, of football and 'The Troubles,' has thus far neglected. Understandably, studies of the sport during the period have focused on how the game functioned in, and was affected by, a divided society. As David Goldblatt has maintained, 'the game starkly highlighted the fundamental issues ... that fuelled the conflict in the North.'[6] Whilst Jonathan Magee has contended the 'study of soccer in Northern Ireland has been dominated by [reference to] cross-community tension and sectarian rivalry.'[7] This article considers those community divisions in the latter years of 'The Troubles' and how football played a role in bridging some of the gulf apparent in Northern Irish society. Furthermore, the article rejects the claim, made by Mike Cronin, that during 1992, Linfield departed from its 'unofficial bar on Catholic players.'[8] There was no bar on Catholic players operating.

The United Kingdom's longest reigning monarch, Queen Elizabeth II, famously described 1992 as an 'AnnusHorribilis.' Her remarks, on November 24, of the said year, came during a speech rendered at a luncheon held in London's Guildhall.[9] Four days prior to this, Elizabeth's favourite house, Windsor Castle, had been greatly damaged. On November 20, a fire broke out, which lasted for several hours. Such was the extent of the blaze, it was estimated that £40million worth of damage was caused.[10] Given the castle's iconic status, images of the building in flames were arresting. They were though, also analogous of the 'AnnusHorribilis,' which Linfield had experienced to that point. On the pitch, the team was struggling; off it, there were regular media attacks made on the club's reputation. As the side's crest was (and still is) emblazoned with a depiction of the royal castle, the catastrophe seemed to reflect the tumultuous year at the Belfast Blues.

Throughout 1992, critics of the Blues had centred their condemnation on the claim that the club operated a sectarian transfer policy. Prior to that year, only one Catholic player had turned out for Linfield's first team since the late 1940s. When he, Tony Coly – a Senegalese international, signed in July 1988 (on loan from Belgian side Brugge KV), sections of Northern Ireland's media were incredulous that the Blues had actually signed a Catholic. Six days after Coly's move was confirmed, one of the Sunday papers led with an 'exclusive' on the deal. The front page of the *Sunday News* screamed 'YOUR [Linfield's] NEW STAR IS A CATHOLIC!'[11] Mike Scrivener of the paper warned that Coly faced a 'hot reception from the soccer club's true blue fans.'[12] When a bewildered Roy Coyle, the then Linfield manager, read the newspaper headline, his first thought was that the club had signed a player without informing him. Coyle had been unaware of Coly's faith, and later explained: 'I didn't ask the lad, 'By the way what religion are you?' The manager never ascertained a player's place of worship before a potential transfer, and he was never instructed to do so.[13]

The *Sunday News* hyperbole gave an indication of just how big a deal it was considered for Linfield to field a Catholic. Critics who maintained that Linfield was sectarian drew parallels with Glasgow Rangers. At the time of Coly's move to Linfield, no Catholic had represented Rangers since the 1920s. By the second half of the twentieth century, this was a phenomenon, which according to Ronnie Esplin and Graham Walker was 'widely perceived as unacceptably discriminatory.'[14] This only changed in the late 1980s as part of the 'Souness Revolution,' which transformed Rangers on and off the field. On July 10, 1989, manager Graeme Souness stunned the footballing world with the signing of Maurice 'Mo' Johnston. Johnston was Catholic and joined from French side Nantes. Given his religion, and that he had previously played for Celtic, the news sent the media into frenzy. After the transfer was confirmed, television cameras waited expectantly outside Rangers' home ground, Ibrox, to catch the reaction of supporters. What they captured was the initial shock of the news and a degree of unease. Some fans burned scarves; others tore up season ticket booklets, whilst a wreath was laid lamenting the loss of '116 years of tradition.' Despite these isolated histrionics, the vast majority of supporters took the transfer in their stride. Fans voted with their feet as they packed out Ibrox to witness Johnston and Rangers claim the 1989/90 league title. At the start of that season, 2000 Rangers' shareholders had attended the AGM in August. Souness was warmly received with loud cheers at the meeting when he explained that he bought Johnston to cement Rangers as Scotland's number one team. Alan Montgomery, Rangers' chief executive, was afforded a similar reception when he articulated that sectarianism was not confined to football in Scotland. Montgomery maintained that religious bigotry was a societal issue that stemmed from separate schooling.[15]

Glasgow Rangers were confident in asserting their position during the media frenzy that resulted from the Johnston signing. The same was not the case for Linfield during the furore caused by The *Sunday News* story. Club officials at the Blues were uncomfortable in making comment on the religious angle of the Coly transfer. A week after *The Sunday News* front-page headlines, the same newspaper complained that Linfield had 'BLACKBALLED' their reporters. A disgruntled article stated 'Club secretary Derek Brooks was said to be 'not available' to Sunday News.'[16] The shunning of *Sunday News* reporters was indicative of the club's reluctance to comment on the sensitive subject. Instead of rebutting claims that the club had operated a sectarian transfer policy, Linfield officials kept their counsel. The Blues' silence on the matter thus left a vacuum for others to consolidate a historical narrative that portrayed the club in an uncomplimentary light.

Four years later, when the Northern Ireland media, and this time outlets further afield, were again awash with stories about Linfield's supposed transfer policy, silence was not an option. On this occasion, it was actually the club's manager who had highlighted the issue. Near the end of 1991, Eric Bowyer (Roy Coyle's successor) gave an interview to *One Team in Ulster*, an unofficial club fanzine, which blew the matter wide open. This came during a period (1989–93) that Gordon Gillespie has identified as the 'golden age' of Northern Irish fanzines. These publications were high in number and at times achieved notable prominence.[17] Indeed, the impact of *One Team in Ulster*'s Christmas 1991 edition was enormous. Below the front cover's picture of Bowyer as a player was a tagline that read 'Eric Bowyer Talks to OTIU [*One Team in Ulster*] – And We Can't get him to Shut Up! [*sic*].'[18] The fanzine editorial acknowledged, 'we've managed a bit of a scoop [in getting] Eric Bowyer to be our interviewee.' It then added 'we hope you'll find it interesting reading!' The entire interview was published over 13 pages and covered a variety of topics. Bowyer answered questions on his team's current form, his views of the press, and the Irish League in general. He also touched on the topic that the Linfield hierarchy traditionally shied away from. Near the end of the interview, Bowyer was asked, 'How do you feel about the club's image as a sectarian club ... Can you ever see that image changing?'[19]

Eric Bowyer realized that answering a question on 'the club's [sectarian] image' was potentially explosive. Yet, instead of ducking the issue, he gave a hard-hitting critique of Northern Irish society and how the Blues operated within it. The manager explained that 'The Troubles' fostered conditions which made it difficult for Linfield to sign Catholics.[20] In articulating this, he wanted to provoke debate. Bowyer recalled that: 'part of me wanted this to open up because I wanted to sign Catholic players ... I didn't see any sense in cutting half of the footballing population off.'[21] The manager's response began by maintaining that he did not like 'the whole idea of sectarianism.' Then he pointed out that he was a

> realist and I know that there are major problems in our society ... I would sign [Cliftonville player] Peter Murray tomorrow, because I know how good a player he is – but that just wouldn't have worked. It wouldn't have worked for a whole variety of reasons. It wouldn't have worked because Peter Murray couldn't have lived in Northern Ireland society. Even if he'd wanted to come here ... The crowd mightn't have liked it, but the more important thing is that when he went back to live in North Belfast, his life would have been miserable. Getting shot would not be an impossibility. I mean, Mo Johnston's ok – he got a million and a half in his hand to live in Edinburgh after two years. You can't do that here! So, with the best will in the world, it would be almost impossible for us to sign Catholics [*sic*].[22]

Bowyer was right to point to the financial differences between the likes of Mo Johnston and Irish League players. For the vast majority of Irish League players, the wages received from a club came on top of a full-time occupation. In Northern Ireland, players have normally lived in the same communities as fans.

Very soon, Bowyer's provocative musings were gracing a much wider audience than the *One Team in Ulster* readership. In the first weekend of 1992, a *Sunday Life* headline read 'NO GO FOR CATHOLICS: LINFIELD BOSS SPELLS OUT WHY HE'LL NOT BE SIGNING RC [Roman Catholic] PLAYERS.'[23] The tabloid paper carried quotes from Bowyer in which he explained, 'If any man or boy from the nationalist community were ever to join us, their life would be unbearable and that's a simple fact … What I am saying is that in our society in Northern Ireland it would be idiotic to think differently.' Bowyer reiterated the comparison with Mo Johnston and maintained that any Catholic who signed for the Blues 'would not be able to escape the enormous pressures when he returned to his own community.'[24]

The *Irish News* (an overtly nationalist paper) weighed in on the story on January 6, claiming that given Bowyer's comments, Linfield 'might be investigated by the Fair Employment Commission.'[25] An unnamed source in the Commission was quoted as saying, 'Officials believe that what has happened here is that the club has decided to virtually flaunt the fair employment laws.'[26] On top of this, the paper's editor, Nick Garbutt, let fly with an opinion piece.[27] Garbutt made the unwarranted accusation that 'Linfield FC … never wants any Catholics in its first team … By keeping the Taigs [an offensive term used to describe Roman Catholics and Irish nationalists] out, Linfield FC perpetuates sectarianism, and gives it a 'respectable' face … it is difficult to understand why UEFA continues to allow Linfield to play in European tournaments.'[28] The *One Team in Ulster*'s interview had opened debate, but in doing so brought denunciation of the club.

By the end of January, criticism of Linfield had spread to the other side of the Atlantic. The Irish National Caucus (INC), an Irish-American lobby group, learned of Bowyer's comments and initiated a campaign against the club. On account of the Blues' supposed sectarian policies, the Caucus demanded, that the Irish Football Association (IFA) cut all links with Linfield and the club's home ground, Windsor Park (which Northern Ireland had a contract to play at). Heading up the campaign and the Caucus was Northern Irish born priest and political lobbyist, Father Seán McManus. He promised that if Northern Ireland qualified for World Cup 1994, the INC would picket and protest the team. The *Sunday Life* quoted McManus saying: 'Linfield must be expelled from all soccer games and Windsor Park must be formally shunned before the World Cup is played in the USA.' He then threatened that if the IFA did not take 'appropriate action there is a real – a very real – possibility that Northern Ireland could be banned from the finals … Linfield's publically stated position is the equivalent of an American sports coach saying he could not hire a black or a Jew.'[29]

When the IFA responded to McManus' comments, the body was quick to reject his analysis. The Association's Secretary, David Bowen, refuted McManus' 'outrageous and totally unjustified attack.' Bowen acknowledged 'the problems facing Linfield in this most difficult of countries,' but maintained that the IFA did not 'regard Linfield as a sectarian club in any way.'[30] However, Bowen's estimation did not placate McManus and the Caucus. The INC continued efforts with gusto and its message struck a resonance within the United States' political establishment. The US Congressional Committee for Irish Affairs wrote to FIFA in support of the INC position and called for the Irish League to throw Linfield out of the competition.[31]

By mid-February, the Caucus was declaring a first scalp in its campaign. An *Irish News* headline declared, 'Pressure group claims victory after Linfield lose sponsorship.'[32] The sponsorship that the story referred to was 'Thorn Security.' In that 1991/92 season, the company's logo had adorned the Linfield kit. Henry McDonald informed *Irish News* readers that a 'major American electrical company announced yesterday that it has withdrawn its sponsorship of Linfield ... it was revealed last night that an Irish-American pressure group met Thorn Security's parent US company two weeks before the multi-national announced it would stop sponsoring the Windsor Park side.'[33]

There was, however, no correlation between loss of sponsorship and the lobby group's efforts. Months before the news broke, Linfield's board was aware that Thorn would not fulfil its sponsorship deal. In late November 1991, the Finance Committee discussed a Thorn Security decision, which had indicated the company was 'unable to honour its agreement with the Club for season 1991/92.'[34] Then after the story broke Thorn's public relations – officer Julia Kisch stressed that the Caucus' adverse publicity played no part in matters. Kisch maintained that the company had taken 'a purely commercial decision and no other factors came into account.'[35] *Look at Linfield* (the club's programme) expanded further on the loss of sponsorship. An editorial explained that after new management assumed control of Thorn Security, 'redundancies at the Belfast branch ... made the sponsorship deal ... untenable.'[36]

Caring little for the nuances of the story, Father McManus was quick to capitalize on the withdrawal of sponsorship, as he called on 'all fair minded companies' that backed Linfield to follow Thorn's lead. McManus outlined that the Caucus wanted to 'pressurise major companies to stop supporting ... Linfield until they change the policy of discrimination.' Businesses that sponsored the Northern Ireland national team were also targeted. According to McManus, the IFA's defence of the Blues placed the body 'right up to its neck' in terms of guilt.[37] Therefore, the INC approached companies, like General Motors and Coca-Cola, that gave financial backing to Northern Ireland. The lobby group's expressed aim was to dry up sponsorship for both teams. Father McManus argued, 'The way to stop discrimination in its tracks is to find the connection between discrimination in Northern Ireland and US funding.'[38]

For all the bluster of McManus, the INC struggled to get sponsors to back the campaign. As St Patrick's Day approached, the Caucus' leader informed the press that the INC would step up efforts. He promised that the body would 'make life uncomfortable' for companies that did not support the cause.[39] Coca-Cola was singled out. The soft drink manufacturer had advertising hoardings on Windsor Park's North Stand, but was not prepared to remove them. Thus on March 15, McManus issued a call for a boycott of Coca-Cola products.[40] All 'Irish Americans, as well as all lovers of peace and justice' were urged to join this action. Coke, New Coke, Sprite, TAB, Fanta, Five Alive and Bacardi Tropical Mixers were all amongst an extensive list of products that the INC blacklisted.[41]

Coca-Cola did not give in to the boycott initiated by the Caucus; the company's North Stand hoardings remained at Windsor. Indeed, Linfield did not lose money over the Caucus' campaign, but it did lose face. Over a three-month period, the club's name had been dragged through the mud in the local press and on the international stage. Throughout this time, the adverse publicity caused considerable discomfort for the Linfield Management Committee. The press coverage and the Caucus campaign were regularly discussed at board level.[42] Yet the club was reluctant to make official comment. Linfield's hierarchy did not like engaging in debate over the perceived sectarian image. The press debacle over Tony Coly's 1988 signing had proved this. That said, the 1992 controversy was very different in nature to the 1988 furore. In 1988, the bad press about the club had died down quickly. This time a political lobby group kept the story in the public eye. The club could not stick its head in the sand and hope everything would blow over. Action was needed and this came on 18 March, (a few days after McManus had called for the Coca-Cola boycott). That evening, Linfield's board issued a lengthy response (agreed upon unanimously) to refute the claims of a sectarian signing policy at the club.[43]

The statement (which was published in full by the *Irish News*) explained that Linfield did 'not have a policy to exclude from its staff anyone by reason of colour; race or religion.' Elaborating on the issue of supposed religious discrimination, the board made clear the 'known fact that there never has been a bar on Roman Catholics playing for Linfield at any time in its history including the present.' The statement pointed out: 'More than 70 Roman Catholic players ... have worn the famous royal blue colours of the club.'[44] Examples of Linfield greats who happened to be Catholic were then listed. What the statement had aimed to show, was that Catholic players and coaches were steeped in the history of Linfield Football Club. Amongst the list of players were two former goalkeeping captains Sylvester Bierne and Tommy Breen. There was also mention of the illustrious Gerry Morgan.[45] As a member of Linfield's 1921/22 Seven-Trophy winning side (a clean sweep of all domestic competitions), Morgan was a revered Linfield player. Yet, Gerry Morgan was more than an acclaimed footballer. From 1939 until he died in 1959, Morgan was the first team's trainer. Gerry Morgan was known as 'Mr Linfield.' Bairner and Walker have maintained that although the club was 'justifiably criticized over many years' for its sectarian image, the prominence of Gerry Morgan at Linfield over a 40-year period should not be 'dismissed as unimportant or simply ignored ... the relationship between sport, especially football, and society is frequently more complex than initial appearances might suggest.'[46]

After rejecting claims that the club had ever employed a sectarian recruitment policy, the statement then addressed the reasons for the lack of Catholic players in recent years. Blame was apportioned to the 'climate created by the present Ulster troubles.' Against this backdrop, Linfield had struggled to attract Catholics on account of the 'distinctly British and Ulster ethos' at the club. The Blues board made no apology for that 'quite legitimate ethos ... which [was] just as strong today as it was in the early formative years' when Linfield was established 'by a group of millworkers in the strongly Protestant district of Sandy Row.' The identity had though posed problems when trying to entice Catholic players to the club during 'The Troubles,' and the statement provided anecdotal evidence of this from 'the early 1970s.' 'Back then ... Linfield signed a promising young Roman Catholic player from west Belfast, but after he and his family reassessed the situation in the light of the serious civil unrest ... the move was abandoned.' The failed bid was not unique. 'Other attempts [had] been made to sign Roman Catholic players of proven ability, but they were [also] unsuccessful.'[47] Given what Bairner and Shirlow have maintained, many supporters followed the Blues to 'avail themselves of the opportunity to exhibit their sense of what it means to be Ulster Protestants,' it was thus understandable that Catholic players were put off by the club's image.[48]

In the early-1990s, Northern Irish society was, as the Board had stated, polarized 'along religious and political lines.' On the ground, there appeared to be no end in sight for 'The Troubles.'[49] During the three-month period between Bowyer's interview and the Board's statement, the province witnessed two very dark days. On January 17, the PIRA murdered eight Protestant workers in a bombing at Teebane Crossroads, County Tyrone. Then on February 5, a loyalist paramilitary group, the Ulster Freedom Fighters (UFF), killed five Catholics in a bookmakers shop on the Ormeau Road, Belfast.[50] 'The Troubles' had spilled into every aspect of life and local football was very much afflicted. A 1990 Irish Cup game between Linfield and Donegal Celtic, which witnessed serious and sustained rioting, had highlighted this, as had a Linfield versus Cliftonville Budweiser Cup semi-final during the 1991/92 season. On that occasion, UFF members attacked Cliftonville fans at the game by throwing a shrapnel grenade in their direction. No injuries resulted, but the attack's life-threatening potential was obvious.[51] The harsh reality of Northern Ireland's 'Troubles' was depressing and the Management Committee argued this had prevented Linfield from signing Catholic players.

Unwilling to engage with the nuances at play in early 1990s Northern Ireland, the INC rebuffed Linfield's statement. McManus commented, 'If there is anything, more offensive than Linfield's record, it is its attempts to cover up that bigotry.'[52] Back in Northern Ireland, there was a quick dismissal of McManus' retort. The *Belfast Telegraph* (a moderate/establishment Unionist paper) gave little credence to the 'trouble-stirring' Caucus' remarks. However, a comment piece in the paper argued that if Linfield wanted to silence its critics, 'the best way to answer is to become beyond reproach.' An editorial maintained, 'Linfield's reply to the latest criticisms ... does not go far enough.'[53] The paper spelt out that change was required if the club was to shake off the unwanted image.

Within days, evidence of change was apparent. The press was awash with reports of a bid for Jim McFadden of Cliftonville. McFadden was a North Belfast Catholic. The New Lodge man was, however, unreceptive to the bid from the Blues. The *Irish News* reported that he turned down a move to Linfield that offered 'three or four times' his current salary.[54] McFadden denied he rejected the deal because of the Caucus campaign. Instead, he did so because 'the climate was simply not right ... It would be difficult to envisage any Catholic player from Northern Ireland signing for Linfield.'[55] The Blues had launched a bid for McFadden four weeks prior to the news breaking. The move was therefore not linked to the increased pressure from McManus and the INC. It was though an indication that Bowyer's provocative fanzine interview had significantly altered things. Jim McFadden would not break the mould at Linfield, but speculation over his potential transfer suggested change might be on the way.

When McFadden rejected Linfield's approach in March 1992, he maintained that it didn't appear 'viable' for a Catholic from Northern Ireland to join the club.[56] Yet within a matter of months, the seemingly unfeasible became a reality. In early June, press reports linked the Blues with a young utility player from Cliftonville (a team that in the main drew its support from a nationalist fanbase). His name was Chris Cullen. On June 9, Cullen told the press that being the first Northern Irish-born Catholic to play for the Blues in years did not worry him 'at all.' The only thing he wanted to do was 'play football.'[57] On July 3, Chris Cullen became a Linfield player. In public, the Blues refused to comment on the political and religious significance of the signing. Club secretary, Derek Brooks, played down the importance of Cullen's arrival and stated the 21-year-old was 'only another player.'[58]

Linfield had endured a difficult six months and officials were anxious to avoid further controversial headlines. Further scandal would, though, rock the club the day after the transfer was announced. The *Irish News* exclaimed that as Cullen's signing was confirmed, a 'mock threat,' made against Father McManus 'came to light.'[59] By the time the *Irish News* exposed the 'threat' it had been in the public domain for three months. The paper's story referred to material that had appeared in *'The Blues Brothers'* fanzine: a publication, which modelled itself as a Rangers-Chelsea-Linfield magazine. In the offending April 1992 edition, a photograph of McManus appeared with a target on his forehead. This was accompanied by the comment 'Blues sign new Target Man.'[60] According to the fanzine editors, 'This was meant as a joke, a football pun' – though an outraged McManus did not find the caption amusing.[61] He maintained that he had set out to expose 'the ... anti-Catholic, sectarian ethos at Windsor Park and ... the picture proved the point graphically ... it reflects the thinking of fans, which in turn reflects the ethos that is tolerated.'[62]

At the end of July, a United States Congressional body weighed in on the latest fanzine controversy. The ad hoc Congressional Committee for Irish Affairs argued that the reception to the publication indicated a 'condoning [of] anti-Catholic bigotry' in Northern Irish football. The body wrote to IFA secretary, David Bowen, stating that the fanzine picture had a 'very clear [meaning] – shoot Father McManus.' The letter criticized the Association for 'shirking its responsibility ... by remaining silent' and not condemning the picture.[63] Over 50 Congressmen signed the letter. They asserted that the IFA was wrong to avoid comment on the contentious subject.[64] Yet, on the day that the *Irish News* had highlighted the picture, Blues secretary, David Brooks, pointed out that the fanzine had 'nothing to do with Linfield Football Club.'[65] His swift rejection of the publication's legitimacy displayed anything but acceptance of the 'joke.' There wasn't much more for the IFA to add.

The furore over *'The Blues Brothers'* fanzine marked the high-water mark of the McManus – led crusade. Whilst the boycott of Coca-Cola remained and the INC did its best to keep pressure on the club, the ferocity of the campaign died down. Earlier in 1992 a *Belfast Telegraph* editorial had spelt out that the best way to answer criticism was for Linfield 'to become beyond reproach.'[66] If Chris Cullen could become just another Linfield player (and other Catholic players could follow), then the sting of Caucus' criticism would be nullified. Cullen's first interaction with supporters came on the afternoon of August 1, Linfield's Open Day. This was a chance for fans to meet their idols. Over a two-hour period, supporters mobbed the young player with requests for pictures and autographs. By the end of the afternoon, Cullen quipped 'My hand's sore ... At Cliftonville I was only asked for my autograph twice.'[67]

Cullen's first game for the Blues arrived on September 12, against Bangor in a Gold Cup (one of the Irish League's minor competitions) tie that finished 1–1. The Downpatrick man was named as a substitute and came on with 50 minutes gone for the injured Martin McGaughey. *Ireland's Saturday Night* (part of the *Belfast Telegraph* group of newspapers) reported that Cullen's arrival 'brought a mixed reaction from the Blues supporters with some cheers and some boohs, but generally the 'clapometer' was registering on the high side.'[68] Chris Cullen had proved that a Northern Irish Catholic could sign and play for Linfield. The symbolism of his appearance against Bangor was monumental. Ten months beforehand, Blues boss Eric Bowyer rated the chances of Linfield signing a Catholic as 'almost impossible,' but it had happened.[69] Although Cullen's reception was not one hundred per cent welcoming, any hostility soon dissipated. Cullen became just another Linfield player. Unfortunately for the player, he never held down a regular first team place.

Less than two weeks after Cullen's debut, the Blues lifted the first piece of silverware of the season. On the evening of September 23, Linfield defeated Ards 2–0 in the final of the Ulster Cup (another minor competition). Manager Eric Bowyer hoped this success was only a 'start.' He told the press 'I believe we have the ability to make a big impression.'[70] When the League programme kicked off in the early autumn, there was, though, little sign of this. The hallmark of recent seasons – inconsistency – was in evidence. Linfield had not lifted the League since 1989 and at Windsor Park, this was not acceptable. After four games played, the Blues had won two, drawn one and lost one. Bowyer's men went into the fifth league match, away to Distillery, under considerable pressure. However, the performance and result attained only piled more misery on the club. A 69th-minute goal from Winkie Armstrong settled the tie in Distillery's favour. *Ireland's Saturday Night* reported that as the Linfield players left the pitch, they were 'given "the treatment" by the fans [whilst] management committee members came under a barrage of verbal criticism.'[71]

Two days after the defeat to Distillery, Bowyer was relieved of his duties. Trevor Anderson, a former striker who had scored close to 100 goals for the Blues, would take over on a temporary basis. Anderson's first job as caretaker manager was to assess the quality of his squad. When he looked around the dressing room, he saw 'good players who needed a bit of confidence.'[72] So over the weeks that followed, he went about instilling belief into them. This paid dividends as the first four league games under Anderson ended in victory. In his fifth game, he endured a 7–2 drubbing in the Budweiser Cup. This coincidently arrived on the same day that the Queen gave her 'AnnusHorribilis' speech, and came at the hands of a Portadown side described as 'scintillating' by the press.[73] That freak result aside, the Management Committee had witnessed enough to hand Anderson a contract until the end of the season. On receiving the board's endorsement, Anderson commented that it was 'a great honour.' He knew, however, that the squad needed strengthening and resolved to bring in 'quality.'[74]

A couple of weeks after landing his permanent contract, Anderson followed through with the vow to sign top-notch players. On December 17, Linfield swooped for Dundalk-based forward, Dessie Gorman. When the press got wind of the club's interest, the player's footballing prowess was of secondary importance. The *Belfast Telegraph* labelled the move 'sensational' on account of its 'ground-breaking' significance.[75] Gorman was a Catholic from the Republic of Ireland and it was almost 50 years since Linfield had signed a player from south of the border. Davy Walsh of Limerick at the end of the Second World War was the last southern player to make the move. Fanfare thus greeted Gorman – the Dundalk Hawk – penning a contract. That said, the political and religious ramifications of the deal were played down by the 28-year-old forward. In Gorman's first media duty as a Linfield player, he quipped, 'what's all the fuss about? … Linfield's background may be different to other clubs I have played for but football is the same the world over – the fans want to see their team scoring goals and winning games. That's why I'm here.'[76]

Two days after the deal went through, Gorman made his Linfield debut at home to Ballyclare Comrades. The Dundalk man sparkled in an impressive team performance that ended in a 4–0 rout to the Blues. The striker did not get on the scoresheet but assisted by winning a penalty. Trevor Anderson heaped praise on his new signing and highlighted Gorman's ability to make room and bring players into the game. The striker's new teammates were equally effusive when lauding his performance. Midfielder Lee Doherty explained that Gorman 'held the ball up ... and brought the midfield into it – something we were not doing.'[77] The 4–0 win over Ballyclare began a fruitful Christmas period for Linfield. The games came thick and fast and the players rose to the challenge. Over the festive period, the Blues amassed 13 points out of a possible 15. This form continued in the New Year, and by February, Trevor Anderson had guided Linfield to the top of the Irish League. The arrival of Dessie Gorman had invigorated the team, but also established players had found their feet. As the Blues surged to the top of the tree, goals flowed from all over the team. At the back, the defence was rock-solid. FIFA statistics showed that at that time, the Blues had the best defensive record in world football.[78] By mid-February, Linfield had only conceded six goals in 21 league games.

In early 1993, Trevor Anderson had continued to ring the changes, bringing in more signings to shore up the resurgence in form. The first of these was midfielder Martin Bayly who arrived in January. Bayly joined from League of Ireland side Home Farm. He was thus Linfield's second recruit from south of the border in a matter of weeks. As well signifying a changing social climate in Northern Ireland, the signature was also indicative of an Irish League that was prepared to spend big. In the early-to-mid-1990s, the Irish League was financially an attractive place for the best players in both Northern Ireland and the Republic of Ireland. Dublin-born Martin Russell had joined mid-Ulster side Portadown in 1991, (instead of moving to a club south of the border) after he left Middlesbrough. Whilst at the beginning of 1994, Linfield would sign one of the League of Ireland's best midfielders, Pat Fenlon. When Bayly joined in early 1993, the INC was still maintaining a close eye on Linfield, and noted that his signature took the number of Catholic players at the club to three. A 1993 publication *The MacBride Principles*, penned by Father McManus, implied that the Caucus-led campaign had brought this about at the club.[79] However, it was Eric Bowyer's opening up to *One Team In Ulster* that allowed for change. Forces outside the club may have piled pressure on Linfield, but it was action from within that drove what had taken place at Windsor.

Two more seasoned professionals joined Bayly in signing short-term contracts until the end of the campaign. In late-March, Scottish striker Graham Harvey and Liverpool-born defender Geoff Twentyman agreed deals. Both had vast experience of professional football in Great Britain, and both helped see the Blues over the line. The additions to the squad and the changes Anderson implemented proved masterstrokes. With one game remaining, the new manager guided the Blues to the Irish League. On April 17, title rivals Crusaders and Portadown, both slipped up with a draw and defeat, respectively. This enabled Linfield to (all but mathematically) win the title at the Oval, home of cross-town adversaries, Glentoran. The Glens had led the Blues 1–0 at halftime through a Stephen Douglas goal before Glenn Hunter grabbed an equalizer and Blues substitute Richie Johnston grabbed a dramatic winner. After the game, the away dressing room was awash with euphoria coupled with relief. Captain Alan Dornan had worried that, 'we'd never return to the title [considering it had] been four long years since the last league triumph.'[80] That season Linfield was not alone in ending a barren spell. A couple of weeks later, the inaugural English Premier League was won by a club that had endured a much longer lean spell. When Manchester United was crowned champions, the team ended a 26-year stretch without a league title. In the ecstasy of success, both United and Linfield fans toasted the impact of a mid-season signing. The mercurial talents of Eric Cantona (who famously crossed the Pennines from Leeds) helped inspire the Manchester side's triumph. Whilst at Linfield, Dessie Gorman had 'pepped up' what the *Belfast Telegraph* had described as 'a flat looking attack.'[81] It was as Denis O'Hara in the *News Letter* (a traditional unionist paper) put it, the stuff of 'fairytales [sic].'[82]

Gorman relished the big stage at Windsor, and the limelight that went with it. The Hawk's move had attracted considerable media attention, yet conversely this made playing for the Blues 'the easiest job in the world … all I had to do was play football … and the football I found very easy, so I enjoyed it.'[83] The Hawk was liberated on the pitch and because of his unique circumstances, he played with freedom. The confidence that Gorman displayed inspired others and played a major role in the club's success. The Hawk proved that the *almost impossible* could be embraced, and that there was an appetite for change in the Province. 'The Troubles' would remain part of everyday life for a time to come. Dark days like the Shankill bomb of October 1993, which killed ten people, and the shooting of six people in Loughinisland as they watched the 1994 World Cup Finals were testament to that. But the early 1990s changes at Linfield indicated that brighter days could lie ahead. If perceptions of the Blues could be turned on their head, there was a distinct possibility that other long held-beliefs could be challenged. The events at Windsor during 1992 and 1993 gave an indication that perhaps some of 'The Troubles' deadlock could be broken. As this article has shown, Linfield Football Club's move to sign Catholic players in the early 1990s was significant, however, it was not a new departure for the Blues. Furthermore, the importance of the fanzine comments made by manager Eric Bowyer cannot be underestimated. For, it was his interview that put in motion the chain of events that brought about the arrival of Cullen, Bayly and of course Dessie Gorman. Pressure from outside may have accelerated the process, but it was Bowyer's words that opened things up and allowed for Gorman to shine in a Linfield shirt.

Disclosure statement

No potential conflict of interest was reported by the author.

Notes

1. Roach, 'Comparative Counter-Terrorism Law,' 6.
2. Bartlett, *Ireland*, 560.
3. McKittrick et al., *Lost Lives*, 1266; Bew, *Ireland*, 537–47.
4. Garnham, *Association Football*, 47.
5. Bell, *The Protestants*, 48.
6. Goldblatt, *The Game*, 201–202.
7. Magee, 'Football Supporters,' 172.
8. Cronin, *Sport and Nationalism*, 172.
9. Hurd, *Elizabeth II*, 68.
10. *New York Times*, November 21, 1992.
11. *Sunday News*, July 10, 1988.
12. Scrivener cited in *Sunday News*, July 10, 1988.
13. Coyle interview with author, April 22, 2014.
14. Esplin and Walker, 'Introduction,' 6.
15. Murray, *Bhoys, Bears*, 31, 44–45.
16. *Sunday News*, July 17, 1988.
17. Gillespie, 'Northern Ireland,' 1, 15.
18. Original text appears in block capitals.
19. *One Team in Ulster* 18, 1991.

20. Bowyer cited in *One Team in Ulster* 18, 1991.
21. Bowyer interview with author, April 22, 2014.
22. Original text appears in block capitals; Bowyer cited in *One Team in Ulster* 18, 1991.
23. *Sunday Life*, January 5, 1992.
24. Bowyer cited in *Sunday Life*, January 5, 1992.
25. *Irish News*, January 6, 1992.
26. Unamed source cited in *Irish News*, January 6, 1992.
27. Horgan, *Irish Media*, 156.
28. *Irish News*, January 6, 1992.
29. McManus cited in *Sunday Life*, January 26, 1992.
30. Bowen cited in *Sunday Life*, January 27, 1992.
31. *Irish News*, March 3, 1992.
32. *Irish News*, February 15, 1992.
33. *Irish News*, February 15, 1992.
34. Linfield Football Club Minutes: Meeting of Finance Committee, November 28, 1991.
35. Kisch cited in *Belfast Telegraph*, February 14, 1992.
36. *Look At Linfield*, February 18, 1992.
37. McManus cited in *Irish News*, March 3, 1992.
38. McManus cited in *Irish News*, March 16, 1992.
39. McManus cited in *Irish News*, March 16, 1992.
40. *Irish News*, March 16, 1992.
41. McManus, *MacBride Principles*, 90.
42. Linfield Football Club Minutes: Meetings of Management Committee, January–March 1992.
43. Linfield Football Club Minutes: Meeting of Management Committee, March 16, 1992.
44. Linfield statement cited in *Irish News*, March 19, 1992.
45. Linfield statement cited in *Irish News*, March 19, 1992.
46. Bairner and Walker, 'Football and Society,' 96.
47. Linfield statement cited in *Irish News*, March 19, 1992.
48. Bairner and Shirlow, 'Loyalism, Linfield,' 173.
49. Linfield statement cited in *Irish News*, March 19, 1992.
50. Gillespie, *Years of Darkness*, 214, 217.
51. Kuper, *Football Against*, 213.
52. McManus cited in *Belfast Telegraph*, March 20, 1992.
53. *Belfast Telegraph*, March 19, 1992.
54. *Irish News*, March 23, 1992.
55. McFadden cited in *Irish News*, March 23, 1992.
56. McFadden cited in *Belfast Telegraph*, March 23, 1992.
57. Cullen cited in *Belfast Telegraph*, June 9, 1992.
58. Brooks cited in *Belfast Telegraph*, July 4, 1992.
59. *Irish News*, July 4, 1992.
60. *The Blues Brothers*, November, 1994.
61. Fanzine editors cited in Gillespie, 'Northern Ireland,' 13.
62. McManus cited in *Irish News*, July 4, 1992.
63. Committee cited in *Irish News*, July 30, 1992.
64. *Irish News*, October 13, 1992.
65. Brooks cited in *Belfast Telegraph*, July 4, 1992.
66. *Belfast Telegraph*, March 19, 1992.
67. Cullen cited in *Sunday Life*, August 2, 1992.
68. *Ireland's Saturday Night*, September 12, 1992.
69. Bowyer cited in *One Team in Ulster* 18, 1991.
70. Bowyer cited in *Ireland's Saturday Night*, September 26, 1992.
71. *Ireland's Saturday Night*, October 24, 1992.
72. Anderson interview with author, November 18, 2014.
73. *Belfast Telegraph*, November 25, 1992.
74. Anderson cited in *News Letter*, December 1, 1992.
75. *Belfast Telegraph*, December 14, 1992.
76. Gorman cited in *Belfast Telegraph*, December 18, 1992.

77. Anderson and Doherty cited in *News Letter*, December 21, 1992.
78. Statistics cited in *Belfast Telegraph*, January 15, 1993.
79. McManus, *MacBride Principles*, 89.
80. Dornan cited in *News Letter*, April 19, 1993.
81. *Belfast Telegraph*, April 19, 1993.
82. *News Letter*, April 19, 1993.
83. Gorman interview with author, February 21, 2015.

References

Bairner, A., and P. Shirlow 'Loyalism, Linfield and the Territorial Politics of Soccer Fandom in Northern Ireland'. *Space and Polity* 2, no. 2 (1998): 163–77.
Bairner, A., and G. Walker 'Football and Society in Northern Ireland: Linfield Football Club and the Case of Gerry Morgan'. *Soccer and Society* 2, no. 1 (2001): 81–98.
Bartlett, T. *Ireland: A History*. Cambridge: Cambridge University Press, 2010.
Bell, G. *The Protestants of Ulster*. London: Pluto Press, 1976.
Bew, P. *Ireland: The Politics of Enmity, 1789–2006*. Oxford: Oxford University Press, 2007.
Cronin, M. *Sport and Nationalism in Ireland: Gaelic Games, Soccer and Irish Identity since 1884*. Dublin: Four Courts Press Ltd, 1999.
Esplin, R., and G. Walker 'Introduction'. In *It's Rangers for Me? New Perspectives on a Scottish Institution*, ed. R. Esplin and G. Walker, 5–9. Ayr: Fort Publishing Ltd, 2008.
Garnham, N. *Association Football and Society in Pre-Partition Ireland*. Belfast: Ulster Historical Foundation, 2004.
Gillespie, G. 'Northern Ireland Fanzines'. Unpublished article, held at Linen Hall Library Belfast, 2000.
Gillespie, G. *Years of Darkness: The Troubles Remembered*. Dublin: Gill & Macmillan, 2008.
Goldblatt, D. *The Game of Our Lives: The Meaning and Making of English Football*. London: Penguin Random House, 2015.
Horgan, J. *Irish Media: A Critical History Since 1922*. London: Routledge, 2001.
Hurd, D. *Elizabeth II: The Steadfast*. London: Penguin Random House, 2015.
Kuper, S. *Football against the Enemy*. London: Orion, 1995.
Magee, J. 'Football Supporters, Rivalry and Protestant Fragmentation in Northern Ireland.' In *Sport and the Irish: Histories, Identities, Issues*, ed. A. Bairner, 172–88. Dublin: Dublin University Press, 2005.
McKittrick, D., S. Kelters, B. Feeney, C. Thornton, and D. McVea *Lost Lives: The Stories of Men, Women and Children Who Died as a Result of the Northern Ireland Troubles* 2nd ed., Edinburgh: Mainstream Publishing, 2007.
McManus, S. *The MacBride Principles: Genesis & History and the Story to Date*. Washington, DC: Irish National Caucus, 1993.
Murray, B. *Bhoys, Bears and Bigotry: The Old Firm in the New Age*. Edinburgh: Mainstream, 2003.
Roach, K. 'Comparative Counter-Terrorism Law Comes of Age'. In *Comparative Counter-Terrorism Law*, ed. Kent Roach, 1–46. New York: Cambridge University Press, 2015.

Harry Cannon: a unique Irish sportsman and administrator

Tom Hunt

> Biographical studies provide insights into social, political, economic and cultural changes in society. This biographical essay on Harry Cannon, an Irish international soccer goalkeeper in the 1920s, apart from recreating Cannon's extraordinary sporting career, also enhances our knowledge of how sport was organized in the newly independent Irish Free State and in particular how sport was organized in the army of the new state. The agenda-driven purpose of army sport is highlighted and in particular how it was intended to create an Irish-Ireland. As a result, the sports identified as foreign by the Gaelic Athletic Association were excluded from the army's curriculum of sport. The attempt by the International Olympic Committee to confine Ireland's representation at the Olympic Games to the territory of the Irish Free State is also examined through the prism of Cannon's career.

Introduction

Even the most dedicated follower of Donegal sport might be hard-pressed to identify the first native of the county to play in goal for Ireland in association football. This distinction belongs to Billy O'Hagan, a native of Buncrana who was capped twice during the 1919–1920 season in drawn matches with England and Wales.[1] The subject of this article, also a remarkable Donegal-born sportsman and administrator, Harry Cannon, also achieved a notable goalkeeping first. He represented the then Irish Free State in what is recognized by the Football Association of Ireland as the first international match played by the association. This biographical essay examines the sporting career of Cannon, his contribution to the administration of sport in Ireland and his pragmatism in combining a playing and administrative career for organizations that had very different attitudes to the territorial extent of the unit they represented. Apart from providing some biographical recognition for what was a remarkable sporting life, an examination of Cannon's career provides some significant insights into how sport was promoted and managed in the early decades of the Irish Free State.

Henry James Cannon was born on 11 July 1897 in Dungloe, County Donegal, the son of Thomas and Mary (nee Duffy) Cannon. Thomas Cannon was a carpenter by trade and the family moved to Dublin shortly after the birth of Henry James, universally known as Harry, and this form of identity will be used for the remainder of this feature. In 1901, the Cannon family resided in No. 175 Pembroke Street, Irishtown in Dublin, in a house shared by four families.[2] Economic circumstances were relatively good for Thomas Cannon, a skilled tradesman, and by 1911, the family resided at the more middle-class 4 Herbert Place, Donnybrook in Dublin in a house categorized as second class using the criteria designed by the census officials.[3] During the Irish War of Independence (1919–1921), Harry Cannon was a member of *Fianna Phadraig*, a scout unit founded by Father Pat Flanagan of Ringsend where for three years he acted as a section leader; it is unclear to what extent, if any, he was involved in military activity.

Prior to joining the army of the Irish Free State on 26 August 1922 at Portobello Barracks, Harry Cannon worked as a solicitor's assistant. He enlisted in the Army Corps of Engineers and after two months at the rank of private, he was promoted to the rank of temporary 2nd Lieutenant on 23 October 1922 and was awarded the rank permanently in April 1923. In April 1924, he attained the rank of Lieutenant and became a Captain in October 1929. He died in service on 18 March 1944.[4]

Sport and the army of the Irish Free State

Almost from the beginning, sport played a central role in the newly formed Irish Free State army and this was given formal recognition on 31 March 1923 with the formation of the Army Athletic Association (AAA). According to *An t-Óglác*, the official newspaper of the Irish Army, athletics assisted 'materially in bringing about that condition of physical fitness essential to the complete efficiency of the soldier and stimulate a healthy sporting spirit amongst the men.'[5] However, the agenda-driven organization of army sport went far beyond the development of physical fitness and a sporting spirit. The army scheme was 'carefully constructed and comprehensively designed' so that the soldiers could 'secure plenty of variety in their athletic training without having recourse to other than Gaelic games.' The variety of sports approved by the AAA was claimed to include 'something to suit every taste.' This was fine as long as these tastes did not extend to soccer, rugby, cricket or hockey, the sports designated as foreign by the Gaelic Athletic Association (GAA) and which members of the GAA were forbidden to play or promote. The exclusion of these sports was based on the belief that the Army should provide the backbone of the Irish-Ireland movement. This was elucidated in an *An t-Óglác* editorial that reflected the views of the army's Chief of Staff:

> The young Irishmen in the Army are the bone and sinew of the country and will play a vitally important part in the creation of the Gaelic State to which we all look forward. They will be all the better citizens of that State in consequence of the training they receive in the Army, and the fostering of a love of clean, healthy sport will be by no means the least valuable part of their military education.[6]

The central council of the GAA was represented at the inaugural meeting of the AAA by General Eoin O'Duffy and its secretary Luke O'Toole; A. C. Harty represented the National Athletics and Cycling Association of Ireland (NACAI), the newly formed governing body for Irish athletics and one with a strong nationalist agenda. The case for the exclusion of rugby, soccer, cricket and hockey was made by O'Duffy who explained to the assembled that 'The [GAA] games were Irish of the Irish, and it would be a sad day when the Irish Army left aside their own games for games of foreign origin.' The decision to exclude the four sports from the AAA curriculum was a unanimous one; the Chief of Staff, Peadar MacMahon, thanked the representatives of the GAA for their attendance and explained that 'The Army should be the backbone of the Irish-Ireland movement, and should contribute of its stock to make Ireland a truly Gaelic State.'7 Fourteen different outdoor sports and several indoor ones were included under the AAA umbrella including golf and tennis without any apparent discomfort as to their cultural origins. The organizational mode adopted by the AAA was that used by the GAA with each company having the status of a club, each battalion that of a county and each command and independent corps of more than 1000 members was granted the status of a province. Competitions in the recognized sports were organized at each level.

The question of excluding certain games was also considered at the AAA's first annual convention held on 29 April 1923 when motions were put forward calling for an end to the exclusion rules. A Cork delegate, Fr Cotter, presented the case for ending the system of sporting apartheid: in the Cork Command, at least 35% of the recruits were both soccer or rugby players and the recreational needs of these men were not catered for. 'He had been a Gael all his life, but they had to face the facts,' Fr Cotter explained. The good cleric also offered more nuanced and sophisticated arguments in support of his case that transcended the empirical and emphasized inclusiveness. Acceptance of the Irish Free State made the need for a 'foreign games' rule redundant: 'Not only that, but if Ireland does not wish to remain aloof from the rest of the world she must show some kind of spirit of comradeship towards other nations. She cannot hope to live in a little niche of her own and hope to impress her abilities' on other nations by merely being indifferent from them in everything,' he argued. The fundamental principle of all sports was fair play and on this basis, all sports were entitled to a fair chance and the best game will survive. 'This policy will benefit everybody, for the best game should give the best development.' There was a necessity for the army to set the example. 'If the Army authorities pander to mere insularity now, they will be followers and not leaders,' Fr Cotter maintained. Unity would only be achieved by considering the needs of all classes. 'It would be not only foolish, but harmful to regard one section of the people as the salt of the earth, and the other as mere aliens in a country, of which it should be the earnest wish of every good Irishman that they should regard themselves as equal citizens.' Finally, Cotter concluded his arguments with the more prosaic claim

> that certain games now called foreign suit the temperament of Irishmen. Such games we can make our own, and in them we can undoubtedly make our mark in International Contests ... let us show the world what we can do.[8]

The arguments were in vain as the decision to continue with the ban was approved by a two to one majority. A motion to include tennis and golf in the list of banned sports was overwhelmingly defeated (18–0). At the conclusion of the convention, the President of the GAA, Dan McCarthy (accompanied by the association's honorary secretary, Luke O'Toole), addressed the delegates and presented two cups to the AAA to be awarded to the winners of the hurling and the football championships. The decision to include golf and tennis in the list of approved sports inspired some correspondence to *An t-Óglác*. Lieutenant Tom Scully had little doubt that the decision was wrong: 'To my mind Golf and Tennis are similar to an epidemic of disease, only the disease in this case is the most horrible of all-imperialism. It stinks the very atmosphere where Golf and Tennis are played. Finally, I object to those games because I don't like playing at being aristocrats, especially when in so doing I make a bad fist of it, I being by nature a democrat.' Corporal James Noone offered an alternative viewpoint: 'It is pure hypocrisy for any Irishman to refuse to play English football, and the same evening attend some hall and revel in English dancing, ten times more demoralising than a simple game of football. Hoping the Army Athletic Association, will reconsider their decision regarding football, and thereby cater for many thousands of men at present serving in the Irish National Army.'[9]

Harry Cannon: mould breaker

Harry Cannon was a prominent and active hurling and Gaelic football player when he joined the army in 1922 and is credited with having played with the Fontenoy Hurling Club, the McCracken Gaelic Football Club and the Keating Club, a club with strong Irish-Ireland associations.[10] Membership of the army provided another outlet for Cannon to display his talents and he played at company, battalion and corps levels as he immersed himself in the Irish-Ireland Gaelic games playing milieu of Irish army sport. His General Headquarters Staff hurling team reached the All-Army championship semi-final in 1924 where they were beaten (6–3 to 2–7) by Cork Command in a match played at Croke Park. According to the match report, the Cork side were 'the better balanced, its defence the sounder and its attack the more dangerous' and if it was not for 'the capital display by Cannon, in goal for G.H.Q., the score against his side would have been much larger at the interval.' According to the report, Cannon 'acquitted himself excellently in goal for the losers, saving many scores and showing much coolness.' A week later, the team returned to Croke Park for the Gaelic football final in which they defeated Waterford Command (1–2 to 0–4) in match in which 'Cannon, in outfield, was very fast and clever and gave the Waterford defence much uneasiness.'[11]

His displays in these championships, 'a first class player in goal or in a forward position,' earned him a place on the all-Army Gaelic football team that defeated the reigning All-Ireland champions Dublin in Croke Park (0–5 to 0–1) in what was 'a new departure in the programme of the G.A.A'; the Army team, captained by Bloody Sunday veteran Tommy Ryan, included some of the outstanding footballers of the day and were awarded a set of gold medals 'of equal value but of a different design from the All-Ireland Championship trophies.'[12] The victory validated the standing of Gaelic sport within the army and the team was later entertained to dinner by the AAA Executive Council at Barry's Hotel in Dublin. The relationship between the GAA and the AAA was so close at this stage that the association's secretary Luke O'Toole suggested in his 1924 annual report to the GAA congress that the AAA be made the association's fifth province. This was rejected by the delegates and O'Toole's report was approved after his eccentric suggestion was excluded.

In 1925, Harry Cannon ended his GAA career and began a lifelong association with Bohemians, the leading amateur soccer club in Dublin. He wasn't a total novice to the association game as he played at junior level for the Pembroke Comrades Club during a brief interlude in his GAA career.[13] When his playing career ended, he served the Bohemians club as honorary treasurer, vice-president and committee member.[14] Making the transition from a skilful Gaelic footballer to become a leading goalkeeper in the soccer code was not an easy one and has rarely been successfully accomplished. According to Dick Fitzgerald in his famous instruction manual on how to play Gaelic football, 'The Goal-Keeper, like the poet is born not made.' 'He should have a keen, quick eye, a great pair of hands, and should be a most resourceful kicker with either leg and with as much length as possible in his kicks. He should also be possessed of a fine spirit of fearlessness, combined with great coolness and should have the capacity to do the needful with quick and unerring judgement.'[15] Fitzgerald's words of wisdom might also constitute a description of the skill-set needed for a successful soccer goalkeeper, but the Gaelic football skills did not transfer easily, although Cannon's midfield position in his army matches might have offered a basic preparation for the rigours of his new posting. Gaelic football goalkeepers of the era managed their goal from a position rooted firmly on the goal line and rarely advanced from the relative safety of their position between the posts. Their kicking duties were limited to placing the ball for the fullback to deliver a lengthy downfield toe-poke. This was poor preparation for a position in the soccer code that required the goalkeeper to constantly advance to deal with crosses and other probing passes hit over and through a goalkeeper's defence. There is evidence that Harry Cannon had some difficulty with this aspect of the game and that he may have suffered from a condition that puzzled many goalkeepers: he had trouble dealing with the crossed ball. In its 17 March 1928 preview of the FAIFS Cup final, *Sport* described Cannon as 'a fine all-round custodian but if he has any fault it is his hesitancy in dealing with crosses and corners.' The same journal in its report on the 1929 cup final credited Cannon with 'one of his best displays of the season … He was more safe than usual in dealing with centres and corners.[16] There is no shortage of testimonies to his quality as a goalkeeper. In the Leinster Cup final of 1926, Cannon was 'a brilliant goalkeeper' whose 'sure fielding and a stylish manner of completing his clearances made his work good to watch.' A few weeks later, he was again a brilliant performer in Bohemians 2–1 friendly victory over St Mirren, who fielded the team that had beaten Celtic FC in the Scottish cup final.[17]

The physical obstacles presented by the change were probably the least of Cannon's difficulties. Opting to pursue a new career with Bohemians in the association code was a decision that required the greatest of moral courage. Soccer was a designated foreign game by the apostles of the Irish-Ireland movement and officially excluded as we have seen from the acceptable sporting pursuits appropriate for a soldier or officer of the Irish army. Foreign in this case equated with English and in post-revolutionary Ireland, this designation carried an additional stigma. Cannon rejected a sport that was validated by the army Chief of Staff and this was a move that was unlikely to help him in his army career. His soccer career added an extra layer of meaning to the debate surrounding the exclusion of soccer from the army sports' portfolio and this was reflected in the pages of *An t-Óglác;* some such as 'Gunner' invoked Cannon's name to bolster their arguments:

> Why should 75 per cent. of us suffer for the minority? If it were put to a vote as to which game the Irish soldier had the most interest in Soccer would be an easy first. The game is not an English one, as it originated in Scotland and is now recognised by all countries as an International game. What finer sportsman does the Army possess than Capt. Cannon, the famous Bohemians goalkeeper? His (*sic*) is also a first-class G.A.A. man and is the admiration of all Ireland. There are many more like him, and in my unit alone we have many who can take their place in the hurling, Gaelic, and Soccer. It is all sport, and as we are in a free country why should we not be allowed to cater for the games that we want.[18]

Despite the validity of the arguments, soccer remained an excluded sport as far as the AAA was concerned.

Playing soccer with Bohemians considerably expanded Cannon's sporting horizons. A year after joining Bohemians, he was displaying his talents to a London audience as a member of the Bohemians team that played in friendly matches against London Caledonians and Tottenham Hotspurs. Bohemians were defeated on both occasions but Cannon was 'the man who emerged with highest honours from both encounters.'[19] He captained Bohemians in the 1927–28 season, the finest in the club's history, which ended in May 1928 when the club beat St James Gate 2–1 to win the FAIFS Shield competition and complete the grand slam of available senior titles for the only time in the club's history. The FAIFS Cup, League and Leinster Senior Cup titles were already secured. The success was built on a solid defence with all six members practically ever present for the 36-game season. Harry Cannon played in 35 matches, his two full backs and wing-backs were ever present, with the centre-half absent on only two occasions. The club's only defeats in their league programme were inflicted by Shelbourne and the Fordson club and in the course of the season, 109 goals were scored and 35 conceded.[20] In the course of a 13-season career with Bohemians, Cannon won two Leinster Senior Cup titles, two FAIFS Cup medals (1928 and 1935), four league titles (1928, 1930, 1934 and 1936) and three FAIFS Shield titles (1928, 1929 and 1934).

The Irish Free State and international football

Harry Cannon's good form for Bohemians earned him selection for the first international match played by the FAIFS, 'the most momentous event in the short history of *Saorstat* Soccer' according to the *Irish Independent* correspondent reporting on 20 March 1926. It was the 'most important game engaged in by a representative team of our players who have been sent to establish abroad the reputation for high-class football they have secured at home.'[21] This match was organized by the FAIFS, which was established on 2 September 1921.[22] Prior to this, football in Ireland was organized, promoted and managed by the Belfast-based Irish Football Association (IFA) established in 1880. The break with the IFA took place prior to the partition of the country and was a product of political, organizational and cultural differences in how football was organized. Long-standing differences existed between Belfast and Dublin, the two strongholds of the game at the time, over the nature of the game and where the balance of power and influence should lie. The greatest Dublin grievances centred on the IFA's selection of the international team as well as the choice of venue for Ireland's home internationals. Soccer in industrial Belfast was more professionalized and commercialized than it was in Dublin where the game maintained a gentlemanly amateur ethos. In Dublin, it was primarily a game for players and participation, not for professionals and paying spectators as it was in Belfast. The long-term grievances over bias in international team selection and venues for fixtures reached breaking point in 1921. In the period between 1882 and 1914, 42 international matches were played in Ireland, but only 6 were held in Dublin, the rest in Belfast.[23] It could hardly have been otherwise as the composition of IFA sub-committees was heavily weighted with members from the Belfast-centred north-east division and other divisional associations within the northern region, with just a smattering of delegates from the other regions appointed to committees.[24] The drawn IFA Cup semi-final of 1921 between Glenavon and Shelbourne was played in Belfast and when the replay was fixed for the same city, Shelbourne refused to fulfil the fixture and were eventually expelled from the competition.[25] 'No greater insult has been known in the annals of Irish football,' *Sport* proclaimed, 'Word fails one at the moment to convey adequately the monstrous injustice of the IFA and their decision to make Shelbourne travel for the second time to Belfast.'[26] The immediate fallout from this episode was the withdrawal of the Dublin clubs from the IFA and the eventual formation of their own association, the Football Association of Ireland (FAI).[27] Politics also played a decisive role in the split and its eventual cementing. Once the forces of nationalism took hold in Ireland, the Leinster Football Association was on a collision course with Belfast. Most southern members shared the views that Ireland should be free of British control. The Belfast members shared the opposite view.[28]

In September 1923, the new football association achieved FIFA recognition and this entitled it to participate in international competition. The first post-war congress of FIFA opened on 20 May 1923 in Geneva and the application of the FAI for recognition featured on the agenda. The application was supported by Italy, Norway, Sweden, Finland and Switzerland, with the latter supporting Ireland's immediate admittance. It was eventually decided to leave the issue to the Emergency Committee to ascertain whether the Irish Free State possessed the political status claimed by the delegates and to determine whether the FAI 'conformed to the principles laid down for national associations.' These criteria were fulfilled and the association was admitted to membership on 1 September following FIFA consultation with the British Foreign Office on the constitutional status of the Irish Free State. The newly designated FAIFS was now free to take its place on the international stage.[29]

Ireland competed in the Olympic Games as an independent entity for the first time in 1924. The footballers became the first competitors to represent Ireland at a Games and on 28 May 1924, Bulgaria was defeated 1–0. This qualified Ireland for a quarter-final match against the Netherlands in which the team was defeated (2–1) after extra time. A friendly match against Estonia was also played in Paris and on their return journey, the USA team stopped off at Dalymount Park and played a friendly international against Ireland on 14 June 1924.[30] The significance of the Olympic football tournament of 1924 has been underestimated in Irish football and Olympic history and the four matches played at this time have not been recognized by the FAI as full internationals. This was the first occasion an Irish football team engaged in a match that did not involve one of the 'home nations' as they competed in what was effectively a world championship in the sport. The geographical spread of the competing nations was greater than that in any previous football competition and the presence of Egypt, USA, Mexico and Uruguay amongst the 22 competing countries established its international credibility and despite the absence of Germany and Great Britain, the quality of football was significantly improved on that on offer at previous tournaments. The performance of the eventual champions, Uruguay, unveiled a new formula for playing the game and set new standards of excellence. Their emphasis on skill and accurate passing rather than on the traditional virtues of strength and stamina that epitomized the British game astonished commentators.

As one of the countries that supported the Irish application for FIFA membership, it was appropriate that Italy provided the opposition for the first international played in Turin on 21 March 1926.[31] The selection was confined to the domestic league on this occasion and the selected players of an army officer, three civil servants, three casual dockers, two employees of Henry Ford, a bookmaker and one unemployed individual departed from Dublin on Wednesday evening and arrived in Turin late on Saturday, no doubt exhausted after the long journey by land and sea. Cannon and the three other amateurs involved received inscribed gold medals to the value of three guineas to mark the occasion; the professionals were paid a match fee of £5.[32] The importance ascribed to the match is not reflected in the coverage of the actual event; the newspapers of the day provided only the most basic report of the match. It attracted an attendance of 12,000 and Harry Cannon and Frank Brady excelled as the Irish Free State were beaten 3–0.[33] The players stopped off on the return journey in Paris where they played a friendly match against *Cercle Athlequike de Paris* under the name of the Irish Nomads on 24 March 1926.[34] Harry Cannon made his second international appearance when he was a member of the Irish team that beat Belgium 4–2 in Liege on 12 February 1928, after recovering from a 2–0 half-time deficit. An attendance of 25,000 witnessed the Irish Free State's first international victory in 'violent storms of sleet.'[35] A Cannon penalty save was the first by an Irish goalkeeper in an international match.[36] Therefore, in his brief international career, Cannon earned the distinction of playing in the Irish Free State's first football international, its first international victory and becoming the first Irish goalkeeper to save a penalty in an international match.

Harry Cannon: the sports' administrator

What gives added significance to Harry Cannon's career and makes it worthy of in-depth study is that his playing career was conducted in tandem with an involvement in the administration and management of sport conducted at the highest level. Cannon was introduced to the world of sports' administration through the AAA and through this, he became involved in the Irish Amateur Boxing Association (IABA) which in turn introduced him to the Olympic movement in Ireland. Apart from its commitment to promoting GAA sport, the AAA was innovative in its promotion of boxing; in November 1923, a boxing sub-committee was established within the AAA with a brief to promote the sport in the army and to draft a training programme to prepare boxers for the forthcoming Tailteann Games and to assist in every way in sending a strong team to Paris to compete in the Olympic Games. Tansy Lee, a former British professional boxing champion and the first Scottish boxer to win a Lonsdale Belt outright, was appointed boxing instructor in the army on an annual salary of £300 and the impact was immediate. Six army boxers won national titles and were selected to compete in the 1924 Olympic Games.[37] The boxers were sharp and match-fit and performed with credit in Paris without winning any medals.[38]

Unfortunately, the minutes of both the IABA and of its Dublin branch have not survived so an exact reconstruction of Harry Cannon's career as an official in amateur boxing is limited and confined to sometimes contradictory information gathered from the occasional newspaper report. He was elected treasurer of the Leinster Amateur Boxing Council in 1928 and still held this position in 1932.[39] He also served as president of the county Dublin board of the IABA and was a founder-member of the Islandbridge Boxing Club.[40]

Cannon's association with the Irish Olympic Council began in 1931. He was one of the three high-powered officials of the IABA who combined with officials of the Irish Amateur Swimming Association (IASA) and the National Athletic and Cycling Association of Ireland (NACAI) and forced J. J. Keane to re-engage with the Olympic Movement in Ireland. Keane was the founding father of the movement in Ireland and was elected to the International Olympic Committee on 8 June 1922; this appointment made it possible for Ireland to send competitors to the Olympic Games.[41] Keane provided much of the leadership associated with Ireland's participation in 1924 and 1928, but it is clear from contemporary newspaper reports that officials from the above organizations were forced to take action in 1931 to resuscitate the Irish Olympic Council due to the inaction of Keane and his fellow officers. No meeting of the council had been held since 18 June 1928. On 26 August 1931, officials from the IABA, the NACAI and the IASA held a meeting chaired by the IABA president Major-General W. R. E. Murphy, at which a general discussion on Olympic matters took place. It was decided to invite the three outgoing executive officers of the Irish Olympic Council together with three representatives from the IABA, the NACAI and the IASA to a conference scheduled for the following week 'for the purpose of carrying through arrangements for the Olympic Games of 1932.' Officers from these three federations had undertaken preliminary work on drafting a constitution for the council.[42] The second meeting was held on 30 August and W. R. E. Murphy again presided. The draft constitution was discussed and a motion proposed by J. J. McGilton (NACAI) and P. J. Kilcullen (IABA) that the document be accepted subject to the approval of the associations concerned was unanimously passed. The attendees decided to reassemble on 14 September for the purpose of winding up the outgoing council, approve the new constitution and to elect a new council to prepare for the 1932 Games. Cannon's standing within the IABA was such that he was present at all three of these meetings. The outgoing executive officers were again invited to attend but failed to do so. In their absence, the draft constitution was approved and the 'flag question was considered.' A long discussion took place on the power of those present to form a new Olympic council in view of the fact that the old council was still in existence. Although it was accepted that this was not possible, those present went ahead and elected Eoin O' Duffy (President), Harry Cannon (Secretary) and H. F. Brennan (Treasurer) as the officers of the new committee.

A final ultimatum was delivered to J. J. Keane. He was instructed to call a meeting within two weeks to form a new Olympic council in accordance with the constitution approved by the conference of the three associations; in the event of his failing to do so, it was resolved that the representatives of the three federations would proceed to elect a new Olympic council on 28 September.[43] The ultimatum had the desired effect. The members of the outgoing council as well as representatives of the IABA, the NACAI and the IASA assembled in Jury's Hotel on 29 September. The outgoing committee was dissolved and matters relating to the terms of the council's constitution were discussed.[44] The delegates reassembled on 10 October 1931 at Jury's Hotel at which the preferred officer board of the concerned federations was confirmed. O'Duffy and Cannon were elected president and honorary secretary, respectively, the two key administrative positions at national Olympic committee level. Cannon was the nominee of the IABA and the NACAI and his election was unanimous.[45] The constitution was adopted at this meeting, the terms of which are outside the scope of this study. A few days later, Cannon's resignation from the IABA was reported. He had taken offence to a derogatory comment passed at an earlier meeting, although it was also claimed that this resignation was inspired by his Olympic responsibilities.[46]

The Games of the Xth Olympiad, Los Angeles, 1932

As honorary secretary, Harry Cannon was responsible for the day-to-day administration of the Irish Olympic Council and was a member of its standing committee established in November 1931 'to carry out the routine matters of the council and any other business referred to them by the council.' A month later, this committee became the General Purposes Committee empowered to control all financial matters relating to the council. Cannon was present at all eight council meetings held during the Los Angeles cycle and his chief responsibilities were co-ordinating fundraising, finalising transport arrangements, entering competitors and communicating with the Los Angeles Organizing Committee. At a council meeting on 28 June, he was given an additional responsibility when he was appointed *Chef de Mission* of the Irish team.[47] As such, he was effectively the team manager in Los Angeles and brought the experience of a still-active competitive sportsman to the post for the only occasion in Irish Olympic history. The *Chef de Mission* is a national Olympic committee's main liaison person with the International Olympic Committee, the international federations and the organizing committee and is responsible for all of a team's competitors and officials.

The Irish Olympic Council's time of preparation for the Los Angeles Games was short but in the time available, it showed itself to be a progressive one and approved several initiatives that contributed to Ireland's success at these Games. Many of these were inspired by its president, Eoin O'Duffy, who was the sports' evangelist of the revolutionary generation.[48] Alec Nelson, a coach at the Cambridge University Athletic Club, was recruited to work with the athletes; a training camp was held at Ballybunion, County Kerry prior to departure which allowed the athletes to train on a full-time basis for several days; Tommy Maloney, a boxing instructor attached to the police depot, was included in the party travelling to Los Angeles as a masseur and crucially an early departure was approved for the athletes to allow for acclimatization.[49] On 3 July, the four-man athletics team ('as fit as hands could make them,' according to coach Nelson) sailed from Cobh aboard the White Star liner, the *Adriatic*, accompanied by Tommy Maloney, who worked with the athletes maintaining their fitness levels on the trans-Atlantic journey.[50] The four boxers and Olympic officials including Harry Cannon departed from Cobh on 10 July.[51] As a result of the early departure, the Irish athletic team had acclimatized for eight days in Los Angeles before the Great Britain team arrived. The result was unimagined success for the small eight-man team with Bob Tisdall and Dr Pat O'Callaghan winning Olympic titles, Eamonn Fitzgerald finished in fourth place in the triple jump and boxer James Murphy also finished in fourth place after injury prevented him from competing in the bronze medal box-off.

There were also successes on the diplomatic front. The world governing bodies of the various Olympic sports hold their assemblies in association with the Games and Cannon was elected to the executive board of the *Fédération Internationale de Boxe Amateur* (FIBA), the world governing body of amateur boxing. The International Amateur Athletic Federation (IAAF) postponed making a decision on the dispute between the Amateur Athletic Association and the NACAI on their respective areas of jurisdiction, but this decision postponed what was the inevitable restricting of the latter's jurisdiction to the territory of the Irish Free State.

As honorary secretary of the Irish Olympic Council and *Chef de Mission* in Los Angeles, it was Harry Cannon's duty to present a report on the Irish involvement in the Games. The report was simple, factual and infused with a sense of national pride at the achievements of the small Irish team. At the Parade of Nations segment of the Opening Ceremony, 'Ireland made an imposing display, and received a tremendous reception from the 105,000 people present,' Cannon reported to his fellow council members. Bob Tisdall succeeded in winning 'amid thunderous applause; His time in the final set up a new World Record of 57–7/10 s – a record that will stand for many years.' The first part of this statement was incorrect as Tisdall's mishap when he knocked over the final hurdle disqualified him from establishing a world record. The second half of the statement was prophetic as an Irish runner did not better Tisdall's time until 8 July 1984 when J. J. Barry finally ran 51.56 s. Within an hour of Tisdall's triumph, Dr Pat O'Callaghan won the Olympic hammer title with his final throw. Cannon reported that it was 'impossible to describe the wonderful scene that took –place on that day with the whole Stadium standing during the playing of our National Anthem, and doing honour to our Nation through the deeds of her athletes.' Cannon reported that triple jumper Mr E. Fitzgerald 'was unlucky not to have filled second place' and explains the basis for this opinion:

> On one of his jumps in the final he succeeded in clearing over 51 feet; but when in the air an attendant at the pit started waving a fault flag, and Mr Fitzgerald allowed himself to fall back on landing. The take-off had not been a fault, and the attendant exceeded his duty as he was only there for the purpose of keeping the pit level. The attendant apologised, but that was little consolation to Mr. Fitzgerald ...

Cannon reported that the boxing contingent 'were unlucky in some cases to have the decisions given against them.' In his opinion, Mr Hughes 'won well'; 'the decision in favour of the Argentine was not well received by the audience. After the fight Pereyra was admitted to Hospital, and was unable to take any further part in the competition.' A decision by Mr Smith to 'mix it' in round two of his bout proved costly. This suited his opponent 'who was very clever at infighting and never allowed Mr Smith to hit him.' Private J. Flood 'after a great mill was beaten on points.' After a great and surprising victory over his USA opponent, J. Miler, James Murphy suffered a badly cut eye in his second bout which forced him to retire. 'During the interval he became blind and gave in. Mr Murphy gained fourth place in this weight.' Despite the losses, Harry Cannon identified reasons to be optimistic for the future. Three of the boxers were under 22 years of age 'and with normal development they should win titles at the next Olympics,' Cannon reported.[52] Unfortunately, for these young boxers and several other athletes, the next Olympics for Ireland was to be the 1948 Games as the Irish Olympic Council chose not to enter a team in 1936.

Harry Cannon's serious association with the Irish Olympic Council ended after Los Angeles. In compliance with its constitutional requirements, he presented his official report on 3 February 1933 to a meeting attended by only six members; at the general meeting of the council held on 4 March 1935, he was defeated by P. J. Kilcullen, also of the IABA, for the position of honorary secretary by 11 votes to 4. Kilcullen was the nominee of the IABA and the NACAI with Cannon supported by the IASA delegates.[53] Although he was co-opted as a member of the council, this ended his active association with the body and he attended only one more meeting of the council in October 1936. He was briefly associated with the Council's campaign that began in 1935 to have the island of Ireland recognized as the representative unit for Olympic competition. Ireland as a 32-county entity competed at the Olympic Games of 1924, 1928 and 1932. The first indication that the IOC intended to change this situation came in the December 1934 issue of their official bulletin which used *Etat Libre d'Irlande* rather than the customary *Irlande* to describe Ireland.[54] The timing of the change, coming almost immediately after the IAAF introduced a rule change that confined the jurisdiction of national athletic federations to the political boundaries of the area they represented, suggested that the

IOC intended to adopt a similar model. The repercussions from this decision were to dominate the business of the Irish Olympic Council for the next 22 years. Harry Cannon made the first response on behalf of the council. On 5 February 1935, he contacted A. G. Berdez, secretary-general of the IOC, and initiated an exchange of correspondence that was continued by council officials until November 1956. On this occasion, Cannon played the innocent card and pointed out that Irish officials believed that a mistake was made in the December bulletin. The Irish committee was 'affiliated as *Irlande* since admission to membership of the CIO [IOC]' and the officers were of the 'opinion that it is only necessary to draw your attention to the matter to have same rectified.'[55]

Unfortunately, the matter was far more complicated than a simple case of mistaken identification and Cannon's initial contact began a campaign by the Irish Olympic officials to have Irish nationals declared eligible to represent Ireland in Olympic competition, regardless of their place of residence on the island and to have Ireland recognized as the name of the unit compering in the Olympic Games that only concluded in 1956.[56]

Conclusion

Despite his duties as an administrator of sport, Harry Cannon continued to play soccer at the highest level in the Irish domestic league and he did not retire from Bohemians until the end of the 1936 season. His last game for Bohemians was an unusual one; he emerged from his soccer exile in April 1937 and played with a club selection of retired and contemporary players who defeated a team from the German Battleship *Schleswig-Holstein* (2–1) in a friendly match staged in Dalymount Park. The occasion is of some significance as it was the first occasion Olympic handball was played in Ireland. Two teams of 11 players from the battleship gave an exhibition of what the *Irish Press* described as Fieldball prior to the soccer game. According to the report, the game 'in many respects resembles basket-ball with soccer goal posts.' The game was described as 'a body-builder and muscle developer, and is played extensively in Germany for the training of all athletes, football players, swimmers, boxers, etc.'[57]

Although he retired from top-flight domestic soccer in 1936, Harry Cannon was not finished with competitive sport. He regularly played with the Civil Service Cricket Club where he was a more than useful wicket keeper. He joined the Railway Union Hockey Club and earned his place on the club's first team and won an Irish Senior Cup medal in 1938, inevitably as goalkeeper. This was fitting finale to a remarkable career in sport. The final against Cork Harlequins, played in the headquarters of Irish hockey at Londonbridge Road, ended in a scoreless draw after two periods of extra time. The *Sunday Independent* noted that it was a match in which 'all the fine points of the game were missing,' but one of its redeeming features was 'the excellent goalkeeping of Cannon, whose judgement probably retained for Railway Union an interest in the cup.'[58] According to another report, 'Harlequin's forwards were thwarted of a number of scores by the magnificent goalkeeping of Cannon for Railway Union.' In the replay at Glasheen Road, Cork, Cannon again remained unbeaten as Railway Union secured an only goal victory.[59] Later in the month, Railway Union secured their first Leinster Senior League title since 1932 with another 1–0 victory, this time against Dublin University.[60] It was a remarkable conclusion to the veteran goalkeeper's career who had distinguished himself in the demanding position in hurling, Gaelic football, soccer and hockey.

Harry Cannon belonged to an era when leading sportsmen were administrators while still actively engaged in their sporting career. Some were all-round sportsmen; Harry Cannon displayed more versatility than almost all of his contemporaries. Life as a gifted sportsman was not easy for Cannon as apart from walking away from the army-approved GAA sports and the Irish-Ireland milieu in favour of a sport designated as foreign, he also managed to reconcile the conflicting loyalties of representing the IABA and the Irish Olympic Council and playing under the auspices of the FAIFS. The latter had accepted partition while both the IABA and the Irish Olympic Council jealously guarded their 32-county status. That he managed to reconcile these conflicting demands provides a fine example of the pragmatism of a sportsman who separated and distanced the politics from the sporting endeavour.

Disclosure statement

No potential conflict of interest was reported by the author.

Notes

1. Joyce, *Football League Players' Records*, 220.
2. http://www.census.nationalarchives.ie/pages/1901/Dublin/Pembroke_East__Donnybrook/Irishtown__Pembroke_Street/1285731.
3. http://www.census.nationalarchives.ie/pages/1911/Dublin/Pembroke_East/Herbert_Place/50003/.
4. Military Archives, CathalBrugha Barracks, Rathmines, Abstract of service for Comdt Cannon, Henry James.
5. *An t-Óglác,* 7 April 1923.
6. Ibid.
7. Ibid.
8. Ibid., May 19, 1923.
9. Ibid.
10. *Football Sports Weekly*, March 17, 1928.
11. *An t-Óglác,* January 12, 1924.
12. *Freeman's Journal,* February 25, 1924.
13. *Football Sports Weekly*, March 17, 1928.
14. *Irish Press*, March 16, 1944.
15. Fitzgerald, How to Play Gaelic Football, 19–20.
16. *Sport*, April 6, 1929.
17. *Sport*, April 24, May 1, 1926.
18. *An t-Óglác*, May 8, 1926.
19. *Irish Independent,* August 21, 1926.
20. *Sport*, May 12, 1928.
21. *Sunday Independent*, March 21, 1926.
22. Byrne, *Football Association of Ireland*, 28–30.
23. Garnham, *Association Football*, 196–200.
24. Moore, *Irish Soccer Split*, 101.
25. Byrne, *Football Association of Ireland*, 21.
26. *Sport*, March 12, 1921.
27. Moore, *Irish Soccer Split*, 100–128.
28. Ibid., 129–39.
29. *Irish Times*, May 26, 1923; Lanfanchi et al., *100 Years of Football*, 64–68; Garnham, *Association Football*, 181; and Moore, *Irish Soccer Split*, 140–161.
30. Moore, *Irish Soccer Split*, 169–76; and Carey, *Paris 1924*, 22–25.

31. Cullen, *Ireland on the Ball*, 9.
32. Ryan, *The Boys in Green*, 16.
33. *Irish Independent*, March 22, 1926.
34. Ryan, The Boys in Green, 16.
35. Irish Independent, February 9, 1928; Cullen, Ireland on the Ball, 10.
36. Ibid., March 26, 1944.
37. *An t-Óglác̄*, 3, November 17, 1923, July 5, 1924.
38. *Irish Independent*, May 8, 3, 4, June 7, 1924.
39. *Irish Independent*, August 20, 1936.
40. Ibid., November 13, 1931.
41. McCarthy, *Gold, Silver and Green*, 305–314.
42. *Irish Times*, August 27, 1931.
43. Ibid., 1, September 15, 1931.
44. Ibid., September 30, 1931.
45. Ibid., October 11, 1931.
46. *Irish Independent*, October 15, 1931.
47. Irish Olympic Council, Minute of meetings of November 12, 1931, December 12, 1931, June 28, 1932.
48. McGarry, *Eoin O'Duffy*, 141–169.
49. The *Kerryman*, 11, June 18, 2, July 9, 1932.
50. *Cork Examiner*, July 4, 1932.
51. *Irish Times*, July 11, 1932.
52. National Library of Ireland, O'Duffy Papers, Report of the Honorary Secretary of the Irish Olympic Council, February 4, 1935.
53. *Irish Press*, March 5, 1935.
54. IOC, Bulletin Officiel, 2.
55. Olympics Studies Centre Historical Archive (Lausanne), D-RMO1-Irlan/002, Correspondence of the NOC of Ireland, 9455, H. Cannon to A. G. Berdez, February 5, 1935.
56. Hunt, The Campaign for the Recognition of Ireland, 837.
57. *Irish Press*, April 14, 1937.
58. *Sunday Independent*, March 27, 1938.
59. *Cork Examiner*, March 28, April 4, 1938.
60. *Irish Independent*, April 25, 1932.

References

Byrne, Peter. *Football Association of Ireland: 75 Years*. Dublin: Sportsworld Publications, 1996.
Byrne, Kevin. 'Los Angeles 1932: Monday 1 August 1932: Ireland's Finest Olympic Hour'. *History Ireland* 20, no. 4 (2012): 28–9.
Carey, Tadhg. 'Paris 1924: Ireland's footballers at the Paris Olympics, 1924'. *History Ireland* 20, no. 4 (2012): 22–5.
Cullen, Donal. *Ireland on the Ball: International Matches of the Republic of Ireland Soccer Team. A Complete Record, March 1926 to June 1993*. Dublin: Elo Publications, 1993.
Fitzgerald, Dick. *How to Play Gaelic Football*. Cork: Guy and Company, 1914.
Garnham, Neal. *Association Football and Society in Pre-partition Ireland*. Belfast: Ulster Historical Foundation, 2004.
Hunt, Tom. 'In Our Case it Seems Obvious the British Organising Committee Piped the Tune', The Campaign for Recognition of 'Ireland' in the Olympic Movement, 1935–1956'. In *Sport in Society, Cultures, Commerce, Media, Politics,* ed. Erik Nielsen and Matthew P. Llewellyn, 835–52. Abingdon: Routledge Journals. 2015. Vol. 18, no. 7.
International Olympic Committee. *Bulletin Officiel, du Comite International Olympique, December 1934*. Lausanne: International Olympic Committee, 1934.
Joyce, Michael. *Football League Players' Records, 1888–1939*. Nottingham: Tony Brown, 2012.
Lanfanchi, Pierre, Christiane Eisenberg, Tony Mason, and Alfred Wahl. *100 Years of Football, The FIFA Centennial Book*. London: Weidenfeld and Nicolson, 2004.

McCarthy, Kevin. *Gold, Silver and Green: The Irish Olympic Journey 1896–1924*. Cork: Cork University Press, 2010.

McGarry, Fearghal. *Eoin O'Duffy: A Self-made Hero*. Oxford: Oxford University Press, 2007.

Moore, Cormac. *The Irish Soccer Split*. Cork: Atrium, 2015.

Ryan, Sean. *The Boys in Green: The FAI International Story*. Edinburgh: Mainstream Publishing, 1997.

How it all began: the story of women's soccer in sixties Drogheda

Helena Byrne

There is very little reference to the history of women's soccer in Irish secondary sources. Any sources that do deal with women's soccer usually focus on the developments since the formation of the Ladies Football Association in 1973. There is little reference to the football teams and leagues that were formed before this date. In Drogheda, the earliest reference to women's soccer was in 1966 when an indoor football league was established. Ireland was going through a period of economic growth in the 1960s and employment opportunities for women grew in urban areas like Drogheda. This article will outline the impact this had on women's sport in Drogheda, it will describe the Abbey Ballroom Indoor Football League and discuss the influence this league had on the development of women's soccer in the region. As there is little secondary source material available, the main sources for this research are newspapers and interviews.

Introduction

We weren't just there for a fashion parade[1]

The aim of this paper is to raise a discussion on the early period of women's soccer and outline a viable strategy for other researchers to follow in order fill the gaps that exist in the current literature. This is just one small case study of a much larger project that needs to be undertaken while this period of history is still within living memory. It is hoped that this paper would be a starting point for such a project. As there are no secondary sources dealing directly with women's soccer in the sixties in Ireland the literature review discusses contemporary historical sources that help give context to the period, discusses attitude to women's involvement in sport which includes recent events and then discusses literature about women's soccer in the Republic of Ireland. The Methodology section outlines the strategies I used to gather information and includes an overview of the results of the project. The discussion section of the paper describes the development of women's soccer in Drogheda in the sixties focusing on the period from 1966 to the early 1970s but it mainly focuses on the Abbey Ballroom Indoor Football League that ran from 1966 to 1967.

Literature review

The official recording of the history of women's experiences and viewpoints is a relatively new phenomenon in Ireland.[2] However, there has never been adequate funding set aside for the documentation of women's football in the Republic of Ireland.[3]

In order to bridge the gap between women's and men's sporting history more funding needs to be allocated by the relevant bodies to bridge the current inequalities that exist. As a result, it is unsurprising that with the exception of the GAA, there has been very little documentation of women's sporting history in Ireland.

Any sources that do deal with women's soccer in the Republic of Ireland usually focus on its development since the formation of the Ladies Football Association (LFA) in 1973. The purpose of this concise literature review is to outline the key texts that give context to the events that led to the development of women's soccer in the mid-sixties, as well as a short review of the current literature on women's soccer from an international perspective. The literature available is discussed in terms of the social conditions of Ireland in the sixties, women in sport and more specifically women's soccer in the Republic of Ireland.

Since the new millennium there have been a number of new publications that have dealt with the historical events over the last century. These publications are a form of historical revisionism which expanded the range of subjects discussed and included the negative elements of Irish society that were once ignored. Ferriter has highlighted that there is a 'need to re-examine critically the framework of interpretation scholars have employed to date' in light of the major scandals that were uncovered in recent years.[4] The 1960s have always been described as 'the best of decades'[5] as there was a rise in population, a decrease in emigration and more jobs in industry created.[6] Ferriter, and more recently Holohan, have highlighted that even though there was some economic development, unemployment rates were still high and it was mostly young people who benefited from any job creation.[7] Higher rates of employment for younger people meant that they had more spending power to buy into the popular cultural trends of the time which were largely influenced by Britain and the USA.[8]

Article 41.2 in the Irish Constitution states that a women's place is in the home, since its inception this has caused many barriers for women over the decades to gain access to education, equality in the workplace, keep working after marriage as well as the types of social and sporting activities they could participate in.[9] Despite these barriers women have always been involved in sport. Since Victorian times some of the many arguments as to why women shouldn't play sport included the possibility of damage to their health, especially the possibility that playing sport would affect their ability to bare children.[10] In 1929, the Pope had also declared that girls participating in athletics and gymnastics must take special precaution 'in regard to Christian modesty ..., in as much as it is extremely unbecoming for them to display themselves before the public gaze'.[11] As newspapers like the *Sporting Press* became popular at the start of the twentieth century the papers were used as a platform to propagate the chauvinistic attitudes of the time and to reaffirm that women should feature 'in the scenery, rather than the action'.[12] Although the myths about the impact sport has on women's health have been disproven[13], the misperception of women as physically inferior to men still prevails today, a very common insult towards League of Ireland players who go down after a tackle is 'she fell over', which implies that the player is weak and must be feminine.

In 2014, Republic of Ireland player Stephanie Roche made history by being the first female player to make it to the final three in the *FIFA Puskás Award* after the goal she scored for Peamount United against Wexford Youths went viral.[14] Her goal was captured on a shaky handheld device whereas the goals her male competitors for the award scored were recorded in High Definition at multiple angles by the professional media. Roche's goal was seen as a unique challenge to the male domination of the sport and she has used this opportunity to promote the women's game as her:

> Goal wasn't just a one-off, it wasn't something that one girl scored and no other girl could ever do. There's been more goals scored like that all over the world, they just haven't had the publicity that I was lucky enough to get.[15]

It has been noted that women's experience in all sports not just soccer, 'virtually replicates their more general experience – that they have been treated as not only different to men but also inferior in many respects'.[16]

In recent year's women's experience in soccer as both a participant and as a spectator have become the focus of academic research.[17] Caudwell has highlighted that this avenue of research goes someway to recognize women as serious participants in the sport in addition to challenging the 'inequitable social arrangements between men and women'. In 2003, *Soccer & Society* published a special issue entitled 'Soccer, Women, Sexual Liberation. Kicking off a New Era' which included 15 articles about women's soccer around the world.[18] In the UK, the history of the sport has been documented in a number of publications. However, this was the first time that there was an academic paper published on women's soccer in the Republic of Ireland.

Bourke in 2003 and Liston in 2006 are the only researchers who have made significant contributions about the history of women's soccer in the Republic of Ireland in Irish academia. However, the bulk of their discussions on the early days of women's football is based around the start of the 1970s as this is the time period when the LFA was formed.[19] Noted in all texts related to the sixties in Ireland is the rise in the number of dance halls that opened up around the country during this period.[20] As the market tried to develop different types of entertainment the lines between what was considered entertainment versus sport became blurred, which led to the development of indoor football leagues.

The Abbey Ballroom in Drogheda set-up an indoor football league in 1966 which actively encouraged women's teams to participate in the competition.[21] As this league was seen as entertainment and not sport the women's matches were warmly received, as were the GAA players who participated in the various teams.[22] Most of the men's teams were formed in the workplace or through other sporting groups with a few still involved in full-time education.[23] However, all of the female players interviewed were involved in full-time work, the camaraderie that was common amongst women in female-dominated workplaces made it easier to form teams to participate in the leagues.[24]

Williams has argued that the participation of women in football around the world grew so dramatically in the later part of the sixties that FIFA had no choice but to acknowledge the sport and support the creation of women's football federations. However, this also gave FIFA the power to suppress the expansion of women's soccer by not applying the same development strategies as the men's game.[25] This has meant that the women's game in many countries, and especially in the Republic of Ireland, 'continues to rely largely, though not exclusively, on voluntary networks of people who organize matches, attend administrative meetings, coach and develop young players'.[26] As this is a recurring issue, it is important to document the experiences of these volunteers in order to learn from the mistakes in the past and to analyse what has influenced the development of women's soccer since the 1960s.

Methodology

Materials used in the study

This research area is exploratory in nature. Thus, a combination of qualitative research methods, crowd sourcing through social media, archival research and literature review formed the basis for this project. As there are very few secondary sources related to the history of women's soccer in Ireland available, with little reference to the Abbey Ballroom Indoor Football League in any secondary sources, this study relied heavily on primary sources. The main source of information was through face to face interviews and old editions of the 'Drogheda Independent'. According to Sangster 'oral history is especially useful as a means of probing the subjective areas of experience and feeling' which cannot be found in traditional resources.[27] Grounded theory was used to determine the exact number of interview participants needed. Grounded theory is defined as a 'research tool which enables you to seek out and conceptualize the latent social patterns and structures of your area of interest through the process of constant comparison', by comparing the interviewees responses to the interview questions it was possible to determine what were the shared experiences versus the personal.[28] Individuals who were involved in the Abbey Ballroom Indoor Football league and an outdoor women's team in the sixties were interviewed.

The participants

A combination of contacting former players directly and the snowball sampling technique was used to recruit participants. A call for participants was advertised via local media, websites and through social media.

Most of the interviewees were in their sixties or seventies at the time of the interview, they were in their mid to late teens when they started playing indoor football at the Abbey Ballroom. However, Interview I coached the Lourdes Girl's, which competed in outdoor soccer competitions and Interview J played with an outdoor team in the 1980s. Many of the people who participated in the league as a player, coach or spectator have either emigrated or passed away. These barriers along with health issues had a significant impact on recruiting potential participants for this project.

Research design

An interview guide was developed in order to direct data collection through semi-structured interviews. The interviews were all audio recorded and some were also video recorded. The initial interviews took place in July 2012, while the remainder of the interviews took place between September 2014 and November 2015. The majority of these interviews focused on the Abbey Ballroom Indoor Football league. The interview questions focused on the following themes: the place, the set-up, getting started, the games. There were also some questions added for male interviewees to gauge their opinions on women playing soccer.

All of these interviews are stored in the Drogheda Local Voices archive located at Drogheda Museum Millmount and available to the public and other researchers during office hours. In this paper, I have de-identified the interviewees by giving them the name Interview A, B, C etc. The letter was assigned in chronological order in relation to the date when the interview took place. As seen in the Figure 1 all

Interview/Public Events Details				
Title	Date	Team Name	League	
Abbey Ballroom Indoor Football - 1966/67				
Interview A	18/07/2012	Dedicated Followers of Football	Men's	
Interview B	19/07/2012	United Ladies	Women's	
Interview C	20/07/2012	United Ladies/Lourdes Girls*	Women's	*Interview C played in the Abbey Ballroom with the Untied Ladies and outdoor football with Lourdes girls.
Interview D	20/08/2012	The Independents	Women's	
Project Launch	8/09/2014	General public and former players attended	Men's/ Women's	
LMFM Late Lunch Gerry Kelly	September 2014	3 players from the men's league interviewed		
Interview E	20/02/2015	Rigor Mortis Five	Men's	
Interview F	24/02/2015	Glen Hearts	Men's	
Interview G	5/03/2015	Rollin' Tones/Bluesville**	Women's	**It is believed that in the first league the team was registered as Rollin' Tones and in the other leagues as Bluesville.
Interview H	11/04/2015	Denim Rovers	Men's	
Public Exhibition at Drogheda Museum Millmount	2/07/2015	General public and former players attended	Men's/ Women's	
Outdoor Football - Sixties/Seventies & Eighties				
Interview I	3/11/2015	Lourdes Girls		
Interview J	6/11/2015	Boyne Rovers		

Figure 1. Interview/public event details.

interviewees both male and female are listed with a corresponding date and the name of the team they were involved in. Some former players did not wish to be interviewed during the data collection phase of the project but agreed to an informal discussion on the topic. Although, the formal data collection campaign on this project has come to an end there are some former players who were not available at the time who will be interviewed at a future date, the resulting interviews will also be available in the Drogheda Local Voices archive.

Preparation of research materials

The interview questions for this project were devised after consultation with key texts referenced in the literature review section of this paper. The texts by Dermot Ferriter and Myrtle Hill were significant in shaping my understanding of the economic and social developments that took place in the sixties. In relation to the challenges women faced playing sport Jean Williams publications on women's soccer were invaluable in particular her book 'A Beautiful Game: International Perspectives on Women's Football'.

The 'Drogheda Independent' from 1966 to 1969 was also a vital source of information that shaped the design of the interview questions. Before the league started in May 1966 there was a write up in the 'Drogheda Independent' explaining what the league was about and the rules for the competition. The Abbey Ballroom also advertised the fixtures for the first three competitions in the newspaper. These fixture lists gave team names, where they were from and match times.

Women's participation in sport is well documented in the UK, however very little of this research correlated the experiences of the players interviewed in this project. The player's experiences in the work place and their later involvement in organized sport was very similar to that of Jane Sangster's work on the Westclox factory in Canada.[29] In addition, there was some similarity with that of other female factory workers interviewed in the recent publications 'Irish Women at work 1930–1960: An oral history' and 'Locked Out: A century of working class life' these publications gave context to the interviewees experiences in the workplace. Whereas, Carole Holohan's recent publication on youth clubs in the sixties was invaluable as it gave context to the interviewees' social experiences during this period. Although, the GAA Oral History project is probably the largest project of its kind in Ireland it differed greatly in size and scope to the Abbey Ballroom Indoor Football project. Until a comprehensive history of women's soccer and other sports in the Republic of Ireland is conducted it is not possible to compare the experiences of the female players at this early stage.

Results

When the Abbey Ballroom Indoor Football League project was announced there was a great enthusiasm from many of the former players. Although, not everyone approached wanted to be interviewed there was a good response from the call for information and interview participants in the local media. It became a hot topic once again for the former players who reminisced over the rivalries during the competitions. Many of the people involved in the Abbey Ballroom Indoor Football League wanted to share their experiences and were delighted to see this element of their cultural history documented formally.

Surprisingly, Facebook groups such as *Drogheda Down Memory Lane* and *Dundalk North End and Friends* turned up a wealth of information that would have been very difficult to find using traditional research techniques. Members of these social media groups were willing to share personal collections such as photographs and newspaper collections. They were also very useful in identifying player names from team photos that were published in newspapers during the sixties.

As mentioned above the 'Drogheda Independent' from the 1960s has a wealth of valuable information. Looking through the newspapers prior to May 1966 shows us that the only organized sports available for women at the time were camogie, golf and tennis. However, golf and tennis were expensive sports to participate in which meant the vast majority of women didn't have access to them. Kiely and Leane highlighted that 'occupational and class segregation in leisure pursuits underlined the role the wider social and community environment played in reinforcing worker identities and in maintaining gender, class and occupational divides'.[30] Thus, the indoor football leagues, inter-factory sporting competitions and other work place social activities organized in Drogheda gave working class women more sporting and leisure opportunities that weren't available until the mid-sixties. The fact that the Abbey Ballroom published the team names and where they were from made it easier to track down potential participants for this project. It also demonstrated how popular indoor football was during the sixties as women's teams travelled from all over the north-east and men's teams from as far away as Cork and Cavan came to Drogheda to participate in the competitions. The newspapers also show that women's involvement in soccer predates the establishment of women's Gaelic football which started in County Louth in 1968.[31]

In addition, the entertainment section of the *Drogheda Independent* had advertisements for similar competitions hosted by ballrooms in Dundalk, Blackrock, Navan and Ashbourne. Some of the more dedicated teams participated in a number of these competitions. Some of the male interviewees even commented that one night they played in a competition in Dundalk and then went straight back to Drogheda to play a match in the Abbey Ballroom.[32] Local newspapers in other urban areas would most likely show up similar competitions as indoor football seems to be a popular form of entertainment in the mid-sixties.

In spring of 1967 'The Evening Herald' sponsored the Abbey Ballroom Indoor Football competition. Throughout this competition the paper published results of matches sporadically in the sports section and a few photos of people at the games. The fact that the competition was sponsored by a national paper could have been the reason why the men's teams from Cork and Cavan participated in the competition.

Figure 2 is from the exhibition that was hosted in Millmount Museum, 'The Abbey Ballroom Indoor Football: An Oral History Exhibition' (Panel 2, July–September 2015). This is not an exhaustive list but most of the teams mentioned in the *Drogheda Independent* are marked on the map.

Discussion

Industrial production was booming in Drogheda during the sixties which is why it was chosen as case study for the pilot survey on manpower. The survey was conducted by the Department of Social Science UCD and took place in 1965. This was the first of many surveys that took place in urban towns across the country.[33] As this survey took place in 1965 before the advent of indoor football it is not

Indoor Football

Where Teams Came From

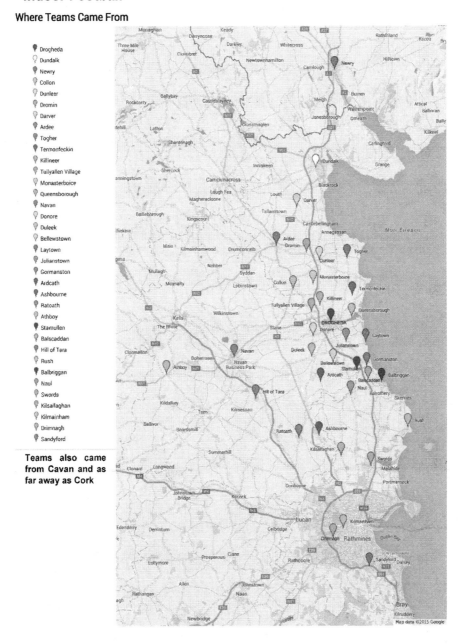

- Drogheda
- Dundalk
- Newry
- Collon
- Dunleer
- Dromin
- Darver
- Ardee
- Togher
- Termonfeckin
- Killineer
- Tullyallen Village
- Monasterboice
- Queensborough
- Navan
- Donore
- Duleek
- Bellewstown
- Laytown
- Julianstown
- Gormanston
- Ardcath
- Ashbourne
- Ratoath
- Athboy
- Stamullen
- Balscaddan
- Hill of Tara
- Rush
- Balbriggan
- Naul
- Swords
- Kilsallaghan
- Kilmainham
- Drimnagh
- Sandyford

Teams also came from Cavan and as far away as Cork

Figure 2. Indoor Football 02 Panel Map, image courtesy of the Abbey Ballroom Indoor Football: An Oral History Exhibition in summer 2015, Drogheda Museum Millmount. This map is an illustration of team locations but it is not exhaustive and some places may not be marked.

surprising that '77% of female respondents said that they had never been members of a sporting group or team' while 11 per cent were.[34] Thus it is easy to see why the answer to question one in Figure 3 was zero. As noted before, a person's social status influenced what type of social and sporting activities they participated in. In

Membership Of Sporting Groups Question 30

Membership	Percentage of female respondents		
	21 Year Olds	Unemployed	Unemployed (Working)
Present member of football club or team	0	0	0
Present member of sporting club or team other than football	11	2	0
Present member of football club or team and other sporting club or team	0	0	0
Past member of football club or team and other sporting club or team	1	1	0
Past member of football club or team	0	0	0
Past member of sporting club or team other than football	9	7	15
No answer	1	1	0
Not applicable – never member of any sporting club or team	77	90	85
Other Answer*	1	N/A	N/A
Total*	100	101	100

*Other answer was not included in the Table 3.25 and 5.25.

*There is no explanation as to why the total number does not add up to 100%.

Adapted from Table 3.25, 5.25 and 8.16 in *Manpower In A Developing Community.*

Figure 3. Manpower Survey Results, adapted from Table 3.25, 5.25 and 8.16 in *Manpower in A Developing Community: A pilot survey in Drogheda by the department of social science, University College Dublin.*

addition, women's working conditions also influenced the type of leisure activities they could participate in. Women involved in factory or public service work could participate in more social activities outside the workplace while domestic workers and hospitality staff participated in more individual leisure activities as they worked unsociable hours or lived in isolated areas.[35]

> One week they'd have the top band in it [The Abbey Ballroom] the next they were playing football.[36]

The Abbey Ballroom was a luxurious place with an excellent dance floor which is probably why it drew large crowds for dances and indoor football.[37]

Indoor football at the Abbey Ballroom was originally set-up as a fundraiser by a small group of local sports people in collaboration with the ballroom manager Ben Gordon in 1966. It quickly became one of the most popular forms of entertainment in Drogheda with large crowds coming both to play and to support the teams.[38] It was advertised in the ballroom and in the local paper, one interviewee recalls 'when you walked in the door there were large posters advertising indoor football'.[39] The week before the first league started there was a call for teams printed in the *Drogheda Independent*. It outlined all the rules of the games and encouraged 'the ladies to come forward with as many teams as possible'.[40] Some players reminiscing about the league remembers that:

> It didn't feature in the sports pages at all. There was an ad on the back page along with the dancing ads and the cinema ads. And eh, you got no notification at all, if you didn't buy the *Drogheda Independent* you didn't know when you were playing.[41]

The playing area was on the dance floor marked out by a partition, those that were used to playing indoor football were able to use it like an extra player.[42] Interview C recalls that the floor had springs underneath it which made it ideal for dancing but also for playing football.[43] Men were allocated twenty-five minutes per game and women were allocated fifteen minutes but they both had a half time break and switched sides.[44]

Some of the men interviewed recall changing for matches in the toilets while others got changed in their car and the women 'changed in the toilets ... there was no such thing as dressing rooms or your name on the door or anything like that and it didn't worry us we didn't even think about it'.[45]

Admission to watch the games varied, admission for the Casino Show band Trophy Competition was 2 shillings, while the Sinalco and Evening Herald leagues were 2 shillings and 6 pence.[46] With matches running from Monday to Thursday it would have been hard for most people to attend every night. There is no explanation given for the increase in the admission fee, but it may have been to cover the expense of maintaining the ballroom.

When the call for teams went out in the *Drogheda Independent* they also published the rules of the game. During the first few weeks of the competitions the teams played friendly matches to allow everyone to adjust to the new sport and then the knock out stages began.

Team organization

As mentioned before people signed up for the leagues through their work places, while some of the men were already involved in soccer teams or heard of it through attending dances at the ballroom.[47] It is not surprising that most of the teams were formed in the work place as several clubs involved in the early stages of the Irish League and the League of Ireland were formed in urban areas and had their roots in factories.[48]

All of the women interviewed formed teams in the workplace and fondly recall the comradery amongst the women they worked with. Interview G recalls that all the women's work stations were lined up on the factory floor and that the person with the best voice at the front would start singing and the rest of the floor would join in.[49] RTÉ, the state broadcaster, had a special report dedicated to women in the workplace in 1968, the narrator remarked on how singing was a sign of high morale which in turn improved the productivity of the factory, were as 'fifty years previously it [singing] was a sackable offence'.[50] Undoubtedly, this practice encouraged more women to form teams to represent their factory with pride in the Abbey Ballroom Indoor Football League.[51] Pride is a common theme that comes up with women involved in manufacturing work. The women interviewed in this study had an enormous sense of pride in their workplace and were proud to represent them even in an unofficial capacity in the leagues. Cullinane highlighted in his research of female textile workers in Cork that pride was the dominant theme that emerged from the women's recollections of their experiences.[52] Similarly, pride was also the primary theme in Sangster's study on the female workers at the Westclox factory in Canada.[53]

As mentioned in the rules, all the teams wore uniforms. Interview A and C both worked in a shoe factory and made their uniforms at home by hand. Interview G recalls:

> The reason why we were so stylish was because we worked in a clothing factory. We were all machinist except for X, ... the company agreed when we approached them and told them what we were going to do, they agreed to sponsor us and give us all the fabrics and we could make it ourselves.[54]

These uniforms helped to establish pride in their team and their workplace. Not everyone registered would have been able to afford the special apparel outlined in Figure 4. Many of the men shared jersey sets and canvas shoes, it is not clear but it is possible that some of the female teams may have shared their playing gear.[55]

All of the women's teams interviewed were coached by men, these men were either partners, co-workers or family members. The United Ladies were coached by one of the player's partners. He showed them a few things to do but the players were very sporty, one of the players had 'a great left kick and even knocked out' an opponent during a match.[56]

The Independents were organized by one of the office managers but Interview D can't recall any formal training sessions. She was from a sporting family and was actively involved in a range of sporting activities, which kept her very fit.[57]

Interview G played for Bluesville, she described herself as a tom boy and was quite active in her free time although she was never involved in any formal sporting clubs. One of the team members was from a Gaelic football family and she believes one of her brothers gave the team some tips on how to play. She also thinks that this is where they got the team name from as this player's brothers played for The Blues.[58]

The only team interviewed from outside Drogheda were the Telstar Beauties. They were from Ashbourne and got involved in the leagues because some of the men from their workplace were playing. All the men's and women's teams had

The Rules of the League

1. What to wear:
    Men: All players must wear shorts and a jersey or shirt
    Women: All players must wear a blouse, shorts or tights
2. Only rubber soled canvas shoes are permitted
3. Each team can register seven players but only five of these players will play in a match.
4. There are no substitutions allowed during play, but a team can alternate between the seven registered players from one game to the next.
5. The choice of players who play in each match is at discretion of the captain.
6. During play the ball must not be handled and the ball must not be played above four feet from the ground.
7. Heading the ball is a foul as it would be a 'high ball'.
8. All free kicks must be indirect; you are not allowed to kick directly at the goals.
9. A penalty kick is kicked directly against the goal keeper.
10. A goal can only be scored inside the goal area parallelogram[1].

Conditions of League

On the 21st of May the "Conditions of League" were printed at the bottom of the fixtures list. This outlined five basic principles:

1. The rules supplied to teams at registration always apply.
2. Each team will play two matches against two different teams as a qualifier.
3. Teams will get points from these matches. Two points for a win and one for a draw.
4. The knock out stages will start after each team has played their qualifying matches.
5. All teams should only play members listed on the original registration form[2].

---

[1] Summarised from - Indoor Football in Drogheda, *Drogheda Independent*, April 30, 1966.
[2] The Casino Showband Trophy Competition, *Drogheda Independent*, May 21, 1966.

Figure 4. Rules of the League. Adapted from the *Drogheda Independent*, 30 April 1966. Conditions of the league. Adapted from the *Drogheda Independent*, 21 May 1966.

Telstar as part of their name. The Telstar Beauties along with the other company teams trained for their matches in the loft of an old barn. One of the players remembers that whenever they hit the ball hard it would rise all the dust from the cereals that was stored there. They only got involved in the competitions because the men's teams were going as it would it would have been difficult to find transport and they wouldn't have had the support of their management when preparing for matches.[59] This demonstrates how sport acted as a tool to cross the gender divide that was common in most workplaces at the time.[60]

The names of the teams that competed in the Abbey Ballroom Indoor Football Leagues reflect the popular culture of the time. Many of the teams took their names from chart music and popular TV programmes or movies, current affairs, their workplace, local sporting teams and even some of the big soccer teams from the UK leagues.

In the men's league Interview A recalls that their team:

> Had the longest name [in both divisions], The Dedicated Followers of Football. The name was picked after a Kinks' song title, The Dedicated Followers of Fashion …, the Kinks themselves were playing in the Abbey Ballroom.[61]

Show bands were a popular inspiration for women's teams such as the Miami Five, the Drifters and Casino Ladies. Some were named after popular films or TV shows of the time such as Thunderbirds, Batgirls as well as Girls from Uncle in the women's leagues and Men from Auntie in the men's league.

Some teams took their names from current affairs for instance the Sputniks and the Busby Babes. While other teams took their names from their workplaces for example The Independents after the Drogheda Independent, Carrollettes after the Carroll's Cigarette Factory in Dundalk and the Symco Ladies from Balbriggan.

Some of the names were very imaginative and added to the fun of the leagues.[62] The variety of names reflects the influence British and American the popular culture had on young people and that the league was very much a social experience as well as a sporting one.[63]

As you can see from Figure 2 teams came from all over the north eastern part of Ireland to compete in the leagues at the Abbey Ballroom. Teams for the women's leagues came from counties Louth, Meath and Dublin. Figure 5 breaks down how many teams from these counties competed in the leagues and what towns they came from. According to the fixture lists in the *Drogheda Independent*, all of the women's teams who competed in the first league came from county Louth, while teams from other parts of the north-east joined later competitions.

Unsurprisingly, the majority of the teams came from Drogheda, with Dundalk second. What is surprising is that of the twenty-five teams from Dundalk who entered the first competition, only three entered the second and only one entered the third competition. Until further research is done on women's soccer in Dundalk during this time period we can only speculate as to the reasons why the numbers dropped so dramatically. One possibility could be that it was difficult for the teams to travel to Drogheda as public transport wasn't running late at night and not many people had cars making competing in local competitions more preferable. During this time period there were regular indoor football competitions running in Dundalk at the Adelphi, during the May Time Festival and at the ballroom in Blackrock as a result the women preferred to focus on these competitions. Another possible reason for the decline is that the Casuals were so tough to beat that the other teams didn't want to compete against them. In the final of the second competition, Interview G recalls that the Casuals were tough 'the reputation came before them and we were kind of afraid of them, I'll put it like that'.[64] The reasons outlined may account for the sudden decline in women's teams from Dundalk.

There were big rivalries between different teams based on a range of factors. The predominant rivalry was between different factories. There was a lot of pride at stake when representing the workplace. Everyone wanted to beat their friends who worked at other factories. Other rivalries were based on geographic location and

Numbers of women's teams that participated

The Casino Showband Trophy Competition May – July 1966 Women's Team Numbers	
Location	**Number of Teams Registered**
Drogheda	42
Dundalk	25
Dunleer	3
Ardee	1
Total*	71

The Sinalco Indoor Football Competition September – January 1966/67 Women's Team Numbers	
Location	**Number of Teams Registered**
Drogheda	30
Dundalk	3
Balbriggan	3
Ashbourne	3
Dunleer	1
Ardee	1
Total**	41

Figure 5. Numbers of women's teams that participated, a breakdown of how many women's teams competed in each competition played at the Abbey Ballroom.

skill and/or physical strength. The players can still remember the teams that they got the most bruises off. In the men's leagues the Seasiders from Clogherhead were the 'tough outfit' to beat, while the women's teams from Dundalk always the strongest.[65] The Casuals were the team that stand out the most when talking to any of the female players as they were 'much stronger than any of us were now, you know. So if you bumped against them ... you could have been knocked out'.[66]

Attitudes towards female players

The men interviewed in this project were delighted to see women get involved in playing indoor football. It was a novelty to see women playing football as this was the first time they were involved in any form of football. In the 1950s there was a big divide between Dubliners who were commonly referred to as 'Jackeens' and country people who were referred to as 'Culchies'.[67] Interview A recalls that there was still a big urban/rural divide in the mid sixties

The Evening Herald Trophy Competition January – June 1967 Women's Team Numbers	
Location	Number of Teams Registered
Drogheda	24
Dundalk	1
Balbriggan	7
Ashbourne	2
Dunleer	1
Ardee	2
Ardcath	2
Ratoath	1
Tara***	1
Dublin	1
Unknown****	1
Total*****	43

*Some inconsistencies with the spelling of team names. Some names appeared with and without 'The' these teams were only counted once.

** There were a few dates when the ladies matches were not listed. Teams not listed on other dates may have competed but it is unlikely. Some inconsistencies with the spelling of team names. Some names appeared with and without 'The' these teams were only counted once

***The team Telstar Chimes is listed as being from Tara on one date and from Ashbourne for the other dates listed. This team was from the business that the other Telstar teams came from in Ashbourne but it is possible that there home address was Tara.

****For one fixture there is a team listed as 'Unknown' it is not clear if a team previously listed played in this match or if it was a new team as they were only listed once with no affiliation. However, there was a team of this name registered in a Dundalk competition.

*****Not all fixture lists were published in the Drogheda Independent. From the 5th of May to the 16th of June the fixtures were posted in the ballroom ticket office window. Some inconsistencies with the spelling of team names. Some names appeared with and without 'The' these teams were only counted once.

Figure 5. (*Continued*)

> There were a few ladies' teams from out the country and eh … there would have been a bit of a banter going on like … the usual insults like where's the cow dung and all this kind of stuff … but in general it was all taken as good fun.[68]

Nevertheless, on the Late Lunch with Gerry Kelly the men interviewed didn't say many positive things about the women's leagues. One interviewee mentioned that some of the men had a great style of play while 'the ladies were interested in the other type of style and there were competitions for who was the best dressed'. Nevertheless, they did recall that the Casuals from Dundalk were 'exceptional … compared to them the other girls didn't have a clue' and that the Casuals were 'so well trained, they passed the ball around so well, they were really really top class'.[69] In response to these remarks interview G stated:

> Well we just didn't go for the style or anything, like we went to play a game of football even though we didn't know an awful lot about it but we knew a certain amount of it, we wouldn't have gone in there and have been totally green. We would've know

anyone who would have seen us play would have known that we knew at least a little bit about it, that we weren't just there for a fashion parade.[70]

Although, some of the teams might not have had 'a clue' as it was the first time that women were involved in organized soccer in Drogheda, the vast majority of teams were serious about it and were out to win (Appendix 1).

Other indoor football leagues

Indoor football was a popular form of entertainment in ballrooms all over the north-east. The entertainment pages of the *Drogheda Independent* from the mid to late sixties were full of adverts for indoor football in places like Blackrock, Dundalk and Navan. There is anecdotal evidence that the first place to start indoor football in the north-east was the Adelphi Ballroom in Dundalk, which started in 1965. This is one full year before indoor football started at the Abbey Ballroom.[71] However, at the beginning of May 1966 was the first time it was introduced to the May Time Festival in Dundalk.[72] This competition was played in the Adelphi Ballroom and sponsored by local brewery Harp, it was called the Harp Lager £350 Indoor Football Competition.[73] If the prize was £350 it is not clear if this was the prize for both the men's and the women's competitions or if it was split between the teams and if so how the money was split. A report on the final in the *Festival Flash* indicates that this was 'the first Indoor Football competition in Ireland', if this is the case then it would disprove the anecdotal claims that indoor football at the Adelphi started in 1965.[74] Nevertheless, this competition did start slightly earlier than the Abbey Ballroom competition giving the Dundalk-based teams a small advantage over the Drogheda-based teams. A write up in the *Festival Flash* in 1967 highlighted how popular indoor football was around Ireland as 'over 2000 copies of the rules have been forwarded by the Indoor Football Association to various organizations'. It is not clear from this report where the Indoor Football Association is based but it does go on to say that:

> Followers of all codes [of football] participate, and may we hope that this will bring closer the day when the barrier, which unfortunately exists between the G.A.A. and other codes is broken down. This in itself would be a major achievement for Dundalk.[75]

This final comment indicates that the newly founded Association was possibly based in Dundalk but this would require further research. The fact that there were participants in the men's leagues that played GAA shows that indoor football was still considered entertainment rather than sport which was something the newly founded association was trying to change. The 1968 May Time Festival indoor football Competition was called the 'Harp Lager All Ireland Indoor Football Championship'.[76] We know that sixteen women's teams entered this competition but it is not clear if there were any teams from other parts of Ireland registered.[77] It is still unknown when these indoor football competitions finished but we know that they were running in the late eighties in the Dundalk area.[78] The *Drogheda Independent* and the *Festival Flash* contained a wealth of information relating to indoor football, thus other local publications could have similar information about other indoor football competitions that ran in their locality.

Outdoor football

It is not clear if indoor football predated women's outdoor football in the sixties or if they started at the same time as there is evidence of a Dundalk team competing against a Waterford side in 1968.[79] However, in the Drogheda area indoor football at the Abbey Ballroom was the first time there was any evidence of organized women's soccer. When the competitions finished up the women involved formed outdoor teams either through friends or their workplaces.

In the later part of the sixties Interview I, who was a youth club leader at a local boy's club, quickly got fed up of the teams from the club not showing up for competitions he was organizing on their behalf. This corresponds with Holohan's finding that youth clubs were in decline in the late sixties as they couldn't compete 'against the excitement of dance halls and rock 'n'roll".[80] However, this worked to the advantage of some girls who hung around the club as he started to coach them and set-up a women's football team called Lourdes Girls to compete in outdoor and indoor competitions. Interview C was also part of this team as they were set-up after indoor football finished at the Abbey Ballroom. They primarily competed against other teams in the town based at factories and even competed for a short while in the Dublin League and played in a friendly match against some teams in Waterford.[81]

Further research is needed to see what influence the decline of the traditional youth club in the sixties had on the development of women's sports. For example, how many club leaders started to coach women's sports teams like Interview I did? From July 1968 women's GAA was established in the area and proved to be very popular as match reviews and photos appeared in the *Drogheda Independent* from that date on.[82] Later that year a women's Ways and Means Committee of Drogheda FC was formed and much to the surprise of the reporter 'twenty-seven ladies – only six of whom are single – were elected on the committee'.[83] Being involved in the Abbey Ballroom Indoor Football league and the activeness of social clubs in the workplace during the sixties had a big impact in developing not only women's sport in Drogheda but also their involvement in other activities outside the home regardless of their marital status.[84] This fed into the social movements and second wave feminist movement that developed in Ireland from the 1970s onwards, which started to see small gains for women's rights in the home and the workplace.[85]

Conclusion

As outlined above there are still major gaps in the documentation of women's football in the Republic of Ireland. In recent years, there has been a more in-depth exploration of the relationship between the work place and sport in Ireland but this research predominately focuses on men's sport. Toms has noted that 'it was rare in the in the hundreds of column inches about soccer in the pages of the Evening Echo, and all of the other provincial newspapers' to report anything related to women's involvement in the sport in the Munster region.[86] Although Toms research focused on the period 1877–1937, there is still very little coverage given to women's soccer in newspapers. As newspaper archives form the basis of most sports history research it is imperative that the gender imbalance in coverage is rectified by documenting women's involvement in soccer through oral history interviews and other research strategies while it is still within living memory. The strategies I used to document the Abbey Ballroom Indoor Football League could easily be applied to any of the other urban areas in Ireland and should yield similar results. The sixties is still within our living history and unless immediate action is taken at a national level to document this period of women's soccer history, it could be lost forever.

Acknowledgements

I would like to thank everyone who supported this project, especially the following people: Julie O'Connor and Arlene Crilly for proof reading this paper. All the volunteers at Drogheda Local Voices that supported this project, Eamon Thornton, Sean Corcoran, Liz King and Anthony McIntyre as well as all the staff at Drogheda Museum Millmount who helped with conducting the interviews and hosting the exhibition in summer 2015. I would also like to thank the UCD SILS Capstone team along with our supervisor Dr Lai Ma that worked to put together the Abbey Ballroom Indoor Football: An Oral History Exhibition in summer 2015. The team members were Andrea Bellomonte, Julie O'Connor, Michael O'Sullivan, Eimear Gaffney and JinShuttleworth. As well as the local media that helped promote this project, the Drogheda Independent, the Drogheda Leader and Gerry Kelly Late Lunch on LMFM. I would also like to thank all my friends and family especially my mother for their support during this project as well as David Toms and Carole Holohan for their advice while writing this paper. Most importantly I would like to thank all the interviewees, without them this project would have been very difficult to research. This project probably would have never happened if it wasn't for Veronica Gallagher, if she hadn't added her team photo with her bio in the local history book *The Marsh Road Scotch Hall Story* I might never had known about the existence of the women's indoor football leagues. I would also like to thank the people on the Drogheda Down Memory Lane and Dundalk North End Facebook groups who helped me source information, especially Charley McCarthy in Dundalk.

Disclosure statement

No potential conflict of interest was reported by the author.

Notes

1. Interview G, March 2015.
2. Hayes and Urquhart, *Irish Women's History Reader*, 1.
3. Bourke, *Women's Football in the Republic of Ireland*, 162.
4. Ferriter, *The Transformation of Ireland*, 2.
5. Ferriter, *The Transformation of Ireland*, 536.
6. Holohan, *Challenges to Social Order and Irish Identity?* 390.
7. Ferriter, *The Transformation of Ireland*, 536; and Holohan, *Challenges to Social Order and Irish Identity?* 390.
8. Hill, *Women in Ireland*, 140; and Holohan, *Challenges to Social Order and Irish Identity?* 390.
9. Hunt, 'Constitutionally, Women are Still Breeding Machines', *Sunday Independent*, May 24, 2015, http://www.independent.ie/opinion/columnists/carol-hunt/constitutionally-women-are-still-breeding-machines-31248545.html (accessed April 13, 2016).
10. Williams, *A Beautiful Game*, 127.
11. Hill, *Women in Ireland*, 7.
12. Rouse, *Sport and Ireland*, 160.
13. Williams, *A Beautiful Game*, 186.
14. FIFA.com, *Roche Recaps Rollercoaster Year*. FIFA, http://www.fifa.com/ballon-dor/news/y=2015/m=10/news=roche-recaps-rollercoaster-ride-2710653.html (accessed January 18, 2016).Topping, 'Forget Van Persie or Costa – Stephanie Roche Shoots for World's Best Goal'. *The Guardian*, http://www.theguardian.com/football/2014/nov/17/stephanie-roche-peamount-united-goal-2014-puskas-award-fifa (accessed January 18, 2016).
15. FIFA.com, *Roche Recaps Rollercoaster Year* (accessed January 18, 2016).
16. Bourke, *Women's Football in the Republic of Ireland*, 163.

17. Williams, *A Beautiful Game*, 112.
18. Caudwell, *Gender, Feminism and Football Studies*, 333.
19. Bourke, *Women's Football in the Republic of Ireland*; and Liston, *Women's Soccer in the Republic of Ireland*.
20. Hill, *Women in Ireland*, 140; Ferriter, *The Transformation of Ireland*, 536; Holohan, *Challenges to Social Order and Irish Identity?* 390; and Rouse, *Sport & Ireland*, 296.
21. Byrne, *The Abbey Ballroom Indoor Football League 1966–67*, 111.
22. Byrne, *Sport or Entertainment?* Sports History Ireland – Conference, September 20, 2014.
23. Interview A, July 2012.
24. Kiely and Leane, *Irish Women at Work 1930–1960*, 136.
25. Williams, *A Beautiful Game*, 14.
26. Liston, *Women's Soccer in the Republic of Ireland*, 375.
27. Sangster, *The Softball Solution: Female Workers, Male Managers and the Operation of Paternalism at Westclox, 1923–60*, 168.
28. Grounded Theory Online, *What is Grounded Theory?* http://www.groundedtheoryonline.com/what-is-grounded-theory/ (accessed April 13, 2016).
29. Sangster, *The Softball Solution: Female Workers, Male Managers and the Operation of Paternalism at Westclox, 1923–60*.
30. Kiely and Leane, *Irish Women at Work 1930–1960*, 140.
31. *Drogheda Independent*, July 5, 1968.
32. Interview F, February 2015 & Interview H, April 2015.
33. Holohan, *Opportunities and Aspirations: Irish Youth in the Sixties.* Ireland Since 1966: New Perspectives – Conference, November 4, 2010.
34. Ward, *Manpower in a developing community*, 15.6.
35. Kiely and Leane, *Irish Women At Work 1930–1960*, 136, 140.
36. Late Lunch with Gerry Kelly, September 2014.
37. Interview A, B, C, D, E, F, G and Project launch.
38. Personal communication.
39. Interview A, July 2012.
40. Indoor Football in Drogheda, *Drogheda Independent*, April 30, 1966.
41. Late Lunch with Gerry Kelly, September 2014.
42. Interview F, February 2015.
43. Interview C, July 2012.
44. Interview A, B, C, D, E, F, G and Project launch.
45. Interview G, March 2015.
46. The Casino Show band Trophy Competition, *Drogheda Independent*, June 4 1966; Sinalco Indoor Football Competition, *Drogheda Independent*, September 17, 1966; and Evening Herald Trophy Competition, *Drogheda Independent*, March 3, 1967.
47. Interview A, B, C, D, E, F, G and Project launch.
48. Toms, *Brightest couple of hours*, 143.
49. Interview G, March 2015 and personal communication, July 2012.
50. RTE Archives, http://www.rte.ie/archives/2013/1120/487850-changing-roles-of-women1968/ (accessed November 20, 2015).
51. Interview B, C and G.
52. Cullinane, *As if You Were Something Under Their Shoe*, 188.
53. Sangster, *The Softball Solution: Female Workers, Male Managers and the Operation of Paternalism at Westclox, 1923–60*.
54. Interview G, March 2015.
55. Interview A, July 2012.
56. Interview B, July 2012.
57. Interview D, July 2012.
58. Interview G, March 2015.
59. Project Launch, September 2014.
60. Kiely and Leane, *Irish Women at Work 1930–1960*, 146.
61. Interview A, July 2012.
62. Millmount Museum, *The Abbey Ballroom Indoor Football: An Oral History Exhibition* (Panel 3, July–September 2015).

63. Holohan, *Challenges to Social Order and Irish Identity?* 393.
64. Interview G, March 2015.
65. The Late Lunch with Gerry Kelly, September 2014.
66. Interview G, March 2015.
67. Garvin, *News from a new Republic*, 6.
68. Interview A, July 2012.
69. The Late Lunch with Gerry Kelly, September 2014.
70. Interview G, March 2015.
71. *Drogheda Independent*, May 9, 1966.
72. Football – New Style, Dundalk Round Table *Festival Flash*, May 17, 1966.
73. Ladies Indoor Football, Dundalk Round Table *Festival Flash*, May 17, 1966.
74. Bank and Janes Win Out, Dundalk Round Table *Festival Flash*, May 19, 1966.
75. Indoor Football One Year Old, Dundalk Round Table *Festival Flash*, May 20, 1967.
76. Indoor Football, Dundalk Round Table *Festival Flash*, May 18, 1968.
77. Indoor Football, Dundalk Round Table *Festival Flash*, May 20, 1968.
78. Interview J, November 2015.
79. *Dundalk Democrat*, August, 1968.
80. Holohan, *A Powerful Antidote?* 193.
81. Interview I, November, 2015.
82. *Drogheda Independent*, July 5, 1968.
83. *Drogheda Independent*, November 8, 1968.
84. Interview C, July 2012; and Interview G, March 2015.
85. Kiely and Leane, *Irish Women at Work 1930–1960*, 146.
86. Toms, *Soccer in Munster*, 145.
87. Drogheda Presentation, *Drogheda Independent*, April 30, 1966.
88. *Drogheda Independent*, January 13 1967.
89. *Drogheda Independent*, April 14 and 21, 1967.
90. *Drogheda Independent*, May 5–June 16, 1967.
91. *Drogheda Independent*, June 23, 1967.
92. Byrne, *The Abbey Ballroom Indoor Football League 1966–67*, 112–4.
93. Millmount Museum, *The Abbey Ballroom Indoor Football: An Oral History Exhibition* (Panel 9, July–September 2015).
94. The Abbey Ballroom fire was the end of an era, *Drogheda Independent*, May 20, 2005.

References

Alan, Hayes, and Diane Urquhart. *The Irish Women's History Reader*, New York: Routledge, 2000.

Bourke, Ann. 'Women's Football in the Republic of Ireland: Past Events and Future Prospects'. *Soccer & Society* 4, no. 2 (2003): 162–81.

Byrne, Helena. 'The Abbey Ballroom Indoor Football League 1966–67. First Women's Football?'. *Journal of the Old Drogheda Society*, no. 21 (2014): 111–8.

Byrne, Helena. 'Sport or Entertainment? The Abbey Ballroom Indoor Football League 1966–1968'. Presentation, Tenth Annual Conference of Sports History Ireland, Dublin, September 20, 2014.

Caudwell, Jayne. 'Gender, Feminism and Football Studies'. *Soccer & Society* 12, no. 3 (2011): 330–44.

Cullinane, Liam. '"As If You Were Something under Their Shoe": Class, Gender and Status among Cork Textile Workers, 1930–1970'. In *Locked Out: A Century of Irish Working-Class Life*, ed. David Convery, 175–91. Dublin: Irish Academic Press, 2013.

Ferriter, Diarmaid. *The Transformation of Ireland, 1900–2000*. London: Profile, 2004.

Garvin, Tom. *News from a New Republic: Ireland in the 1950's*. Kobo ed. Dublin: Gill & Macmillan, 2010.

Hill, Myrtle. *Women in Ireland. A Century of Change*. Belfast: Blackstaff Press, 2003.

Holohan, Carole. 'Challenges to Social Order and Irish Identity? Youth Culture in the Sixties'. *Irish Historical Studies* XXXVIII, no. 151 (2013): 389–405.

Holohan, Carole. 'A Powerful Antidote? Catholic Youth Clubs in the Sixties'. In *Adolescence in Modern Irish History* edited by Catherine Cox and Susannah Riordan, 176–98. Basingstoke: Palgrave Macmillan, 2015.

Joan, Sangster. 'The Softball Solution: Female Workers, Male Managers and the Operation of Paternalism at Westclox, 1923–60'. *Labour/Le Travail* 32, no. 32 (1993): 167–99.

Kiely, Elizabeth, and Máire Leane. *Irish Women at Work, 1930–1960: An Oral History.* Dublin: Irish Academic Press, 2012.

Liston, Katie. 'Women's Soccer in the Republic of Ireland: Some Preliminary Sociological Comments'. *Soccer & Society* 7, no. 2 (2006): 364–84.

Toms, David. *Soccer in Munster: A social history 1877–1937*. Cork: Cork University Press, 2015.

Toms, David. '"The Brightest Couple of Hours": The Factory, Inter-House, Inter-Firm and Pubs Leagues of Ireland, 1922–73'. In *Locked Out: A Century of Irish Working-Class Life*, ed. David Convery, 141–55. Dublin: Irish Academic Press, 2013.

Ward, Conor K. *Manpower in a Developing Community: A Pilot Survey in Drogheda by the Department of Social Science, University College Dublin*. Dublin: AnRoinnSaothair, 1967.

Williams, Jean. *A Beautiful Game: International Perspectives on Women's Football*. New York: Berg, 2007.

Appendix 1. A summary of all competitions held at the Abbey Ballroom from 1966 to 1967.

The first competition was sponsored by the Casino Show Band which ran from May to July 1966, they also formed a team and played a few matches in the competition. There was no write up in the *Drogheda Independent* about the finals of this league. However, there was a photo of the winning men's team being presented with the trophy but the caption didn't mention the winners of the women's competition.[87] It is assumed that the winning women's team was from Dundalk as all the other women's titles were won by Dundalk-based teams.

The second competition was sponsored by the soft drink Sinalco, the competition ran from September 1966 to January 1967. The winners of both the men's and women's competition won gold watches while the runners up received transistor radios. There was a big write up in the *Drogheda Independent* at the end of the competition which also featured photos of both the winning teams being presented with their prizes. The women's title was won by the Casuals from Dundalk who bet Bluesville from Drogheda in the final.[88]

The third competition was sponsored by the *Evening Herald*; it ran from March to May 1967. The winners of this competition are unknown as the last fixture list appeared in the paper appeared on 14th April 1967. During the subsequent weeks there was a notice in amongst the listings for the dances that stated 'Knockout continued – see show window for fixtures'. We do know that the finals took place in the first week of May.[89] The Evening Herald sporadically published the results of the matches in its paper but any reports on the finals if published have yet to be found.

The final competition that appeared in any newspaper ran from May to June 1967. There were no fixture lists printed in the *Drogheda Independent*, but there was a notice for indoor football amongst the dance listings which stated 'see our show window for fixtures'.[90] The finals took place at the start of June as the presentation dance was on the 16th of June. There was a big write up on the finals which appeared in the *Drogheda Independent* the following week. The Sputniks from Dundalk bet the Everglades who were from Drogheda 3–0 in the final. The prizes for this competition were gold watches for the winners while the runners up received cups. This report also mentioned that the ballroom manager, Ben Gordon announced that indoor football would take a break and start up again in the autumn.[91] However, this is the last reference to indoor football in Drogheda in the *Drogheda Independent*. It was originally thought that this was because the leagues were so popular that the ballroom didn't need to advertise it in the newspaper but after reviewing the interviews with former participants this was probably the last competition at the Abbey Ballroom.[92]

No definitive date for the end of the Abbey Ballroom Indoor Football has been established. The evidence suggests that the league ended in 1967 because of the damage caused to the Ballroom's chandeliers and fittings.

Someone asked me onetime, why did it not go on? But I mean there was probably damage being done in the bloody place every night there was a ball kicked. I mean there were chandeliers in the place, there were lights ... there was probably a certain amount of damage done to the ballroom that they decided that it wasn't worth it. Because this wasn't your average barn ... this was a beautiful ballroom.[93]

On the 29th of February 1969, the Abbey Ballroom burnt down as a result of a fire that started in the cinema.[94] Thus, any records of the league that might have survived in an archive are difficult to find now if they even survived when the Abbey Ballroom was redeveloped into a shopping centre.

The development of schoolboy coaching structures for association football in Ireland, 1945–1995

Conor Curran

This article offers a comparison in progress in developing coaching structures for schoolboys' soccer in Ireland in the period from the end of the Second World War until 1995. It will be shown that in Northern Ireland, the Belfast-based Irish Football Association's implementation of coaching courses was at a more advanced level in the decades immediately following the war, while the Dublin-centred Football Association of Ireland was hindered by a lack of facilities and funds for most of the twentieth century. In Northern Ireland, links between soccer organizers and governing bodies for physical recreation were stronger, and the IFA had begun to develop a coherent structure for the qualification of coaches by the early 1950s. This contrasted greatly to the structures put in place by the FAI and it was not until the Jack Charlton era (1986–1995) that they were able to implement a more comprehensive nationwide system.

Introduction

2016 sees the Republic and Northern Ireland both taking part in the finals of a major tournament for the first time. Despite this, soccer in Ireland still awaits an academic publication dedicated to the game's overall development north and south of the border. It is unsurprising then that the historiography of association football in Ireland lacks an analysis of how coaching structures for schoolboys were implemented. A clearer picture of how the game developed at a regional level has only begun to be formed. Initial studies of the game's development by Malcolm Brodie have focused largely on its growth in Belfast, while Neal Garnham's major publication gives little attention to how enthusiasts of the game were actually tutored in its required skills.[1] More recent work by Hunt, Curran and Toms has focused more on the game's regional dimensions but the growth of coaching structures throughout Ireland has not yet been examined in any great detail.[2]

Although Irish professional clubs had used trainers since the late nineteenth century, opportunities for young players to receive coaching at schoolboy level appear to have taken longer to develop.[3] Peter Doherty, who managed Northern Ireland at the 1958 World Cup finals in Sweden, stated in 1946 that 'Ireland is not like England where there are coaches for the schools and colleges, the period when a young footballer is made.'[4] As Matthew Taylor has noted, the English Football Association had focused mainly on coaching schoolboys in the 1930s but after 1945 began to extend its courses to managers and professional footballers.[5] However, English attitudes towards coaching courses for managers and coaches were slow to evolve in comparison with those in continental Europe.[6] Developments in Ireland were slower than in England and both the Irish Football Association (IFA) and Football Association of Ireland (FAI) at times relied on the FA for assistance. Developing structures was not a straightforward process with the level of finance needed, and the difficulties in getting educational authorities on board. This article offers a comparison between strategies for developing coaching structures for soccer in Ireland in the period from the end of the Second World War until 1995. While professionalism was officially legalized by the IFA in 1894,[7] coaching of the game was much slower to be developed. It will be shown that in Northern Ireland, the Belfast-based IFA's implementation of coaching courses was at a more advanced level in the decades immediately following the Second World War, with the Dublin-centred FAI hindered by a lack of facilities and funds for most of the twentieth century. In Northern Ireland, links between soccer organizers and governing bodies for physical recreation were stronger, and the IFA had begun to develop a coherent structure for the qualification of coaches by the early 1950s. Similarly, they had begun to put coaching structures in place for schoolboy players at that time, while youth internationals were also offered the chance to learn the game from formally qualified men. This contrasted to the structures put in place by the FAI, with the implementation of the position of national coach by the Dublin organization lasting only briefly in the 1950s. It was not until a national commission into the state of association football in the Republic was launched in the early 1970s that a new national coach was appointed, but work was hindered by funding problems. With the success of the Jack Charlton era (1986–1995), the FAI were finally able to put in place a nationwide system for the development of the game at grassroots and schoolboy level as interest in the game and sponsorship opportunities improved with its increased acceptance throughout the Republic of Ireland.

Early post-war coaching in Northern Ireland

The IFA, although rejecting a proposal by Peter Doherty in 1945 for a coaching scheme to be set up throughout the country because of the expense involved, enjoyed greater co-operation than the FAI with governmental and educational authorities in the decades immediately following the Second World War.[8] The IFA had their own structured plan in place by the early 1950s for the training of adults to become coaches and for the coaching of young players, having clarified their position on the coaching of underage players in 1948. Their Youth International Committee, at a meeting in July of that year, considered a coaching scheme essential for boys of fourteen to sixteen years and also for youths of sixteen to eighteen years.'[9] They decided to 'advertise for a number of old players to act as coaches' and to ask Stanley Rous of the FA 'to nominate a suitable lecturer' for their coaching courses. It appears he chose Walter Winterbottom who conducted a course at Grosvenor Park, the home of Distillery FC, that year.[10]

This meant that prior to their establishment of a coaching committee in 1950, coaching classes had been held under their Youth International committee in a number of areas, with potential coaches and international youth team players receiving instruction from Winterbottom and RP Fulton, respectively.[11] Fulton appears to have been the only locally based FA-qualified coach the IFA had available at this point and was 'highly recommended' by Winterbottom, who was England manager from 1946 until 1962 and FA Director of Coaching.[12] Some clubs including Linfield and

Derry City had also held coaching classes for youths.[13] By June 1949, a plan for developing the IFA's coaching structure had been drawn up by ETF Spence, the Technical Representative of the Central Council for Physical Recreation, which aimed 'to improve the physical and mental health of the community through physical recreation.' This organization had been set up in 1936 under the patronage of the King and Queen of England and was extended to Northern Ireland in May 1949.[14] In particular, Spence recommended that 'a panel of coaches' be established to give instruction in the basic skills of the game. There were five steps which he felt would benefit overall development, with the appointment of local coaching sub-committees to oversee events in their respective districts recommended. He also encouraged 'propaganda events' to be organized with films and demonstrations deemed necessary while the recruiting of potential coaches, through these local sub-committees in conjunction with the CCPR, was also advised. The IFA was also instructed to put in place a coaching award which would be gained through an examination in local and central venues. Finally, it was felt that the work of the coaches would have to be carefully organized, with the CCPR to act as agents and advisors for the national governing body.[15] The IFA seem to have stuck closely to Spence's plan.

Fulton continued his coaching work under the IFA's new coaching committee, with a coaching course taking place over eight weeks from April to June 1950, with the fifteen participants receiving 'the routine training of every first class coach' with the help of the Distillery and Cliftonville clubs.[16] Gradually, coaching spread to more outlying areas. In October, a coaching course for boys was started in Portadown with the help of the County Armagh Education Committee, the Portadown Technical School Management Committee and the Central Council of Physical Education. Grading of coaches was categorized into two awards by the beginning of 1951, while by April coaching for boys had taken place in Ballymena, Lurgan and Portadown.[17]

Later that year, the IFA added prestige to the qualification by agreeing that a certificate and badge would be given to those who had passed the required exams. Over 100 schoolboys took part in 'open air' coaching in Belfast in the summer of 1951 at three venues, while by the spring of the following year a coaching course for youth leaders had been organized by the Federation of Boys' Clubs in the capital.[18] At this point, the majority of coaching courses appear to have been held in the east of the province, with CCPR-backed courses also taking place in Portrush during the summer months in the early 1950s, although by 1953 international youth trial players from the north-west were also said to be receiving IFA coaching.[19]

The difficulty in implementing Association football in Grammar Schools

Those initially organizing coaching in Northern Ireland had an advantage over their counterparts in the Republic, in that they could attract support from government-sponsored bodies. But difficulties were evident within schools. The IFA's coaching committee were 'co-operating with various local education authorities' by October of 1950.[20] However, implementing the game in grammar schools was awkward, and association football struggled to gain a foothold in many of Ireland's public schools and colleges, with rugby particularly popular in those in Ulster.[21] Educational opportunities at secondary school level were somewhat better north of the border in the decades after the Second World War. Free education had been available in Northern Ireland since 1947, through an Education Act, which was part of wider reforms implemented by the newly elected Labour government at Westminster. This established 'compulsory education for all up to fifteen years' while selection for places in grammar schools, based on the eleven-plus examination, was also introduced.[22] Prior to the Second World War, there were almost 14,000 students attending 66 grammar schools in Northern Ireland, and by 1956 nearly 200,000 additional pupils were enrolled in 'the new tripartite network of intermediate schools.'[23] Despite this, schools in Northern Ireland remained divided on a religious basis for a number of decades afterwards with Jonathan Bardon stating that 'the full social and political impact of educational advance was not felt until the mid-1960s' and 'educational reform had a modernising effect in Northern Ireland only within the limits of a strictly segregated system.'[24]

In the immediate post-war years, as Bardon states, 'the traditional grammar schools successfully resisted direct control and preserved their identity largely intact.'[25] Gaining recognition for soccer in grammar schools was difficult in Northern Ireland, with a government-backed investigation into the attitudes of 44 grammar schools in 1954 revealing that there was much resistance to the idea of implementing soccer.[26] Nineteen replies were received from headmasters and four schools were said to have agreed that 'association football should be allowed the same freedom as the other traditional games', although they did not all play soccer. 'About an equal number' expressed sympathy for the idea but felt that they could not provide the facilities needed for the game. Several of the remainder were said to be 'directly opposed to the suggestion', while others were 'unable or unwilling to consider the introduction of the game.' These schools put forward a number of 'chief difficulties' they felt they had in implementing it, including the view that they could not run two games at the same time, and that neither would succeed if both were played. Playing fields were also said to be lacking, while a scarcity of masters 'capable of supervising, refereeing and coaching association football games' was noted. It was also felt that these men had enough to do without having to take on more work, particularly in smaller grammar schools.[27]

Additionally, some schools felt that with their strong rugby ethos, change would be opposed by 'parents and old boys brought up in that tradition.' Views were also expressed that rugby was a better game for schoolmasters as it gave 'opportunities for star performers' and depended 'much more on the spirit of the team as a whole.' The point about it being easier to arrange fixtures against schools of the same type was made while some schools were opposed to 'soccer's commercialisation and professionalism.' In some cases, it was felt that there were not enough boys in the sixteen–eighteen age group interested in games to justify playing another code. Travelling costs were also said to be a consideration while a number felt 'that the Irish Football Association has not helped its case for association football by the remarks of some of its members, as published in the press, about grammar schools and headmasters.'[28] As Garnham has stated regarding the development of earlier structures for sport within schools in Ulster, the decision of Belfast's elite schools to stick to rugby over soccer 'probably reflected a certain sporting snobbery.'[29] As Sugden and Bairner have noted, from the early 1870s onwards, 'schools rugby has been an important feature of Ulster's social as well as sporting life' and therefore an accommodation of other sports was going to be difficult.[30]

Despite this opposition, the IFA remained steadfast in their efforts to promote soccer amongst schoolboys and to develop coaching structures. By 1954, the annual summer school, again held in conjunction with the CCPR, was staged in

Stranmillis Training College, Belfast, illustrating a shift away from Portrush and a move into a more centrally located educational institution.[31] A schoolboys' course was organized during the Easter holidays with 50 selected players participating in the three-day event, which was the first run in conjunction with the Irish Schools' FA, although the schools' football body did not gain affiliation to the IFA until 1980.[32] In 1955, there was increased involvement with local schools' associations with courses held in Derry, Larne and Carrickfergus, while coaching for schoolboys in Coleraine was also provided in 1956, along with that for a selection of boys from the under-eighteen section of the minor league.[33] Some individual schools, such as Whiteabbey Primary School in 1958, also contacted the IFA about organizing coaching courses, and they generally appear to have facilitated these requests. In December of that year, Gilbert McKenzie, a Grade I IFA coach, was appointed by the Minister of Education and the Belfast Education Committee to assist teachers in various Belfast schools with their coaching.[34]

Further developments

In 1957, the IFA began using films and lectures more frequently under the guidance of their coaching committee chairman, Harry Cavan, with these being held in Belfast, Newry, Ballyclare, Downpatrick, Derry and Armagh with over 1000 boys in attendance. These events were also held in Rathfriland, Newtownards, Enniskillen and Ballymena the following year as they branched out further into the province.[35] A residential course, in conjunction with the Belfast Education Authority, was organized for 'possible' schoolboy international players at Orangefield Boys Secondary School in Belfast in August 1959. The IFA began to take stronger steps to have soccer played in schools through the organization of coaching classes for school teachers and training college students with a summer course held in Stranmillis that year. A school leavers' course was also organized with assistance of the CCPR.[36] By the early 1960s, the IFA were able to offer a subsidy of £200 to assist the Belfast Education Authority with the course at Orangefield. This appears to have been the norm for this event throughout this decade, illustrating their interest in investing in coaching at this time, and the finance they had available to do this.[37] The Northern Ireland Coaches' Association was established in 1966 with Ted Smyth as chairman, while IFA coach Eric Trevorrow took up the role of secretary.[38]

In 1971, 'realising the necessity and demand for coaching facilities at all levels throughout Northern Ireland', the IFA implemented a coaching scheme to cater for 2000 schoolboys at 50 centres in Northern Ireland.[39] A total of 51 courses for schoolboys, grammar schoolboys, potential youth internationals, regular coaches and Irish League club managers and staff coaches were held. The IFA's part-time coaching advisor, Brian Halliday, supervised the scheme, while FIFA technical adviser/coach Detmar Cramer provided instruction for the Irish League managers and staff.[40] Despite this, problems remained in the west of the country. In July of that year, 14 schoolboys attended the first course for these players in Strabane, County Tyrone, with Halliday of the opinion that 'there is a tremendous amount of untapped footballing talent in the area', while one reporter felt that 'it was a breakthrough in this part of the world.'[41] However, the course was cancelled the following year after only six people applied to participate, with a minimum of twelve necessary.[42] Similarly, coaching structures for those in Enniskillen, County Fermanagh appear to have been slow to develop, with one writer expressing hopes that a course scheduled there for under-fifteens during the 1986 Christmas holidays would be 'only the first of many courses of this nature in the area.'[43]

In April 1975, Roy Millar was appointed full-time coaching development officer on a three-year contract, after the Northern Ireland Sports Council had approved the IFA's move.[44] Millar began to give increased attention to university and teacher training colleges with the IFA introducing a new teacher coaching certificate and a teachers' referee course. There was said to be 1483 participants in the 1975–6 season, with eight preparatory coaching courses, six teacher coaching certificate courses, thirteen schoolboy courses, three youth courses, three grade two-coaching courses, one grade-one coaching course and six referees courses taking place.[45]

By the late twentieth century, soccer schools conducted by Irish internationals were being organized for the summer holidays in more regional areas in both the Republic and Northern Ireland. The Packie Bonner Goalkeeping School was staged initially in West Donegal in 1986, while the Gerry Armstrong Soccer School, a three-day event, was first held in Omagh in 1991.[46] By 1993, the Armstrong coaching event was said to be 'the most popular soccer school in Northern Ireland' with 'top IFA qualified coaches in attendance', along with George Best.[47] In 1994, it was estimated that 400 children would attend, 'making the event the biggest of its kind in Northern Ireland.'[48] IFA soccer schools were also operational in more outlying areas of Fermanagh such as Lisnaskea in the early part of this decade, illustrating how these structures had become a lot more firmly implemented by the eve of the twenty-first century.[49]

Coaching in the Republic of Ireland

Coaching structures within schools in the Republic have been slow to become established. Like in Northern Ireland's grammar schools, instruction in soccer techniques suffered as a result of an emphasis on other codes, with Gaelic games prominent in many secondary level schools for much of the twentieth century. This lack of interest on the part of the Department of Education to promote soccer can be seen as a part of a wider attempt by the new Free State government in the inter-war years 'to establish an Irish Catholic nationalist ethos in terms of cultural production, education and general intellectual atmosphere.'[50] Soccer in the Free State received little support from the government or the Catholic Church after 1922 as it was seen as a foreign game.[51] The FAI had noted difficulties in implementing the game in schools and colleges in 1938 and it was decided to attempt to meet with the Minister of Education about this, but there is little evidence of any great change at the time.[52] In 1945, 'the difficulties confronting these [schoolboy] leagues, in view of official school prejudices' was acknowledged in an FAI annual report, which does not suggest much progress.[53] Gaining interest in coaching amongst schools was difficult in some areas as priority was given to other codes and teachers with an interest in soccer were not always to be found. One reporter stated in December 1952 that despite the monopoly enjoyed by rugby and Gaelic football in the Republic of Ireland's schools, there were 200 schoolboy soccer teams in operation throughout the country. However, he also felt that 'the majority of these are run by a couple of senior enthusiasts, or often by the boys themselves.'[54]

The FAI's attempts to develop coaching structures seem to have increased around the same time as those of the IFA in the post-war years. In 1948, one journalist felt that League of Ireland clubs should look to younger players and 'devise ways and means of providing them with proper coaching and training.'[55] It was felt by another reporter that year that while 'the continental countries' had 'made such rapid strides that they are almost on a level with English and Scottish standards', the FAI had only begun to look at using international coaches. In bringing English international George Hardwick of Middlesbrough to Dublin to instruct local coaches, they were making progress in that regard, but the journalist felt that 'this coaching scheme must be speeded up and enlarged upon and extended to the provincial areas.'[56] The following year saw Republic of Ireland and Manchester United star Jackie Carey conduct a three-day coaching clinic organized by the Galway FA, while in the summer of 1950, the FAI organized a coaching course in Dublin with Scottish international, Ken Chisholm, conducting matters.[57] Coaching films and lectures on developing soccer skills were also initiated around this time.[58] This general interest in the value of coaching culminated in the FAI appointing Scot, Dougald Livingtone, as national coach in 1951.

'The chief of the new Saxon recruiting campaign'

Livingstone identified 'three great needs' that he saw soccer in Ireland as having: improved playing pitches; a higher quality of training facilities with heated dressing rooms; and a better standard of coaching.[59] His efforts did not go unnoticed by the president of the Gaelic Athletic Association, M.V. O'Donoghue, who claimed at the their annual congress in 1953 that Livingstone was in fact 'the chief of the new Saxon recruiting campaign' and had been 'busy enticing young Irish boys by various inducements to become happy little English children, and heirs to the joy of a soccer paradise.'[60] This 'campaign', which included giving lectures and instruction in areas as peripheral as Westport in County Mayo, appears only to have lasted briefly but these comments are indicative of the anti-soccer feeling amongst some sections of Irish society and the abuse its organizers received.[61] By July 1953, Livingstone had left his job, having been appointed as coach to the Belgium FA for a salary of £3000, and was replaced by former Everton and Ireland inside-right, Alex Stevenson.[62] Not all League of Ireland clubs were in favour of the appointment of a national coach as they would have to help 'foot the bill' and this is illustrative of the difficulties in financing this position.[63] The following year, Stevenson resigned from the £600 a year FAI coaching position in order to take up a vacancy as player-coach with St Patrick's Athletic, citing the lack of day-time activity as national coach as a factor in this decision, and the FAI did not reappoint a national coach until the early 1970s.[64]

Despite this, by the middle of the 1950s, coaching of young players was gaining a lot more support at club level, with current and ex-players keen to get involved. Leading Irish schoolboy club Home Farm's eleven teams each had their own coach in 1956 and it was reported that 'these volunteer enthusiasts, former club players, have attended summer courses given by international player Noel Kelly, holder of an FA coaching certificate.'[65] Coaching courses were also organized by the Dublin-based United Churches' League, with examinations taking place for the FA's Coaching Certificate.[66] These catered for 'club coaches, games masters, youth leaders and players' while schoolboy sessions were also organized.[67] By the end of the decade, funding for coaching was still said to be a problem for the FAI with sponsorship from 'private bodies' said to be necessary in the organization of coaching courses.[68]

In 1960, there was said to be 'between twenty and thirty preliminary certificate coaches in [the Republic of]Ireland and most of these gained the award at courses organised by the United Churches League.'[69] It was also the first year that a full FA coaching award was available in the Republic of Ireland. Despite this progress, by the beginning of 1963, structured coaching throughout the Republic was still in its infancy, with Professional Footballers Association of Ireland secretary Alan Glynn expressing hopes that 'a proper coaching scheme' would be established as he felt that 'there are not enough good coaches in this country.'[70] This came at a time when the recruitment of coaches by League of Ireland clubs was becoming more firmly established. Glynn hoped that the English FA would be of assistance in this attempt to improve the standard of football at senior and junior level. In addition, a lack of coaching facilities was also said to still be a problem at this time, with Shamrock Rovers sending their coaches to English Sports Schools 'for specialised training' by the middle of the 1960s.[71]

Attempts to develop coaching in schools

Relationships between soccer organizers and educational bodies have been slow to evolve in the Republic of Ireland. One reporter contrasted these with developments in West Germany in 1959 when he stated that 'all their football is integrated from the schools upwards. The [West] German FA as distinct from our own, get 100 per cent co-operation from their education authority.'[72] By the middle of 1967, it was reported that facilities for sport in vocational schools were improving, but difficulties remained in many counties, with the Meath Vocational Education Committee rejecting an application from local club Parkvilla to have soccer coaching implemented in a technical school in Navan that year.[73]

The following year, a five-day coaching course 'for games masters', under the guidance of Bohemians' manager, Sean Thomas and organized by the Irish Universities and Colleges Football Union, was held at Belfield having gained recognition from the FAI. This was said to be 'the latest stage in the proposed development of soccer in Irish Secondary Schools.'[74] By the middle of 1969, the course had been recognized by the Department of Education who sent a lecturer to talk about 'educational aspects of soccer and sport in general' with a medical doctor also present to speak about injuries. Applications were received from 'schoolmasters as far apart as Donegal and Cork' with written and oral exams part of the week's activities.[75]

Writing in 1969, one reporter felt that in the Republic of Ireland, 'PE has been almost totally absent from most primary schools due to two factors- lack of trained teachers and an over-constricted curriculum.'[76] A lack of emphasis on Physical Education at primary and secondary school level had been evident until the late 1960s, but this was also changing with a new syllabus being introduced by 1971 and specialized instruction given at the PE department of the new teacher-training college for secondary school teachers in Limerick. Previously, physical training had been implemented in some schools by drill instructors focusing on fitness, but this was to become a thing of the past with PE said to be 'almost the direct opposite' of this style of learning.[77]

A policy of providing free education for secondary school students (up to intermediate level) was implemented in 1969 having been announced by Minister for Education, Donogh O'Malley, in 1967. Funding applications for schools' sports facilities were encouraged by Brian Lenihan, who took up this ministerial role the following year. Community and comprehensive schools were also established towards the end of the decade.[78] By 1970, the FAI did have a coaching committee in operation, although one journalist felt that the finance simply was not there to develop a national coaching course.[79] Despite this, a 'countrywide coaching scheme' for secondary school students, teachers and other adults involved in schools soccer was set up by the FAI with the aid of a FIFA development grant.[80] Initial sessions, with the help of former Manchester United goalkeeper Ray Wood, an FA coach, were organized for Cork and Dublin and other provincial centres that year.[81]

A new national director of coaching

On 27 August 1973, 'the biggest coaching scheme ever attempted in Ireland' was launched. The was organized by the National Commission for Amateur Football, which had been set up in 1972, through government involvement, to investigate the state of soccer in the Republic of Ireland.[82] Funding for the new coaching scheme was to be provided via a grant from COSAC, the National Council for Sport and Recreation. The course lasted for five days with a number of League of Ireland clubs participating, and was developed around the plans of the English FA's Amateur Midland Regional Coach, John Jarman, who had overseen a 'pilot scheme' in Dublin the previous year.[83] Jarman was appointed FAI national coach later that year and took up the post in 1974.[84]

The same problems experienced by Dougald Livingstone were obvious early in Jarman's tenure. Despite trips to regional areas throughout Ireland such as Athenry, Sligo and Letterkenny in 1974, and a proposal drawn up by Jarman to be viewed by government officials in the hope of gaining more concrete support in the form of funds, facilities and finance remained problematic for the development of the game at grassroots and schoolboys level.[85] In November, Jarman called on the FAI to establish an £11,000 a year scheme for a permanent coaching structure. A year and a half into his contract, he felt that unless the scheme could be implemented, his work in Ireland was more or less finished, with the development of soccer being impeded by the lack of a regional administrative structure.[86] He felt that this was not something new, it being 'one of the principal recommendations' of the Football Commission in 1973. This lack of finance was a common problem within Irish soccer at this point, with one reporter noting its 'poverty-stricken state' in October 1975.[87] Jarman wanted to see the setting up of more regional centres for coaching, as although seven had been established, they did not have the proper facilities. He also felt that 'the schoolboys and youths of Ireland are crying out to be helped', while one reporter was of the view that the Welshman had 'virtually revolutionised the Irish soccer set-up at grass-roots level.' Improvements were shown in the fortunes of the Republic of Ireland's schoolboys and youths teams, while 250 teacher-coaches had passed exams in coaching.[88] Jarman had also established a scheme for 280 boys in St Anne's Park in Dublin that summer, while eighteen former Irish internationals passing preliminary exams and eighteen Bohemians players receiving teacher awards. College students, including those of the National College of Physical Education in Limerick, had also passed exams along with army men, while an interprovincial youth tournament had been held in Limerick.[89] Jarman's efforts were at times hindered by poor attendances in some counties while what he termed 'parochial attitudes' were said to be evident in Sligo, where he felt that 'everybody wants to develop his own corner but nobody is interested in co-operation with the result that all suffer.'[90] He added that 'nothing could develop properly in those circumstances', although he felt that there was 'a slight foundation' there already but it was 'not very solid.'[91] Jarman was also critical of the Irish government's minister 'responsible for sport', John Bruton, in 1976, and called for clarification on his policy towards sport and facilities. He also felt that Department of Education grants were 'totally inadequate' in helping to keep people interested in the game.[92] The country, he suggested, was 'at least 15 years behind' Wales, Belgium and Holland 'in acquiring adequate facilities for sport.' In July 1977, he resigned from the role, citing family commitments as being key to this, despite reports highlighting tensions in his relationship with international manager John Giles and the FAI during his three-and-a-half years as National Director of Coaching.[93] For all Jarman's hard work, in January 1977, one reporter felt that progress in 'successfully organising a coaching policy throughout the country' was hindered by 'the lack of playing and coaching facilities, the lack of freedom of choice for boys who would like to play soccer at school, and the lack of trained personnel to continue where he himself has engendered enthusiasm into hitherto untapped areas.'[94]

Earlier that year, it was noted that less than half of the 14 major recommendations of the 1973 Commission had been implemented, with Shamrock Rovers director Louis Kilcoyne noting that the FAI was in 'a serious financial debt.' Plans to bring in a levy with each player in the country contributing £1 had not materialized and the move did not have the support of the junior clubs, with whom the majority of the players were registered. The FAI chairman at the time of the report, Donie O'Halloran, believed that not enough progress had been made in setting up divisional structures.[95]

The impact of international success on coaching infrastructures

By the middle of the 1980s, soccer in the Republic was still struggling to cement a coherent nationwide infrastructure, with one Cork-based correspondent to a national soccer magazine stating that the game was 'going through a very bad period.' He made a number of observations, with a lack of facilities again highlighted. He also recommended the building of a national stadium, the promotion of soccer in schools, the implementation of more coaching courses and the provision of a lottery by the FAI to help grassroots clubs reach a decent standard.[96] This situation was to change with the Republic of Ireland's qualification for Euro '88 following the appointment of Jack Charlton as international manager in 1986. A lack of success at international level and the poor state of the game in Ireland had meant that many Irish people could not properly embrace soccer.[97] The Republic of Ireland team's performance in Euro '88, in beating England, drawing with the USSR and narrowly being defeated by the Netherlands, meant that interest in soccer grew, particularly in areas where soccer had struggled to gain a foothold at schoolboy level, with the South Donegal Schoolboys' League founded in September of that year.[98] This progress at international level also had a strong effect on the development of coaching. In the winter of 1989, FAI Director of Coaching, Noel King, noted that

> The level of interest nationwide has been enormous and more counties and people have become involved than ever before. Courses have taken place in Mayo, Clare, Limerick, Cork, Meath, Galway, Sligo, Donegal and, of course, north and south Dublin. Throw in the teachers' association, the V[ocational] E[ducation]C[ommittee] and you begin to

feel the growth that we are experiencing…Undoubtedly, this is largely due to the success of the national team, but regardless of the reason, the facts are that we are in the process of creating a coaching structure that can mean something and have a genuine effect on the future of many children, now and well into the future…with every region now forming coaching associations, it may be possible to effect, not only potential coaches, but more importantly, potential players with the introduction of schools of excellence, FAS courses and so on.[99]

International success meant greater sponsorship opportunities and more finance. One journalist was of the opinion that year that 'the first signs of benefits from the national team's success on the field of play showed themselves when the FAI announced a number of grants and interest free loans to various soccer bodies throughout the country.'[100] The Avonmore Ireland Cup, sponsored by a milk company, was said to be 'the first schoolboy international tournament to be held in Ireland', with 'in excess of 1200 boys at under 12, under 14, under 16 and under 18 years of age' taking part in this competition in April 1988 in Dublin.[101] In February 1990, in the build up to the World Cup, a joint venture between the confectionary manufacturer Mars and the FAIS saw soccer skills competitions established, with three age groups, under nine, under eleven and over eleven put into place. One hundred and six schools were to take part with regional winners going through to the finals at Lansdowne Road, scheduled to be held before an international match. This system was devised by Noel King with over 2000 children participating in the 1990 programme.[102] In 1995, there were 133 new school entries, bringing the overall total of schools involved to 500, within 18 regions.[103] The dissemination of soccer in Irish primary schools was also helped by the Football Association of Ireland Schools' publication of a book on the game, said to include lesson plans, and sent to every school in the country. Having been written by three primary school teachers, it was launched by the Minister for Education, Liam Aylward, in April 1994.[104] In 1992, Coca Cola became involved in FAI coaching clinics, providing £150,000 to the FAI over three years, although this was not the first time they had been involved in sponsorship for soccer coaching in Ireland.[105] This appears to be part of a broader Coca Cola policy to involve itself in football generally, and youth football specifically, at a global level.[106]

The development of schoolboys' soccer in Ireland was also helped by a shift in attitudes towards the game in some educational institutions. Some traditional GAA playing schools began to accommodate the game in the late twentieth century, with students at St Kieran's in Kilkenny, an institute said to be 'devoid of any kind of a tradition in the game of billions', benefiting from the input of Tipperary-born teacher Jim Carew to win the Leinster Schools' Senior Cup for the first time in 1993. The game had first been included as part of their sporting calendar during the 1975–6 season.[107] A similar development occurred at St Macartan's College in Monaghan in the 1980s where 'maths teacher and enthusiastic football fan' Aidan McCabe was behind the development of soccer in what was traditionally a Gaelic football college.[108] It is important to note that in both of these second-level institutions, these teachers were helped by the co-operation of their principals, who were both clergymen. This illustrates a change in attitudes towards soccer from the stance of many members of the clergy which had been evident for much of the twentieth century, particularly in Christian Brothers' Schools.[109] In addition, there is some indication that schools traditionally known for their rugby-playing prowess in the Republic are becoming more open to playing soccer at a serious schools' level, with Blackrock

College, who hold the record number of Leinster Schools' Senior Cup titles in rugby, winning the All-Ireland Senior Schools soccer competition for the first time in 2003.[110] Their opponents in the final in 2003 were a school with a strong GAA tradition, St Patrick's of Cavan. North of the border, there has also been progress made in establishing soccer's place within Northern Ireland's schools. In 2015, The Royal Belfast Academical Institution won their first ever soccer trophy, the Belfast Under-18 league title.[111] This development was said to be the result of structures put in place by teacher Paul McKinstry in the late 1970s, while traditional rugby-playing educational institutions Methodist College and Campbell College also now have soccer teams.[112]

Conclusion

As shown above, those attempting to implement coaching structures for young players in Ireland have faced many challenges at local, regional and national levels. Northern Ireland, in contrast to the Republic of Ireland, received some of the benefits of the post-war consensus in Britain that saw, and encouraged, the state as a benign and beneficent facilitator in people's lives and this impacted on implementation and organization of coaching. While the IFA had a smaller area to work with than the FAI, they too had to face competition from other sports and indifference from those running educational institutions. However, it appears that financially, the former body were initially able to cope a lot better in organizing coaching structures than those in Dublin, and support from government and educational bodies came a lot quicker in the decades immediately following the war.

Despite recent improvements, progress has not always been smooth, and some problems remain, particularly in more peripheral areas. Prior to the FAI's Emerging talent Scheme being initiated in 2006, it was reported in one provincial newspaper that there was 'no consistent, integrated and structured coaching and development programme for the most talented Irish players.' A 'representative squad structure' had existed, but this was 'more advanced in some parts of the country than in others.' Additionally, it was stated that 'the quality and quantity of the training sessions for these squads' was varied.[113] However, it must be noted that much progress has been made since the opening decade of the twenty-first century through the new scheme, with 12 Emerging Talent centres now in operation.[114]

In Northern Ireland, centres of excellence have also been put in place, although the financial considerations of the attendance fee and transport may hinder some families from sending their children.[115] In addition, the 'Small-Sided Games' strategy has been implemented as a model for primary school children participating in football with 15 centres for this development established by 2012.[116] Thirty specialist coaches are now employed as part of the IFA's Curriculum Sports Programme within 270 Northern Ireland Schools.[117] The IFA implemented their new strategy, 'Let Them Play', in 2015, with a view to improving participation of young players in soccer. This is supported by UEFA and includes a plan to develop a pathway for young players to progress further in the game.[118]

While developments in the Republic of Ireland were hindered by the game's lack of a national identity in many areas, it would be interesting to know if qualification for a major international tournament prior to the late 1980s would have boosted interest in developing soccer, not only through player participation, but also in the attitudes of those in the government, educational establishments and businesses. It is difficult to establish the impact of qualification for Sweden '58, Spain '82 and Mexico '86 on soccer in Northern Ireland at these times, although the game there has also faced difficulties with the Troubles and the identity associated with the national team. Whether or not Euro 2016 will lead to a boost in developments in the game's coaching structures at schoolboy level in both countries remains to be seen, while more research needs to be undertaken on the impact of international tournaments on other less successful footballing nations at grassroots level so that a more transnational comparison can be made.

Acknowledgements

I wish to express my thanks to the Irish Football Association and the Deputy Keeper of Records, Public Records Office of Northern Ireland, for granting me permission to publish material from their archives in this article. I am also grateful to the Football Association of Ireland for granting me access to their archives. Finally, I would like to thank Professor Matthew Taylor and Dr David Toms for advice given on an initial draft of this article.

Disclosure statement

No potential conflict of interest was reported by the author.

Notes

1. Brodie, *The History of Irish Soccer*; *100 Years of Irish Football*; Garnham, *Association Football and Society*.
2. Hunt, *Sport and Society*; Toms, *Soccer in Munster*; Curran, 'Networking Structures' and *The Development of Sport*.
3. Garnham, *Association Football and Society*, 93.
4. *Irish Independent*, August 9, 1946.
5. Taylor, *The Association Game*, 219.
6. Carter, *The Football Manager*, 107.
7. Garnham, *Association Football and Society*, 69.
8. Doherty, *Spotlight on Football*, 113–5.
9. IFA, Youth International Committee Minutes, July 6, 1948.
10. IFA, Youth International Committee Minutes, December 7, 1948.
11. IFA, Youth International Committee Minutes, December 7, 1948 and March 22, 1949.
12. IFA, Council Minutes, November 29, 1949; and 'Sir Walter Winterbottom.'
13. IFA, Council Minutes, November 29, 1949.
14. Northern Ireland Ministry of Education, Explanatory Memorandum, 1950.
15. IFA, Youth International Committee Minutes, June 22, 1949.
16. IFA, Coaching Committee Minutes, June 21, 1950.
17. IFA, Coaching Committee Minutes, June 21, 1950, January 3, 1951 and April 19, 1951.
18. IFA, Coaching Committee Minutes, August 29, 1951 and April 19, 1952.
19. IFA, Youth International Committee Minutes, October 8, 1953.
20. IFA Council Minutes, October 24, 1950.
21. Garnham, *Association Football and Society*, 23–6.
22. 'CAIN Service: Discrimination and Education.'
23. Fleming, 'Education since the late Eighteenth Century', 222.
24. Fleming, 'Education since the late Eighteenth Century', 222 and Bardon, *A History of Ulster*, 596. In 1981, the first co-educational second-level school in Northern Ireland to integrate Catholics and Protestants, Lagan College, was opened.
25. Bardon, *A History of Ulster*, 595–6.
26. IFA Council Minutes, June 29, 1954.
27. IFA Council Minutes, June 29, 1954.

28. IFA Council Minutes, June 29, 1954.
29. Garnham, *Association Football and Society*, 23.
30. Sugden and Bairner, *Sport, Sectarianism and Society*, 55.
31. IFA, AGM, May 29, 1954.
32. IFA, AGM, June 28, 1980.
33. IFA, AGM, May 28, 1955 and May 26, 1956.
34. IFA, Miscellaneous, Referees and Coaching Committee, August 13 and December 5, 1958.
35. IFA, AGM, May 31, 1958 and May 31, 1959.
36. IFA, AGM, May 28, 1960.
37. IFA Referees and Coaching Committee Minutes, March 11, 1964 and January 31, 1967.
38. Brodie, *100 Years of Irish Football*, 120.
39. IFA, AGM, April 30, 1971; and *Irish Independent*, March 23, 1971.
40. IFA, AGM, April 30, 1971.
41. *Strabane Chronicle*, July 10 and 17, 1971.
42. *Strabane Chronicle*, July 1, 1972.
43. *Fermanagh Herald*, December 20, 1986.
44. IFA, AGM, May 30, 1975.
45. IFA, AGM, April 30, 1976.
46. *Derry People and Donegal News*, April 14, 1986; and *Ulster Herald*, March 21, 1992.
47. *Ulster Herald*, May 15, 1993.
48. *Ulster Herald*, May 28, 1994.
49. *Fermanagh Herald*, July 18, 1992.
50. Delaney, *Irish Emigration since 1921*, 30.
51. Cronin, *Sport and Nationalism*, 125.
52. FAI, Junior Committee, February 24, 1938 and September 2, 1943.
53. FAI, Junior Committee Annual Report, 1944–5.
54. *Sunday Independent*, December 21, 1952.
55. *Irish Press*, April 27, 1948.
56. *Irish Independent*, October 5, 1948.
57. *Western People*, October 1, 1949; and *Irish Press*, May 4, 1950.
58. *Sunday Independent*, May 14, 1950.
59. *Irish Examiner*, August 30, 1951.
60. *Irish Independent*, April 6, 1953.
61. *Connaught Telegraph*, July 4, 1953.
62. *Connaught Telegraph*, June 11, 1953 and *Irish Independent*, September 10, 1953.
63. *Irish Independent*, August 5, 1953.
64. *Irish Independent*, January 27, 1954; *Irish Press*, September 28, 1954. See also *Sunday Independent*, January 31, 1971. Livingstone and Stevenson were full-time coaches but were not in charge of Inter-League selections.
65. *Sunday Independent*, April 22, 1956.
66. *Irish Independent*, November 5, 1957.
67. *Irish Independent*, August 4, 1958.
68. *Munster Express*, May 9, 1958.
69. *Irish Press*, May 31, 1960.
70. *Irish Press*, January 1, 1963.
71. *Irish Independent*, March 31, 1965.
72. *Irish Independent*, May 15, 1959.
73. *Connacht Sentinel*, June 13, 1967 and *Meath Chronicle*, July 29, 1967.
74. *Irish Independent*, June 26, 1968.
75. *Irish Independent*, June 21, 1969.
76. *Irish Press*, March 4, 1969.
77. *Irish Press*, March 4, 1969.
78. *Irish Press*, March 4, 1969.
79. *Irish Press*, November 18, 1970.
80. *Irish Independent*, June 16, 1970.
81. *Irish Independent*, June 16 and December 1, 1970.

82. *Irish Press*, April 12, 1972.
83. *Irish Press*, August 4, 1973.
84. *Irish Examiner*, December 29, 1973.
85. *Connacht Tribune*, July 5, 1974, *Sligo Champion*, July 19, 1974, *Donegal News*, August 3, 1974, *Irish Independent*, August 29 and November 28, 1974 and *Irish Press*, December 30, 1974.
86. *Irish Examiner*, September 4, 1975.
87. *Irish Press*, October 21, 1975.
88. *Irish Press*, September 4, 1975.
89. *Irish Examiner*, September 4, 1975.
90. *Donegal News*, September 27, 1975; and *Sligo Champion*, November 14, 1975.
91. *Sligo Champion*, November 14, 1975.
92. *Irish Press*, April 30, 1976.
93. *Irish Examiner*, July 23, 1977.
94. *Irish Examiner*, January 17, 1977.
95. *Irish Press*, January 12, 1977.
96. *Soccer Magazine*, 5, 1985, 22.
97. Cronin, *Sport and Nationalism*, 129.
98. *Sunday Independent*, February 13, 2011.
99. *Soccer Magazine*, 48, 1989, 26.
100. *Soccer Magazine*, 47, 1989, 3.
101. *Soccer Magazine*, 33, 1988, 10.
102. *Soccer Magazine*, 59, 1990, 25.
103. *Soccer Magazine*, 96, 1995, 26.
104. *Eleven-a-Side*, 2, 5, 1994, 3.
105. *Donegal News*, August 22, 1992; *Soccer Magazine*, 68, (1992), 18; and *Irish Press*, March 16, 1979.
106. 'Coca-Cola.'
107. *Eleven-a-Side*, 1, 1993, 16–9.
108. *Eleven-a-Side*, 7, 1993, 6–9.
109. *Irish Independent*, June 12, 1970.
110. *Irish Times*, April 10, 2003.
111. 'RBAI Football Champions.'
112. 'Sport and Games' and 'Football Results 2015–6.'
113. *Leinster Express*, December 21, 2006.
114. 'Emerging Talent.'
115. 'Enrolment Fees.'
116. 'Small-sided Games Strategy.'
117. 'Grassroots.'
118. 'IFA Launches Youth Football Strategy.'

References

Bardon, J. *A History of Ulster*. Belfast: Blackstaff Press, 2005. [New updated edition].
Brodie, M. *The History of Irish Soccer*. Glasgow: Arrell Publications, 1968.
Brodie, M. *100 Years of Irish Football*. Belfast: Blackstaff Press, 1980.
'CAIN Service: "Discrimination and Education" from "Perspectives on Discrimination and Social Work" in Northern Ireland'. Available online at http://cain.ulst.ac.uk/issues/discrimination/gibson1.htm.
Carter, N. *The Football Manager: A History*. Oxon: Routledge, 2006.
'Coca Cola'. Available online at http://www.fifa.com/about-fifa/marketing/sponsorship/partners/coca-cola.html.
Cronin, M. *Sport and Nationalism in Ireland: Gaelic games, soccer and Irish identity since 1884*. Dublin: Four Courts Press, 1999.
Curran, C. 'Networking Structures and Competitive Association Football in Ulster, 1880–1914'. *Irish Economic and Social History* 41 (2014): 74–92.
Curran, C. *The Development of Sport in Donegal 1880–1935*. Cork: Cork University Press, 2015.

Delaney, E. *Irish Emigration Since 1921*. Dundalk: The Economic and Social History Society of Ireland, 2002.
Department/Ministry of Education Papers. Ed/13/36. Educational Services (Central Council of Physical Recreation) Regulations (Northern Ireland) 1950, Explanatory Memorandum.
Doherty, P. *Spotlight on Football*. London: Art and Education Publishers, 1947.
'Emerging Talent'. Available online at http://www.fai.ie/domestic/take-part-programmes/emerging-talent.
'Enrolment Fees'. Available online at http://www.irishfa.com/kit/model/11/player-development-programme/.
FAI Minutes. P137/31. Junior Committee Annual Report, 1944–5.
Fleming, N.C. 'Education since the late Eighteenth Century'. In *Ulster since 1600: Politics, Economy and Society,* ed. Kennedy, L. and Ollerenshaw, P. 211–27. Oxford: Oxford University Press, 2013.
Football Association of Ireland Papers. Junior Committee Minutes, P137/28-9.
'Football Results 2015–16'. Available online at http://www.methody.org/School-Activities/Sport–Games.aspx.
Garnham, N. *Association Football and Society in Pre-Partition Ireland*. Belfast: Ulster Historical Foundation, 2004.
'Grassroots'. Available online at http://www.irishfa.com/grassroots/primary-school-coaching-programme/.
Hunt, T. *Sport and Society in Victorian Ireland: The Case of Westmeath*. Cork: Cork University Press, 2007.
'IFA Launches Youth Football Strategy'. http://irishfa.com/news/item/10103/ifa-launches-youth-football-strategy/.
IFA Papers. Coaching Committee Minutes. D/4196, Q/1.
IFA Papers. Annual General Meetings. D/4196/ U/1, Annual Reports, 1954–80.
IFA Papers. Council Meeting Minutes. D/4196/ A/6.
IFA Papers. T/5, Miscellaneous, Referees and Coaching Committee.
Irish Football Association Papers. Youth International Committee Minutes. D/4196/ F/1.
'RBAI Football Champions'. Available online at http://www.rbai.org.uk/index.php?option=com_content&view=category&layout=blog&id=89&Itemid=372.
'Sir Walter Winterbottom'. http://www.theguardian.com/news/2002/feb/18/guardianobituaries.football1.
'Small-sided Games Strategy 2013–4'. Available online at http://www.irishfa.com/fs/doc/Irish_FA_Small-Sided_Games_Strategy_120613.pdf.
'Sport and Games'. Available online at http://www.methody.org/School-Activities/Sport–Games.aspx.
Sugden, J., and Bairner, A. *Sport, Sectarianism and Society in a Divided Ireland* [Paperback version]. Leicester: Leicester University Press, 1995.
Taylor, M. *The Association Game: A History of British Football*. Harlow: Pearson Education Limited, 2008.
Toms, D. *Soccer in Munster: A Social History 1877–1937*. Cork: Cork University Press, 2015.

Pedagogy, game intelligence & critical thinking: the future of Irish soccer?

Seamus Kelly

> Utilizing data gathered from over 20 action research workshops involving over 350 participants with clubs in the UK and Ireland, this paper examines how coaching pedagogy facilitates the development of young soccer players in general and their perceptual cognitive skills in particular. This paper argues that in order to enhance player learning, coaches and managers would benefit from an understanding of the many theoretical frameworks underpinning the process of learning. This pedagogical knowledge assists in understanding how specific practices such as critical thinking, reflection, questioning and feedback facilitates the enhancement of player learning and in the assessment and development of perceptual cognitive skills. The value of this paper lies in its potential to stimulate debate, discussion and sensitize Irish coaches and managers, at all levels, to the way in which they, and their players, learn and to stimulate a critical evaluation and reflection of their current coaching and management practices.

Introduction

The opportunity to present this longitudinal research is timely considering that national youth development structures in Ireland are currently being revised. More specifically, the FAI Player Development Plan, produced in 2015, is designed to facilitate the development of soccer players in Ireland. This plan – produced by Ruud Dokter, the High Performance Director and his FAI colleagues – identifies a number of recommendations for the development of Irish players at all levels. Some of these recommendations involve: new structured pathways consisting of underage Regional and National Leagues; collaboration between senior and schoolboy clubs; and age-specific non-competitive football incorporating smaller pitches and increased game time. However, numerous commentators within the Irish media have argued that Ruud Dokter is fighting against an ingrained culture involving a deep-seated ignorance and resistance.

Some of this resistance may be due, in part, to some Irish clubs tradition of producing players in general and at schoolboy level in particular. For example, many Irish schoolboy clubs have a proven track record of producing players for elite levels both in Ireland and abroad. In particular, the Dublin District Schoolboy League is the largest of its kind in Europe with over 200 clubs and 16,000 players competing from the ages of eight to eighteen. Historically, the migration of Irish footballing talent was a prominent feature of professional football in the UK.[1] However, there has been a notable reduction in the number of Irish players progressing to elite and professional levels in the UK. More specifically, the majority of Irish players migrating to the UK never play at the highest level of English League football or represent their country at senior international level.[2] This reduction may be a reflection of some English clubs greater emphasis on the recruitment of cheaper, more experienced high-profile players from abroad.[3] Potential sources of resistance may also emerge from Irish coaches lack of openness and receptiveness regarding new coach education initiatives which may partly question their existing coaching practices and knowledge.

Arguably, any current or potential resistance to these new player development plans, regardless of their source or level, can be addressed through communication, negotiation, participation, involvement and education. Regarding the latter, this paper argues that the future of Irish soccer lies in education and engagement with a growing body of scientific evidence. For example, we know that the identification and development of talent in soccer is a multifaceted approach involving the systematic assessment of players' physiological, technical, tactical, social and psychological characteristics.[4] In addition, a number of studies have identified the importance of player development pathways and supportive talent development environments consisting of holistic, more person-centred approaches.[5] In the context of player development, Martindale et al. have argued that one of the most crucial 'factors influencing athletes at all levels of performance is the quality of the coaching environment.'[6] In this regard, the science of coaching has been examined from a number of theoretical perspectives such as psychological, social psychological, philosophical, sociological and pedagogical.[7] For example, we know that coaches that are more 'athlete-centred and less ego-orientated' tend to connect better with their athletes needs,[8] while some coach behaviours or leadership styles are more effective than others in particular contexts.[9] In addition, the coach–player relationship not only influences player motivation, but also their continued participation in soccer. It is argued that Irish coaches and managers should also 'consider the philosophical assumptions and practical applications of pertinent learning theory'[10] which will assist them in developing expert knowledge.[11] This growing body of scientific knowledge can assist coaches and managers in solving a number of problems they face regarding aspects of player development in general and in the assessment and development of what is arguably one of the most difficult skills in soccer: perceptual cognitive skills, or in soccer parlance 'knowledge of the game' or 'game intelligence.' Before critically evaluating how the academic literature could assist in the assessment and development of young Irish soccer players' perceptual cognitive skills, the following section outlines the research methods used in this study.

Research methods

This paper is guided by longitudinal research, still underway, gathered from over 20 action research workshops involving over 350 participants. The participants were coaches, managers and player development officers who were currently employed within national Football Associations or within the league structures in the UK or Ireland. The coaching and managerial careers of the participants lay between the extremes of outstanding professional success and more modest success. More specifically, some of the participants had coaching and managerial experience at English Premier League Academies, National Football Association's and at underage international level, while others had spent their entire careers at grassroots or youth level in the lower leagues. The participants possessed various levels of coaching experience and qualifications from UEFA B-Licence up to and including the UEFA Pro-Licence.

The purpose of these workshops was to critically evaluate how academic literature could assist participants in the assessment and development of players in general and their perceptual cognitive skills in particular. The workshops lasted between 90 and 120 min and were participatory in nature where participants were given individual and group tasks which preceded an opportunity to engage in group dialogue and debate. More specifically, participants were given open-ended unstructured questionnaires and required to answer three questions: What is game intelligence?; How do we coach game intelligence?; and finally, how do we know that players know, understand and display game intelligence? This latter question was of considerable importance because game intelligence components are arguably the most difficult skills to assess and develop in soccer. Therefore, these questions sought to ascertain participant's knowledge and understanding of the various components of game intelligence and how these skills could be assessed and developed. Participants were required, after each question, to discuss their responses in pairs followed by group discussion and debate. Participant's attention was then drawn to the academic literature on pedagogy and game intelligence which was an attempt to enhance and expose them to scientific evidence not identified in the group discussions. Arguably, these workshops facilitated participants learning through their process of engaging in practice-based inquiry which involved critical evaluation and discussion concerning aspects of game intelligence and coaching pedagogy. The key learning processes adopted by the author in the workshops involved observing, listening, questioning, feedback and combining challenge and support within a critical dialogue.[12]

In this paper, no attempt is made to attain ecological validity or argue that game intelligence can be developed utilizing reductionist processes, but to present an overview of the main results gathered to date. More specifically, this is the first of two papers that explores how pedagogical knowledge may assist in the assessment and development of game intelligence in soccer. Thus, the purpose of this paper is to identify some of the key principles and practices that could be utilized by coaches and managers in their assessment and development of game intelligence. Moreover, the paper is structured as a form of critical review of the academic literature guided by workshop participants' lived experiences and experiential knowledge of (professional) soccer. Thus, the value of this paper lies in its potential to stimulate debate, discussion and to sensitize Irish coaches and managers to the ways in which they and their players learn. One recurring theme, which emerged from the workshops, was recognition by the participants of the importance of critically evaluating their current management and coaching practices. Therefore, the paper is structured and presented in such a way as to not only question current and aspirant coaches' and managers' knowledge and skills but, to provide some basic practical, scientific and evidence-based guidelines for those interested in understanding how to enhance player learning and the process of assessing and developing game intelligence in particular.

Before we present the results of the data gathered in the above-mentioned workshops, the next section critically evaluates pedagogy in the context of both player development and game intelligence. Subsequent sections then examine how additional practices such as reflection, questioning and feedback assist in enhancing player learning and in developing young soccer players' game intelligence. The final section illustrates the central role of critical thinking in facilitating both the development and application of knowledge.[13] This is important for both academic and practical purposes. As we shall see later, critical thinking questions the appropriateness of coaching practices in other countries and clubs and their application and adaptation to Irish clubs and players in particular. Moreover, the usefulness of conducting a critical review of the scientific evidence in performance analysis will be particularly evident and relevant for Irish coaches and managers. In the conclusion, omissions and avenues for further reading are identified.

Pedagogy

While pedagogy is viewed as any conscious activity by one person designed to enhance learning in another, there are many ways in which coaches and managers can facilitate the enhancement of player learning.[14] Firstly, coaches and managers need to understand the basic communication process. If the communication channels utilized (e.g. verbal, written, audio and visual) by coaches and managers as part of the sender encoding process are not applied properly, meaning can be distorted. Feedback can overcome this distortion and facilitates understanding by ensuring that messages are correctly perceived as intended by the receiver.[15] This is important because people encode, process and decode (reconstruct) information such as visual (watching) or auditory (listening) in different ways. However, quite often, coaches solely focus on kinaesthetic (doing) as demonstration of understanding (outcome). Before viewing such common sense knowledge with cynicism, it might be useful if coaches reflect on what methods of communication and feedback, other than verbal, are incorporated in their coaching practice. Moreover, because coaching is a mulitsensory experience, it is important that coaches communicate messages to players through different sensory modes and communication channels in order for messages to be fully understood.[16] I will return to this point later. Secondly, in order to facilitate player learning, coaches and managers would benefit from an understanding of the many theoretical frameworks underpinning the learning *process*. This knowledge will not only inform and guide their practices, assist in enhancing player learning, but also in dealing with the many challenges and problems that they encounter.

Many different theoretical approaches exist which facilitate an understanding of the learning process. One approach views learning as a persisting *change* in human performance, or performance potential, that may be brought about as a result of the learner's interaction with their environment. Moreover, learning also involves the relatively permanent or enduring *change* in a person's knowledge or behaviour due to experience, or in the capacity to behave in a given fashion. Implicit in the above is the importance of change. Therefore, it is argued that coaches adopt, like their players, a growth mindset in which they are open to understanding the learning process. However, one recurring theme from workshop participants concerned how their exposure to complex theoretical frameworks resulted in stress, hostility and consciously incompetent[17] fears concerning their levels of coaching knowledge. As discussed during the workshops, such fears are normal, but participants were encouraged to strive for an openness and awareness that not only facilitates an engagement in developing new knowledge in general, but an ability to critically evaluate the practical application of scientific knowledge in particular.

Learning is a broad complex concept involving many different perceptions, theoretical frameworks and assumptions. Perspectives of learning may be categorized under headings such as behaviourism, cognitivism and constructivism, with the latter being subdivided into psychological and social.[18] This paper will focus on a constructivist orientation underpinning learning. Constructivism holds that learning is an active, constructive process that is learner-centred where learners arrive with prior knowledge that they can use as building blocks for acquiring new knowledge.[19] What this means is that the learner is an information constructor where new information is linked to prior knowledge. It is important for coaches to recognize that the learner is not a blank slate (*tabula rasa*) but brings past experiences and cultural factors to a given situation. This is important because players will have been previously subjected to various different sports, learning styles and coach behaviours. Constructivism emphasizes learning in context through meaningful activities and a focus on high-level thinking activities. This not only facilitates the development of a players' cognitive flexibility and ability but might also assist them in identifying and pursuing their own specific learning goals. Therefore, coaches and managers need to simplify tasks for a player that facilitates how they solve complex problems by providing tools, strategies and practices that are viewed as an essential part of the learning process. For example, this can be accomplished by embedding learning in complex, realistic and relevant coaching environments, while critical thinking, reflection and feedback are also strategies that support the learning process. Related to the learning process is how higher mental processes are developd through social interactions between coaches and players. For example, the use of questions, discussion and debate may also assist players develop and defend individual perspectives while recognizing those of other players and coaches. As we shall see later, learning can also be facilitated through peer-to-peer learning, guided discovery and discovery learning, while a vibrant learning environment tends to be player-centred involving active player engagement.

Another core aspect of constructivism is self-direction. What this means is that players are actively involved in determining what their own learning needs are and how those needs can be satisfied, rather than being purely passive recipients of coaching instructions. Thus, coaches share in the learning process, rather than controlling it. Moreover, the purpose of learning is for an individual to construct his or her own meaning and not just memorize the 'right' answers and replicate someone else's meaning. In this regard, coaches can facilitate this learning process with players by utilizing scenarios and problem-based learning[20] in a kind of whole-part-whole approach involving game-based plays, progressions and set pieces, etc. Thus, coaches can facilitate learning where players solve problems and coaches observe and intervene, only if necessary, with appropriate feedback and encouragement. Coach feedback and observation will be discussed later. Moreover, to facilitate the learning outcomes of a coaching session, all drills and practices should be constructively aligned and incorporate an appropriate non-pressurized climate conducive to learning.

At a more advanced level, because learning involves a little bit of uncertainty and insecurity, coaches may utilize activities such as stress inoculation practices. Such practices involve taking players out of their comfort zone and have been widely used by Sir Alex Ferguson.[21] In addition, it is well known that situated learning facilitates talent development and skill learning in youth soccer,[22] while random practice incorporating contextual interference facilitates a greater learning experience for the more skilled players.[23] Moreover, to facilitate greater learning, a little bit of chaos,[24] trauma[25] and specificity of training[26] may also be utilized. Now that we have a broad understanding of the learning process, a useful starting point to facilitate coaches in the assessment and development of player's game intelligence might be to describe its various components.

What is game intelligence?

In comparison to anthropometric and physiological attributes, perceptual cognitive skills are viewed as being more likely to predispose players towards success in soccer and at the elite level in particular.[27] Perceptual cognitive skills, often referred to by coaches as 'knowledge of the game' or 'game intelligence' incorporate a player's ability to read the game, anticipate an opponent's intentions and involve key skills such as creativity, innovation and decision making.[28] Perceptual cognitive skills also refer to a players' cognitive ability to utilize strategies that assist them in actively thinking about and modifying their actions during games, which facilitates their expectation of what is likely to happen, given a particular set of circumstances.[29] Because players are confronted with a complex and rapidly changing playing environment, they must pick up information from the ball, team-mates and opponents before deciding to select and execute an appropriate action in a given situation. Such in-game decisions may also be influenced by game strategies, tactics and specific action constraints such as their technical ability and physical capacity.[30] These decisions are often made under pressure, where opposition players are trying to restrict both their 'time' and 'space.' Perceptual cognitive skills incorporate a number of key components or cognitive factors, such as enhanced knowledge of situational probabilities, recognizing patterns of play, utilizing visual search strategies and processing of contextual information.[31]

Processing of contextual information and advance cue utilization (e.g. picking up key postural cues) refers to a player's ability to anticipate an opponent's actions and to make accurate predictions based on partial or advanced sources of information arising from an opponent's posture and bodily orientation.[32] While most research on postural cue utilization has been undertaken using penalty kicks, expert outfield players possess superior ability in using similar sources of information in reliably anticipating an opponent's actions.[33] For example, we know that the more skilful soccer players utilize more pertinent visual search strategies that involve a greater number of fixations of shorter duration on more relevant sources of information.[34] This transfers to an ability to know 'where' and 'when' to look and gives players a better than average idea of what to anticipate from an opponent's actions in general and in anticipating the destination of an opponent's pass in particular.[35] It is important to note that expert players do not possess superior visual skills or abilities such as visual acuity, depth perception and peripheral awareness.[36] However, higher skilled players do have a greater awareness of opposition players' position and movement 'off the ball,' thus reducing the possibility of them being caught 'ball watching' and subsequently being caught out of position.

Visual search strategies differ in terms of viewing the whole field (e.g. 11 vs. 11 situations), micro-states of the game (e.g. 1 vs. 1, 3 vs. 3 situations) and between defensive and offensive patterns of play. In addition, expert soccer players are better at recognizing and recalling structured patterns of play because their accumulated knowledge allows them to 'chunk' or group perceptual information items (e.g. players' positions) into larger and more meaningful units (e.g. patterns of play), thus enabling them to recognize the emergent features of a pattern of play early.[37] This better recall of the more experienced soccer players is due to enhanced task-specific knowledge bases and more rapid and efficient retrieval of this information from memory. These 'knowledge bases or structures,' which may be a result of experience, direct players' visual search strategies towards more pertinent areas of the display based on their expectations (i.e. knowledge of situational probabilities) and more effective processing of contextual information (e.g. pattern recognition and advance cue utilization). For example, while defenders may utilize game plans, match strategy and tactics, they may also be constrained by a priori expectations and instructions where they must respond to opponents' actions in attempting to prevent goal scoring opportunities. Now that we have a basic understanding of the components of game intelligence, the next section will explore some of the ways in which these components can be developed and tested through various practices and activities.

How do we coach game intelligence?

Some coaches and managers might argue that game intelligence is 'a result of playing experience, innate, not amendable to practice and instruction' and that it is not possible – or at least too difficult – to develop structured training programs to improve these skills.'[38] However, compelling empirical evidence now exists to indicate that anticipation and decision-making skills, underlying game intelligence, are amenable to appropriate training, practice and instruction and can be acquired and developed using appropriate interventions and testing mechanisms.[39] For example, testing soccer players' perceptual cognitive skills may incorporate match simulations and film-based anticipation, recall and recognition tests.[40] In this regard, we know that in tests utilizing video clips, experienced players encode soccer-specific information to a deeper and more conceptual level and recognize previously viewed action sequences more accurately than their less-experienced counterparts.[41] In terms of developing and enhancing the cognitive knowledge bases underlying perception cognitive skills in soccer, coaches may also utilize video simulations where the appropriate displays (e.g. 1 vs. 1 defensive plays or penalty kicks) are filmed from the players' perspective and then played back to them with varying degrees of coach instruction and feedback.[42]

The variability inherent within dynamic open-play in soccer ensures that the development of appropriate interventions is a complex proposition. However, with the advent of less-expensive and more 'user-friendly' digital video-editing systems, coaches are now able to recall specific plays and replay them to players.[43] Combining quantitative performance statistics with video footage regarding the moves and actions typically performed by forthcoming opponents improves a players' ability to make accurate predictions regarding the opposition's intentions during a forthcoming match. For example, the recognition of offensive patterns of play such as overlap runs, split runs or third player running can be improved through repeated exposure to a variety of related action sequences using video simulations.[44] In this regard, the use of opposition video clips, distributed to players via their mobile phones, is a practice that is widely used in many professional football clubs and by Sam Allardyce at a number of his former clubs and at Stoke City FC in particular. While recent advances in virtual reality technology offer many exciting opportunities for those interested in creating realistic simulations for the purpose of performance enhancement, a growing body of neuroscience research utilizing fMRI has examined player's perceptual-cognitive superiority in anticipating their oncoming opponent's moves.[45] In this regard, fMRI research may assist in a greater understanding of the impact specific coaching methods – such as the integration of brain-centred learning adopted by Michel Bruyninckx in Belgium – might have on the acquisition and development of perceptual cognitive skills.

We know that the possession of superior perceptual cognitive skills is a function of players' enhanced task-specific knowledge bases which is developed through experience, quality of practice and coaching instruction. In addition, engagement in soccer-specific practice activities during adolescence and sports-specific play activities during childhood in particular is a contributing factor in the development of perceptual cognitive skills.[46] In this regard, considerable evidence supports how small-sided games involving game-specific contexts and situations facilitate the development of player awareness (e.g. patterns of play, spatial recognition) and problem-solving capabilities which quite often assists players in making quicker, more efficient decisions during games.[47] We also know that Teaching Games for Understanding,[48] guided discovery,[49] learning through understanding[50] and reflection during (in action) and after (of action) competitive games and training sessions facilitate learning. Reflection will be discussed later. The aforementioned approaches require coaches to question their existing practices, move outside their comfort zone and to be highly creative in designing practice games and conditions that advance player learning and provide them with an opportunity to acquire game intelligence knowledge implicitly. As we shall see later, coach feedback is crucial in facilitating learning. Moreover, feedback assists players expected response requirements, refinement of specific perceptual cognitive skills and in improving their ability to pick up advance information cues from an opponents' postural orientation in particular.

The take-home message is that players' perceptual cognitive skills are amenable to practice and instruction and, consequently, the important challenge for coaches is to determine how best to design, implement and evaluate appropriate training programmes and practices.[51] One final question remains; How do coaches know that players know and understand what game intelligence is? One obvious answer is kinaesthetic where coaches observe players executing or replicating game intelligence skills, or its components, in training and in competitive matches. However, one major issue when designing practice activities concerns 'the retention and transfer of learning from that activity to the complexity of field performance.'[52] In this regard, it is argued that specific practices exist that coaches and managers can utilize to enhance player learning, develop game intelligence and decision making in particular.

Feedback

It is important that players, coaches and managers have a shared knowledge and understanding of the important role feedback plays in the learning process. This is because individual and personalized coach feedback facilitates the improvement of sport skill performance,[53] increases the long-term motivation of athletes and impacts positively on athlete self-concept.[54] Thus, when coach–athlete interactions are characterized by high amounts of instruction, feedback and encouragement[55] and delivered in a positive manner by coaches, it elicits positive athlete outcomes such as enjoyment, self esteem and persistence.[56]

Feedback is any information, verbal and non-verbal, conveyed to athletes about the extent to which their behaviours and performance correspond to expectations and is viewed as a crucial coaching behaviour.[57] Central to the learning process is the provision of objective coach feedback[58] in general and augmented feedback in particular.[59] A growing body of academic research has examined the role of coach feedback,[60] how coaches modify coaching practices using post-match feedback, the systematic manner in which feedback is delivered to athletes and an appropriate timescale for delivering feedback.[61] More specifically, it is well known that the appropriateness, contingency and quality of coach feedback is more critical than its frequency or quantity.[62] Coach feedback can be characterized as positive, encouraging, supportive, instructionally based, and punishment orientated or ignoring.[63] We also know that less prescriptive, more divergent (i.e. analytical) as opposed to convergent (i.e. recall) questions, as a form of feedback, facilitates players' cognitive development, awareness, reflection and problem-solving skills.[64] Thus, in one-to-one meetings with players, coaches could consider utilizing divergent questions regarding the various sources of information from the ball, team mates and opponents that players utilized in deciding to select and execute an appropriate action in a given match or training situation.

In addition to the time-consuming and laborious nature of collecting feedback and disseminating its results, problems exist concerning coaches' ability to observe, recall and analyse key events during training sessions, competitive games and in-game observations in particular.[65] In response, technology and mobile phone applications not only assist in dealing with many of these problems, but may also facilitate individualized personal feedback between coaches and athletes concerning aspects of their performance.[66] In addition, coaches may also utilize the *One Minute Paper*. This task, widely used in education is a confidential, anonymous, efficient exercise in which players respond, in writing, to two or three simple questions after training sessions. For example, players may be asked what did you like about the session, what did you learn during the session or what problems are still in your mind after the session?

At a more advanced level, it would be useful if coaches and managers could develop an understanding of the knowledge, skills and methods that facilitate an observation *of* player learning. As a form of feedback, it has been argued that coaches should consider employing observation during their coach–athlete interactions and during coaching practices in particular.[67] Moreover, Jones et al. argue for a more specific type of observation; one that facilitates witnessing or noticing *of* player learning.[68] More specifically, because 'noticing becomes intake for learning,' coaches could adopt 'disciplined glances' that incorporate 'seeing the non-visible.'[69] This involves the ability to being sensitive to the moment or 'sensitized to notice' where coaches not only decide 'on what to notice' but perhaps may try and observe 'what's not happening.'[70] This is important because being 'sensitised or primed to notice certain things often distinguishes the ordinary coaches from the really good ones.'[71] In this regard, it might be a worthwhile exercise for coaches and managers to examine the observation methods employed by Sir Alex Ferguson.[72] For example, quite often coaches and managers notice the achievements and shortcomings of their players, how they get on with each other and the dressing room cliques. However, what informs your decision to stop a particular session and is this decision guided by what you expect to see? This is an important question, as quite often coaches and managers see what they want to see (e.g. mistakes), which provides them with the opportunity to stop the practice and intervene, which may in fact inhibit rather than facilitate player learning. Moreover, in the context of game intelligence, while most coaches and managers possess the ability to observe instances when players are caught 'ball watching' or 'out of position,' perhaps they could adopt 'disciplined glances' and observe players positioning and visual search strategies, such as their head movements, during games and preceding such instances in particular. This may provide some indication of 'where,' 'when' and 'what' they specifically observed. In this regard, subsequent coach feedback, incorporating divergent questions, may facilitate cognitive development and a greater awareness of the importance of both positioning and visual search strategies. As we shall see in the next section, reflection can also facilitate the learning process by encouraging coaches and managers to question and self-assess their own practices and behaviours.

Reflection

Conceptualized in different ways and incorporating many different levels, reflection involves both self-awareness and self-disclosure which can assist coaches, players and managers in a number of ways.[73] Moreover, reflection facilitates an understanding and exploration of their complex, messy, unpredictable, untidy and constantly changing soccer environment. Because of the considerable frustration inherent in coaching and management, reflection facilitates the deduction of practical and meaningful insights. However, to facilitate player learning, coaches and managers would benefit from an understanding on the importance of reflection and how it is utilized. Reflection is central to the learning process and involves thinking back on what you have done in order to discover how our knowing in action may have contributed to solving a problem or dealing with surprises or unexpected phenomena.[74]

Some obvious questions are *what* do we reflect on, *how* do we reflect and *when* do we reflect? Regarding the latter, coaches and managers may reflect after (reflection on action) or may pause in the midst (reflection in action) of a training session or game. What this means is that we reflect on our understandings that are implicit in the action and then critique, restructure and embody the practice in future action. Regarding *what*, reflection may be technical (e.g. session structure and format, drills), practical (e.g. personal feelings and emotion focused account of practice, communication and feedback, coaching style and behaviour) and critical (e.g. social, economic, cultural factors and values underpinning players behaviours). Moreover, reflection involves viewing both sides (e.g. coach and player or defender and attacker) of an issue and assessing and interpreting information objectively. Thus, in an attempt to attain greater objectivity, coaches and managers may reflect on their subjective assessment of a player's attitude or ability. This is important because traditionally managers and coaches have subjectively assessed playing talent based on their emotions, intuition and gut feeling.[75] In the context of game intelligence, coaches may reflect on the percentage of time allocated to feedback and 'playing form' or 'training form' activities that replicate game-related conditions.[76] Moreover, coaches may reflect on what percentage of their time consists of coach instruction and player feedback? It might also be useful for coaches to critically evaluate and reflect on how their coaching behaviour and style contrasts with coaches in Spain[77] and England.[78] Reflection may also be utilized by players to assist them in assessing their in-game decisions. This is important because the encouragement of athletes to engage in structured reflection concerning aspects of their performance and decision-making can have significant benefits.[79] Research, currently underway, suggests professional soccer players' engagement in structured reflection after training and competitive performances significantly impacts the development of their in-game decision making.

Regarding *how* to reflect, reflection must be somewhat structured. In this regard, the Gibbs[80] reflective model is a useful framework to assist players, coaches and managers reflect on aspects of their performance and critical incidents in particular. Consisting of six different steps, from description to action plan, this model facilitates greater efficiency in analysing problems and is a valuable learning tool. Some writing techniques to facilitate reflection include diaries, field notes, photographs and videos, while some coaches utilize Dictaphones to record what they see, think and feel. There exist many different types of reflective writing such as: descriptive writing, descriptive reflection, dialogic reflection and critical reflection, where levels of reflection are generally seen as a continuum from a lack of reflection to critical reflection.[81] The depth of reflection is related to the quality of reflective writing which involves adopting a 'writing to learn' paradigm that views writing as a learning mechanism rather than merely as evidence of learning.[82] For example, while descriptive writing (technical writing) is not reflective and merely consists of a description or report of events, descriptive reflection is an attempt to provide reasons or justifications for the events or actions taken. Dialogic reflection is a type of reflective writing which generally demonstrates a 'stepping back' from the events and/or actions, leading to a discourse with the self. Critical reflective practice is a process, where coaches and managers philosophically contest, challenge and alter various aspects of their practice. For example, critical reflective practice might involve discussion and debate between managers, coaches and backroom staff regarding aspects of player assessment or coaching practices which may assist in alleviating any potential confirmation bias[83] and facilitate consensual decision making. On a deeper level, critical reflection involves a type of reflective writing that demonstrates awareness that actions and events are not only located in, and explicable by, reference to multiple perspectives but are located in, and influenced by, multiple historical and sociopolitical contexts.[84] This involves a description of events that occurred and may assist in providing comprehensive reasons or justification for events or actions taken.

Finally, coaches and managers require an absorption in the reflective process and being open to the discovery of new phenomena which involves a process of discovery, reframing and questioning of their opinions and beliefs. This is important because central to reflection is a desire to engage with opposing views and assume a certain level of responsibility which quite often involves recognition of errors and mistakes made in the past. What this means is that the consequences of your actions are considered and accepted. While reflection can facilitate the development of an increased self awareness, reflection is time-consuming, intellectually and emotionally challenging.[85] In this regard, the Gibbs reflective model is a useful framework in assisting coaches and managers in overcoming their fear of regressing into a state of continual reflection or paralysis by analysis.[86] For example, it well known that Sam Allardyce, Aidy Boothroyd, Eddie Howe and Sir Alex Ferguson are keen endorsers of reflection as part of their coaching and management practice.

Critical thinking and performance analysis

Defined in numerous ways, critical thinking is, despite being a specialist skill, something which is learned with practice.[87] Critical thinking refers not only to skills, but also as an orientation to engaging with the (de)construction of knowledge, conventions and norms and as a navigation of one's position in relation to them. Critical analytical thinking has been used in a number of different academic domains (e.g. psychology, philosophy and science), extensively in educational settings[88] and is regarded as essential in progressing and growing knowledge. In this regard, many third-level academic institutions – delivering courses in coaching science and sport management – recognize the importance of practising skills that facilitate critical thinking as part of the learning process. Arguably, the integration of a 'critical review' into formal coach education promotes an orientation to learning preparedness, critical thinking and scholarly writing by equipping learners with both content-specific knowledge and generalizable skills.[89] Moreover, the critical review, as an assessment, can be used across a diversity of learning environments, thus enhancing the development of a learning culture.[90] A useful starting point for coaches, managers and players to develop critical thinking skills might be to adopt the critical incident technique. Critical incident technique, developed during Second World War, is widely used in the educational environment.[91] Critical incidents are not necessarily sensational events but quite often involve minor incidents that coaches, players and managers experience on a daily basis. Their classification as critical incidents is based on the significance and the meaning that the learner attributes to them. Thus, critical incidents can be positive, negative, or both.[92]

Critical analytic thinking is 'thought to be a prerequisite to determining the best course of action in important, complex decisions'[93] and is considerably useful when incorporated into various methods for enhancing coach, manager and athlete learning. While most Irish managers and coaches have critically evaluated the application, usefulness and appropriateness of *gegenpressing* or *tiki-taka* to Irish Soccer, a useful exercise might be to evaluate the scientifically proven processes and practices that coaches adopt for improving decision making in sports such as volleyball, basketball, netball, rugby union and in teams such as the New Zealand All-Blacks.[94] Critical analytic thinking assists in the reflection process and assists learners in two specific ways. Firstly, it assists learners in identifying, then evaluating key dimensions of discipline-specific academic literature. Secondly, by allowing learners to reflect upon and communicate how their understandings and views might be influenced or challenged by their understanding of the academic literature. To illustrate its usefulness, a very brief attempt will be made to examine the role that critical thinking plays in assessing the current academic knowledge in performance analysis.

Performance analysis (PA) is firmly embedded within the coaching process[95] and can facilitate the process of improving player performance.[96] However, despite a significant growth in performance analysis research, a number of issues and questions remain concerning the progress of the field and the assumptions underpinning PA research.[97] For example, in 2013, Mackenzie & Cushion argued that the adoption of a reductionist approach has resulted in PA research consistently reducing the complexity of performance by portraying it as a series of steps to be followed in an overly descriptive, systematic and unproblematic process with little regard of how this knowledge is transmitted from coach to athlete.[98] They also argued that PA research has been driven to establish causal relationships between isolated performance variables in an attempt to predict outcomes. Isolated performance variables are independent variables that are directly associated with match outcomes in isolation without acknowledging potentially confounding variables or providing sufficient context to the variable itself. Moreover, Mackenzie & Cushion argued that variables have been measured as a result of availability with little attention paid to the applicability of performance variables in the context of complex sporting performances.[99] Patton was also sceptical of objective approaches such as notational analysis and suggested that numbers might disguise instead of protecting against bias. This is important because 'all statistical data are based on someone's definition of what to measure and how to measure it.'[100] In response, Mackenzie & Cushion identified a number of possible solutions to some of the aforementioned issues with PA research that are worth exploring. Firstly, they argued that it is important to understand the nature of the competition that is to be investigated and the context to the sample used (i.e. location, period of season, opposition faced, etc.). Secondly, further research is required to identify comprehensive and published operational definitions for the variable(s) under investigation. Thirdly, there is a need for the dissemination and use of PA research in applied settings and the impact PA has on athlete learning and information retention as part of their performance feedback process in particular. In this regard, coaches might find research examining the pedagogical impact of performance analysis and technology useful.[101]

Finally, Bampouras et al., has argued that the 'locking-out' of the athlete from the PA process 'reflects a short-termist, ends oriented technical rationality.'[102] In this regard, coaches may benefit from examining how a coach-led, player-driven evidence-based approach to performance analysis assists in the development of players' decision making capabilities. For example, both the excellent research conducted by Professor Bill Gerrard and his applied work at both Saracens and Bolton Wanderers is worth exploring. This is important because the inclusion of players in the process of goal setting and development of individual and team metrics and performance measures might not only engage players, create team cohesion, but also facilitate a shared understanding of the very performance components coaches and managers strive to measure.[103] This is an important point because we know that providing athletes with greater autonomy and the empowerment of athletes through their inclusion in a variety of decision-making activities can have a variety of positive performance-functional outcomes and a constructive impact on their motivation in general.[104]

Conclusion

This paper has explored the central role of pedagogy in developing players in general and their game intelligence in particular. This pedagogical knowledge may also inform and guide coaching and management practices, behaviours and assist in facilitating an understanding of how learning is transferred from them to their players. This paper also examined how the role of critical thinking, reflection, questioning and feedback assists in enhancing player learning and development of game intelligence. However, due to space restrictions, there are a number of obvious and considerably important omissions.

First, there is no mention of how specific coaching behaviours and interactions in training and competitive matches facilitate player development and learning.[105] Second, there is no examination of how emotional intelligence (EQ) assists in understanding coach–athlete relationships, facilitates athletes' ability to perform and think for themselves or how EQ may support coaches and managers in dealing with the potential stress and conflict when dealing with fans and parents.[106] Third, one neglected approach to learning and development is 'active adaption' which involves the sharing of player and coach knowledge through conversations, group reflective practices, communities of practice and mentoring.[107] Fourth, there was no discussion on the relationship between habits and decision making,[108] or how the excellent work of Bill Beswick and Dan Abrahams[109] may assist coaches and managers in the assessment and development of soccer players. Finally, one crucial omission is how our individual-level values[110] act as guiding principles for decision making in general and in the formulation of a coaching philosophy[111] in particular. This is important because a vague or uncertain coaching philosophy quite often leads to inconsistency in coaching behaviours and practices.

In conclusion, change quite often produces fear, anxiety, uncertainty and hostility which may be due, in part, to a lack of understanding and knowledge. In this regard, and as argued earlier, if the future of Irish soccer lies in education, then it is hoped that this paper provides a useful starting point in stimulating debate, discussion and a critical evaluation and reflection of our current coaching and management practices in general and how we develop our players in particular.

Acknowledgements

I wish to thank the anonymous reviewers and Susan Giblin, Ruud Dokter and Gavin Fleming for their considerably helpful suggestions and comments on an earlier draft. A special word of thanks to the editors of this special issue for their advice, support and considerable patience. Finally, considerable gratitude is owed to the workshop participants for their assistance, advice and engagement with this research.

Disclosure statement

No potential conflict of interest was reported by the author.

Funding

This work was supported by UCD Seed Funding [42808].

Notes

1. Poli et al., *Annual Review of the European Football*.
2. Curran, 'Post-Playing Careers,' 1273–86.
3. Walters and Rossi, 'Labour Market Migration in European Football.'
4. Williams, *Science and Soccer*.
5. Ivarsson et al., 'The Predictive Ability,' 15–23; Williams, *Science and Soccer*; and Kidman, *Athlete-centred Coaching*.
6. Martindale et al., Quest, 353.
7. Cassidy et al., *Understanding Sports Coaching*.
8. Barić and Bucik, 'Motivational Differences in Athletes,' 181.
9. Renshaw et al., 'Insights from Ecological Psychology,' 540–602.
10. Roberts and Potrac, 'Behaviourism, Constructivism and Sports,' 180.
11. Jones et al., *Sports Coaching Cultures*.
12. Higgs and Titchen, 'Knowledge and Reasoning,' 23–32.
13. Stoszkowski and Collins, 'Sources, Topics and Use,' 1–9; and Stoszkowski and Collins, 'Using Shared Online,' 23.
14. Roberts and Potrac, 'Behaviourism, Constructivism and Sports,' 180–87.
15. Januario and Rosado, 'Variables Affecting.'
16. Ibid.
17. Murray, 'Intuitive Coaching-Summary,' 203–6.

18. Cassidy et al., *Understanding Sports Coaching*.
19. Ibid.
20. Jones and Turner, 'Teaching Coaches to Coach,' 181–202.
21. Elberse, 'Ferguson's Formula,' 116–25.
22. Christensen et al., 'Situated Learning,' 163–78.
23. Porter et al., 'When Goal Orientations Collide,' 935–43.
24. Porter et al., 'When Goal Orientations Collide,' 935–43; and Light et al., Improving 'At-action' Decision-making 258–75.
25. Collins and McNamara, The Rocky Road to the Top.
26. Hodges and Franks, 'Modelling Coaching Practice,' 793–811.
27. Williams and Reilly, 'Talent Identification and Development,' 657–67; and Williams and Davids, 'Visual Search Strategy,' 111–28.
28. Roca et al., 'Developmental Activities,' 1643–52; Reilly et al., 'A Multidisciplinary Approach,' 695–702; and Williams and Reilly, 'Talent Identification and Development,' 657–67.
29. Williams, *Science and Soccer*; and Gray and Plucker, 'She's a Natural,' 361–80.
30. Morris, 'Psychological Characteristics,' 715–26.
31. Williams, *Science and Soccer*; Williams and Reilly, 'Talent Identification,' 657–67; and Williams and Davids, 'Visual Search Strategy.'
32. Williams, *Science and Soccer*.
33. Williams et al., 2005, 'Perceptual-cognitive Expertise,' 283–307; and Carling et al., *Performance assessment*.
34. Williams and Davids, 'Declarative Knowledge,' 259–75; and Williams and Davids, 'Visual Search Strategy.'
35. Williams and Davids, 'Declarative Knowledge,' 259–75; Williams and Davids, 'Visual Search Strategy'; Vaeyens et al., 'The Effects of Task Constraints,' 147; and Vaeyens et al., 'Mechanisms Underpinning,' 395–408.
36. Williams and Hodges, 'Practice, Instruction and Skill,' 637–50; and Williams and Davids, 'Visual Search Strategy.'
37. Williams, *Science and Soccer*; Bishop et al., 'Telling People Where to Look'; and Vaeyens et al., 'The Effects of Task Constraints,' 147.
38. Williams and Hodges, 'Practice, Instruction and Skill,' 646.
39. Williams and Hodges, 'Practice, Instruction and Skill,' 637–50; Williams, *Science and Soccer*; and Broadbent et al., 'Perceptual-cognitive Skill Training.'
40. Roca et al., 'Developmental Activities,' 1643–52; and Williams and Davids, 'Declarative Knowledge,' 259–75.
41. Williams and Davids, 'Declarative Knowledge,' 259–75; Ericsson et al., *Complex Information Processing*, 235–67; Ericsson et al., 'Long-term working,' 211; O'Donoghue, *An Introduction*; and O'Donoghue, 'Research methods.'
42. Williams, *Science and Soccer*; and Williams and Davids, 'Declarative Knowledge,' 259–75.
43. Groom et al., 'The Delivery of Video-based,' 16–32.
44. O'Donoghue, 'Research Methods.'
45. Bishop et al., 'Neural Bases for Anticipation,' 98–109.
46. Roca et al., 'Developmental Activities,' 1643–52; and Ford et al., 'An Analysis of Practice Activities,' 483–95.
47. Davids et al., 'How Small-sided and Conditioned Games,' 154–61; and Partington and Cushion, 'An Investigation of the Practice Activities,' 374–82.
48. Light et al., 'Improving 'At-action' Decision-making,' 258–75; Light, 'An International Perspective,' 211; Grehaigne et al., 'Modelling Ball Circulation,' 257–70; and Harvey et al., 'Teaching Games for Understanding,' 29–54.
49. Cassidy et al., *Understanding Sports Coaching*.
50. Hauw, *Reflective Practice*, 341–52.Richards et al., 'Developing Rapid High-pressure,' 407–24.
51. Williams and Hodges, 'Practice, Instruction and Skill,' 637–50.
52. Broadbent et al., 'Perceptual-cognitive Skill Training,' 328.

53. Williams, *Science and Soccer*; Cassidy et al., *Understanding Sports Coaching*; Potrac et al., *Routledge Handbook of Sports Coaching*; Jones et al., *Sports Coaching Cultures*; and Jones, et al., *The Sociology of Sports Coaching*.
54. Stein et al., 'Influence of Perceived,' 484–90; and Carpentier et al., 'When Change-oriented,' 423–35.
55. Cushion and Jones, 'A systematic observation,' 354; and Ford et al., 'An Analysis of Practice Activities,' 483–95.
56. Smoll et al., 'Enhancement of children's,' 602.
57. McGarry et al., *Routledge Handbook*.
58. Laird and Waters, 'Eyewitness Recollection,' 76–84; and Carling et al., *Handbook of Soccer Match Analysis*.
59. Groom and Cushion, Using of video based coaching, 40–6; and Carling et al., *Handbook of Soccer Match Analysis*.
60. Jones et al., 2013; Ambiguity, 'Noticing and Orchestration,' 276–7; and Partington et al., 'The Impact of Video Feedback,' 700–16.
61. Partington and Cushion, 'An investigation,' 374–82; and Wright et al., 'An Analysis of Elite Coaches,' 436–51.
62. Chelladurai, 'Discrepancy between preferences,' 27–41; Smith and Smoll, 'Self-esteem and Children's Reactions,' 987; and Smith et al., 'Effects of a Motivational Climate,' 39.
63. Smith et al., 'Effects of a Motivational Climate,' 39; Smoll et al., 'Enhancement,' 602; and Smith and Smoll, 'Self-esteem and Children's Reactions,' 987.
64. Partington and Cushion, 'An Investigation of the Practice Activities,' 374–82; Harvey et al., 'Teaching Games for Understanding,' 29–54; and Davids et al., 'How Small-sided and Conditioned Games,' 154–61.
65. Frank and Miller, 'Training Coaches to Observe,' 285–97; Laird and Waters, 'Eyewitness Recollection,' 76–84; and Carling et al., *Handbook of Soccer Match Analysis*.
66. Kelly and McGann, 'Exploring the Role of Mobile.'
67. Turnnidge et al., 'A Direct Observation,' 225–40.
68. Jones et al., 2013; Ambiguity, 'Noticing and Orchestration,' 276–7.
69. Ibid.
70. Ibid.
71. Ibid.
72. Elberse, 'Ferguson's Formula,' 116–25.
73. Schön, *The Reflective Practitioner*; and Van Manen, 'On the Epistemology,' 33–50.
74. Gibbs, *Learning by Doing*.
75. Christensen, 'An Eye for Talent,' 365–82.
76. Partington and Cushion, 'An Investigation of the Practice Activities,' 381; Partington et al., 'The Impact of Video Feedback,' 700–16; Cushion et al., 'Coach Behaviours,' 1637; and Williams & Hodges, 'Practice, Instruction and Skill,' 637–50.
77. Balaguer et al., 'Coaches' Interpersonal Style,' 1619–29.
78. Ford et al., 'An Analysis of Practice Activities,' 483–95.
79. Partington et al., 'The Impact of Video Feedback,' 700–16; Cushion et al., 'Coach Behaviours,' 1637; Jones, 'The Sports Coach as Educator,' 405–12; and Jones, et al., *The Sociology of Sports Coaching*.
80. Gibbs, *Learning by Doing*.
81. Hatton and Smith, 'Reflection in Teacher Education,' 33–49.
82. Jasper, 'Nurses' perceptions,' 452–63.
83. Tversky and Kahneman, 'Availability: A Heuristic,' 207–32.
84. Cassidy et al., *Understanding Sports Coaching*; and Peel et al., 'Learning through Reflection,' 729–42.
85. Cassidy et al., *Understanding Sports Coaching*. Peel et al., 2013.
86. Gibbs, *Learning by Doing*.
87. Elander et al., 'Complex skills,' 71–90; and Davies, 'Not Quite Right,' 327–40.
88. Byrnes and Dunbar, 'The Nature and Development,' 477; and Schneider, 'Looking outside Education,' 119.
89. Saltmarsh and Saltmarsh, 'Has Anyone Read the Reading,' 621–32.
90. Ibid.

91. Flanagan, 'The Critical Incident Technique,' 327.
92. Shapira-Lishchinsky, 'Teachers' Critical Incidents,' 648–56.
93. Byrnes and Dunbar, 'The Nature and Development,' 477.
94. A number of studies have examined the processes and practices that coaches adopt for improving decision making in volleyball (Macquet, 2009) basketball (Bar-Eli & Tractinsky, 2000) netball (Richards et al., 2012) and rugby union (Light et al., 2014) and in teams such as the New Zealand All-Blacks Kidman (2010)
95. MGarry et al., 2013, *Routledge Handbook of Sports*; Carling et al., *Performance assessment*; Groom et al., 'The Delivery of Video-based,' 16–32; and Groom et al., 'The Delivery of Video-based,' 16–32.
96. Bampouras et al., 'Performance Analytic Processes,' 468–83.
97. Mackenzie and Cushion, 'Performance Analysis in Football,' 639–76; and Carling et al., 'Comment on 'Performance Analysis.'
98. Ibid.
99. Ibid.
100. Patton, 'Qualitative Interviewing,' 574.
101. Groom et al., 'The Delivery of Video-based,' 16–32.
102. Bampouras et al., 'Performance Analytic Processes,' 468–83.
103. Senecal et al., 'A Season-long Team-building,' 186; and Mallett and Hanrahan, 'Elite Athletes: Why Does,' 183–200.
104. Cassidy et al., *Understanding Sports Coaching*.
105. Potrac et al., 'It's All about Getting Respect,' 183–202; and Jones, et al., *The Sociology of Sports Coaching*.
106. Cooper and Sawaf, *Executive EQ*; Thelwell et al., 'Examining relationships,' 224–35; and Lane et al., 'Emotional Intelligence,' 195–201.
107. Cassidy et al., *Understanding Sports Coaching*; Culver and Trudel, 'Clarifying the Concept,' 1–10; and Horgan and Daly, 'The Role of the Coach.'
108. Duhigg, *The Power of Habit.*
109. Beswick, *Focused for Soccer* or Abrahams (2012, 2013); Abrahams, *Soccer Brain*, 2013; and Abrahams, *Soccer Tough*, 2012.
110. Van Mullem and Brunner, 'Developing a Successful Coaching,' 29–34.
111. Renshaw et al., 'Insights from Ecological Psychology,' 540–602.

References

Abrahams, Dan. *Soccer Tough: Simple Football Psychology Techniques to Improve Your Game*. Birmingham, AL: Bennion Kearny, 2012.

Abrahams, Dan. *Soccer Brain: The 4C Coaching Model for Developing World Class Player Mindsets and a Winning Football Team*. Birmingham, AL: Bennion Kearny, 2013.

Balaguer, Isabel, Lorena González, Priscila Fabra, Isabel Castillo, Juan Mercé, and Joan L. Duda. 'Coaches' Interpersonal Style, Basic Psychological Needs and the Well-and Ill-being of Young Soccer Players: A Longitudinal Analysis'. *Journal of Sports Sciences* 30, no. 15 (2012): 1619–29.

Bampouras, Theodoros M., Colum Cronin, and Paul K. Miller. 'Performance Analytic Processes in Elite Sport Practice: An Exploratory Investigation of the Perspectives of a Sport Scientist, Coach and Athlete'. *International Journal of Performance Analysis in Sport* 12, no. 2 (2012): 468–83.

Bar-Eli, Michael, and Noam Tractinsky. 'Criticality of Game Situations and Decision Making in Basketball: An Application of Performance Crisis Perspective'. *Psychology of Sport and Exercise* 1, no. 1 (2000): 27–39.

Barić, Renata, and Valentin Bucik. 'Motivational Differences in Athletes Trained by Coaches of Different Motivational and Leadership Profiles'. *Kineziologija* 41, no. 2 (2009): 181–94.

Beswick, Bill. *Focused for Soccer*. Champaign, IL: Human Kinetics, 2010.

Bishop, Daniel, Gustav Kuhn, and Claire Maton. 'Telling People Where to Look in a Soccer-based Decision Task: A Nomothetic Approach'. *Journal of Eye Movement Research*. 7, no. 2 (2014): 1–13.

Bishop, Daniel T., Michael J. Wright, Robin C. Jackson, and Bruce Abernethy. 'Neural Bases for Anticipation Skill in Soccer: An FMRI Study'. *Journal of Sport & Exercise Psychology* 35 (2013): 98–109.

Broadbent, D.P., J. Causer, A.M. Williams, and P.R. Ford. 'Perceptual-cognitive Skill Training and Its Transfer to Expert Performance in the Field: Future Research Directions'. *European Journal of Sport Science* 15, no. 4 (2015): 322–31.

Byrnes, James P., and Kevin N. Dunbar. 'The Nature and Development of Critical-analytic Thinking'. *Educational Psychology Review* 26, no. 4 (2014): 477–93.

Carling, Christopher, Craig Wright, Lee John Nelson, and Paul S. Bradley. 'Comment on 'Performance Analysis in Football: A Critical Review and Implications for Future Research''. *Journal of Sports Sciences* 32, no. 1 (2014): 2–7.

Carling, Christopher, Tom Reilly and A. Mark Williams. *Performance Assessment for Field Sports*. London: Routledge, 2008.

Carling, Christopher, A.M Williams, and T. Reilly. *Handbook of Soccer Match Analysis: A Systematic Approach to Improving Performance*. London. Routledge. (2005).

Carpentier, Joëlle, and Geneviève A. Mageau. 'When Change-oriented Feedback Enhances Motivation, Well-Being and Performance: A Look at Autonomy-supportive Feedback in Sport'. *Psychology of Sport and Exercise* 14, no. 3 (2013): 423–35.

Cassidy, Tania G., Robyn L. Jones, and Paul Potrac. *Understanding Sports Coaching: The Pedagogical, Social and Cultural Foundations of Coaching Practice*. London: Routledge, 2015.

Chelladurai, Packianathan. 'Discrepancy between Preferences and Perceptions of Leadership Behavior and Satisfaction of Athletes in Varying Sports'. *Journal of Sport Psychology* 6, no. 1 (1984): 27–41.

Christensen, Mette Krogh. 'An Eye for Talent: Talent Identification and Practical Sense of Top-level Soccer Coaches'. *Sociology of Sport Journal* 26 (2009): 365–82.

Christensen, Mette Krogh, Dan Nørgaard Laursen, and Jan Kahr Sørensen. 'Situated Learning in Youth Elite Football: A Danish Case Study among Talented Male under-18 Football Players'. *Physical Education & Sport Pedagogy* 16, no. 2 (2011): 163–78.

Collins, Dave, and Aine McNamara. *Sports Medicine* 42, no. 11 (2012): 907–14.

Cooper, Robert K., and Ayman Sawaf. *Executive EQ: Emotional Intelligence in Leadership and Organizations*. New York: Penguin, 1998.

Culver, Diane, and Pierre Trudel. 'Clarifying the Concept of Communities of Practice in Sport'. *International Journal of Sports Science and Coaching* 3, no. 1 (2008): 1–10.

Curran, Conor. 'Post-Playing Careers of Irish-Born Footballers in England, 1945–2010'. *Sport in Society* 18, no. 10 (2015): 1273–86.

Cushion, Christopher J., P.R. Ford, and Mark Williams. 'Coach behaviours and practice structures in youth soccer: Implications for talent development'. *Journal of Sports Sciences* 30, no. 15 (2012): 1631–41.

Cushion, Christopher J., and R.L. Jones. A Systematic Observation of Professional Top-level Youth Soccer Coaches. *Journal of Sport Behavior* 24, no. 4 (2001): 354.

Davids, Keith, Duarte Araújo, Vanda Correia, and Luís Vilar 'How Small-Sided and Conditioned Games Enhance Acquisition of Movement and Decision-Making Skills'. *Exercise and Sport Sciences Reviews* 41, no. 3 (2013): 154–61.

Davies, Martin W. "Not Quite Right': Helping Students to Make Better Arguments'. *Teaching in Higher Education* 13, no. 3 (2008): 327–40.

Duhigg, Charles. *The Power of Habit: Why We Do What We Do and How to Change*. London: Random House, 2013.

Elander, James, Katherine Harrington, Lin Norton, Hannah Robinson, and Pete Reddy. 'Complex Skills and Academic Writing: A Review of Evidence about the Types of Learning Required to Meet Core Assessment Criteria'. *Assessment & Evaluation in Higher Education* 31, no. 1 (2006): 71–90.

Elberse, Anita with Sir Alex Ferguson. Ferguson's Formula. *Harvard Business Review*, October, 116–25, (2013).

Ericsson, K. Anders, and Walter Kintsch. 'Long-Term Working Memory'. *Psychological Review* 102, no. 2 (1995): 211.

Ericsson, K. Anders, and James J. Staszewski. Skilled Memory and Expertise: Mechanisms of Exceptional Performance. *Complex Information Processing: The Impact of Herbert a. Simon 2* (1989): 235–67.

Flanagan, John C. The Critical Incident Technique. *Psychological Bulletin* 51, no. 4 (1954): 327–58.

Ford, Paul R., Ian Yates, and A. Mark Williams. 'An Analysis of Practice Activities and Instructional Behaviours Used by Youth Soccer Coaches During Practice: Exploring the Link between Science and Application'. *Journal of Sports Sciences* 28, no. 5 (2010): 483–95.

Franks, Ian M., and Gary Miller. 'Training Coaches to Observe and Remember'. *Journal of Sports Sciences* 9, no. 3 (1991): 285–97.

Gibbs, Graham. *Learning by Doing: A Guide to Teaching and Learning Methods.* Oxford: Oxford Brookes University, 1988.

Gray, H. Joey, and Jonathan A. Plucker. 'She's a Natural: Identifying and Developing Athletic Talent'. *Journal for the Education of the Gifted* 33, no. 3 (2010): 361–80.

Gréhaigne, Jean-Francis, Didier Caty, and Paul Godbout. 'Modelling Ball Circulation in Invasion Team Sports: A Way to Promote Learning Games through Understanding'. *Physical Education and Sport Pedagogy* 15, no. 3 (2010): 257–70.

Groom, Ryan, and Chris Cushion. 'Using of Video Based Coaching with Players: A Case Study'. *International Journal of Performance Analysis in Sport* 5, no. 3 (2005): 40–6.

Groom, Ryan, Christopher Cushion, and Lee Nelson. 'The Delivery of Video-based Performance Analysis by England Youth Soccer Coaches: Towards a Grounded Theory'. *Journal of Applied Sport Psychology* 23, no. 1 (2011): 16–32.

Harvey, Stephen, Christopher J. Cushion, Heidi M. Wegis, and Ada N. Massa-Gonzalez. 'Teaching Games for Understanding in American High-School Soccer: A Quantitative Data Analysis Using the Game Performance Assessment Instrument'. *Physical Education and Sport Pedagogy* 15, no. 1 (2010): 29–54.

Hatton, Neville, and David Smith. 'Reflection in Teacher Education: Towards Definition and Implementation'. *Teaching and Teacher Education* 11, no. 1 (1995): 33–49.

Hauw, Denis. 'The Predictive Ability of the Talent Development Environment on Youth Elite Football Players' Well-being: A Person-Centered Approach'. *Reflective Practice* 10, no. 3 (2009): 341–52.

Higgs, Joy, and Angie Titchen. 'Knowledge and Reasoning'. *Clinical Reasoning in the Health Professions* 2 (2000): 23–32.

Hodges, N.J., and I.M. Franks. 'Modelling Coaching Practice: The Role of Instruction and Demonstration'. *Journal of Sports Sciences* 20, no. 10 (Oct 2002): 793–811.

Horgan, Peter, and Pat Daly. The Role of the Coach Developer in Supporting and Guiding Coach Learning: A Commentary. *International Sport Coaching Journal* 2 (2015): 354–6.

Ivarsson, Andreas, Andreas Stenling, Johan Fallby, Urban Johnson, Elin Borg, and Gunnar Johansson. 'The Predictive Ability of the Talent Development Environment on Youth Elite Football Players' Well-Being: A Person-Centered Approach'. *Psychology of Sport and Exercise* 16 (2015): 15–23.

Jacobs, Heidi LM. Information Literacy and Reflective Pedagogical Praxis. *The Journal of Academic Librarianship* 34, no. 3 (2008): 256–62.

Januario, Nuno, Antonio F. Rosado, and Isabel Mesquita. 'Variables Affecting Athletes' Retention of Coaches Feedback'. *Perceptual & Motor Skills* 117, no. 2 (2013): 389–401.

Jasper, Melanie A. Nurses' Perceptions of the Value of Written Reflection. *Nurse Education Today* 19, no. 6 (1999): 452–63.

Jones, Robyn. 'The Sports Coach as Educator: Reconceptualising Sports Coaching'. *International Journal of Sports Science and Coaching* 1, no. 4 (2006): 405–12.

Jones, Robyn L., Kathleen M. Armour, and Paul Potrac. *Sports Coaching Cultures: From Practice to Theory.* London: Routledge, 2004.

Jones, Robyn L., Jake Bailey, and Andrew Thompson. Ambiguity, Noticing and Orchestration: Further Thoughts on Managing the Complex Coaching Context. In *Routledge Handbook of Sports Coaching,* 271–83. ed. Potrac, P., Gilbert, W., and Denison, J. London. Routledge. (2013).

Jones, Robyn L., Paul Potrac, Chris Cushion, and Lars Tore Ronglan, eds. *The Sociology of Sports Coaching.* London. Routledge, 2010.

Jones, Robyn L., and Poppy Turner. 'Teaching Coaches to Coach Holistically: Can Problem-Based Learning (PBL) Help?' *Physical Education & Sport Pedagogy* 11, no. 2 (2006): 181–202.

Kelly, S., and Ronan McGann. 'Exploring the Role of Mobile Phone Applications in the Assessment and Development of Elite Athletes'. Presentation at the European Association for Sport Management Congress. Coventry, 2014.

Kidman, Lynn. *Athlete-centred Coaching: Developing Decision Makers*. Worcester, MA: IPC Print Resources, 2010.

Laird, Peter, and Laura Waters. 'Eyewitness Recollection of Sport Coaches'. *International Journal of Performance Analysis in Sport* 8, no. 1 (2008): 76–84.

Lane, Andrew M., Richard C. Thelwell, James Lowther, and Tracey J. Devonport. 'Emotional Intelligence and Psychological Skills Use among Athletes'. *Social Behavior and Personality: An International Journal* 37, no. 2 (2009): 195–201.

Light, R. 'An International Perspective on Teaching Games for Understanding'. *Physical Education and Sport Pedagogy* 10, no. 3 (2005): 211.

Light, Richard L., Stephen Harvey, and Alain Mouchet. 'Improving 'At-action' Decision-making in Team Sports through a Holistic Coaching Approach'. *Sport, Education and Society* 19, no. 3 (2014): 258–75.

Mackenzie, Rob, and Chris Cushion. 'Performance Analysis in Football: A Critical Review and Implications for Future Research'. *Journal of Sports Sciences* 31, no. 6 (2013): 639–76.

Macquet, A.C. 'Recognition within the Decision-making Process: A Case Study of Expert Volleyball Players'. *Journal of Applied Sport Psychology* 21, no. 1 (2009): 64–79.

Mallett, Clifford J., and Stephanie J. Hanrahan. 'Elite Athletes: Why Does the 'Fire'burn So Brightly?' *Psychology of Sport and Exercise* 5, no. 2 (2004): 183–200.

Van Manen, Max. 'On the Epistemology of Reflective Practice'. *Teachers and Teaching: Theory and Practice* 1, no. 1 (1995): 33–50.

Martindale, Russell J., Dave Collins, and Jim Daubney. 'Talent Development: A Guide for Practice and Research within Sport'. *Quest* 57, no. 4 (2005): 353–75.

McGarry, Tim, Peter O'Donoghue, and Jaime Sampaio. *Routledge Handbook of Sports Performance Analysis*. London: Routledge, 2013.

Morris, T. 'Psychological Characteristics and Talent Identification in Soccer'. *Journal of Sports Sciences* 18, no. 9 (September 2000): 715–26.

Van Mullem, Pete, and Dave Brunner. 'Developing a Successful Coaching Philosophy: A Step-by-step Approach'. *Strategies* 26, no. 3 (2013): 29–34.

Murray, Eileen. 'Intuitive Coaching-summary'. *Industrial and Commercial Training* 36, no. 5 (2004): 203–6.

O'Donoghue, Peter. *Research Methods for Sports Performance Analysis*. London: Routledge, 2009.

O'Donoghue, Peter. *An Introduction to Performance Analysis of Sport*. London: Routledge, 2014.

Partington, Mark, and C. Cushion. 'An Investigation of the Practice Activities and Coaching Behaviors of Professional Top-Level Youth Soccer Coaches'. *Scandinavian Journal of Medicine & Science in Sports* 23, no. 3 (2013): 374–82.

Partington, Mark, Christopher J. Cushion, Ed Cope, and Stephen Harvey. The Impact of Video Feedback on Professional Youth Football Coaches' Reflection and Practice Behaviour: A Longitudinal Investigation of Behaviour Change. *Reflective Practice* 16, no. 5 (2015): 700–16.

Patton, Michael Quinn. 'Qualitative Interviewing'. *Qualitative Research and Evaluation Methods* 3 (2002): 344–7.

Peel, John, Brendan Cropley, Sheldon Hanton, and Scott Fleming. 'Learning through Reflection: Values, Conflicts, and Role Interactions of a Youth Sport Coach'. *Reflective Practice* 14, no. 6 (2013): 729–42.

Poli R, L. Ravenel, and R. Besson. *Annual Review of the European Football Players' Labour Market*, Neuchatel: Professional Football Players Observatory, 2012.

Porter, C.O., J.W. Webb, and C.I. Gogus. 'When Goal Orientations Collide: Effects of Learning and Performance Orientation on Team Adaptability in Response to Workload Imbalance'. *Journal of Applied Psychology* 95, no. 5 (September 2010): 935–43.

Potrac, Paul, Wade Gilbert, and Jim Denison. *Routledge Handbook of Sports Coaching*. London: Routledge, 2013.

Potrac, Paul, Robyn Jones, and Kathleen Armour. 'It's All about Getting Respect': The Coaching Behaviors of an Expert English Soccer Coach'. *Sport, Education and Society* 7, no. 2 (2002): 183–202.

Reilly, T., A.M. Williams, A. Nevill, and A. Franks. 'A Multidisciplinary Approach to Talent Identification in Soccer'. *Journal of Sports Sciences* 18, no. 9 (September 2000): 695–702.

Renshaw, Ian, Keith W. Davids, Richard Shuttleworth, and Jia Yi Chow. 'Insights from Ecological Psychology and Dynamical Systems Theory Can Underpin a Philosophy of Coaching'. *International Journal of Sport Psychology* 40, no. 4 (2009): 540–602.

Richards, Pam, Dave Collins, and Duncan RD Mascarenhas. 'Developing Rapid High-pressure Team Decision-making Skills. The Integration of Slow Deliberate Reflective Learning within the Competitive Performance Environment: A Case Study of Elite Netball'. *Reflective Practice* 13, no. 3 (2012): 407–24.

Roberts, Simon, and Paul Potrac. 'Behaviourism, Constructivism and Sports Coaching Pedagogy: A Conversational Narrative in the Facilitation of Player Learning'. *International Sport Coaching Journal* 1, no. 3 (2014): 180–7.

Roca, A., A.M. Williams, and P.R. Ford. 'Developmental Activities and the Acquisition of Superior Anticipation and Decision Making in Soccer Players'. *Journal of Sports Sciences* 30, no. 15 (2012): 1643–52.

Saltmarsh, David, and Sue Saltmarsh. 'Has Anyone Read the Reading? Using Assessment to Promote Academic Literacies and Learning Cultures'. *Teaching in Higher Education* 13, no. 6 (2008): 621–32.

Schneider, Jack. 'Looking outside Education: Expanding Our Thinking about Moving Research into Practice'. *Education Policy Analysis Archives* 23 (2015): 119.

Schön, Donald A. *The Reflective Practitioner: How Professionals Think in Action*. Vol. 5126. New York. Basic books, 1983.

Senécal, Julie, Todd M. Loughead, and Gordon A. Bloom. 'A Season-long Team-building Intervention: Examining the Effect of Team Goal Setting on Cohesion'. *Journal of Sport & Exercise Psychology* 30, no. 2 (2008): 186.

Shapira-Lishchinsky, Orly. 'Teachers' Critical Incidents: Ethical Dilemmas in Teaching Practice'. *Teaching and Teacher Education* 27, no. 3 (2011): 648–56.

Smith, Ronald E., and Frank L. Smoll. 'Self-esteem and Children's Reactions to Youth Sport Coaching Behaviors: A Field Study of Self-Enhancement Processes'. *Developmental Psychology* 26, no. 6 (1990): 987.

Smith, Ronald E., Frank L. Smoll, and Sean P. Cumming. 'Effects of a Motivational Climate Intervention for Coaches on Young Athletes' Sport Performance Anxiety'. *Journal of Sport and Exercise Psychology* 29, no. 1 (2007): 39.

Smoll, Frank L., Ronald E. Smith, Nancy P. Barnett, and John J. Everett. 'Enhancement of Children's Self-Esteem through Social Support Training for Youth Sport Coaches'. *Journal of Applied Psychology* 78, no. 4 (1993): 602.

Stein, Jonathan, Gordon A. Bloom, and Catherine M. Sabiston. 'Influence of Perceived and Preferred Coach Feedback on Youth Athletes' Perceptions of Team Motivational Climate'. *Psychology of Sport and Exercise* 13, no. 4 (2012): 484–90.

Stoszkowski, John, and Dave Collins. Using Shared Online Blogs to Structure and Support Informal Coach Learning – Part 1: A Tool to Promote Reflection and Communities of Practice. *Sport, Education and Society* 20 (2015): 1–24.

Stoszkowski, J., and D. Collins. Sources, Topics and Use of Knowledge by Coaches. *Journal of Sports Sciences* 34, no. 9 (2016): 1–9.

Thelwell, Richard C., Andrew M. Lane, Neil JV Weston, and Iain A. Greenlees. 'Examining Relationships between Emotional Intelligence and Coaching Efficacy'. *International Journal of Sport and Exercise Psychology* 6, no. 2 (2008): 224–35.

Turnnidge, Jennifer, Jean Côté, Tom Hollenstein, and Janice Deakin. 'A Direct Observation of the Dynamic Content and Structure of Coach-Athlete Interactions in a Model Sport Program'. *Journal of Applied Sport Psychology* 26, no. 2 (2014): 225–40.

Tversky, Amos, and Daniel Kahneman. 'Availability: A Heuristic for Judging Frequency and Probability'. *Cognitive Psychology* 5, no. 2 (1973): 207–32.

Vaeyens, Roel, Matthieu Lenoir, A. Mark Williams, and Renaat M. Philippaerts. 'Mechanisms Underpinning Successful Decision Making in Skilled Youth Soccer Players: An Analysis of Visual Search Behaviors'. *Journal of Motor Behavior* 39, no. 5 (2007): 395–408.

Vaeyens, Roel, Matthieu Lenoir, A. Mark Williams, Liesbeth Mazyn, and Renaat M. Philippaerts. 'The Effects of Task Constraints on Visual Search Behavior and Decision-making Skill in Youth Soccer Players'. *Journal of Sport and Exercise Psychology* 29, no. 2 (2007): 147.

Walters, G., and G. Rossi. Labour Market Migration in European Football: Key Issues and Challenges. *Birkbeck Sports Business Centre Research Paper Series*. (2) 2 (2009).

Williams, A. Mark, Paul Ward, J. Bell-Walker, and P.R. Ford. 'Perceptual-cognitive Expertise, Practice History Profiles and Recall Performance in Soccer'. *British Journal of Psychology* 103, no. 3 (2012): 393–411.

Williams, A.M. *Science and Soccer: Developing Elite Performers*. London: Routledge, 2013.

Williams, Mark, and Keith Davids. 'Declarative Knowledge in Sport: A by-Product of Experience or a Characteristic of Expertise?' *Journal of Sport and Exercise Psychology* 17 (1995): 259–75.

Williams, A.M., and K. Davids. 'Visual Search Strategy, Selective Attention, and Expertise in Soccer'. *Research Quarterly for Exercise and Sport* 69, no. 2 (June 1998): 111–28.

Williams, A.M., and K.A. Ericsson. 'Perceptual-cognitive Expertise in Sport: Some Considerations When Applying the Expert Performance Approach'. *Human Movement Science* 24, no. 3 (June 2005): 283–307.

Williams, A.M., and N.J. Hodges. 'Practice, Instruction and Skill Acquisition in Soccer: Challenging Tradition'. *Journal of Sports Sciences* 23, no. 6 (June 2005): 637–50.

Williams, A.M., and T. Reilly. 'Talent Identification and Development in Soccer'. *Journal of Sports Sciences* 18, no. 9 (September 2000): 657–67.

Wright, Craig, Steve Atkins, and Bryan Jones. 'An Analysis of Elite Coaches' Engagement with Performance Analysis Services (Match, Notational Analysis and Technique Analysis)'. *International Journal of Performance Analysis in Sport* 12, no. 2 (2012): 436–51.

Supporter ownership as a method of football governance: the concept of a Supporters' Trust and its operation within England and the Republic of Ireland

Shane Tobin

> This paper seeks to analyse and evaluate the subject of supporter ownership as a form of football governance. The historical evolution of football has seen the game transform into a contemporary global product that transcends geographical boundaries, culture and tradition. The formation of Supporters Direct in 2000 represents the formalization of supporter activism as supporters sought to promote democratic practices within the game in search of a sustainable sport. The emergence of Supporters' Trusts across the UK and Ireland symbolizes a significant shift in the governance of football. The embracement of community as a concept and an awareness of group ideology, has enabled the Supporters' Trust model to prosper at a lower level of the game. This paper seeks to trace the conditions which contributed to the emergence of supporter ownership; explore how the concept has been formalized; and examine the role of active supporters in the League of Ireland.

In order to understand the contemporary condition of professional football and the role supporters play within the game, it is important to examine the historical and cultural context in which the game evolved. Football's growth from a disorderly pastime into one of the most global and popular sport has radically changed the structure and make-up of the game. The relationship between supporters and their clubs has been reorganized due to the influx of neo-liberal ideology in English football in the 1980s and consequent shift in social relations. The Taylor Report and the birth of the Premier League in 1992 can be seen as key events that contributed to the globalization of elite English football. The breakaway of the Premier League from the Football League marked an end to over a century-long tradition of interventionist governance and administration. The breakaway permitted Premier League clubs embrace free market policies and light regulation. The legal requirement of all-seated stadia, introduced as a result of perilous stadiums that contributed to the Heysel, Bradford and Hillsborough Stadium disasters, combined with lucrative television deals has resulted in the increased commercialization of the game.

English football's attempt to attract a more 'affluent consumer' in pursuit for further commodification has left many 'traditional' supporters' feeling isolated. This feeling of seclusion has resulted in supporters' seeking to play an active role in the overall make-up of their clubs. The notion of supporters' as active stakeholders was promoted by New Labour and Third Way ideology. The idea of supporters' as active citizens, and the quest to re-embrace community resulted in the foundation of Supporters Direct, a formal initiative that seeks greater influence for supporters in the running of their clubs. One of the key functions of Supporters Direct and Supporters' Trusts in general, is to move 'beyond moral and value-led arguments' for fan ownership and to provide a systematic and practicable approach for greater supporter involvement.[1]

This paper will analyse the feasibility of Supporters' Trusts and examine some of the key dimension of such a mode of governance. Drawing on new social movement theory and theories of community, Supporters' Trusts cannot simply be defined as a universalist and linear concept, but something that is particular and unique. The sheers size of Premier League clubs' and the problem of raising sufficient finance to compete with shareholders could be seen as one of the key obstacles to the Supporter Trust movement. A clear lack of tradition and culture of supporter ownership in England is reflected in the absence of supporters' in legislation and governance policies. In contrast, fan activism and supporter ownership in European leagues, and in particular the German Bundesliga, are often highlighted as democratic modes of ownership capable of raising the required finance to compete at an elite level while preserving supporters' as a central stakeholder.

The German Bundesliga has demonstrated that the role of supporters' as a central stakeholder has helped develop a competitive and sustainable football league that is accessible to all social groupings. In contrast, the Premier League and the reputed 'gentrification' of football has prevented Supporters' Trusts from achieving success at an elite level. The Supporters' Trust model and its apparent failure to penetrate top-flight English football can be analysed within the overall context of the failure of Third Way politics. Its pragmatic attempt to demarcate neo-liberalism whilst preserving capitalism as the dominant economic system is reflected in football. Supporters' quest for inclusion does not attempt to revamp the economic relations of the game. It simply seeks greater participation through democratic principles in which a sustainable model of football can be implemented. This fails to initiate change and combat the problems of extreme financial expenditure at a premier level. The 'bottom-up' policies of Supporters' Trusts and its inability to infiltrate top-flight English football can be seen as a consequence of the failure of English governing bodies to thoroughly regulate professional football, ultimately creating a highly unequal structure that prevents social mobility.

According to David Goldblatt, 'football, in its transition from a chaotic folk ritual to a sector of the global entertainment industry',[2] has encountered a dilemma which has been torn apart by the forces of money and power. The Premier League and its incorporation of globalization and its characteristics is in polar opposite to the League of Ireland. Supporter activism amongst League of Ireland clubs has failed to receive appropriate attention and could be seen to be somewhat of an exemplification to smaller leagues and clubs across Europe. This paper seeks to highlight the accessibility of supporters' organizations to their League of Ireland clubs who seek greater involvement with their clubs. The League of Ireland can be portrayed as an extremely localized league, free from commodification. In spite of a comprehensive licensing system that closely inspects the financial state of clubs, the League has been plagued by issues of financial uncertainty. It is the aim of this paper to undertake a study of the League of Ireland, and in particular Cork City FC, and examine how periods of financial uncertainty can contribute to supporters gaining a potent role in the operation of their club.

The League of Ireland & Cork City FC

The globalized and monetized spectacle of Europe's major leagues that derive much of their income from colossal television and commercial deals, as well as incredibly high attendances, portrays European professional football as a global and glamorous entity with infinite resources. In reality, for the majority of European professional football leagues, the heterogeneous and fashionable manner in which the 'big five' European leagues is presented is in stark contrast to the reality of European football on a wider scale. According to the UEFA European Club Licensing Benchmarking Report 2011, 'nearly half of all top division clubs (48%) attract an average of less than 3000 spectators'.[3] This statistic presents European top flight football as a much smaller economy, something that is much more localized and confined than what is generally perceived.

The League of Ireland – the Republic of Ireland's national association football league consisting of a Premier and First Division – can be categorized as a European domestic football league that is very much free from the constraints of globalization and its characteristics. The League of Ireland consists of twelve Premier Division and eight First Division clubs. The administration of the League has been under the control of the Football Association of Ireland (FAI) since 2006. Participation in the league is subject to an FAI Licensing system that was introduced 'in 2004 to ensure that clubs participating in the League of Ireland were maintaining certain standards'. The FAI licensing system monitors clubs in five key areas: sporting, infrastructure, legal personnel and administrative.[4] The licensing system is a coherent attempt to promote sustainability and regulate League of Ireland clubs primarily through strict budget controls. Under the license participation agreement, clubs are required to provide monthly Management Accounts alongside an Annual Financial Statement to be 'prepared and audited by independent auditors'.[5]

Regular financial auditing of League of Ireland clubs' accounts is to ensure that the Salary Cost Protocol, section 10.10 of the FAI licensing system is being adhered to. The criteria of the Salary Cost Protocol requires the licensee not to 'incur related expenditure on player, management and coaching salary costs greater than 65% of its relative income for the corresponding financial year'.[6] Undeniably, the FAI licensing system is a comprehensive regulatory framework that seeks to limit clubs financial expenditure by promoting an ethos of sustainability and encouraging clubs to live within their means. Current chairman of Cork City FC, Pat Lyons, while speaking at the Supporters Summit: Financial Fair Play – at Home and Abroad workshop, paid tribute to the FAI club licensing system, and in particular the '65% rule', describing them as 'very important' as clubs strive to develop an 'ethos of transparency'.[7] Despite a central governing body undertaking a prominent interventionist position in the League's internal affairs, the League of Ireland, regardless of the introduction of a club licensing system in 2004, has been dominated by financial irregularities.

Although governance structures have improved, League of Ireland clubs have experienced increased registration fees combined with a series of cuts to prize money and television revenue. Despite promises of 'record prize money'[8] and increased television coverage since the FAI's takeover of the League in 2006, financial downsizing has occurred. From the beginning of the 2011 season, 'the total prize pot available to Premier Division clubs has been reduced from €700,000' in 2010 to €223,500, while €91,000 has been assigned to First Division clubs – 'down from €161,000. This means a combined drop between the two division of €546,500'.⁹ The collapse of the Irish economy in 2008 undoubtedly placed enormous pressure on the FAI's financial resources with redundancies and staff pay cuts common practice. It could be suggested that League of Ireland clubs faced the burden of the FAI's restructuring policies that seeks to cut resources. Under the guidance of the FAI, affiliation fees for the 2007 season – the first under FAI control – was €17,000 per team, 'a 70% increase from the previous year'. Television money for the same season was cut from €5000 to €3000.[10] Today, League of Ireland clubs do not receive any income for the right of RTÉ or Setanta Sports to broadcast matches live, leaving Irish clubs in somewhat of an unusual position in a European context.

With increased affiliation fees, reduced prize money, and no income from television revenue, means of generating revenue for League of Ireland clubs is limited, and somewhat reliant on supporters as a means of fundraising. The 500 Club and Supporter Patrons Scheme at Sligo Rovers and St. Patrick's Athletic, respectively, illustrate supporters' attempts to raise finance on behalf of the club. The focus of St. Patrick's Athletic's Patron Scheme is to 'increase the playing budget of the team manager'[11] by subscribers paying €20 on a monthly basis. By the end of 2013, the Sligo Rovers' 500 Club in its eleven years of existence have paid over €850,000 to the club.[12] The initiatives demonstrated by Sligo Rovers and St. Patrick's Athletic supporters highlight the proactive and influential role supporters play in raising finance for League of Ireland clubs. The modest and localized nature of the League of Ireland places increased emphasis on supporters as a source of revenue in comparison to more affluent European leagues. Nevertheless, while the 500 Club and Supporter Patron Scheme raise vital finance for their clubs, the role of both initiatives is simply limited as a system of fundraising. Such schemes bear no legal or administrative right in the supervision of their football clubs.

Evidently, supporters of League of Ireland clubs are an important mechanism in terms of raising finance. For the past ten years, issues of financial difficulties have dominated the League. A number of high-profile clubs have entered Examinership– rescue process whereby the protection of the Court is obtained to assist the survival of the company – and three clubs; Dublin City, Sporting Fingal, and Monaghan United have withdrawn from the League for various reasons. It is somewhat of a rarity for a League of Ireland club to have not experienced some form of financial difficulty in recent times. Cork City FC, Derry City FC, Shamrock Rovers, Bohemian FC, Drogheda United, Dundalk FC, Shelbourne FC and Galway United are just some of the clubs to have struggled financially. Shelbourne FC in their quest for European success amassed debts of approximately €9 million. Shelbourne FC enjoyed a highly successful period under the stewardship of Ollie Byrne – lifelong Shelbourne fan and board member since 1976 – winning a number of domestic titles and relative success in European competitions. Shelbourne FC reached the Uefa Champions League third qualifying round in 2004, a hugely successful European campaign by Irish standards. Despite Shelbourne almost making €700,000 from four out of their six Champions League qualifiers, the club accumulated a loss of €1.7 million for the 2004 season.[13]

As a result of excessive spending in the pursuit of on-the-field success, Shelbourne were denied a Premier Division License for the 2007 season by the FAI licensing committee. The impulsive nature of Shelbourne FC under the guidance of Ollie Byrne has left the club in an uncertain position. John Phelan, former

Commercial Manager of Shelbourne FC, highlights the irresponsible and tactless dealings of the club at the time: 'Some weeks we'd only get €20,000 in gate receipts', yet, 'players wages was over €40,000 a week'.[14] Shelbourne FC effectively operated on borrowed money in the hope of on-the-field success. The actions of Ollie Byrne could be portrayed as somewhat egoistical. However, Shelbourne FC represented a microcosm of wider Irish society. As Ireland 'could go straight from the almost pre-modern to the post-modern, skipping ahead to the bright, supercharged, ultra-connected future',[15] the League of Ireland attempted to reach the pinnacle of European football without a systematic structure or coherent ideology. The example of Shelbourne FC is one of extreme negligence in the hope of interim success. This model of disregard is arguably an innate characteristic of the mentality of those running League of Ireland clubs, and of particular relevance to the history of association football in Cork.

The history of association football in the city of Cork is of a cyclical nature of boom-to-bust-to-boom again, as no less than eleven clubs have represented the city since Fordson's in the 1920s. Fordson's was a football club representing the Ford plant built in the City's marina in 1917, and would prove to be one of the largest sources of employment in the city.[16] Since then, association football in Cork has been characterized by a variety of clubs in various configurations. For the purposes of this article, I will concentrate on Cork City FC, founded in 1984 and the longest serving Cork side in the League of Ireland. Cork City FC's thirty-two year history has seen the club enter Examinership on three occasions, with two of those coming successively in 2008 and 2009. The unstable position of the club provided Foras the unique opportunity to takeover Cork City FC for the beginning of the 2010 season. This marked the first time supporters' owned their football club in the history of Cork association football. Foras were officially formed in 2008 by supporters not with the intention of ownership of the club, but, rather as a group who could provide financial assistance for infrastructural projects and as a form of custodianship of the club.

> Forás in our native native tongue means development or evolution, in domestic football, FORAS, the 'Friends of the Rebel Army Society' is a supporters' trust that will provide supporters the opportunity to become guardians of the clu, ensuring its future and aiding its development through regular, long term support, Foras will raise direct funding for Cork City FC and Foras will provide a reserve for emergencies faced by projects undertaken by CCFC.[17]

Although Foras was established with the purpose of being a 'guardian' of the club, the group got the opportunity to mobilize and generate public support for the Supporters' Trust model due to the mismanagement and unrealistic intentions of consecutive owners. The first of these was Arkaga– a private equity fund that invest principally in the healthcare, property, media and leisure sectors.[18]

Arkaga was founded by Gerard Walsh, who 'by 2005 at the latest, was, or had become, a fraudster', as described by a Jersey court in a case which awarded Nolan Transport €15 million 'after they fell victim to fraud when they invested in a raft of investments sold by a businessman'.[19] Arkaga's period of control of Cork City FC is somewhat blurred. There is a clear lack of public information about the company's dealings and Arkaga's motive for investing in Cork City FC is also somewhat unsure. According to an article in the *Irish Independent*, the incentive 'for Arkaga investing in Cork has never been established', but it is believed the private equity fund were 'strong supporters of an All-Ireland League and are thought to be frustrated about the obstacles that stand its way, with the FAI and IFA (Irish Football Association) unwilling to buy into the idea'.[20]

Arkaga's investment in Cork City FC poses many questions. Arkaga's apparent reliance on the development of an All-Ireland League and its failure to materialize resulted in the group ceasing to invest in the club. In a statement, Akraga claimed to devote €2.4 million into Cork City, making the club the 'single biggest benefactor in the League of Ireland'. Under the ownership of Arkaga, Cork City FC accumulated a reported debt of €750,000, ultimately forcing the club to enter Examinership in September 2008.[21] The uncertainty surrounding the future of Cork City FC resulted in the official formalization of Foras on 1 September 2008. Foras legally registered as an Industrial and Provident Society, and within the first few days of its existence assembled 'over 120 members' raising €13,000 (O'Sullivan, 2008).[22] An Industrial and Provident Society is more commonly known as a Co-operative and is bound by set of rules that governs the society with each member having equal voting rights. With the help of Cork City FC successfully emerged from Examinership. Tom Coughlan, property developer and former member of the Progressive Democrats – a conservative-liberal political party which was dissolved in 2009 – was chosen as the preferred bidder for the club. Commenting on Tom Coughlan's acquisition of the club, newly appointed CEO Gerry Nagle outlined the future projects for the club:

> For the club to survive long term it must be at the heart of the sporting community in Cork…We want to bring back volunteers to Cork City FC and deliver top class football to our supporters, fans and our sponsors… Following recent discussion we are looking forward to working closely with Foras… Realistic cost structures are a key component in terms of our long terms plans for the club.[23]

Tom Coughlan's attempt to restructure the club while delivering 'top class football' is extremely naive. Despite Nagle's pledge for a 'sustainable future for the club'.[24] Coughlan in an interview with Liam Mackey of the *Irish Examiner* (2009), outlines his dream of a '20,000-seater stadium plus convention centre and hotel for the city'.[25] Coughlan's zealous pursuit for a club embedded within the city's framework was heavily reliant on success on the field. The impractical objectives of achieving success on the pitch within months of exiting Examinership, combined with Coughlan's unreasonable long-term vision for the club illustrate the irrational framework in which the club operated. Just two months into the 2009 season, the club faced further financial difficulties regarding tax liabilities. The 2009 season under Tom Coughlan can be seen as a watershed moment for Foras and supporters of Cork City FC. A series of dealings with the Office of the Revenue Commissioners, numerous court appearances, threats of industrial action by employees of the club, and the subsequent damage to the reputation and status of the football club offered Foras an ideal opportunity to galvanize support for fan ownership as a feasible and realistic alternative.

With Revenue Bills exceeding €439,000 and players' believed to be owed in the region of €150,000, the FAI Independent Disciplinary Committee issued a twelve month ban against Tom Coughlan 'from football related activity for bringing the game into disrepute'.[26] Charges brought against Coughlan by the Independent Disciplinary Committee 'relate to allegations that he failed to pay employees on time, failed to meet obligations to revenue, failed to pay insurance premiums on time, failed to pay ESB resulting in supply being cut off, bounced cheques to referees and revenue, failed to pay transport costs and was involved in two high profile winding up proceedings'.[27] The chaotic administration of Cork City FC under Tom Coughlan left supporters feeling aggrieved. Under the banner of Foras, supporters' mobilized and issued protests in 'solidarity and support for the proposed industrial action by players', and, imperatively, sought to raise awareness within the FAI that CCIFL – Cork City Investments FC Limited, the parent company of Cork City FC – under Mr. Coughlan are not suitable license holders and should not be awarded a license for next season'.[28]

Supporters' efforts to organize and create a harmonized Supporters' Trust resulted in Foras applying for a First Division License for the 2011 season. The application was submitted as a 'Plan B' to secure League of Ireland football in Cork, with the expectation that CCIFL would fail in its attempt for a Premier Division License due to outstanding debts with the Revenue. Consequentially, CCIFL were denied a Premier Division License, allowing Forasto preserve the tradition of League of Ireland football in Cork through Cork City Foras Co-op – later changed to Cork City FC when the trust completed the purchase of the liquidated assets of Cork City FC Investments FC Ltd. A new era of supporter ownership underpinned by an ethos of community, sustainability and transparency emerged. Foras' initial efforts to save the club and eventual restructuring of Cork City FC, both on and off the pitch, must be commended. Nevertheless, the case of Cork City FC and the various instances of financial tribulation throughout the League suggests that despite a regulatory framework in operation, it has failed to detect and prevent clubs from the erroneous actions of its directors. Further to this, clubs need to take responsibility for their own actions. Reckless spending on players wages, inadequate planning, and the small-time approach of many clubs has resulted in a league that has failed to attract investment. As a result, facilities are largely decrepit, and attendances remain low.

The active role of supporters in League of Ireland clubs gives some hope. The recent success of supporter-owned Shamrock Rovers in the Europa League illustrates that clubs can operate on limited budgets and still achieve success. It is hoped the ethos of sustainability, community, and transparency, as promoted by Cork City FC, can be transferred to other clubs, and can become the dominant ideology in a league that lacks guidance and leadership. The collapse of the Irish economy in 2008 and the prevailing economic cutbacks prompted by the FAI, and endured by League of Ireland clubs, has resulted in the league taking several steps backwards. A retreat was needed in order for clubs and supporters to think. The establishment of a number of Supporter Trusts' across the island, and the promotion of supporters' as an almost citizen-like entity with various rights and responsibilities, could develop a new form of shareholding within League of Ireland circles. Commenting on the FAI's takeover of the League of Ireland in City Edition, Brian Lennox (Chairman and owner of Cork City FC at the time) duly notes: 'So here we again. A new league with a new logo, new ideas, new promises, big prize money and a huge budget to invest in marketing yet the same old story. Same old suits just a different tie'.[29] The notion of grande ideas being promoted by an archaic directory is very much institutionalized. Having said that, the emergence of a new supporter may encourage change.

Supporters' relationship with governing bodies

A survey amongst eight European countries, including the Republic of Ireland, commissioned by Supporters Direct Europe and published by Substance, illustrates the general feeling amongst supporters in their respective countries regarding issues relating to governance. The survey had almost 12,000 participants, representing a significant sample size. Overall, 39% of supporters said they were 'almost completely ignored' at club level in relation to their involvement with their club. This is in comparison to 73% of supporters who felt they were almost 'completely ignored' at a national level.[30] There is a clear disparity between supporters' and their governing associations. The dissatisfaction felt by supporters is strongly embodied in the Republic of Ireland, where a total of 89.35% of respondents were either 'unsatisfied' or 'very unsatisfied' with how football was being run in the country.[31] The distrust experienced between supporters and their governing bodies undoubtedly complicates relations. For a systematic and comprehensive governance structure to function, there needs to be a clear understanding of both parties obligations. If supporters are to play a significant role in the governing of the game, a coherent relationship needs to exist with its governing association.

As part of the survey, participants were asked to put forward two separate, single words to describe the running of football in their country. In Ireland, Illustration 1 depicts the FAI as an 'amateur', 'disorganised' and 'unprofessional'[32] organization. Despite the FAI's detailed licensing system, financial irregularities are still a common occurrence. The FAI's lack of investment in the League – as demonstrated by a number of financial cuts, and its apparent emphasis on the Men's Senior National Team, has created a clear disconnection between supporters of League of Ireland clubs and their governing body. This feeling of isolation is also apparent in English football. Speaking via video at the Supporters Summit, Wembley Stadium, 2014, Chairman of the FA, Greg Dyke, proclaims: 'Whether supporters have a big enough voice in the FA is up for discussion'.[33] Dyke's comments could be seen to lack conviction and fail to inspire change. The perception that supporters' are under-represented at a national level and the sense of distrust amongst fans towards the FA was clearly expressed by Dr John Beech. Beech who is an Honorary Research Fellow at Coventry University, declared at the Supporters Summit, 2014, that 'The FA are part of the problem rather than a solution' and that 'strong and good leadership'[34] was needed which the FA does not provide (Figure 1).

In contrast, in Germany and Sweden where there is a culture and history of supporter participation, supporters were 21% more likely to be satisfied or very satisfied with the running of football in their country and 25% more likely to be satisfied or very satisfied with the running of football at their club.[35] The importance of an all-encompassing governance system that is dynamic in its approach and has a clear recognition for aspects of tradition and culture has resulted in greater supporter gratification. It could be argued that the tradition and culture of supporter participation in Germany and Sweden is the biggest obstacle facing supporters in countries such as England and the Republic of Ireland. The emphasis on supporters as a key stakeholder is confirmed in legislative and governance frameworks in Germany and Sweden, thus providing supporters' with a definite status. Tony Erst, a member of Svenska Footballs support erunionen and a participant of the European Commission: 'Improving Football Governance' project notes: 'In many places in Europe there is certainly a cultural tradition of community ownership in sport. And so for us to

Figure 1. NB: The larger the word, the more times it was used.

think less like customers and more like stakeholders is probably easier than it is for an English football fan'.[36] The interpretation of supporters as 'consumers' by football clubs in England can be seen as a reconfiguration of supporters' relationship with their club, ultimately creating a new framework which does not entail a role for fans to have active participation in affairs. In contrast, the League of Ireland is not a commercialized and globalized commodity. Therefore the League of Ireland could be portrayed as an economy where the concept of supporter ownership can develop and become a prominent mode of governance.

Community

The globalization of the Premier League and its embrace of globalization's characteristics has posed a substantial challenge to the traditional and historical fabric to the game. In this sense, globalization can be seen as a tool that confronts traditional norms and values. The transition of elite levels of English football to a highly globalized entity has placed enormous pressure on the traditional structures of English football, most notably issues regarding governance and supporters. The laissez-faire approach of the FA and its associated bodies has positioned football as the 'worst governed sport in the country',[37] as described by Hugh Robertson, UK Minister of Sport. A lack of regulation and a disregard of tradition has enabled elite English football to restructure itself as a global commodity. The local community is no longer the epicentre of a football club's social relations. The ability of the Premier League to transcend global boundaries and create a communal identity regardless of space and time illustrates a significant shift for the concept of community within football. Globalization, in effect, 'creates the possibility of new modes of transnational social organisation ... making communities in particular locales vulnerable to global conditions or developments'.[38]

The transformation of the Premier League as a global economy is juxtaposed to the alteration of community as a classical sociological concept. Gerard Delanty notes that the concept of community 'has been challenged by developments relating to postmodernism, globalisation, the Internet, and 'third-way' style politics'.[39] The extension of community as a concept that can operate without a spatial boundary has been central to the rise of the Premier League. The global interconnectedness conceived by elite English clubs has had significant consequences for its local social relations. Supporters feeling aggrieved by the direction of the sport and an increased sense of exclusion amongst fans has resulted in the formulation of an active category of supporter that seeks greater representation within the game. The establishment of Supporters Direct under the rhetoric of Third Way ideology has given supporters a formalized and coherent network in which democracy and sustainability are central to their overall framework. The Supporters' Trust movements failure to influence relations at elite English clubs and its apparent reliance on periods of financial insecurity to gain influence raises important questions regarding the overall practicality of the Supporters' Trust model.

The understanding of Supporters' Trusts as a democratic vehicle of power is extremely difficult to comprehend in its current extensive and loose configuration. For example, Manchester United Supporters' Trust (MUST) overall aims and its understanding of concepts like community is vastly different to those of a Supporters' Trust at a League of Ireland club. Issues of place and locality for League of Ireland clubs is very much parochial and is drawn on a clear boundary setting. A sense of belonging and group ideology is demonstrated in the case of Shamrock Rovers and Drogheda United. According to Shamrock Rovers FC official website, aspects of community and identity are very much confined; 'Founded in Ringsend, resident in Milltown for over six decades,...Along with Tallaght, these areas will be regarded as our three spiritual homes'.[40] Drogheda United present themselves 'as an important part of the social and sporting fabric of the area. It represents Drogheda and keeps the name of our town on the national stage'.[41] Evidently, League of Ireland clubs' operate within a localized environment, relatively free from the characteristics of globalization. In this sense, community is very much understood and operated in a traditional sense.

The historical connotation of community as a 'particular form of social organization based on small groups, such as neighbourhoods, the small town or a spatially bounded locality' is perhaps best applied to League of Ireland clubs and their supporters. A sense of collective identity and intimacy has allowed supporters' of League of Ireland clubs to mobilize. Literature regarding theories of community suggests that a growing sense of individualism has somewhat deteriorated the concept. Research on new social movement theory suggests that individualism 'is in fact the basis of a good deal of communal activity and that what sustains any kinds of collective action is precisely strong individualism'.[42] In the case of the League of Ireland, clubs are reliant on volunteers to fulfil a number of roles. A policy framework titled Millennium Volunteers, launched in the UK in 1998, outlined that the proposed beneficiaries voluntary activity are threefold: first, the young person, who will gain in self-confidence and key skills and become more employable; second, the communities in which they are volunteering, and third, the society as a whole as the young people recognize and understand their rights and responsibilities as a citizen.[43]

The notion of voluntary work as a mechanism that enhances an individual's skills and knowledge has a clear correlation to Third Way politics. Foras Member 3, a voluntary member of Cork City FC's Marketing Committee, declares that 'one of the reasons I'm doing it' is to build up expertise. 'I'm giving ten hours a week to the club because I love the club, but I need to do it for personal reasons as well'.[44] An individual's quest for self-fulfilment can be integrated into the overall experience of a collective movement, thus benefiting both parties in equal measure. League of Ireland clubs' operation as a traditional form of community symbolized by place in a broader social environment distinguished by increased interconnectedness, growing individualism, and a global culture places demand on clubs to interact with their local environment. Supporters Direct definition of a Supporters' Trust outlines the role of Trust as 'strengthening the links between the club and the community it serves'.[45] The theme of 'community' is almost always used as a positive concept within public policies and frameworks. The positive perception of 'community' is something that League of Ireland must exploit and illustrated throughout the Conroy Report – a consultation review of the League published in 2015.

As a supporters-owned club, Cork City FC as an active, participatory club, engaged with community-based projects is somewhat limited by a lack of resources. Foras Member 1 declared; 'City don't have money to be spending on community (projects)'.[46] Former Foras Board Member A outlines; 'A community programme that is accessible and extensive is going to take years. To sum up Cork City, the ethos and ideal is right, but there's a lot of work to be done on planning an execution'.[47] Cork City FC as a supporters-owned and run club is in its infancy. A lack of resources and reliance on volunteers to initiate projects has resulted in a form of community ownership that has not yet realized its potential. Supporters' Trust have proved to be a lucrative form of governance at League of Ireland and lower-league English clubs. Former Board Member B describes the Supporters' Trust model as 'made for the League of Ireland'. However, issues relating to raising finance to achieve further success, both on and off-the-field, places strain on the model. Erik Samuelson, Chief Executive of supporter-owned AFC Wimbledon notes:

> Money's importance has never changed. And sadly, the higher up you progress in the pyramid the more important money becomes. Right now, we've got enough to compete with our peers financial muscle, which was derived from our relatively large fan base. The time might come when we have to decide whether supporter ownership is something that the fans think is a price worth paying for limited horizons on the football front.[48]

What is the future for Supporters' Trusts?

The concept of Supporters' Trusts as a mode of governance is an extremely new concept in association football's 153 year history. The Trust model has achieved considerable success in the League of Ireland and for certain lower-league clubs in England. The success of the Supporters' Trust model has been reliant on periods of crisis to ignite support and conduct change. The majority of clubs that are supporter-owned, or, where supporters tend to have influence, have all undergone some period of crisis, whether it be financial – in the case of Portsmouth FC, Swansea FC, Exeter City, Shamrock Rovers and Cork City FC – or some threat to the identity and historical structure of the club – FC United of Manchester and AFC Wimbledon. As a supporters owned and run club, Cork City FC underwent consecutive seasons in Examinership before Foras garnered control of the club. The actions of former club directors' functioned as a form of recruitment tool for Foras. Former Board Member A and Foras Member 1 describe Tom Coughlan as 'the best thing that ever happened' in terms of gathering support and momentum for Foras as an alternative mode of ownership.[49,50]

Former Board Member B declares: 'The greatest unifier was not the white knight on the white horse, but the black knight on the black horse', when describing the role Tom Coughlan played in fusing support for Foras. This theory of having a common enemy in order to bolster support for the project is in tandem with Anthony Downs *Up and down with ecology – the 'issue attention cycle'*. Down's declares 'gathering support for attacking any problem is always easier if its ills can be blamed on a small number of 'public enemies', especially 'if the enemies exhibit extreme wealth and power'.[51] Tom Coughlan's portrayal as the 'other' had a significant impact on initial membership figures for Foras. In 2010, Foras had 587 active members. Recent figures suggest that as of August 2014, there are 365 active members of Foras. The initial uptake in membership and the subsequent decline could be perceived in various ways. Foras' development corresponds to the distinct stages of social movement life cycles. The unrest amongst Cork City supporters and their distrust of Tom Coughlan is evident in the coalescent stage – the second of four distinct stages of contemporary social movement theory – of the group, a period where discontent becomes 'focalised and collective', and the movement becomes 'organised and strategic in their outlook'.[52]

In the five seasons since the 'coalescence' period of 2010, where the group experienced a significant uptake in membership, subscribers to the Trust have steadily declined. The successful acquisition of Cork City FC by Foras went beyond the original targets and aims of the organization. Niamh O'Mahony (former board member of Foras), declares that 'Foras fell into ownership by accident'. She claims that Foras 'never intended to take ownership of the club' and 'events overtook us'.[53] Foras has since become institutionalized as a custodian of Cork City FC, greatly exceeding initial expectations. The pace at which Foras succeeded meant that the organization proceeded through the 'bureaucratisation' process extremely quickly. Former Board Member A explains: 'It's ultimately a happy ending for us as we took control of the club, but now starts another era altogether and that's running it successfully. Because there's no crisis now and there's a feeling that everything is grand, year in, year out, the Board of Cork City will put in a load of work and will still need volunteers'.[54] The speed of success enjoyed by Foras and the formalization of the grouping as owners of Cork City FC has presented a new challenge in terms of attracting and maintaining members. The ethos of sustainability has presented a period of normality for the club. With no financial crisis and no apparent enemy or 'other', the Trust needs to readjust its targets and goals to preserve interest and affinity to the Supporters' Trust model.

Laurence Overend, chair of The Exeter City Supporters' Trust – majority shareholder of Exeter City FC – reiterates the importance of maintaining interest amongst members once normality resumes:

> 'The sense of fear and desperation that almost going out of business created was, ironically, a great motivator. My concern is that the further away we move from that time, combined with the fact that Exeter are now in sound financial shape, might make people less inclined to get involved.'[55]

The fact that Supporters' Trusts as vehicles of ownership and greater supporter involvement are relatively new, it is difficult to gauge if the movement has experienced substantial decline. Numerous Supporters' Trusts have relied on creating goals and targets to remain competitive. For AFC Wimbledon, since the club has reached the Football League, its objective and aspirations have had to be readjusted and reformulated, ultimately placing increased demands on the Trust model as it requires extra finance to be able to compete at higher levels. In this sense, once the primary motives of the movement is realized, it is imperative that the movement outlines what it has achieved, and construct innovative and realistic strategies capable of motivating, sustaining, and, fundamentally, developing its membership.

Foras Member 2 declares that for Foras to continue to be a practical and sustainable mode of governance, it will 'continuously need new people', and for this to occur, it is important that 'theTrust needs focus, it needs something to aim for'.[56] The requirement for Supporters' Trusts to identify and manufacture new objectives is further emphasized by Former Board Member B. When asked what the future for Foras entailed, Former Board Member B revealed, 'We need to get our own base whether that be a clubhouse or training ground, but we need to have something concrete to show what we've done'.[57] By constructing new objectives and constantly striving to meet these demands, focus and support for the movement can be prolonged. It crucial to note that the notion of increased supporter involvement and fan activism is not applicable to all supporters of a club.

Cleland and Dixon (2014) distinction of 'active' and 'passive' fans is critical to the overall understanding of supporter ownership. 'Active' fans are those who seek 'a greater sense of inclusion in the club-fan relationship', while 'passive' supporters are define as those fans who do not actively engage with other fans, clubs, supporter organisations or the media.[58] The distinction and lack of unity between 'active' and 'passive' supporters poses perhaps one of the greatest challenges to supporter movements in their pursuit of legitimacy and rationalization. From supporter groups initial mobilization and emergence, until their eventual decline, the need for an effective correspondence between 'active' and 'passive' supporters is apparent. With this in mind, 55% of respondents in Supporter Direct Europe's 2013 survey said that they were interested in joining a supporters' organization that sought to gain or maintain ownership at their club,[59] representing a significant proportion of participants. It could be perceived that this figure signifies considerable appeal towards the idea of supporter ownership, and could perhaps provide optimism for the future of the movement in Europe.

Evidently, the notion of supporter ownership and the vehicle of a Supporters' Trust to obtain influence is an extremely diverse and multifaceted concept. The overall aim of each individual Trust is unique and dependent on the culture and magnitude of their respective club. For instance, Katrina Law, Secretary of Tottenham Hotspur Supporters' Trust (THST), outlined at the Supporters Summit: Supporters' Trust workshop, that the THST 'were never going to own the club', but could campaign on behalf of supporters on issues regarding 'cheaper tickets' for adolescents.[60] THST's acceptance that ownership of a Premier League club is beyond the capability of a Supporters' Trust does not completely fracture the movement. Instead, its aspirations are manufactured to the environment in which the Trust operated. Lee Daly, Chair of Shelbourne's 1895 Trust, declaration that 'supporter ownership is not a panacea',[61] illustrates the complex and problematic domain in which the movement operates. It does not seek to solve the adverse dimensions of football. It is simply an instrument in which democratic practices can promote an ethos of sustainability and transparency in the overall structure of the game.

Conclusion

The formalization of supporter activism through organizations such as Supporters Direct has enabled supporters to mobilize coherently. The emphasis of Third Way ideology on the reconfiguration of community and its relationship with the individual is clearly illustrated in the Supporters' Trust movement. Supporters' Trusts can be seen as collective organizations with a common ideology which seek to alter the governance structures at their clubs and achieve meaningful input for supporters in football. The political framework which has authorized the movement signifies the important relationship between the political and the social with regard to sport. In this sense, the Supporters' Trust model can be seen as the first legitimate and meaningful attempt by supporters to gain influence within the relations of the game. A clear lack of tradition and culture of supporter involvement at a prominent level in English football's has placed strain on the relation with the governing associations as supporters seek greater involvement within the hierarchy of the game.

In the Republic of Ireland, the development of the concept of supporter ownership could be perceived as somewhat unpremeditated. The frequency of financial difficulties experienced by League of Ireland clubs and the possibility of companies becoming insolvent, supporter ownership became somewhat of a last resort. A lack of policy and ideology from the FAI regarding supporter ownership resulted in the movement being somewhat inorganic in its primitive phase. The 500 Club's successful acquisition of Shamrock Rovers in 2005, followed by Foras taking control of Cork City FC in 2010, has contributed to the League of Ireland becoming an environment where purposeful supporter ownership in the form of a Supporters' Trust is possible and could be seen as somewhat as a benchmark for similar sized leagues and clubs across Europe. The confined and intimate nature of the League allows supporters to undertake a proactive role in the running of their clubs. If a methodical and amalgamated approach to the operation of the League is incorporated, the concept of supporter ownership and the Supporters' Trust template may prove to be an attractive and sustainable form of governance that is universal, and not just particular to individual clubs. Commenting on The Heart of the Game, the Irish segment of the European Commission: 'Improving Football Governance' Project, Michael D. Higgins, President of Ireland, notes, 'I am very encouraged to see football supporters coming together like this for the first time to develop ways of addressing the long-term challenges facing football in Ireland'.[62]

Overall, this article outlined the complex and demanding relations which underpin the supporter movement, and how its desire to embrace elements of place and community is reflected in its overall trajectory. This article provides a critical evaluation of the concept of supporter ownership, especially in relation to the Republic of Ireland. The primitive nature of the subject makes it difficult to display a veracious understanding of the concept of supporter ownership. It is interesting to note that in a globalized and contemporary age, the idea that supporters should have influence within the relations of their club is not an extremely innovative or glamorous abstraction, but could be seen as a retreat to the norms and values of society that places themes of tradition and heritage over prosperity.

Disclosure statement

No potential conflict of interest was reported by the author.

Notes

1. Supporters Direct, 'The Social and Community Value of Football.'
2. Goldblatt, *The Ball is Round*, xiv.
3. UEFA, *The European Club Licensing Benchmarking Report*.
4. The FAI, 'Club Licensing Manual.'
5. Ibid.
6. Ibid.
7. Lyons, 'Financial Fair Play at Home and Broad.'
8. Foras, 'Foras', 38.
9. O'Connor, '€546,500: FAI Slash League Prize Money.'
10. Lennox, 'Lennox's Take: A word from the Chairman', 2.
11. Supporter Patron Scheme, *Supporter Patron Scheme*.
12. Sligo Rovers FC, 'Join the Sligo Rovers 500 Club.'
13. Newstalk, 'Never Ignored.'
14. Ibid.
15. O'Toole, *Ship of Fools*, 100.
16. Toms, 'Notwithstanding the Discomfort Involved.'
17. Foras, 'Foras', 38.
18. Irish Independent, 'Who are the owners of Cork City FC?'
19. Mulligan, 'Wexford Transport Dynasty Awarded €15m after Jersey Fraud.'
20. Irish Independent, 'Who are the owners of Cork City FC?'
21. Mackey, 'Arkaga Defends Its Role at Cork City.'
22. O'Sullivan, 'Here Today, Here Forever.'
23. Cork City FC News, 'Club Statement.'
24. Ibid.
25. Cork City FC News, 'Interview with Tom Coughlan.'
26. SSE Airtricity League, 'FAI Call on Tom Coughlan to Consider His Position at Cork City FC.'
27. RTÉ, 'Coughlan Case Thrown Out of Court.'
28. Riordan, 'Cork City Fans to Stage Pitch Protest.'
29. Lennox, 'Lennox's Take', 2.
30. Supporters Direct Europe, 'Improving Football Governance through Supporter Involvement and Community Ownership.'
31. Adam Brown, 'European Fans' Survey.'
32. Ibid.
33. Dyke, 'England Commission Report.'
34. Beech, 'Supporters Summit.'
35. Supporters Direct Europe. 'Improving Football Governance through Supporter Involvement and Community Ownership', 20.
36. Keoghan, *Punk Football*, 2958.
37. Gibson, 'Hugh Robertson.'
38. Held and McGrew, *The Global Transformation Reader*, 7.
39. Delanty, *Community*, 1.
40. ShamrockRovers FC, 'Members Club Aims.'
41. Drogheda United FC, 'Drogheda Untied is a Member Owned club', *Drogheda Untied FC*, 2010.
42. Delanty, *Community*, 120.
43. Eley and Kirk, *Developing Citizens through sport*, 152–153.
44. Interview with member of Foras.
45. Supporters Direct, 'What is a Supporters' Trust?'
46. Interview with member of Foras.
47. Interview with board member of Foras.
48. Keoghan, *Punk Football*, 1319.
49. Interview with member of Foras.
50. Interview with board member of Foras.
51. Downs, 'Up and down with Ecology – The 'Issue-attention Cycle'', 47.
52. Christiansen, 'Social Movements & Collective Behaviours.'
53. Off The Ball, 'The Off the Ball Football Show.'

54. Interview with board member of Foras.
55. Keoghan, *Punk Football*, 1589.
56. Interview with member of Foras.
57. Interview with board member of Foras.
58. Cleland and Dixon, 'Black and Whiters.'
59. Supporters Direct Europe, 'Football Governance through Supporter Involvement and Community Ownership.'
60. Law, 'Supporters Trusts.'
61. Off The Ball, 'The Off the Ball Football Show.'
62. Supporters Direct Europe, 'Improving Football Governance through Supporter Involvement and Community Ownership.'

References

Brown, A. 'European Fans' Survey: Interim Report 1: Ireland', *Supporters Direct Europe*, Manchester: Substance, 2012.

Christiansen, J. 'Social Movements & Collective Behaviours- Four Stages of Social Movements', in *EBSCO Research Starters*, 2009. Available at http://www.ebscohost.com/uploads/imported/thisTopic-dbTopic-1248.pdf.

Cleland, J., and K. Dixon 'Black and Whiters': The Relative Powerlessness of 'Active' Supporter Organisation Mobility at English Premier League Football Clubs'. *Soccer & Society* 16, no. 4 (2014): 540–54.

Cork City FC News. 'Club Statement'. *Cork City FC*, 2008. Available at http://www.corkcityfc.ie/home/2008/12/09/club-statement-15/.

Cork City FC News. 'Interview with Tom Coughlan'. *Liam Mackey*, 2009. Available at http://www.corkcityfc.ie/home/2009/03/07/interview-with-tom-coughlan/.

Delanty, G. *Community*, New York: Routledge, 2003.

Downs, A. 'Up and down with Ecology – The 'Issue-attention Cycle'. *Public Interest* 28 (1972): 38–50.

Drogheda United FC. 'Drogheda Untied is a Member Owned Club', *Drogheda Untied FC*, 2010. Available at http://www.droghedaunited.ie/membership.php.

Eley, D., and D. Kirk 'Developing Citizen through Sport: The Impact of a Sport-based Volunteer Programme on Young Sport Leaders'. *Sport Education and Society* 7, no. 2 (2002): 151–66.

Foras. 'Foras'. *City Edition* 24, no. 2 (2007): 38.

Gibson, O. Hugh Robertson: 'Football is Worst Governed Sport in UK'. *The Guardian* (Online). http://www.theguardian.com/football/2011/jan/20/hugh-robertson-football-worst-governed (accessed January 20, 2010).

Goldblatt, D. *The Ball is round: A Global History of Football*, London: Penguin Books Ltd, 2006.

Held, D., and A. McGrew, eds. *The Global Transformation Reader: An Introduction to the Globalisation Debate*. Cambridge: Polity Press, 2000.

Irish Independent. 'Who Are the Owners of Cork City FC?'. *Irish Independent* (Online). http://www.independent.ie/sport/soccer/who-are-the-owners-of-cork-city-26469325.html (accessed August 15, 2008).

Keoghan, J. *Punk Football: The Rise of Supporter Ownership in English Football*. Durrington: Pitch Publishing, 2014, eBook.

Lennox, B. 'Lennox's Take: A Word from the Chairman'. *City Edition* 24, no. 2, 2007: 2.

Mackey, L. 'Arkaga Defends Its Role at Cork City', *Irish Examiner* (Online). http://www.irishexaminer.com/sport/soccer/domestic/arkaga-defends-its-role-at-cork-city-70090.html (accessed August 18, 2008).

Mulligan, J. 'Wexford Transport Dynasty Awarded €15m after Jersey Fraud', *Irish Independent*. http://www.independent.ie/business/irish/wexford-transport-dynasty-awarded-15m-after-jersey-fraud-30440156.html (accessed July 18, 2014).

Newstalk. 'Never Ignored: Ollie's Reds', *Newstalk Documentaries* (Podcast). http://www.newstalk.ie/never-ignored-ollies-reds (accessed August 16, 2014).

O'Connor, R. '€546,500: FAI Slash League Prize Money', *Irish Independent* (Online). http://www.independent.ie/sport/soccer/league-of-ireland/546500-fai-slash-league-prize-money-26694874.html (accessed February 12, 2011).

O'Sullivan, J. 'Here Today, Here Forever'. *City Edition* 25, no. 17, 2008: 20.

O'Toole, F. *Ship of Fools: How Stupidity and Corruption Sank the Celtic Tiger*. London: Faber & Faber, 2010.

Off The Ball. 'The Off the Ball Football Show', *Newstalk* (Podcast). http://media.newstalk.ie/podcast/72565/?uniqueID=125238 (accessed March 28, 2013).

Riordan, J. 'Cork City Fans to Stage Pitch Protest', *Irish Examiner* (Online). http://www.irishexaminer.com/sport/soccer/cork-city-fans-to-stage-pitch-protest-103372.html (accessed October 15, 2009).

RTÉ. 'Coughlan Case Thrown out of Court', *RTÉ* (Online). http://www.rte.ie/sport/soccer/irish-soccer-league/2010/0127/260178-corkcity_coughlant/ (January 27, 2010).

ShamrockRovers FC. 'Members Club Aims', *ShamrockRovers FC* (Online). Available at: http://www.shamrockrovers.ie/members/club-aims.

Sligo Rovers FC. 'Join the Sligo Rovers 500 Club', *Sligo Rovers Football Club* (Online), 2013. Available at: http://www.sligorovers.com/join-sligo-rovers-500-club.

SSE Airtricity League. 'FAI Call on Tom Coughlan to Consider His Position at Cork City FC', *FAI* (Online), 2009. Available at: http://www.sseairtricityleague.ie/about/press-office/1345-fai-calls-on-tom-coughlan-to-consider-his-position-at-cork-city-fc.

Supporter Patron Scheme. 'Supporter Patron Scheme: 600 People, One Grid, One Team, One Dream', *Supporter Patron Scheme* (Online), 2010. Available at: http://www.stpatsfc.com/downloads/patron_book.pdf.

Supporters Direct. 'The Social and Community Value of Football – Summary Report', *Supporters Direct*, 2010. Available at: http://www.supporters-direct.org/wp-content/uploads/2013/04/svoff-summary-report.pdf.

Supporters Direct. 'What is a Supporters' Trust?', *Supporters Direct* (Online), 2014. Available at: http://www.supporters-direct.org/homepage/what-we-do/faqs.

Supporters Direct Europe. 'Improving Football Governance through Supporter Involvement and Community Ownership', *Supporters Direct Europe*, 2013. Available at: http://www.supporters-direct.org/wp-content/uploads/2013/06/Final_Report_EN.pdf.

The FAI. 'Club Licensing Manual', *The FAI*. Available at: http://www.fai.ie/sites/default/files/atoms/files/2014_Final_Club_Licensing_Manual.pdf.

Toms, D. "Notwithstanding the Discomfort Involved': Fordson's Cup Win in 1926 and How 'the Old Contemptible' Were Represented in Ireland's Public Sphere during the 1920s'. *Sport in History* 32, no. 4 (2012): 504–25.

UEFA. *The European Club Licensing Benchmarking Report*. Geneva: UEFA, 2011. Available at: http://www.uefa.org/MultimediaFiles/Download/Tech/uefaorg/General/01/91/61/84/1916184_DOWNLOAD.pdf.

Rule changes and incentives in the League of Ireland from 1970 to 2014

David Butler and Robbie Butler

We consider how five rule changes in the League of Ireland have affected the amount of goals scored in the domestic league from 1970 to 2014. Altering the rules represents a significant departure from the previous season and changes the incentive structure for teams. Numerous individual rule changes were imposed on the league during this period, each with the intention of improving playing standards and incentivizing more attacking football. This paper describes the impact of three new points systems introduced in 1981–1982, 1982–1983 and 1993–1994, the introduction of the First Division League in 1985–1986, and the switch to a single calendar year league with a March–November schedule in 2003 known as *Summer Soccer*. A retrospective analysis of goals per season and single match outcomes suggests that changes to the points system have not resulted in an increase in the number of goals scored in the Premier Division, nor has the introduction of the First Division.

Introduction

In a broad sense, institutions act as the 'rules of the game'. These exist in conjunction, and are reliant upon, the individuals that use them. The structure of institutions change the behaviour and choices individuals make. Rules are one form of an institution and are formal constraints that establish the incentive structures in which humans interact.[1] Alterations to the rules of a society are often a product of relatively minor events and can cause critical junctures in a state's history, ultimately leading to different cultural, social and economic developments.[2,3]

One can draw parallels with this to football where minor events induce rule changes. Historically, relatively negligible events on the field of play have invoked rule changes by football authorities that have altered the incentive structure for teams and had important long-term consequences. There are many examples of this. For instance, additional time was introduced due to an incident in 1891, when the Aston Villa goalkeeper Albert Hinchley kicked the ball out of the stadium (that could not be retrieved) after a penalty was awarded to Stoke.[4] In 1927 a rule was introduced to ensure that all goalkeepers stay on their line for penalty kicks after Dubliner Tom Farquharson, who played for Cardiff City, was named the 'Penalty King' for continually rushing off his line as a penalty was about to be taken.[5] In 1992 the back-pass rule was introduced. The establishment of this rule was linked to the actions of Irish goalkeeper 'Packie' Bonner in the 1990 World Cup. *The Guardian* newspaper argued that Ireland's defensive displays at the tournament caused the Fédération Internationale de Football Association (FIFA) to 'rethink the laws of the game ... in particular one passage of play in the group match between the Republic of Ireland and Egypt [saw] the Irish keeper hold the ball for almost six minutes [cumulatively] without releasing it'.[6] The lesson we take from such narratives is that changing the rules can be important – both socio-economic interactions and modern football are structured by cumulative rule changes.

This paper provides a retrospective analysis of how five rule changes in the League of Ireland (hereafter LoI) have affected the amount of goals scored in the league, from 1970 to 2014. We analyse both goals per season and single match outcomes. Such instances are interesting to study from an economic perspective as they constitute institutional variations in a natural setting, where the resulting change in behaviour can be observed. Given that the LoI competition design has repeatedly transformed since 1970, we do not intend to provide a detailed empirical analysis of each rule change. We nest these five changes within a wider context, considering the evolution of the LoI from 1970 to 2014.

In each case, altering the rules represents a significant departure from the previous season(s) and changes the incentive structure for teams. While the rule changes considered in this paper were not a consequence of individual actions on the field of play, like those of the narratives introduced above, the alterations were done so with the intention of improving playing standards and incentivizing more attacking football. We explore how three different points systems, the introduction of a new division, and the switch to a single calendar year league affected the number of goals scored in the league. While other rule changes did occur from 1970 to 2014, we consider these five the most important.

This paper continues as follows. The next section provides a background on the specific rule changes considered since 1970. Following this, data are presented on the number of goals scored and results in the LoI from 1970 to 2014. An analysis of goals scored and the distribution of score lines for the period is also provided. The paper concludes by discussing the impact and effectiveness of these rule changes in increasing the number of goals in the League.

LoI Rule Changes 1970–2014

From 1970 to 2014 five major rule changes occurred in the LoI. Each one signified an effort to increase the attractiveness of the game to audiences and encourage more attacking play. In this section we explain each specific rule change. From 1970 until 1981 either fourteen or sixteen clubs competed in the LoI. Two points were awarded for a win and one point was awarded for a draw. The original two-point winning system in operation existed in England until the 1981–1982 season and is suggested to have emerged directly from challenge matches where two teams would compete for a prize pot. As noted in the *The Guardian* on 5 February 2009, if a game was won, the winner would take the prize pot but if the match was drawn the pot would be split equally. For the 1981–1982 season, the FA introduced a three-points system in its place. The Irish football authorities however conducted an alternative trial.

1981–1982 Season Experiment

For the 1981–1982 season, the LoI conducted an experiment by altering the points awarded for winning and drawing teams depending on the location of a match. Prior to this trial, winning teams were awarded two points for a win and one point for a draw, regardless of match venue. For the 1981–1982 LoI season, teams were awarded four points for an away win and three for a home win. Additionally, if a team drew away from home they were awarded two points while the home team was awarded one. Logically, the rule change sought to incentivize greater attacking play, particularly from the visiting team. Achieving a draw away was now worth an additional point, while winning away from home merited double the points of achieving the same result in previous seasons.

1982–1983 Season Experiment

For the 1982–1983 season, a second experiment was conducted in the LoI. Winning teams were awarded three points for a win and one point for a draw regardless of the venue. Draws were now relatively devalued with less tied matches expected. At the end of the 1982–1983 season, the LoI decided against adopting either of the points systems trialled in the previous two seasons and opted to revert to the older scheme where two points were awarded for a win and one point for a draw, regardless of the venue. This system was maintained in the LoI until the end of the 1992–1993 season.

Introduction of the First Division 1985–1986

Prior to the 1985–1986 season, only one league existed (Division A) in the LoI and there was no promotion or relegation. The First Division was inaugurated for the 1985–1986 season and saw ten out of twenty-two LoI clubs compete in a smaller, lower grade division. The top twelve teams from the previous 1984–1985 season automatically qualified for the newly constituted Premier Division. A system of promotion and relegation commenced between the two tiers. The bottom two teams in the Premier Division would be relegated and replaced by the winner and runner-up of the First Division for the following season. Given these incentives, one would expect greater competition nearing the end of a season among those bidding to stay in the elite division. Since the First Division was introduced, the mechanism to decide relegation and promotion has been tumultuous as the LoI iterated between a ten club and twelve club Premier Division. As was the case with other rule changes in the LoI, this innovation aimed to generate greater excitement for fans.[7]

During the 1992–1993 season, the potential for a third team to be relegated/promoted was introduced via a play-off mechanism between the club finishing third from bottom in the Premier Division and the club finishing third in the First Division. For the 2001–2002 season, further changes to the specifics regarding relegation and promotion occurred. These changes were made to reverse the number of places in both leagues; the Premier Division became a ten team League and twelve teams competed in the First Division. The bottom three teams in the 2001–2002 Premier Division were relegated and the team finishing ninth entered a play-off with the runner-up in the First Division. Only the champions of the First Division were automatically promoted. In the 2002–2003 season, only the bottom placed team in the Premier Division and the champions of the First Division were automatically relegated and promoted, respectively. The second last team in the Premier Division and the second to fourth teams in the First Division entered a knock-out play-off competition.

Further promotion and relegation changes occurred in the 2004 season under the new 'Summer Soccer' fixture schedule. The LoI sought to revert to a twelve team Premier Division, with only the bottom club automatically relegated. The top three First Division clubs were promoted. In 2007 the bottom placed team in the Premier Division and the champions of the First Division were automatically relegated and promoted respectively while a three-way play-off occurred, where the second and third placed teams in the First Division played each other to decide who met the second last Premier League team in the play-off final. In 2008, a ten team Premier Division was reinstated as three teams were relegated automatically from the Premier Division and only the champions of the First Division were automatically promoted. Finally, in 2009 there was no automatic relegation.

A mechanism to create relegation from the First Division was established in 2008. The bottom First Division club would enter a play-off with an 'A' League Championship club for the right to play in the First Division the following season. The 'A' League Championship was a third tier established by the FAI to aid a club's progression to the LoI. The 'A' League Championship was abolished at the end of the 2011 season. No relegation mechanism from the First Division currently exists.

The Dawn of the Modern Points System

The LoI changed the points system again for the 1993–1994 season. This move constituted the most recent change to the amount of points allocated for different results. Three points were again awarded for a win and one point for a draw. As mentioned earlier, this change occurred far earlier in England in response to falling attendances. The motivation for the change was another attempt to alter incentives, encourage more attacking from teams and achieve more goals per match. Given that this system did not come to fruition earlier, despite it being experimented with in the 1982–1983 season, one could assume this change was motivated by influences external to the league, in particular international trends in the sport.

Notably, FIFA supported the move to a three-points system. The three-point innovation aided the development of the game internationally and was particularly relevant given that the FIFA World Cup was due to be hosted in America in 1994. American sport audiences were generally unfamiliar with the concept of a tied game. In June 1993 Joseph (Sepp) Blatter, General Secretary of FIFA, announced that the number of points awarded to a team for winning a group stage game at the 1994 World Cup was to increase from two to three points. An *LA Times* article in 1993 suggested that 'an underlying reason for FIFA's action … was the feeling that American fans, used to higher-scoring American games, would be much less tolerant and much more quickly turned off than a more traditional soccer audience by an early parade of 0-0 and 1-1 results'.[8] An article from the *New York Times* in 1994 concurred with this sentiment, suggesting that the change 'increased optimism that teams will emphasize offense and produce a scoring spectacle in the World Cup'.[9]

Although this change occurred for the World Cup in 1994, moving to a three-points system did not uniformly occur across European league competitions. At the start of the 1995–1996 season FIFA introduced an international rule change making the three-points system compulsory. Economists have since developed a formal model[10] to consider this unilateral change and have conducted empirical studies on the effects of the rule in European countries outside of Ireland. Interestingly, empirical studies addressing the effects of adopting a three-points system for a win find that the change did the opposite to what it intended to achieve. Data from referee post-match reports for the 1994–1995 and 1995–1996 in Spain's *La Liga* indicate that teams in a winning position were more likely to commit offences and incur punishment, with a higher probability of red cards occurring in matches with a three-points system.[11] After the points system change, winning teams adopted more defensive tactics in the German *Bundesliga* which led to both teams having fewer shots on goal.[12] Further studies of the German *Bundesliga* show only minimal evidence exists to suggest that the three-points system increased the number of second-half goals by losing first-half teams. No evidence exists that the rule made games more decisive.[13] However, a study from the Portuguese league, *Primeira Liga*[14] finds evidence of 'some positive effects in the game' but that the general effect was modest and non-uniform, impacting the strategies of different teams (such as underdogs) in different ways.

The Summer Soccer Era (2003 – to date)

For the 2002–2003 LoI season the league was purposefully condensed to aid a transition to *Summer Soccer*. This was a switch to a single calendar year league in 2003. The term *Summer Soccer* was used to describe this shift. The LoI moved from a model where the season began in August and played through the winter months in the Northern Hemisphere (concluding in May) to a model where the season would commence in March with the majority of the fixtures being played through the summer months (concluding in November).

There were many motivations for introducing this change. Firstly, given the inclement Irish winters, it was likely players would be playing in better conditions and on playing surfaces more conducive to attractive football. As a corollary of the on-field climatic motivations, it was deemed that supporters were more likely to enjoy attending live football in warmer conditions. A further motivation for the switch related to player fitness and Irish club involvement in European competitions. European competitions start in July. This would now be mid-season for Irish clubs following the switch to *Summer Soccer*, but pre-season for the majority of other European clubs. Irish teams therefore would have a fitness advantage over European counterparts who were only returning for pre-season training.

To understand the possible impact of rule changes to the points system, the inauguration of relegation, and a move to a single calendar season on the number of goals scored, an overview of the League from 1970 to 2014 is presented in Table 1.

Data and Descriptive Statistics

To establish the impact these rule changes have had on the number of goals scored in the LoI, data are collected from 1970 to 2014 on all matches played in the top tier of the domestic league. Following the establishment of the First Division, the top tier is referred to thereafter as the Premier Division. The data are sourced from *Republic of Ireland Football League Tables and Results 1921–2012* and from official LoI records for the last two years of the data-set. The sample under consideration covers a total of forty-five completed seasons, consisting of 8,655 individual

Table 1. The League of Ireland structure, points system and calendar: 1970–2014.

Year	No. Premier Clubs	No. 1st Div. Clubs	Relegation places	Premier play-off	1st Div. relegation	Win Pts	Draw Pts	Calendar
1970–1977	14	–	–	–	–	2	1	Winter
1977–1981	16	–	–	–	–	2	1	Winter
1981–1982	16	–	–	–	–	3–4	1–2	Winter
1982–1983	14	–	–	–	–	3	1	Winter
1983–1984	14	–	–	–	–	2	1	Winter
1984–1985	16	–	4	–	No	2	1	Winter
1985–1992	12	10	2	No	No	2	1	Winter
1992–1993	12	10	3	Yes	No	2	1	Winter
1993–2001	12	10	3	Yes	No	3	1	Winter
2001–2002	12	9**	4	Yes	No	3	1	Winter
2002–2003	10	12	2	Yes	No	3	1	Winter
2003	10	12	2	Yes	No	3	1	Summer
2004	10	12	1	No	No	3	1	Summer
2005	12	10	2	Yes	No	3	1	Summer
2006	11**	10	–	Yes*	–	3	1	Summer
2007	12	10	2	Yes	No	3	1	Summer
2008	12	10	3	No	Yes	3	1	Summer
2009–2010	10	12	2	Yes	Yes	3	1	Summer
2011	10	11**	1	Yes	No	3	1	Summer
2012	11**	8	1	Yes	No	3	1	Summer
2013–2014	12	8	2	Yes	No	3	1	Summer

*The Football Association of Ireland took over the running of the LoI in 2007. For the 2007 LoI season an Independent Assessment Group established by the Football Association of Ireland determined which clubs would enter the Premier League and First Division. Although there was a play-off in the 2006 season, which Dundalk F.C won, the club was not selected to enter the 2007 Premier League. Thus, despite the play-off occurring in 2006, the result had no bearing on the teams in the Premier Division for the subsequent year.
**Years where an odd number of teams competed in the LoI refers to a case where a team did not complete the season after they were accepted to enter. In 2001–2002 St. Francis FC withdrew from the First Division before the start of the season. In 2006 Dublin City disbanded during the season for financial reasons and their results were erased. In 2011 Drogheda United were reinstated to the Premier League, even though they were relegated the previous year, as Sporting Fingal withdrew from the League in February 2011. In June 2012 Monaghan United withdrew and their results were erased. These represent unique cases as previously teams that withdrew before the start of the season may have been replaced, as was the case for the 1996–1997 First Division when St. James Gate FC were replaced by St. Francis FC before the league commenced.

match observations. Table 2 presents descriptive statistics on matches from 1970 to 2014.

The number of games per season varied. The sixteen team leagues of the late 1970s and early 1980s played 240 games in total per season. The number of clubs in the top division has changed regularly, and has ranged from between ten and sixteen. As a result the number of goals per season has been irregular, depending mainly on the number of games per season. A mean of just over 500 goals per season is found between 1970 and 2014, with a standard deviation of almost 93 goals. Figures 1 and 2 examine this more closely. Figure 1 illustrates the number of goals scored per season (left-hand axis) in both Division 'A' (1970–1985) and Premier Division (1985–2014). The right-hand axis on the graph plots the number of matches in the division each season. As expected, the number of goals per season is highly correlated to the number of matches ($R = 0.81$).

Table 2. LoI 1970–2014 Descriptive Statistics.

Variable	Total	Mean	St. Dev.	Min	Max
Games	8,655	192.94	(25.22)	132	240
Clubs in Division 'A'/Premier Division	–	12.62	(1.79)	10	16
Goals	22,581	501.80	(92.94)	333	725

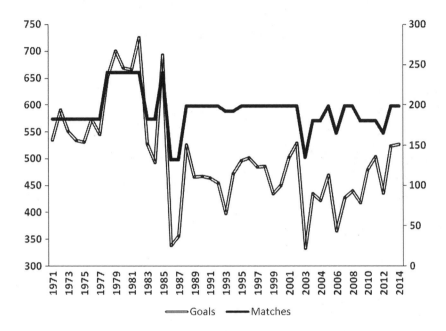

Figure 1. Number of goals & matches 1970–2014.

Interestingly, the highest number of goals in a single season occurred during the 1981–1982 campaign, the same year the points system was altered so that four points were awarded for an away win and two for an away draw. The introduction of the First Division for the 1985–1986 season coincides with a dramatic fall in the number of goals. This is primarily due to the reduction in the number of games. However, an increase in the number of matches from the 1987–1988 season to the 2001–2002 season does not see a return to the number of goals from 1970 to 1977, when a similar number of games per season were played. A reduction in the number of Premier Division teams in 2003, resulted in the lowest number of goals (333) in any season in the sample. This can be explained by the shortened league season, to accommodate the switch to *Summer Soccer*.

Figure 2 illustrates the mean number of goals per club across each season from 1970 to 2014. Again, a strong positive relationship exists between the two. A reduction in the number of matches, most notably from 1985 to 1987 and again during the 2002–2003 season, resulted in a sharp drop in the average number of goals scored by each club ($R = 0.60$)

It is worth noting that there is an annual increase in the average number of goals scored per club from 2007 to 2011. A total of 503 goals were scored by the ten

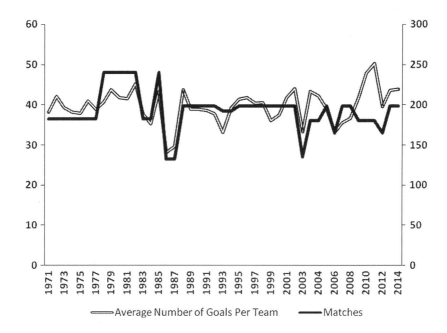

Figure 2. Mean number of goals per club and number of matches 1970–2014.

Premier Division teams in 2011, making this season the only time teams ever surpassed the 50 goal average and 500 goal total for a season. The following season (2012) reports a fall to just fewer than 40 goals per season. The evolving league structure makes it difficult to interpret Figures 1 and 2. However, Figure 3 controls for changes in the number of matches played each season and the number of teams involved in each league campaign.

Despite a relatively stable mean number of goals per club (Figure 2) the mean number of goals per game has declined over the entire sample period. In the LoI, as in many other leagues worldwide, goals are becoming scarcer.[15] Despite various rule changes to the points system, little has been done to arrest the continuous decline in the number of goals per game. This decline, further emphasized by the linear trend line, reaches its nadir during the 1992–1993 season, when just 2.07 goals per game were scored on average. It is noteworthy that since this low point, the average number of goals per game has slightly increased between the years 1993 and 2014 when three points are awarded for a win. This is primarily influenced by the annual average increases between the years 2006 and 2011.

As a corollary, it is interesting to compare goals in the FAI Cup to the League competition. Accurate data for FAI Cup matches are accessible for a ten-year period from 2004 to 2014 from The *Rec.Sport.Soccer Statistics Foundation*. Table 3 displays the average number of goals per round for the FAI Cup from 2004 to 2014. The average number of goals ranged from 3.04 (maximum) to 2.47 (minimum). These averages are comparable to the current goal scoring trends in the league.

The next part of this analysis considers single match outcomes. This is undertaken to determine if individual rule changes have had a significant impact on the outcome of individual matches. Again, we initially provide an overview of

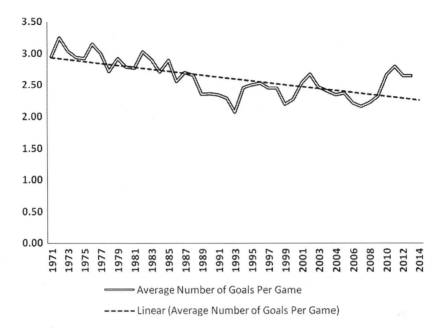

Figure 3. Mean number of goals per game 1970–2014.

Table 3. Mean number of goals per round in the FAI Cup 2004–2014.

	2004	2005	2006	2007	2008	2009	2010	2011	2012	2013	2014
Qualifier	–	–	–	–	2.27	3.25	3.00	2.00	–	–	–
Round 1	3.00	2.69	3.30	2.40	2.11	3.27	2.33	2.29	3.00	2.73	3.29
Round 2	3.61	2.50	2.53	2.84	2.89	3.62	3.10	3.53	3.33	3.56	3.00
Last 16	2.50	2.64	2.30	2.50	4.25	1.45	2.30	3.09	2.50	3.10	2.36
Quarter Final	2.86	3.25	3.40	2.80	1.33	2.13	4.00	2.00	5.00	2.60	3.43
Semi-Final	2.00	2.00	2.33	1.50	2.50	3.50	2.00	2.33	2.67	2.00	3.67
Final	3.00	2.00	7.00	1.00	4.00	3.00	0.00	2.00	5.00	5.00	2.00
Average	3.04	2.61	2.81	2.52	2.48	2.92	2.73	2.78	3.00	2.47	2.98

individual match outcomes from 1970 to 2014. Table 4 presents a matrix of possible results and covers 8,655 games. The results from the LoI are not dissimilar to those found for the Football League in England.[16]

The most frequent score in the LoI from 1970 to 2014 is a 1-1 draw. The second most common result is a 1-0 home win, followed by a scoreless draw, and 1-0 away win. More than 40% of LoI matches end in one of these four outcomes. Including games that finished 2-0, 2-1, 2-2, 0-2 and 1-2, more than 71% of matches are covered by these nine possible score lines. Including score lines 3-0, 3-1, 3-2, 3-3, 0-3, 1-3 and 2-3, we find that 89% of games end in results ranging from scoreless draws at one extreme, to games where both teams scored three goals each, with the match ending tied at 3-3.

Next we consider how each of the five rule changes mentioned impact upon the frequency of match outcomes over the course of the rule changes. Given that almost

Table 4. Frequency of League of Ireland results from 1970 to 2014.

		Away Team Goals							
		0	1	2	3	4	5	6	7+
Home Team Goals	0	9.07%	8.87%	5.55%	2.39%	0.82%	0.34%	0.09%	0.06%
	1	10.24%	12.19%	6.46%	2.92%	0.99%	0.29%	0.11%	0.05%
	2	6.70%	7.62%	4.41%	1.78%	0.53%	0.22%	0.06%	0.01%
	3	4.05%	3.92%	2.13%	0.72%	0.28%	0.13%	–	0.01%
	4	1.53%	1.55%	0.72%	0.24%	0.08%	0.05%	0.02%	0.01%
	5	0.65%	0.58%	0.27%	0.09%	0.02%	0.01%	–	–
	6	0.39%	0.21%	0.12%	0.04%	0.01%	–	–	–
	7+	0.16%	0.13%	0.06%	0.02%	0.02%	–	–	–

90% of games are covered by the score lines with all combinations of one, two and three goals for both home and away teams, the matrices for each season are presented with only these results included.

Comparing across tables it is evident the rule changes have a negligible effect on match outcomes. The tables do point to an increase in the incidence of scoreless draws. While just 6.82% of games from 1970–1981 (Table 5), and just over 5% of games in the 1981–1982 (Table 6) season ended scoreless, the past thirty years have seen an increase. Table 7 and Table 8 present data on the one-year three-points system during the 1982–1983 season and the return to the two point winning system from

Table 5. 1970–1981 (win 2 points).

		Away			
		0	1	2	3
Home	0	6.82%	7.70%	4.68%	2.29%
	1	8.92%	10.77%	6.38%	3.41%
	2	6.29%	8.24%	5.21%	2.44%
	3	4.04%	4.48%	2.39%	1.02%

Table 6. 1981–1982 trial system (4-3-2-1).

		Away			
		0	1	2	3
Home	0	5.02%	7.11%	5.44%	2.93%
	1	9.62%	9.62%	6.28%	4.18%
	2	7.11%	5.44%	5.02%	2.93%
	3	5.44%	4.60%	2.09%	1.67%

Table 7. 1982–1983 (win 3 points).

		Away			
		0	1	2	3
Home	0	7.14%	7.69%	5.49%	2.20%
	1	8.79%	13.19%	7.14%	3.85%
	2	6.04%	6.04%	3.30%	1.65%
	3	2.20%	5.49%	1.10%	1.10%

Table 8. 1983–1993 (win 2 points).

		Away			
		0	1	2	3
Home	0	10.76%	8.51%	5.57%	2.41%
	1	9.90%	13.17%	6.42%	3.16%
	2	6.85%	8.08%	3.48%	1.55%
	3	3.80%	3.59%	1.98%	0.59%

Table 9. 1993–2003 (win 3 Points).

		Away			
		0	1	2	3
Home	0	9.94%	9.94%	5.47%	1.79%
	1	11.42%	13.36%	6.26%	2.16%
	2	7.05%	7.84%	4.21%	1.21%
	3	4.05%	3.68%	2.10%	0.84%

Table 10. 2003–2014 (Summer Soccer).

		Away			
		0	1	2	3
Home	0	9.60%	9.64%	6.43%	2.95%
	1	10.98%	11.92%	6.74%	2.72%
	2	6.70%	6.88%	4.69%	1.74%
	3	4.33%	3.66%	2.14%	0.31%

Table 11. Match outcomes 1970–2014.

	Home (%)	Draw (%)		Away (%)
1970–1981	43.71	24.07		32.21
		(6.82)	(17.25)	
1981–1982	44.77	21.34		33.89
		(5.02)	(16.32)	
1982–1983	41.21	24.72		31.87
		(7.14)	(17.58)	
1983–1993	40.26	28.05		31.69
		(10.76)	(17.29)	
1994–1903	40.84	28.50		30.66
		(9.65)	(18.84)	
2003–1914	40.49	26.54		32.95
		(9.60)	(16.94)	

*The outcomes for drawn games, also report in parenthesis, whether the game finished scoreless (left) or was a score draw (right).

1983 to 1993, respectively. Since the permanent introduction of the three points system, almost one in ten games has finished without a goal (Table 9 and Table 10). The trial 4-3-2-1 points system introduced during the 1981–1982 season did have an impact on match outcomes (Table 6). 0-0 are reported at their lowest level

(1 in 20 matches) for the entire sample, while 1-3, 2-3 and 3-3 occur more frequently than in any of the other five tables. Away teams, it appears, did attack more; however, when one considers the distribution of possible match outcomes over the six periods, very little change has occurred despite the multiple rule changes. Table 11 provides a breakdown of match outcomes.

Little variation has occurred in match outcomes, despite the various rule changes seeking to elicit more attacking football. The only noteworthy trend is a movement away from home wins towards more drawn games, albeit a minimal change (approximately 3%). Away wins have remained almost constant, with roughly one in three away teams emerging victorious.

Discussion

Despite the many attempts by the LoI and later the FAI to incentivize more attacking football, no significant and lasting increases in the number of goals scored are observed over the course of the past forty-five seasons. There are some signs of increased attacking effort in the 1981–1982 season but the difference between this season and others is negligible. Over the period an increasing amount of draws are observed. The permanent move to three points for winning a match in 1993 served to stem the declining trend in the number of goals per game in the LoI from 1970 to the early 1990s, rather than increase the amount. The average number of goals scored in the FAI cup between 2004 and 2014 is comparable to the recent goal scoring trends in the league.

While defensive football is not necessarily worse football, the objective of increasing goals per game with rule changes has, for the most part, been ineffective in the LoI. We suggest three explanations why modifications to the structure and seasonal timing of the league, as well as alterations in the points system have been unsuccessful in incentivizing more attacking football, as measured by goals scored. All three are conjectural.

Firstly, one could argue tactical developments in the football rather than rule changes have caused the downward trend in the number of goals scored. In particular, football in the twentieth century saw an increased emphasis on defensive tactics. Historically, teams lined out in relatively attacking formations. These included the WM or Meodo formations (5 forwards, 2 midfielders and 3 defenders), and the Pyramid or Danubain formations (5 forwards, 3 midfielders and 2 defenders). All four involved having five attacking players on the pitch at all times. Football formations have evolved towards including a greater number of defensive minded players over the course of the twentieth century.[17] The period considered coincides with Irish teams participating in European competitions. Exposure to 'foreign' tactics may have affected Irish clubs. This in turn could have spread to other domestic clubs. There is a possibility that tactical innovations in the LoI may have derived from exposure to European practices. The diffusion of tactical knowledge from European clubs to Irish clubs is an area open to future research. Today, teams commonly start a match with just one recognized attacking player, or in some cases play without a recognized attacking player, otherwise known as the False Nine formation. This general movement in tactics, away from traditional attacking play, has likely impacted the number of goals scored in each game as teams not only have fewer players attacking the opposition goal, but also a greater number of players to defend their own goal.

The second reason for the decline in the number of goals could be due to convergence between football clubs. While often spoken about in an economic sense, where poorer countries grow more quickly and tend to catch up with richer countries, convergence in a football sense refers to the fact that the weaker teams in the LoI today are more competitive than they have been in the past. An improvement and standardization of coaching practices, and advances in sports science and dietary requirements has resulted in all clubs having access to information concerning the best methods regarding physical, mental and tactical preparation for a match. UEFA licensing prerequisites and the requirement for clubs training personnel to hold coaching qualifications has served to further this standardization. Improved information has removed a degree of uncertainty clubs would have faced in the past when meeting an opponent. Technological advances, in particular the advent of televised football, have allowed clubs to reduce information barriers regarding an opponent's strengths and weaknesses. The use of technology in football has advanced rapidly since 1970. In the modern game, teams can prepare tactically days in advance by accessing sophisticated statistical information about the opponent.

A third reason may relate to non-rational responses. From a behavioural perspective the concept of loss aversion is important.[18] Individuals treat losses differently to gains. In short, losses loom larger and the pain of losing is psychologically approximately double that of gaining. Loss aversion has been found to exist in other high stakes sporting environments.[19] If individuals are averse towards losses, offering greater incentives to teams to score more goals may not sufficiently incentivize more attacking play. A winning team may be purely interested in protecting a lead once it is achieved. This may be of particular importance to this period of the leagues history as it has become more professional during this time. Naturally losses may have become more costly to managers and players. Furthermore, one could argue that rational actions on the field are not susceptible to minor tweaks to the incentive structure. Decisions on the field of play are often more attributable to emotions than to rational behaviour.[20] Calculated responses to incentives are not usually attributed to high stakes sporting environments where time pressures exist.

Conclusion

We consider five individual rule changes that are imposed on the LoI from 1970 to 2014. These were intended to incentivize more attacking football. By considering goals per season and individual match outcomes, we reason that changes to the points system have not resulted in a considerable increase in the number of goals scored in the top division, nor has the introduction of relegation.

We are cognizant of the limitations of this study. Firstly, our analysis of individual rule changes relies upon the *ceteris paribus* assumption. This constrains the inferences one can make. The benefit of making this assumption is that it makes specific rule changes more amenable to analysis. Secondly, we focus upon external incentives. Given the complexity of the task, we do not consider the role of incentives within clubs, or those faced by coaches and management. This study does however provide evidence that historical changes to the point structure negligibly affected the observed outcomes of matches and the amount of goals scored in the league. We speculate why these changes may not have achieved their desired effect and suggest that our conjecture may form the basis of future research into the LoI.

Disclosure statement

No potential conflict of interest was reported by the authors.

Notes

1. North, 'Economic Performance Through Time', 360.
2. Acemoglu and Robinson, *Why Nations Fail.* Chapters 11–12.
3. Mokyr, *The Enlightened Economy*, 20.
4. Nawrat and Hutchings, *Sunday Times Illustrated History of Football.*
5. Toms, *Darling of the Gods*, 5–8.
6. *The Guardian*, January 28, 2014, https://www.theguardian.com/sport/football-cliches/2014/jan/28/memory-legal-backpasses-jones-souness-dixon.
7. Whelan, *Who Stole our Game?*, 127.
8. *The LA Times*, December 17, 1993 http://articles.latimes.com/1993-12-17/sports/sp-2890_1_world-cup-competition.
9. *New York Times*, January 4, 1994 http://www.nytimes.com/1994/01/04/sports/world-cup-update.html.
10. Brocas and Carrillo, 'Do the "Three-point Victory" and "Golden Goal" rules make soccer more exciting?' 169–85.
11. del Corral et al., 'The Effect of Incentives on Sabotage'.
12. Dilger and Geyer, 'Are Three Points for a Win Really Better Than Two?'
13. Hon and Parinduri, 'Does the Three-point Rule Make Soccer More Exciting?'
14. Guedes and Machado, 'Changing Rewards in Contests'.
15. Anderson and Sally, *The Numbers Game*.
16. Fivethirtyeight.com, 2015 http://fivethirtyeight.com/features/in-126-years-english-football-has-seen-13475-nil-nil-draws/.
17. Wilson, *Inverting the Period.*
18. Kahneman and Tversky, 'Prospect Theory'.
19. Pope and Schweitzer, 'Is Tiger Woods Loss Averse?'
20. Elster, *Explaining Social Behaviour*, 76.

References

Acemoglu, D., and J. Robinson. *Why Nations Fail: Origins of Power, Poverty and Prosperity.* London: Crown, 2012.
Anderson, C., and D. Sally. *The Numbers Game: Why Everything You Know About Football is Wrong.* London: Viking. 2013.
Brocas, I., and J.D. Carrillo. 'Do the "Three-point Victory" and "Golden Goal" Rules Make Soccer More Exciting? A Theoretical Analysis of a Simple Game'. *Journal of Sports Economics* 5 (2004): 169–85.
del Corral, J., J. Prieto-Rodriguez, and R. Simmons. 'The Effect of Incentives on Sabotage: The Case of Spanish Football'. *Journal of Sports Economics* 11 (2010): 243–60.
Dilger, A., and H. Geyer. 'Are Three Points for a Win Really Better Than Two?: A Comparison of German Soccer League and Cup Games'. *Journal of Sports Economics* 10 (2009): 305–18.
Elster, J. *Explaining Social Behavior: More Nuts and Bolts for the Social Sciences.* New York: Cambridge University Press, 2007.
Fivethirtyeight.com. 2015. *In 126 Years, English Football Has Seen 13,475 Nil-Nil Draws*, http://fivethirtyeight.com/features/in-126-years-english-football-has-seen-13,475-nil-nil-draws/ (accessed 2015).
Graham, A. *Republic of Ireland – Football League Tables & Results 1921–2012.* South Humberside: Soccer Books Ltd, 2013.
Guedes, J.C., and F.S. Machado. 'Changing Rewards in Contests: Has the Three-point-rule Brought More Offense to Soccer?' *Empirical Economics* 27 (2002): 607–30.
Hon, L.Y., and R.A. Parinduri. 'Does the Three-point Rule Make Soccer More Exciting? Evidence from a Regression Discontinuity Design'. *Journal of Sports Economics* 17 (2016): 377–95.

Kahneman, D., and A. Tversky. 'Prospect Theory: An Analysis of Decision under Risk'. *Econometrica* 47 (1979): 263–91.

Mokyr, J. *The Enlightened Economy: An Economic History of Britain 1700–1850*. London: Yale University Press, 2009.

Nawrat, C. and S. Hutchings. *The Sunday Times Illustrated History of Football*. London: Hamlyn, 1998.

North, D.C. 'Economic Performance Through Time'. *The American Economic Review* 84 (1994): 359–68.

Pope, D.G., and M.E. Schweitzer. 'Is Tiger Woods Loss Averse? Persistent Bias in the Face of Experience, Competition, and High Stakes'. *The American Economic Review* 101 (2011): 129–57.

Toms, D. '"Darling of the Gods": Tom Farquharson, Irish Footballing Migrant'. *Soccer & Society* 16 (2014): 1–13.

Whelan, D. *Who Stole Our Game? The Fall and Fall of Irish Soccer*. Dublin: Gill & MacMillian, 2006.

Wilson, J. *Inverting the Pyramid: The History of Football Tactics*. London: Hachette, 2010.

Index

Note: Boldface page numbers refer to tables & italic page numbers refer to figures. Page numbers followed by "n" refer to endnotes.

AAA *see* Army Athletic Association (AAA)
Abbey Ballroom Indoor Football League 112, 115; attitudes towards female players 123–5; interviews and data collection 113, *114,* 115; map of 116, *117*; playing area 119; 'pride' 120; rules and conditions *121*; team organization 119–23, *123*, *124*
Acheson, James 20
action research workshops 149–50
Adelphi Ballroom, in Dundalk 125
AFA *see* Army Football Association
alcohol consumption, in inter-war Ireland 60
'A' League Championship 190
Allen, Walter 15
all-Ireland Football Federation 70
all-Ireland soccer team 67–9
Alton United 41
Anderson, Trevor 90, 91
Andrews, David 68, 69
Andrews, Todd 36
Anglo-Celt 37, 56
Anglo–Irish football relations 4
Anglo-Irish War, soccer violence during 52–5
'AnnusHorribilis' speech 82, 90
An t-Óglác 96, 97, 99
Arkaga 174; investing in Cork City FC 174–5; Walsh, Gerard 174
Armstrong, Winkie 90
Army Athletic Association (AAA) 96–9, 102
Army Football Association (AFA) 23
Association Football and English Society, 1863–1915 (Mason) 1
Association Football and Society in pre-partition Ireland (Garnham) 1
'Association Nearly Played Out' *12*
Athenry (Dr Croke) FC 15
Athenry GAA 19
Athlone FC 13

Austria, soccer crowds 51
Avonmore Ireland Cup 142
Aylward, Liam 142

back-pass rule 187
Bairner, Alan 73
Ballinrobe FC 13
Ballyhaunis FC 13, 21
Barry, J. J. 105
Bartlett, Thomas 81
Bayly, Martin 91
Beech, John 177
Belfast 52, 53; Catholics 55, 66; gunfire in, soccer match 54; hooliganism 55
Belfast Agreement 81
Belfast Celtic club 53–5, 66
Belfast Telegraph 88–90, 92
Bell, Geoffrey 82
Berdez, A. G. 106
Bessel, Richard 51
Best, George 5, 66, 67, 76
Bierne, Sylvester 87
Biggs, Richard 19
Bingham, Billy 73, 75
Blake, Valentine J 13
Blaxnit Cup 67
bloody ethno-nationalist conflict *see* Troubles, The
Bloody Sunday 98
Blues 83, 85, 87–9
Blues Brothers, The 89
Bohemians club 98
Borough, Sligo 12
Bowen, David 75, 85, 89
Bowyer, Eric 84, 85, 89–92
Brady, Liam 67, 70, 71, 76
brain-centred learning 155
Bray Unknowns 56
Breen, Tommy 87
Brennan, H. F. 103
British army regiments 17
British Home Championship 73

203

INDEX

British imperialism 16
British military soccer teams 18
Brooks, David 89
Brooks, Derek 72, 84, 88
Brown, Daniel 3
Bruton, John 141
Bundesliga 191
Butler, David 2
Butler, Robert 2
Byrne, Helena 2
Byrne, Ollie 173–4
Byrne, Peter 72

Cannon, Harry 3, 95, 103; Bohemian Football Club 100, 106; Fianna Phadraig, member of 96; Irish Olympic Council 102–6; Irish Senior Cup medal, 1938 106; in military activity 96; sporting career of 98–100; sports' administrator 102–3
Cantona, Eric 91
Carew, Jim 142
Carey, Jackie 138
Castlebar FC 13
Castle Catholics 38
Catholic players 82–4, 87, 88, 91
Cavan, Harry 68–71, 73, 136
CCIFL *see* Cork City Investments FC Limited
Cercle Athlequike de Paris 102
ceteris paribus assumption 199
Charlton, Jack 141
Chef de Mission 104
Chisholm, Ken 138
club-fan relationship 182
coach–athlete interactions 155, 156
coaches: basic communication 151; dictaphones 158; grading 134; One Minute Paper task 156; perceptual cognitive skills 153; qualification of 133; recruitment of 134, 139; social interactions 152; stress inoculation practices 152; visual search strategies 153, 157
coach feedback 155–7
coaching: behaviour 157; courses 134; environments 152; infrastructures 141–3; mulitsensory experience 151; performance analysis 159–60; practices 151; science of 149
coaching structures, for schoolboys: developments 136–7, 139–40; difficulty in grammar schools 134–6; early post-war coaching 133–4; impact of international success 141–3; Jarman, John 140; Livingstone, Dougald 138, 140; national director 140–1; in Republic of Ireland 137–8; residential course 136; Saxon recruiting campaign 138–9; Stevenson, Alex 138; summer course 136
coach–player relationship 149
Co. Antrim Football Association 53

Coca-Cola boycott 86, 87, 89
Collingwood Cup 4, 60
Coly, Tony 86
Commercials of Sligo Foot Ball Club 12
community 178–80
Connacht: commercial capital 19; Connacht Union 22–3; Irish Football Association 25–6; military unit 16; multi-causal soccer agency 18; Muscular Christianity 15; population 15, 17; soldiers 16–17; urbanization 15
Connacht Union 22–3
Connaught Rugby Union 19
Connolly, Sean 75
constructivism 152
Cooper, Ivan 69
Coote, Orlando R. 12; coaching 12; legacy and stonyhurst rules 22
Cork: association football in 174; Cork City FC 174
Cork City FC 174; Arkaga's investment 174–5; Cork City Investments FC Limited 176; Coughlan, Tom 175–6, 180–1; examinership 175, 180
Cork City FC's Supporters' Trust 2
Cork City Investments FC Limited (CCIFL) 176
Cork *vs.* Cavan match 6
Cotter, Fr 97
Coughlan, Tom 175–6, 180–1
Council of Europe Parliamentary Assembly report (1999) 59
County Armagh Education Committee 134
county Galway 17
Coyle, Roy 83
Craig, David 68
Cramer, Detmar 136
critical reflective practice 158
critical thinking 151, 158–60
Croke Park, Dublin in 98
Cronin, Mike 1, 10, 15–16, 82
Cullen, Chris 88, 89
Curran, Conor 3
Cusack, Michael 34

Daly, Gerry 71
Daly, Lee 182
Davis, Frank 71
Dawn of the Modern Points System 190–1
Derry City 67, 74
dialogic reflection 158
Diocesan School FC 12
Doherty, Lee 91
Doherty, Peter 133
Dokter, Ruud 148
Donegal 36–8
Donegal Celtic 74
Dornan, Alan 91

INDEX

Dougan, Derek 67, 68, 76
Douglas, Stephen 91
Dowdall, Jack 55
Drennan, William 67
Drogheda Down Memory Lane 116
Drogheda Independent 113, 115, 116, 119, 125
Drogheda, women's soccer in: Article 41.2 statement 111; *Drogheda Independent* 113, 115, 116, 119, 125; Drogheda Local Voices archive 113; Facebook groups 116; Ferriter, Dermot 111, 115; *Festival Flash* 125; grounded theory 113; Hill, Myrtle 115; Holohan, Carole 111, 115, 126; Ladies Football Association 111; outdoor football 126; overview of 110; Pope's view 111; Roche, Stephanie 111–12; Sangster, Jane 113, 115; 'Soccer, Women, Sexual Liberation: Kicking off a New Era' 112; *Sporting Press*' support for 111; survey 116, *118*; Toms research 126; Williams, Jean 112, 115 *see also* Abbey Ballroom Indoor Football League
Dublin 53; Alton United 41; association football clubs 35; hooliganism 52, 54; lower middle-class denizens 38; popularity of soccer 38; soccer 16, 51, 55
Dublin Association FC 13
Dublin District Schoolboy League 148
Dundalk, Adelphi Ballroom in 125
Dundalk club 56–7
Dundalk Hawk 82, 90
Dundalk North End and Friends 116
Dunning, Eric 50, 58
Dyke, Greg 177

East Lancashires 18
Education Act 134
Eleven of The Rest 12
Elias, Norbert 50, 62n2
Elizabeth II 82
Emmet Gaelic Athlone Club 21
emotional intelligence (EQ) 160
English football 170
English Football Association 132
English League football 149
English Premier League 91
EQ *see* emotional intelligence
Etat Libre d'Irlande 105
European Championship 69, 70, 71, 73, 76
European countries: fitness advantage 191; soccer game 51; supporters' relationship 177; three-points system 190
European Football Championship 68
European professional football 172

Facebook groups, Drogheda women's soccer 116
FAI *see* Football Association of Ireland
FAI Cup Final 5
FAIFS *see* Football Association of the Irish Free State
FAIFS Cup final 99
Fair Employment Commission 85
False Nine formation 198
Fannin, Alfred 38
Farquharson, Tom 187
Farrell, John 73
Fédération Internationale de Boxe Amateur (FIBA) 104
Fédération Internationale de Football Association (FIFA) 66, 85; Blues 91, 188; Cavan, Harry 69; football association 101; Irish National Caucus 85; membership application 101; post-war congress of 101; support to three-points system 190, 191
female players, attitudes towards 123–5
Fenlon, Pat 91
Ferriter, Dermot 111, 115
Ferriter, Diarmaid 52, 60
Festival Flash 125
Fianna Phadraig 96
Fiat Justitia Ruat Caelem 15
FIFA *see* Fédération Internationale de Football Association
First World War 35, 51–2, 60
Fitzgerald, Dick 98
Fitzgerald, E. 104, 105
fMRI research 154–5
folk-football 3
Football Association of Ireland (FAI) 62n7, 63n27, 68, 70, 76, 95, 101, 133, 172, 192; coaching course in Dublin 138; Coca Cola 142; Connolly, Sean 75; Cork City Investments FC Limited 176; Davis, Frank 71; disciplinary committees 55; financial resources 173; Independent Disciplinary Committee 175; Irish Football Association 65, 66, 69, 76; Jarman, John 140; Kilcoyne, Louie 73; lack of investment 177; licensing system 172; membership application for 74; O'Driscoll, Peadar 72; Player Development Plan 148; 'recent unfortunate occurrences' 72; restructuring policies 173; serious financial debt 141; soccer game in schools and colleges 137; supporter ownership 171, 182, 183
Football Association of the Irish Free State (FAIFS) 56–8, 65
Football Sports Weekly 40, 41
FORAS *see* Friends of the Rebel Army Society
forces of unionism 16
Ford, Henry 101
Fordson club of Cork 59
foreign game 5
formalization, of supporter activism 183

INDEX

Foster, Roy 52
Freeman's Journal 41, 54; murder of a referee 55; Sligo's inhabitants 19
Free State Cup final 51
Friends of the Rebel Army Society (FORAS) 174
Fulton, RP 133–4

GAA *see* Gaelic Athletic Association
GAA's Oral History Project 63n46
Gaelic Athletic Association (GAA) 10, 16, 21, 34, 58, 61, 62n10, 96–8, 102, 138; contribution to Irish society 4; dominance of sport 6; Oral History Project 115
Gaelic football 18–21, 24, 37, 38, 137, 142
Gaelic football enthusiasts 18
Gaelic football final 98
Gaelic football National League 5
Gaelic games 4, 17, 38, 137; interiorization and folklorization 23
Gaelic nativism *vs.* pervasive British imperialism 10
Galway 19; football club 21; old Spanish colony 19; population 15, 19; township 16–17, 19; township's population 19
Galway Commercials GAA 19
Galway Queens College FC 19
game intelligence 150, 153–5, 157, 160
Garbutt, Nick 85
Garnham, Neal 1, 34, 35, 51
'garrison game' 1, 2, 3, 6, 15–17, 34–5
Gerry Armstrong Soccer School 137
'Giant and Dwarf' *13*
Gibbs reflective model 158
Gibson, Darron 75
Giles, John 67, 76, 141
Gillespie, Gordon 84
Gillespie, Neil 35
Glasgow Celtic 74
Glentoran team 54, 66, 91
globalization: elite English football 170; League of Ireland 171; of Premier League 178
Glynn, Alan 139
Goldblatt, David 6, 50, 59, 62n1, 82
Gold Cup 89
Good Friday Agreement 75
'Go on De Wet' *14*
Gordon, Ben 119
Gorevan, Charlie 22
Gorman, Dessie 82, 90–2
Government of Ireland Act of 1920, 65
grammar schools: compulsory education 135; implementing association football 134–6; Irish Football Association 135; recognition for soccer 135; rugby 135; Second World War 134–5

Great Britain: bombing campaign across 82; professional football in 91; quality of football 101; roundtable talks 82
grounded theory 113
Guardian, The 187, 188
Gunning, Paul 3

Halliday, Brian 136
Hamilton, Brian 68
'Harp Lager All Ireland Indoor Football Championship' 125
Harte, Jim 7
Harty, A.C. 96
Harvey, Graham 91
Hill, Myrtle 115
Hinchley, Albert 187
Hockey Association 71
Holohan, Carole 111, 115, 126
hooliganism *see* soccer hooliganism
Hunter, Alan 68
Hunter, Glenn 91
Hunt, Tom 3

IASA *see* Irish Amateur Swimming Association
IFA *see* Irish Football Association
IFA Cup semi-final (1921) 100
IFA Junior Cup (IJC) 25
INC *see* Irish National Caucus
Independent Disciplinary Committee 175
indigenous Gaelic sports 15
individualism 179–80
indoor football leagues 125 *see also* Abbey Ballroom Indoor Football League
Industrial and Provident Society 175
International Amateur Athletic Federation (IAAF) 104, 105
International Olympic Committee, 1922 102
internment camps 36
inter-war soccer hooliganism 59–60
IRA *see* Irish Republican Army
Ireland's Saturday Night 89, 90
Irish Amateur Athletics Association 34
Irish Amateur Boxing Association (IABA) 102, 103, 105
Irish Amateur Swimming Association (IASA) 102, 103, 105
Irish-American 86
Irish Association football 35
Irish athletic team 104
Irish Civil War 36, 41
Irish Constitution 111
Irish Cup 51, 67; Glentoran and Belfast Celtic 66; Linfield and Donegal Celtic 74, 88; between Shelbourne and Glentoran 54
Irish Football Association (IFA) 55, 62n7, 63n27, 65, 66, 68, 76, 85, 89, 100, 101, 133, 135;

INDEX

Cavan, Harry 68, 136; coaching award 134; coaching scheme 136; coaching structure 134, 137; Connacht in 25–6; Cramer, Detmar 136; Football Association of Ireland 65, 66, 69, 76; Halliday, Brian 136; King, Noel 141, 142; summer course 136; teacher coaching certificate 137; Trevorrow, Eric 136; Wilton, James 66
Irish Football League 65, 66, 68
Irish Free State 3, 60, 65; Cannon, Harry 95; and international football 100–2; international victory 102; Irish Independent correspondent reporting 100; Olympic Games, 1924 101; sport and army of 96–8; training camp 104; Xth Olympiad Games, 1932 103–6
Irish Free State Cup 41
Irish Independent 50, 53, 54, 56, 100, 174, 175
Irish-Ireland Gaelic games 98
Irish-Ireland movement 96, 99
Irish League 53, 55, 70, 85, 91
Irish National Army 98
Irish National Caucus (INC) 85, 86, 88; Coca-Cola, boycott of 86, 89
Irish News 74, 85–9
Irish Olympic Council 102–6
Irish Press 57, 106
Irish Republican Army (IRA) 3, 34, 35, 41–2, 52, 54, 55, 71
Irish revolutionaries 36
Irish Soccer Split, The 65
Irish soldiers 16
Irish sporting administration 3
Irish Times 70, 75
Irish Universities Football Union 69
Irish War of Independence 36, 40, 96
Irlande 105, 106
Islandbridge Boxing Club 102

Jack, Bob 57
James, Harold 51
Jarman, John 140–1
Jennings, Pat 68
Johnston, Mo Maurice 83, 84, 85
Johnston, Richie 91
Jordan, Willie D'Exeter 13

Keane, J. J. 102, 103
Keane, Roy 75
Kelly, James 3
Kelly, Noel 138
Kerryman newspaper 71
Kilcoyne, Louie 68, 73
Kilcoyne, Louis 141
Kilcullen, P. J. 103, 105
Kilmarnock, Lord 20
King, Noel 141, 142
Kisch, Julia 86

Ladies Football Association (LFA) 53, 56, 111, 112
laissez-faire approach 178
La Liga 191
Lambert, John 18
Laochra Gael (Gaelic heroes) 5
Laochra Sacair 5
Lawlor, Mick 72
League of Ireland (LoI) 6, 70, 171, 187, 188, 192; active role of supporters 176; competition design 188; and Cork City FC 172–6; descriptive statistics **193**; financial auditing 172; First Division 189, 190; governance structures 172; loss aversion 199; match outcomes, rule changes effect on 196, **196, 197,** 198; mean number of goals per game **195,** *195*; number of goals and matches *193, 194*; 1981–1982 season 188–9; 1982–1983 season 189; 1985–1986 season 189–90; 1993–1994 season 190–1; Premier Division 189, 190; raising finance 173; reasons for modifications in 198–9; results from 1970 to 2014 **196**; revenue 173; structure, points system and calendar **192**; Summer Soccer era 191; supporters' relationship with governing bodies 177–8
learning 151–2; constructivism 152; feedback 155–7; person's knowledge 151; perspectives of 151–2; styles 152
Lee, Tansy 102
Leinster Amateur Boxing Council (1928) 102
Leinster Cup final (1926) 99
Leinster Football Association (LFA) 53, 62n7, 65, 101
Leinster Senior League, 1932 106
leisure concept 51
Leitrim Observer 57
Lennon, Neil 74
LFA *see* Ladies Football Association; Leinster Football Association
Linfield Football Club 82, 85, 92; 'all fair minded companies' 86; 'blackballed' 83; Caucus-led campaign 91; Cliftonville Budweiser Cup *vs.* 88, 90; criticism of 85; English Premier League 91; history of 87; Northern Irish Catholic 89; sign Catholic players 82, 92; sponsorship withdrawn of 86; supporters 67, 72
Linfield Management Committee 86
Linfield's Open Day 89
Little Belfast 18
Livingstone, Dougald 138, 140
LoI *see* League of Ireland
Look at Linfield 86
Los Angeles Organizing Committee 104
loss aversion concept 199

INDEX

MacBride Principles, The 91
MacMahon, Peadar 96
Madras Light Infantry 12
Magee, Jonathan 82
Major McBride AFC 23
Maloney, Tommy 104
Manchester United 91
Manchester United Supporters' Trust (MUST) 179
Marist Brothers FC 12, 22
Mason, Tony 1
McCann, Patrick 36
McCarthy, Dan 97
McClean, James 75
McDonald, Henry 86
McFadden, Jim 88
McGaughey, Martin 89
McGilton, J. J. 102
McGivern, N.P. 74
McKnight, Allen 74
McLoughlin, Alan 75
McManus, Séan 85, 86
Michael Cunningham's Boyle FC 13
migratory labour 4
military association football teams 34
Millar, Roy 137
Moles, Thomas 66
Moore, Cormac 3
Moore, W. 54
Morgan, Gerry 87
Mr Eades' Diocesan School 12, 19, 20
Mr Shekleton's Primrose Grange 20
Munro, Alex 20
Murphy, James 104
Murphy, W. R. E. 103
MUST *see* Manchester United Supporters' Trust

NACAI *see* National Athletic and Cycling Association of Ireland
Nagle, Gerry 175
National Athletic and Cycling Association of Ireland (NACAI) 96, 102–5
National College of Physical Education 140
National Football Association 149
national Olympic committee 103
Nelson, Alec 104
News Letter 92
New York Times 190
non-Gaelic games 35, 36
Noone, James 97
Northern Ireland: 'anti-Catholic bigotry' in 89; bombing campaign across 82; Catholic player 83; dark days in 88, 92; financial backing to 86; hard-hitting critique of 84; international players 74; in 1990 Irish Cup 88; soccer supporters 74; study of soccer in 82; turbulent in 81–2; wide-scale violence in 76; World Cup 1994 73, 85, 92
Northern Ireland Coaches' Association 136
Northern Ireland Sports Council 137
Northern Ireland Troubles 65, 66; all-Ireland dream 71–6; all-Ireland international team 66–8; IFA–FAI talks 69; Irish Universities Football Union 69
North Sligo Football Association (NSFA) 25

O'Brien, Samuel 56
O'Callaghan, Pat 104, 105
O'Connell, Patrick 5
O'Donoghue, M.V. 138
O'Driscoll, Peadar 72
O'Duffy, Eoin 96, 103, 104
Offaly's Banagher FC 13
O'Hagan, Billy 95
O'Hara, Denis 92
O'Kane, Liam 68
Olympic Games, 1924 101
Olympic movement, in Ireland 102
O'Mahony, Niamh 181
O'Malley, Donogh 6
Ó Maonaigh, Aaron 3
O'Neill, Martin 68
One Team in Ulster 84, 85, 91
Orange March 82
O'Toole, Fintan 75
O'Toole, Luke 96
Oughterard Celtic FC 17, 23
outdoor football 126
Outdoor Relief Riots of 1932 58, 63n41
Overend, Laurence 181

PA *see* performance analysis
Packie Bonner Goalkeeping School 137
patriotism 20–2
pedagogical knowledge 150, 160
Pembroke Comrades Club 98
perceptual cognitive skills 153–5
performance analysis (PA) 159–60
Phelan, John 173
physical and mental health, of community 134
PIRA *see* Provisional Irish Republican Army
Player Development Plan 148
player learning 150–2
Plymouth Football Club 57
Premier Ambitions 5
Premier League 171, 190; community 178–80; globalization 178; transformation 178
Primeira Liga 191
Primrose Grange FC 19, 20
Professional Footballers Association of Ireland 139
Provisional Irish Republican Army (PIRA) 82
Pyramid or Danubain formations 198

INDEX

Rangers-Chelsea-Linfield magazine 89
Raphoe's Gaelic football club 7
reflection, coaches 157–8
'remarkable "feat" on the football field' *11*
Republic of Ireland Football League Tables and Results 1921–2012 191
revitalization of Irish sports 33
revolutionary soccer players 36
Robertson, Hugh 178
Roche, Stephanie 111–12
Rod Squad, The 5, 8n23
Rogan, Anton 74
Roscommon's Castlerea FC 12
Rous, Stanley 67
RTÉ television documentary 5
RUC 74
'rules of the game' 187
Russell, Martin 91
Russian Revolution of 1917 51
Ryan, Tommy 98

Sangster, Jane 113, 115
Saxon recruiting campaign 138–9
science of coaching 149
Scottish Football Association 69
Scroope, Simon H 22
Scully, Tom 97
Second World War 133, 134
self-direction 152
seoininism 36
Setanta Cup 75–6
Shamrock Rovers FC 56, 179
Shamrock Rovers selection 4
Shelbourne FC 63n23, 173–4
Sinclair, James 20
Sir Alex Ferguson 152, 156
Sir Henry Gore-Booth 20
Sligo: Gorevan, Charlie 22; Little Belfast 18; population 19; post factum 18; Primrose Grange FC 19; shipping trade and customs returns 19; Sligo FBC 19; sportive acculturation 19
Sligo Agricultural Society's Show Grounds 6
Sligo Amateurs FC 18, 23
Sligo FBC 12, 19, 20
Sligo United YMCA 12
Smyth, Ted 136
Soccer and Irish Identity since 1884 (Cronin) 1
soccer clubs 6–7
soccer hooliganism 3, 50, 61–2; Anglo-Irish War, soccer violence during 52–5; deconstructing trend of violence 58–61; European society and 51; inter-war 59–60; Ireland 52, 58; 'terrorism' of soccer supporters 55–8
soccer organizers 6
soccer schools 137

soccer's coloeur locale 23–4
Soccer & Society 112
soccer techniques 137
'Soccer, Women, Sexual Liberation: Kicking off a New Era' 112
soccer World Cup Finals 71
'socker code' in Connacht (1879–1906) 10; British Army 16; coloeur locale 23–4; Connacht Union 22–3; garrison game 15–17; keystone local mythos disassembled 17–18; Little Belfast, Sligo v old spanish colony, Galway 18–20; sham patriotism 20–2; sojourned in 'blessed isolation' 25–6; 'The Lemonaders' and social respectability 24; Ulster Association 11
So Far So Good: A Decade in Football (Brady) 67
Sport and Nationalism in Ireland: Gaelic games (Cronin) 1
Sporting Press 111
Staunton, Niall 4
Stevenson, Alex 138
St James's Gate players 55
St Patrick's Day 86
Sugden, John 73
Summer Soccer era (2003 – to date) 191
'Summer Soccer' fixture schedule 190
Sunday Independent 53, 55
Sunday Life 85
Sunday News 83, 84
Sunningdale Agreement 69
supporter activism 171
supporter ownership 171, 182, 183
Supporters Direct 171, 177, 179, 180, 183
supporters' relationship 177–8
Supporters' Trusts model 171; future for 180–2; vehicles of ownership 181

television advertising 4
'terrorism' of soccer supporters 55–8
TG4 5
'the Blaxnit All-Ireland' cup competition 66
The Buffs 23
The Leader 37
theory of the civilization process 50
'The Silent Final' 67
Thorn Security decision 86
three-points system 190–1
THST *see* Tottenham Hotspur Supporters' Trust
Tisdall, Bob 104, 105
Tobin, Shane 2
Todd Andrews, Christopher Stephen 37–8
Toms, David 60
Tottenham Hotspur Supporters' Trust (THST) 182
Towerhill FC 13
Traynor, Oscar 5, 35, 39–42
Trevorrow, Eric 136

INDEX

Troubles, The 81, 82, 84, 87, 88, 92
Tuam FC 15, 21
Tuam Herald 21
Tullamore FC 13
Twentyman, Geoff 91
Tynan, Mark 3

UEFA 72; B-Licence 150; Europa League game 1; licensing prerequisites 199; Pro-Licence 150
UFF *see* Ulster Freedom Fighters
Ulster Association 11
Ulster Cup 90
Ulster Freedom Fighters (UFF) 88
Ulster Spinning Company Mill 82
United Irish League (UIL) 24
United Soccer Association 4
United States Congressional body 89
University of Ulster 74
'Up the UVF' 67
US Congressional Committee 85

visual search strategies 153, 157

Walsh, Davy 5, 7, 90
Walsh, Gerard 174
Waterford club 57, 58
West Britainism 16, 36
West Donegal Gweedore Celtic club 6
Whelan, Gerard 58
Williams, Jean 112, 115
Wilton, James 66
Windsor Castle 82
Windsor Park 67
WM or Meodo formations 198
Wolff, Alexander 73
women's soccer participation 112
World Cup 68, 69, 71, 73–5, 85, 132, 142, 187, 190

Young, James 92
Youth International committee 133